GW00685391

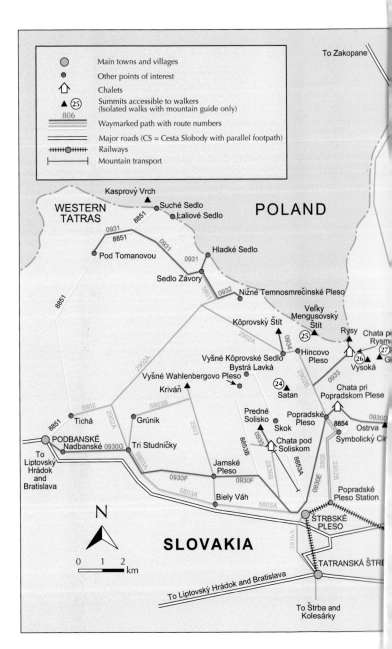

THE HIGH TATRAS

SLOVAKIA AND POLAND
INCLUDING THE WESTERN TATRAS
AND WHITE TATRAS

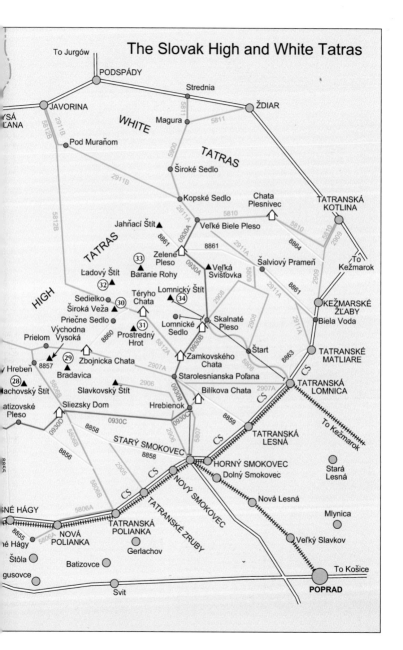

The Slovak High and White Tatras

To Jurgów

PODSPÁDY

Strednia

JAVORINA

ŽDIAR

WHITE

Magura

5811

Pod Muraňom

TATRAS

Široké Sedlo

Kopské Sedlo

Chata
Plesnivec

TATRANSKÁ
KOTLINA

Veľké Biele Pleso

To
Kežmarok

TATRAS

Jahňací Štít

8861

Zelené
Pleso

Veľká
Svišťovka

Šalviový Prameň

(33)

Baranie Rohy

HIGH

Ladový Štít

(32)

Sedielko

Téryho
Chata

Lomnický Štít

(34)

KEŽMARSKÉ
ŽLABY

Široká Veža

(30)

Biela Voda

Priečne Sedlo

Lomnické
Sedlo

Skalnaté
Pleso

Východna
Vysoká

(31)

Prostredný
Hrot

Prielom

8860

Štart

TATRANSKÉ
MATLIARE

Hrebeň

8857

(29)

Zbojnická Chata

Zamkovského
Chata

(28)

Bradavica

Starolesnianska Poľana

TATRANSKÁ
LOMNICA

achovský Štít

Slavkovský Štít

2906

Bilíkova Chata

CS

atizovské
Pleso

Sliezsky Dom

Hrebienok

To Kežmarok

8858

STARÝ SMOKOVEC

8859

TATRANSKÁ
LESNÁ

8856

8858

HORNÝ SMOKOVEC

Dolný Smokovec

Stará
Lesná

SNÉ HÁGY

NOVÝ SMOKOVEC

Nová Lesná

8855

NOVÁ
POLIANKA

TATRANSKÁ
POLIANKA

TATRANSKÉ
ZRUBY

Mlynica

né Hágy

Gerlachov

Štôla

Batizovce

Veľký Slavkov

gusovce

Svit

To Košice

POPRAD

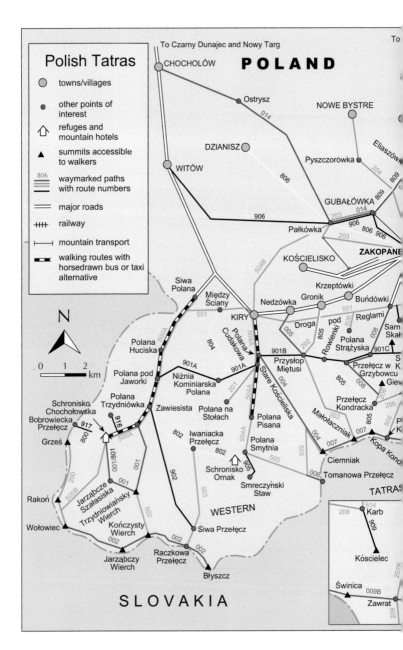

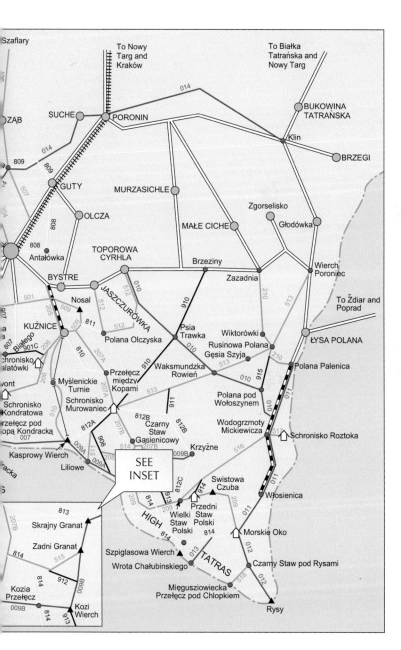

About the Authors

Colin Saunders has wide experience of walking in many parts of Britain and Europe. He has written books on walking in London and southeast England and is a member of the Outdoor Writers and Photographers Guild. After a career in the travel trade, Colin became a consultant on walking to charities and other organisations, and was the first route manager of the Capital Ring, a 78-mile trail around London, which is part of the London Strategic Walks Network, supported by Transport for London.

Renáta Nárožná was born and bred in the Slovak Tatras, and worked as a mountain guide for the state tourism organisation, Čedok. After Czechoslovakia's 'Velvet Revolution', Renáta ran her own travel company in the Tatras for a while, then she was appointed manager of the Vienna branch of the Slovak tourism organisation. In a complete career change, Renáta became the organisational director of Greenpeace in central and eastern Europe and is now the Treasurer of Doctors without Borders in Austria and the Czech Republic.

Other Cicerone guides by Colin Saunders
London – The Definitive Walking Guide (Cicerone, 2002)

THE HIGH TATRAS

SLOVAKIA AND POLAND
INCLUDING THE WESTERN TATRAS
AND WHITE TATRAS

by
Colin Saunders and Renáta Nárožná

2 POLICE SQUARE, MILNTHORPE, CUMBRIA LA7 7PY
www.cicerone.co.uk

© Colin Saunders and Renáta Nárožná 1994, 2006, 2012
Third edition 2012
ISBN: 978 1 85284 682 4
Second edition 2006
ISBN-10: 1 85284 482 5
ISBN-13: 978 185284 482 0
First edition 1994
ISBN: 1 85284 150 8

Printed in China on behalf of Latitude Press Ltd.

Maps originated by Barry Saunders and redrawn by Clare Crooke.
All photographs are by Colin Saunders, except where indicated.

Acknowledgements

With special thanks to Janusz Arnold, Director of Trip Travel in Zakopane, and a mountain guide, for his invaluable help with and advice on the section on the Polish Tatras.

Thanks also to Peter Chudý, Michal Labus, Ian Mitchell, Peter Šperka, Julian Tippett and Ronald Turnbull; members of the Anglian Fell and Rock Club and the Vanguards Rambling Club; and the staff of T-Ski Travel Agency in Starý Smokovec and Waymark Holidays in England, all of whom provided help and encouragement for the first and second editions.

Advice to Readers

Readers are advised that, while every effort is made by our authors to ensure the accuracy of guidebooks as they go to print, changes can occur during the lifetime of an edition. Please check Updates on this book's page on the Cicerone website (**www.cicerone.co.uk**) before planning your trip. We would also advise that you check information about such things as transport, accommodation and shops locally. Even rights of way can be altered over time. We are always grateful for information about any discrepancies between a guidebook and the facts on the ground, sent by email to info@cicerone.co.uk or by post to Cicerone, 2 Police Square, Milnthorpe LA7 7PY, United Kingdom.

Front cover: Ascending Skupniów Upłaz en route to Schronisko Murowaniec (Poland, route Blue 207A).

CONTENTS

PREFACE

In August 1988 I had the very good fortune to be sent, all expenses paid, by my then employers, a tour operator specialising in walking holidays, to undertake a feasibility study into the High Tatras as a new walking centre. I was most impressed, not only by the beauty of the area, but by the enthusiasm of the local people for their mountains, none more so than that of my guide, Renáta Nárožná. She was then working for the Czechoslovak state travel agency, without whose say-so no progress could be made – at that time.

Two years later I read somewhere that there was no English language guide to the High Tatras, and suggested to Renáta that we give it a try. By this time both of us had set up our own businesses, and we believed that, with me doing the writing and her providing the local knowledge, we had a reasonable chance of producing the goods. This book is the result.

Much has happened since Renáta and I first met. The Velvet Revolution of 1989, which overthrew the communist regime, was followed by the Velvet Divorce of 1993, which saw Czechoslovakia split into its two constituent parts – the Czech Republic and the Slovak Republic (although the latter is commonly referred to as Slovakia). Now the Tatras find themselves shared by the republics of Poland and Slovakia.

Equally profound changes were taking place simultaneously in Poland, and Cicerone Press felt that it would make good sense to include the Polish part of the Tatras in the same book. We were fortunate to enlist the help of a Polish mountain guide, Janusz Arnold, whose extensive knowledge of the walking north of the Polish–Slovak border has proved invaluable.

Since my first visit in 1988, I have visited the Tatras six times, exploring new territory on each occasion. Even so, I still have much ground to cover, which gives you an idea of the scope for walkers in this comparatively small area. Renáta, Janusz and I hope that you will be encouraged by this book to visit the Tatras, and that it will provide a great deal of help in finding your way around, and play some part in the enjoyment of your stay.

Recent history has shown how quickly the political situation can change, especially in the former Iron Curtain countries, to an extent that would have been inconceivable not so long ago. When I first visited what was then Czechoslovakia, a visa was necessary and it took 90 minutes to pass through three separate passport, visa and customs checks at Prague Airport. These days visas are no longer necessary for most English-speaking visitors to the Czech Republic, Slovakia or Poland, and border formalities are quick. Indeed, now that both Slovakia and

Poland are members of the European Union, there are no border controls when travelling between the two countries.

Both Slovakia and Poland became full members of the European Union in May 2004, and the Tatras have been designated a 'Euroregion', which means that development on both sides of the border should be coordinated, with the help of EU funding, for the benefit of residents, visitors and the environment. On my visit in July 2005, the change since my first visit in 1988 was profound. The communist era is a distant memory, and younger children do not remember it at all. People are relaxed and forthcoming, instead of restrained and secretive, and they are working harder. The area looks more prosperous, instead of run down, and the atmosphere in the mountain resorts is very similar to that prevailing in Alpine countries where tourism has flourished for decades.

As a small example, I remember that, when visiting one of the few food shops in 1988, there were long queues for a basket, and unless you had one you could not enter to buy from a very limited range. Now there are many more shops, cafés, bars, hotels and pensions to choose from, and few if any shortages.

Tourism in the Tatras started in the late 18th century, and the region was much visited by English-speaking people until world wars and political dogma interfered during the 20th century. At the time of writing, such people are beginning to drift back, and it is hoped that sensible proposals to encourage sustainable tourism development in the region will attract more people seeking the healthy benefits of clean air and exercise. After all, why should such beautiful scenery be kept hidden from the world?

In preparing the second and third editions, I was delighted that both Renáta and Janusz were still in a position to help. Apart from political developments, the most noticeable change since my previous visits was the effect of the Tatranská Bora – an ill wind if ever there was one. For more details of this calamitous cloud over the Slovak side – but possibly bearing a silver lining – see page 72.

Colin Saunders
May 2011

SECTION 1
AN INTRODUCTION TO THE TATRAS

Approaching from the plain of the Poprad river in Slovakia, the sight of the craggy peaks of the High Tatras mountains is unforgettable, beautiful and dramatic. Soaring abruptly skywards, they are like a phalanx of gigantic sentries barring the way to and from the north. With a dusting of snow and a swirl of mist, they assume the ghostly appearance of a phantom army.

Travelling by road or rail from Bratislava, you approach through the narrow, pretty valley of the River Vah, with castles balanced precariously on high cliffs above. As you progress eastwards, the Western Tatras seem quite impressive, but your first sight of broad-shouldered Kriváň in the High Tatras will take your breath away – no wonder this is the national symbol of Slovakia!

On the Polish side, approaching from Kraków, your first sight of the High Tatras comes as you pass the town of Nowy Targ. They are preceded by several ranges of low hills, so the impact is not quite so impressive as in Slovakia, yet even here these awesome mountains stamp their authority as a force to be reckoned with.

A phalanx of gigantic sentries! The High Tatras from near Poprad, Slovakia (photo: J Rizman)

Orla Perć – at Zmarzła Przełęcz
(Red 009B, Poland) (photo: R Turnbull)

From either side, the mountain faces are forbidding and steep, the ridges narrow and turreted. Yet as you close in, reaching the small towns and villages that line the slopes at around 1000m above sea level, you discern the valleys that separate the peaks, and realise that there are ways of overcoming and surmounting these resolute watchmen.

This is easier than may at first seem possible, because a network of well-engineered, waymarked paths links the resorts with peaks, lakes and mountain chalets. On some paths a good head for heights is needed, as there is scrambling, exposure and the use of fixed wires. (If these terms are strange to you, all is revealed in Paths and Waymarking, page 45.) Other routes lead gently through meadows and forests, yet still within sight of the fearsome summits above.

To find the High Tatras on a physical map of Europe, first imagine the Alps in the form of an antique pistol. Its butt lies near the Mediterranean Sea, the handle curves through France into Switzerland, and the barrel stretches on into Austria. The pistol is fired at Vienna, point blank; the bullet leaves the gun and passes over the city and across the Danube, but after travelling just half the barrel's length, it strikes a range of mountains beyond. They are the High Tatras, straddling the border between Slovakia and Poland.

For over 120 years, from the late 18th century to the early 20th century, these mountains were much visited by royalty and nobility from Austria–Hungary and other nearby states, and by discerning travellers from all over Europe, but their custom fell away during the political upheavals and wars of the 20th century. During the communist era, these peaks became very well known to Central and Eastern Europeans, because this was the only accessible region of high mountains for those who lived behind the Iron Curtain. Then, in 1991, Count Otto von Habsburg, the senior surviving member of the famous Austro–Hungarian ruling dynasty, revived the earlier tradition with a visit to the Tatras, accompanied by his family, as recorded in the visitors' book at the National Park Museum in Tatranská Lomnica.

People from the western side of the former Iron Curtain have only recently been reintroduced to these mountains, but now that they can visit the Tatras with a minimum of fuss, we hope that this book will encourage them to fully explore. To visit either Poland or Slovakia, most English-speaking visitors do not require a visa for a visit of less than 90 days.

The High Tatras are the highest and most northerly part of the Carpathian Mountains, a sickle-shaped range, 1200km long, which starts near Bratislava, then passes through Slovakia, the Czech Republic, Poland, Hungary, Ukraine and on into Romania, to finish at the Kazan Gorge on the Danube. In general, the Carpathians are not very high as mountains go – over half the peaks fail to reach 1000m. But the High Tatras are a notable exception – nearly 100 of their

15

more than 500 rocky summits surpass 2000m, ten come very close to or exceed 2500m, and the highest reaches 2654m. With so many walking routes surrounding the summits, you can view most of them from many different angles – even set yourself 'name that peak' competitions.

A miscellany of delights is provided by this compact microcosm of alpine scenery, which has been designated a World Biosphere Reserve by UNESCO. This designation gives strict protection to a wide variety of natural habitats and an immense diversity of wildlife, through the existence of neighbouring national parks in Slovakia and Poland, which together cover all of the High Tatras, as well as the adjoining White Tatras and most of the Western Tatras.

The High Tatras were one of the few parts of the Carpathians to be glaciated during the last ice age, and in an area just 27km by 10km there is much evidence of this. Small glaciers formed dozens of valleys containing more than a hundred lakes and tarns, and left moraines and moulded corries, ravines and basins.

The erosion of many different types of rock – granite, gneiss, sandstone, limestone and schists – has resulted in a wide variety of beautiful scenery, recalling that of the Alps, yet in a much smaller area. In just one day you may see needle-point summits, toothy ridges, massive cliffs, deep valleys, mirror-surfaced tarns, tinkling streams and splashing waterfalls. Other areas recall English landscapes on a grand scale – graceful, grey, rounded domes with grass-covered shoulders, shallow valleys and dry streambeds.

Though most of the villages are purpose-built mountain resorts, some date from the late 18th century, and several distinct traditional styles of architecture are on display. Many of the buildings are full of character, with much use of wood. Blending well with the pine trees, the colours chosen to decorate walls, beams, balconies and window frames offer a soothing mixture of mustard, custard, chocolate and cream, while rust-red dominates the roofs.

Every upside must have its downside though, and to appreciate the picturesque you will sometimes have to tolerate the grotesque – the architecture of the 1970s and 1980s did no favours for the Slovak Tatras. Now, because of the fragile ecology, and in realisation of the mistakes of the past, there is a ban on major new developments in the national park areas. (An 'ill wind', the Tatranská Bora – see page 72 – while opening up some splendid views, also exposed some of the concrete horrors that had previously been hidden by trees.)

Zakopane and its surrounding villages, in Poland, have retained their attractive and very distinctive styles of architecture, but some walkers may find the popularity of parts of this side of the Tatras rather off-putting, as a large proportion of Poland's 38 million population makes its way to these gorgeous mountains for holidays and weekends. Fortunately, they tend to congregate in half a dozen honeypots, leaving most of the footpath network relatively uncrowded.

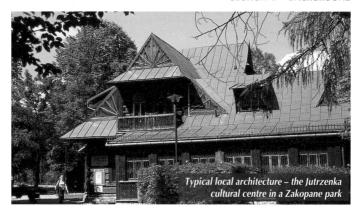

*Typical local architecture – the Jutrzenka
cultural centre in a Zakopane park*

For the urban-dwelling visitor, the air of the High Tatras seems incredibly pure, enhanced by the altitude, the scent of pine and (except in Zakopane) the low level of motorised traffic, which is banned from the mountain valleys, even where there are roads. This is an ideal location for a mountain holiday, and especially for the adventurous walker. It is an area that offers enough variety to fill a fortnight, yet small enough to provide the satisfaction of being able to explore it reasonably thoroughly in the same period.

The walking in the area covered by this book falls fairly distinctly into the Slovak and Polish sectors, so it is convenient to place the route descriptions in a separate section for each country. In Slovakia, as the Western Tatras is quite difficult to reach from the main resorts, nearly all the walking covered by this book is in the High Tatras, plus a small amount in the White Tatras. In Poland, much of the Western Tatras is easily accessible from the main resort of Zakopane, so these as well as the Polish High Tatras are included. We start, though, with an overview of general topics common to both countries.

BACKGROUND

Tatras is the word used by English-speakers as the plural of Tatra, though in both Polish and Slovak the plural form is Tatry. It applies to several mountain ranges, in total 78km long and on average 10km wide, that straddle the border between Slovakia and Poland. There is also the completely separate Low Tatras range to the south, wholly within Slovakia, and not covered by this book. The diagrammatic maps in this book (on pages 2–3 and 4–5) provide a general overview of the area, but to familiarise yourself with these ranges it will be more helpful to refer to one of the larger scale walking maps described on pages 40–45.

Written across and around the mountainous areas on these walking maps are several names in capital letters. The two largest are simply POLSKO (Poland) and SLOVENSKO (Slovakia). Next comes TATRY (Tatras), which applies to the whole region, both in Slovakia and Poland. It stretches from the town of Zuberec in the west to the valley of the Biela river in the east, and between the line of valleys to the north (in one of which lies the Polish town of Zakopane) and the Sub-Tatras Basin (the broad valleys of the rivers Poprad and Vah) to the south.

Next in size come ZÁPADNÉ TATRY (Slovak) or ZACHODNIE TATRY (Polish), meaning Western Tatras; VYSOKÉ TATRY (Slovak) or WYSOKIE TATRY (Polish), meaning High Tatras; and BELIANSKE TATRY (Slovakia) or BIELSKIE TATRY (Polish), meaning White Tatras. On some maps you may see Východné or Wschodnie Tatry (Eastern Tatras), but this term is rarely used.

Surrounding the mountain ranges are the low-lying regions of Podtatranská Kotlina (Sub-Tatras Basin), Liptov and Spiš in Slovakia, and Podhale (Below the Mountain Meadows) and Rów Podtatrzański (Sub-Tatras Trench) in Poland. These do not concern us much, except that you will frequently be overlooking them from the mountains.

Some maps may show neighbouring, lower ranges of hills or mountains. To the north, Pasmo Gubałówskie (Gubałówka Range) features in the walking from Zakopane as described in this book, but most of them will only be seen in the distance from high vantage points in the Tatras: in Slovakia – Skorušinské Vrchy (Front Hills), Chočské Vrchy, Nízke Tatry (Low Tatras), Kozie Chrbty (Goat Ridge), Levočské Vrchy (Lion Hills) and Spišská Magura; in Poland – Zamagurze Spiskie and Pieniny.

The **High Tatras** extend for 27km in the form of a shallow, upside-down arch, and consist mostly of granite and gneiss rock. With six peaks exceeding 2600m (culminating in Gerlachovský Štít at 2654m), this range lays claim to several 'highest' titles – in the Tatras, in Slovakia and in the whole Carpathian chain.

There are many short lateral spurs, most of which descend northward into Poland. A much longer spur extends southwestward into Slovakia for 7km, from near the bottom of the huge crook in the border with Poland to the valley of Kôprová Dolina. Another of 9km reaches north to Lysá Poľana.

The official dividing point between the High and White Tatras is Kopské Sedlo, due north of Starý Smokovec. The dividing point between the High and Western Tatras, depending on whose authority you follow, is one or other of two neighbouring saddles on the Slovak–Polish border northwest of Štrbské Pleso. For Slovakia, it is Ľaliové Sedlo (Liliowe in Polish); for Poland, it is Sucha Przełęcz (Suché Sedlo in Slovak). This dichotomy results in the intervening summit, Beskyd

Approaching Vyšné Kopské Sedlo in the White Tatras (Green 5900, Slovakia) (photo: R Turnbull)

(Slovak) or Beskid (Polish), not knowing whether it belongs to the High or Western Tatras. The valley called Tichá Dolina, which runs southwestwards from Ľaliové Sedlo, is generally considered to be in the High Tatras, though on the maps it appears to lie in the Western Tatras. This may seem nitpicking, but for local people it is a matter of some importance.

The **Western Tatras** form the second highest mountain range in the Carpathians, with some 20 summits above 2000m, the highest being Bystrá (2248m). While the slate peaks of the Western Tatras are generally lower and less spectacular than those of the High Tatras, there are some fine ridge walks. These are longer, more numerous and more accessible to walkers without a guide than in the High Tatras.

The range includes several sub-groups, including Czerwone Wierchy (Polish) or Červené Vrchy (Slovak), both meaning Red Hills, Osobitá, Roháče, Liptovské Tatry and Liptovské Kopy.

Two particularly worthwhile waymarked ridge walks in the Western Tatras follow separate sections of the border between Slovakia and Poland. However, because of difficulty with access, the westernmost of these requires a two-day expedition, with a long descent into a valley for overnight accommodation.

There is not enough space in this book to describe the Western Tatras in Slovakia, which in any case are not easy to reach from the High Tatras resorts, though you may see them from some vantage points. From Zakopane in Poland, however, some fine routes in the Western Tatras are easily accessible, and so are included in this book.

The **White Tatras** are a distinctive, 13km long range of pale-grey, limestone peaks rising from grassy slopes. They adjoin the High Tatras transversely, like a hammerhead, at Kopské Sedlo, and have six summits over 2000m, the highest being Havran (Raven, 2152m).

In 1978 the whole of the White Tatras was closed to tourists, apart from two short, low-level walking routes. This was because the routes to the summits and along the ridge had become very badly eroded, and the delicate ecology was under threat. In 1993 the whole range was handed over to the Urbariat (Association of Historical Landowners) of the village of Ždiar, who decided to reopen one route across the range to link up with the High Tatras network, and this is described in the relevant section of this book. However, even after three decades of closure, other parts of the White Tatras, once the location of high-level walking routes, had still not recovered enough to be reopened, and they are likely to remain closed for the foreseeable future.

If you do not manage to get into the White Tatras range itself, you can still admire its graceful beauty from several points in the eastern High Tatras, such as

*The White Tatras from Veľké Biele Pleso
(Blue 2911A, Slovakia) (photo: R Turnbull)*

Jahňací Štít and Kopské Sedlo, or from the top of the cable-car at Lomnický Štít, or even from the main road at Ždiar to the east.

Adjoining the Tatras, and just creeping onto some maps, are the lesser ranges of **Skorušinské Vrchy** to the west and **Spišská Magura** to the east, in Slovakia, but as these are not parts of the main Tatras ranges, they are not covered in this book. Neither are the completely separate **Pieniny** to the northeast in Poland, nor the **Nízke Tatry** (Low Tatras) to the south in Slovakia. They are, nevertheless, very attractive areas for walkers, and good walking maps of all these other ranges are available in bookshops and tourist offices in the Tatras and in specialist bookshops abroad.

Altitudes

As altitudes (heights above mean sea level) feature prominently in this book, it is important to point out that you may see different figures quoted, depending on the source of your information, especially where summits are concerned. This is because they have been measured by various authorities from three reference points – the Baltic Sea, the Adriatic Sea and satellites. Sea level varies from the mean in different parts of the world, and large bodies of water that are almost detached from the oceans, such as the Baltic and the Mediterranean, may vary more than most.

Traditionally, and naturally, Poland has taken the Baltic as its reference, while Slovakia has used the Adriatic. However, as the technology used for measurement improves, altitudes are being corrected from time to time. Satellite technology has only recently begun to be used for this purpose, and in due course it seems likely that this will allow such details to settle down to a standard figure. In this book, we have as far as possible used the altitudes accepted by our principal local sources of information.

EARLY HISTORY

Though the origin of the word 'Tatra' and its variants is not certain, it seems likely that it comes from the Old Slavonic word *trtra*, meaning high cliff – of which there are certainly plenty in these rugged mountains. The first record of the name so far discovered, in the form 'Tritri', is dated 1086 and comes from the archives of the archbishopric of Prague. The first instance of the present spelling, Tatry, was used in a handwritten document dated 1255, and in print in 1545.

Much of the rock that forms the Tatras was created 300 million years ago, by sediment deposited in a huge ocean. A hundred million years ago, over a period of several thousand years, the immense force of a collision between the once separate tectonic plates that carried what is now Italy and the rest of Eurasia created what is now the Alps and, behind them, the Carpathians. So great was this force that some of the land that lay to the south was pushed up and over what is now the High Tatras, to form the hills now lying on the north side.

During various ice ages the Tatras region was one of the few parts of the Carpathians to be covered by glaciers, and successive glacial periods shaped the peaks, gouged the valleys, and left the moraines that dammed the tarns.

Evidence of Late Stone Age human activities (about 5000 years ago) has been unearthed at several locations in the Tatras foothills, including the skull of 'Ganovce Man', a cast of which now lies in state in the National Museum in Prague. In the early Bronze Age (about 3000 years ago) the area to the south was densely settled by Turkic people, engaged mainly in sheep farming and other agricultural activities, who appear to have been much influenced by the Mycenean culture of the eastern Mediterranean. Many of their settlements were sited to afford a view of the High Tatra peaks, and it has been suggested that this may have some connection with the religious customs of the time, or it may simply have been to provide better protection from, and a lookout for, approaching enemies.

The land to the north of the Tatras was uninhabited at this time.

Subsequent history is related under 'Later History' at the beginning of each of Sections 3 and 4 on Slovakia and Poland.

VEGETATION AND WILDLIFE

Flowers should be at their best in early July, but please remember that **picking flowers, fruit or fungi, and taking cuttings, is strictly forbidden** in the Tatras National Park.

Because of the fragile nature of the local wildlife, there are restrictions on taking dogs into the national park areas. In Slovakia they are only allowed in the national park if muzzled and on a lead, but they are not allowed into nature reserves at all. In Poland dogs are not allowed into the national park area at all.

It has been established that some 1300 plant species can be found in the ranges that make up the Western, High and White Tatras, including at every level the most primitive of plants – lichens and mosses – clinging to rocks and dead wood.

In autumn, frost burns the leaves of many of the shrubs and trees to a whole variety of rich hues, from orange and gold to purple and dark brown, enhanced by early morning frost and perhaps a dusting of snow.

There is animal life in abundance in the Tatras, but most species are extremely shy and keep well away from the waymarked walking routes. However, as a result of protection, some species are currently increasing in number and are beginning to lose their fear of humans. On a recent visit, the authors saw chamois, a marmot and a bear in broad daylight at comparatively close quarters.

If you wish to see the more unusual varieties, the best time is early in the morning, when the nocturnal ones are returning to their homes, and before most walkers have arrived. Keep very quiet and wear dark clothes. Take binoculars if you have them – they will help to identify the many species of birds, as well as animals in the distance.

Vegetation and wildlife in mountainous regions are strongly affected by the altitude and prevailing weather. The mountains can be divided into a number of biological zones, described below. The altitudes are given as a general guide, but there will be many variations in particular areas, influenced by location, prevailing weather and rock type.

Sub-Tatras Basins (below 700m)

Approaching the High Tatras from the Podtatranská Kotlina (Sub-Tatras Basin) in Slovakia, or Podhale in Poland, you are surrounded by rather poor-quality **agricultural land**, which mainly produces crops such as potatoes and oats, and to a lesser extent rye and millet. Farming communities at between 700m and 900m mark the edge of the agricultural plains. In Slovakia, these include Tatranská Štrba, Mengušovce, Batizovce, Gerlachov, Nová Lesná, Stará Lesná and Stráne pod Tatrami. In Poland, Chochołów, Poronin and Bukowina Tatrańska.

The Sub-Tatras Basin from near Štrbské Pleso, Slovakia (photo: J Rizman)

In and around these villages, as well as the common birds seen in most parts of Europe, and of course cattle and sheep, you may see **white storks** nesting in the spring, and perhaps some **black grouse**.

Forest Zone (700m to 1600m)
In the Slovak Tatras the forest zone is reckoned to occupy the territory between 700m and 1600m. However, in November 2004 the Taranská Bora (see page 72) destroyed most of the trees below 1250m, so at present the forest zone starts at around this level. The dominant tree species is **spruce**, with occasional interlopers such as **larch**, **pine**, **birch**, **mountain ash** and **willow**. In the lower affected areas, it seems likely that in due course this will be replaced by a regime of mixed forestry, containing coniferous and deciduous species in equal proportions. In some places the forest may be allowed to revert to meadows.

A string of villages and hamlets lines the southern slopes of the Tatras giants between 900m and 1300m, taking advantage of the clean air and pure spring water to pronounce themselves mountain resorts or spas: Štrbské Pleso, Vyšné Hágy, Nová Polianka, Tatranská Polianka, Smokovce (the Smokovec villages), Tatranská Lesná, Tatranská Lomnica and Tatranské Matliare.

In Poland the town of Zakopane and its satellites have spread up the valley of the Cicha Woda (Quiet Water) and adjoining hillsides between 800m and 900m, while the expanding communities of Kościelisko, Murzasichle and Małe Ciche occupy neighbouring valleys and ridges. Higher up, apart from the tourist station of Kuźnice, there are just occasional collections of shepherd huts in the valleys and meadows. Tourism now dominates Zakopane and, though still basically farming communities, the surrounding villages are developing their facilities with many new hotels, guest houses and restaurants having opened in recent years.

In forested areas a few shrubs can be found in the undergrowth: **bilberry**, **cranberry**, **mountain strawberries** and **raspberries**, the poisonous **daphne** and the alpine **clematis**. But the best floral displays occur in the spring and summer, taking over the clearings and meadows. At various times, **crocus**, **cowslip**, **daisies**, **buttercups**, **foxglove** and **golden lily** are in abundance, while in certain areas rarer species such as **orchids** (including lady's slipper) may be spotted. A wide variety of **fungi** can be seen.

During the daytime, **roe deer**, **red deer** and **foxes** may run across the meadows, or browse among the trees within sight of the paths. Early risers may see a **badger**, **otter**, **weasel** or **stoat**. On autumn evenings the baying and bellowing of the deer can be heard for miles. In the parks and woods of the mountain resorts **black and brown squirrels** run riot, and on the Slovak side **red squirrels** may also be spotted in more remote areas.

Less likely to be seen, in areas rarely visited by (and in some cases barred to) walkers, are **wildcats**, **martens**, **lynxes**, **wolves**, **wild boar** and even **bears**. These are mostly on the eastern, western and northern fringes of the High Tatras. Bears tend to hibernate in Poland as the snow lies longer there. Remember that these potentially dangerous animals are very rarely seen by tourists, and even more unlikely to attack unless provoked. If you are nervous about meeting such creatures, and if you visit the less crowded areas, do not go alone, but with a number of companions. Check the current situation at an information office (and see also page 329).

Something that may surprise you, if you have visited other mountainous parts of Europe such as the Alps or Pyrenees, is the lack of cattle and sheep on most mountain pastures. A law was passed in the 1950s forbidding farming because livestock were considered to have caused too much soil erosion. This has been relaxed a little on the Polish side, to keep up the shepherding tradition, where cattle and sheep can now be seen, and the gentle tinkling of cowbells heard, at Polana Chochołowska, Dolina Kościeliska and Hala Kalatówki in the Western Tatras, and at Hala Kopieniec and Rusinowa Polana in the High Tatras. You may sometimes find sheep's-milk cheese on sale there.

Among the birds, **woodgrouse**, **woodcock** and **partridge** abound, and you may hear the distinctive song of a **thrush**, or the mocking call of a **cuckoo**. Darting over and around the many turbulent streams, you will surely spot a **dipper**, or

Anemone narcissiflora

a **yellow wagtail**, and in the streams themselves swim several varieties of **trout**. Colourful butterflies, including **red admiral**, **brimstone** and **peacock**, flutter among the flowers and sheep in fields and meadows.

Sub-Alpine (Dwarf Pine) Zone (1600m to 1850m)

At around 1600m the lofty conifers run out of soil deep enough for their sprawling roots. Here, densely huddled for protection against the fierce winter wind and cold, **dwarf pines**, with their shorter roots, take over for another 250m or so, before the ground becomes too rocky even for the grip of these tenacious little trees. Here the **anemone**, **edelweiss**, **gentian**, **helianthemum** and other hardy species thrive.

Alpine Zone (1850m to 2300m)

From 1850m upwards, the surface is predominantly bare rock that seems to have no capacity to harbour life, yet life can be found in the cracks – usually tufts of grass or a stunted dwarf pine. There are some grassy alpine meadows, too, where flowers will bloom briefly in July and August, but at this altitude only the hardiest plants manage to exist.

Helianthemum grandiflorum

A strikingly deep blue gentian (*Ciminalis clusii*)

You will see an occasional lone giant, or a small clump of them, among the dwarves, and sometimes even higher. Usually they are oval-crowned **limba-fir** (*sembra*), defiantly thrusting roots through cracks in the rock to find soil. The outermost limbas in a clump will be branchless on their northern sides, where they are battered by the prevailing winter winds – they are called **flag-trees**. Sometimes a **birch**, **mountain ash** or **willow** may occur in the dwarf pine belt. The fruit of the limba was once collected by shepherds to provide an aromatic additive to the oil used in spa treatments, but this activity is now banned in the national parks.

You should watch out particularly for the shiny **black moss** that covers some granite boulders high up above the tree-line – it is very slippery when wet, and rough enough to cut your skin.

You are likely to see on distant rocks a single **marmot**, or a whole family basking in the sun. This large brown rodent is closely related to the squirrel, but in size and shape comparable to the badger. You will probably hear its gull-like yelp, even if you fail to see the animal itself. Also above the tree-line you may see groups of **chamois** – the symbol of the TANAP national park in Slovakia, and of the mountain guides in Poland – springing nimbly from ledge to precarious ledge. Binoculars would certainly be an advantage at this level.

High above, the rock eagle may be seen hovering, then perhaps swooping down on its unsuspecting prey.

Sub-Nival Zone (above 2300m)

The very highest part of the High Tatras is called the sub-nival ('below the snow-line') zone, that is, below the level where snow always exists (of course, in this area, that only occurs close to the highest summits). Even at this altitude a wide variety of very tough species can be found if you look carefully, such as **mosses**, **lichens**, and in summer the **glacier gentian**.

Among the fauna, birds of prey are predominant, especially **eagles**, yet even among the rocks such creatures as **ermine**, **snow-vole** and species of **mountain mice** may be hiding. Some lower areas in the north-facing Polish High Tatras, where snow always exists, are in effect 'sub-nival' – in particular Kociol Mięguszowiecki to the south of Morskie Oko, the big tarn in the southeast corner.

WEATHER

As in all mountain ranges, one thing you can be sure of in the Tatras is that the weather will be changeable. The High Tatras are even more exposed to climatic changes than most other ranges, because of their comparatively small area and great elevation at the heart of Europe, and the weather in the mountains may be completely different from that in the surrounding plains.

Summer is a short season in the mountains – from the beginning of July to the end of August. The Tatras experience high precipitation, which may fall as snow on higher ground. July and especially August are generally the warmest months, but as usual in mountains the hotter the weather the greater the likelihood of thunderstorms – the areas in Slovakia around Veľka Svišťovka, and in Poland around Giewont, Morskie Oko and Czerwone Wierchy, are particularly prone to thunderstorms between noon and 2pm.

The average daytime temperature in the mountain resorts in summer is 20–22°C (68–72°F), but it may be much cooler first thing in the morning and in the late evening.

It is often the case in summer that there are blue skies in the morning, a gathering of clouds during the late morning and early afternoon, followed by a heavy downpour and perhaps a thunderstorm, then the blue skies return in the evening. Do not let this weather pattern detract from the enjoyment of a day's excursion, but allow for it in the plan. Be ready to set off early on a fine morning, so that you can either be back in the village when the storm breaks, or enjoy an extended lunch in a hospitable chalet.

In late June and early July you can expect to find some paths blocked by snow for short stretches, but in most cases walkers will have trodden a path across it.

Autumn is the best season for many walkers, from the end of August to mid October, when the weather is more settled, warmer than in spring, the air is clear and crisp, and the walking is delightful – though sometimes restricted by early snow at higher levels. The average daytime temperature in the resorts is

10–12°C (50–54°F), but it should be warmer at the end of August and beginning of September.

Winter walking (November to March) can be invigorating and charming, providing you take wise precautions – see Winter Walking, page 59.

Spring is not generally a good time for walking in mountains. In late March and April there is a high risk of avalanches. In May and early June the lower routes are awash from melting snow.

In Slovakia the higher routes are closed from 1 November until 15 June, to protect hibernating animals during the winter, and baby wild animals being reared in spring. In Poland there is no formal closure period, but in practice some routes are impassable at times – you can check at the national park information office on the way to Kuźnice, or at the huts where entry fees are collected. In this book, an indication is given for each route as to whether it is likely to be open or closed during this period.

Avalanche warnings are posted when necessary at the start of walking routes. In Poland a grading system applies, ranging from Level 1 (slight) to Level 5 (severe). Obviously if there is danger of an avalanche you should avoid that area.

There are as yet no **weather forecasts** in English by radio or telephone, but you should be able to get information about the weather in English from your hotel reception, or at tourist or national park information offices, or on the internet. Mountain rescue stations (see Appendix F) will have weather forecasts, though the staff may not be able to communicate in English.

Please read Mountain Safety and Emergency Services, page 54, regarding wind chill and altitude factors.

NATIONAL PARKS

The whole of the High and White Tatras ranges, as well as most of the Western Tatras, are included in the Tatransky Národny Park (TANAP) in Slovakia, or the Tatrzański Park Narodowy (TPN) in Poland (both mean Tatras National Park). Established in 1949 (Slovakia) and 1954 (Poland), the two organisations on either side of the border work closely together to protect the natural environment and provide facilities for rest and enjoyment. Together they cover approximately 730sq km, of which 70% lies in Slovakia, 30% in Poland.

Most facilities you will use while walking in the Tatras are provided by the national park authorities: path building and maintenance, waymarking, nature trails, guides and wardening.

As in all national parks, there are strict prohibitions to protect the environment. These are really just common sense, and would be followed as a matter of normal practice by all readers of this guide, but for the record you are forbidden to: walk away from the waymarked routes, or take short cuts on bends; pick flowers, mushrooms or fruits of the forest; break off branches; set up tents anywhere except in designated campsites; light fires; swim or use boats anywhere except places specified for these activities; leave litter; damage or remove any notices or waymarks. Failure to observe these very sensible rules may result in a heavy fine. See the Mountain Code and Visitors' Charter in Appendix E.

National park rangers in both Slovakia and Poland wear a green uniform and a badge, which in Slovakia bears the words 'Strážca Tanapu' (TANAP Ranger), and in Poland an edelweiss emblem. Mountain rescue personnel and guides wear red sweaters bearing the mountain rescue badge.

The administrative headquarters of the Slovak TANAP is in Tatranská Lomnica, in a modern building 500m east of the railway station. It also contains a research institute and an interesting museum, which displays various aspects of life in the park. The reception counter sells a range of maps and guides in English (including a guide leaflet to the museum), and there is an audio-visual display in the morning and afternoon. There is also a TANAP office in Tatranská Štrba.

In Poland the headquarters of TPN and mountain rescue are at Kuźnice, on your left as you approach the cable-car station. They also run an information office and small museum, easily recognised by its impressive carved wooden colonnades, beside the roundabout at the foot of the approach road (Rondo Jana Pawła II).

LANGUAGES

English is becoming more widely spoken as a result of the increase in English-speaking visitors, and because children are learning it at school. German is widely spoken on the Slovak side of the Tatras – indeed, it is the native language of many older people who were brought up in what was the German-speaking Austro–Hungarian province of Zips (now Spiš) in that area. Even so, it will help visitors to have an understanding of the Polish and Slovak languages, the pronunciation of place names and the meaning of some words.

Both are descended from Old Slavonic, which was almost universally spoken by Slav peoples until the Middle Ages, and there are still many similarities between the two languages. Slovak is also very similar to Czech, but there are some subtle and some substantial differences.

The pronunciation of Slav languages can be very difficult for English speakers. Some words appear impossible to pronounce, with far too few vowels, or even none at all, in relation to the number of consonants, especially in Polish, where the faint-hearted may give up halfway through the first syllable of some words. The single letters k, s, v and z in Slovak, and w and z in Polish, are words in their own right.

In both Slovak and Polish most letters are pronounced as in English – remember that g is always hard, as in 'goat' – and the stress nearly always goes on the first syllable. The differences are described to the best of our ability in Appendix A, though some sounds are almost impossible to explain in writing.

A wide variety of diacritics (accents) appears over some letters, affecting the way they are pronounced – see Appendix A.

There are no definite or indefinite articles in either language. All nouns and place names have gender – masculine, feminine or neuter – and this together with grammatical cases affects the endings of many words in a way that is far too complicated to describe in detail here, but you should be prepared for the names of people and places to appear in a multitude of versions. Tatra can also be seen in Slovak as Tatry, Tatier, Tatrám, Tatrách and Tatrami; in Polish as Tatry, Tatr, Tatrami and Tatrach. Even your name may be rendered in several ways. In Slovak, Colin Saunders can also appear as Colina Saundersa, Colinovi Saundersovi or Colinom Saundersom, while Renáta Nárožná may appear as Renáty Narožnej, Renáte Nárožnej or Renátou Nárožnou. In Polish, also as Colina Saundersa, Colinowi Saundersowi or Colinem Saundersem; Renáty Nárožny, Renácie Nárožnie, Renátę Nárožnę or Renátą Nárožná.

In this book we use where possible the unaffected versions of names for simplicity, but on maps, signposts and so on, you may find the endings altered.

Appendix A contains a glossary of words that you are likely to encounter on the Tatras maps, or in the mountains and villages, as well as some useful words or phrases, for example to help you order a drink or a meal. For further help, you can buy inexpensive pocket dictionaries in bookshops in the Tatras resorts (see Shopping and Services information in Sections 3 and 4 for each country), and in specialist bookshops in English-speaking countries.

PLACE NAMES

In this book we use Slovak or Polish place names as appropriate, and translate them where possible, either in the main text or in the gazetteers, to add interest and help with identification. Note that some places in the Tatras have slightly different names in Slovak and Polish – we use where possible the name that is relevant to the location.

When using Polish and Slovak maps, it is easy to get confused by a number of situations that have arisen over the years. The following is an attempt at clarification, though you may be none the wiser by the end.

On Slovak maps, for names applied to geographical features, you will see that it is customary to use lower case for the initial letter of the type of feature (such as tarn, valley, saddle), whether this comes first or second, such as Skalnaté pleso, Suchý žľab, Lomnicky štít, Kopské sedlo, Kôprová dolina, hrebeň Svišťových veží, pleso Nad Skokom. This looks wrong to English speakers, so in this book we have given capital letters to all the words, to make clear that they are all part of the place name. In Slovak there is an exception to the rule when applied to the names

High up in Malá Studená Dolina
(Green 5812A) (photo: R Turnbull)

of towns or villages, when both words have capital letters, for example Štrbské Pleso, Kežmarské Žľaby.

On Polish maps, as in English, all words in the names of geographical features start with capital letters, except where prepositions are included.

In Slovak place names, as in English, it is usually (but not always) correct to put the type of geographical feature last, such as *chata* (chalet), *dolina* (valley), *pleso* (tarn), *polana* (clearing), *potok* (brook), *sedlo* (saddle or pass) and *vrch* (hill).

In Polish it is usually (but not always) correct to put, for example, *dolina* (valley), *polana* (clearing), *hala* (pasture), *jaskinia* (cave) and *schronisko* (refuge) first, but some Polish mapmakers have chosen to show these terms last in some (but not all) cases. However, *potok* (brook), *przełęcz* (saddle or pass), *staw* (tarn) and *wierch* (hill) nearly always come last on all maps. Sometimes the correct procedure is abandoned, simply because the opposite sounds better to native ears, as in Siwa Polana. In this guidebook we try to follow the correct procedure, but what is correct is not always clear.

Bear in mind that the circumstances and names of some places and chalets shown on older maps may have changed since your map was published. In Slovakia the chalet Chata Kapitána Rašu (near Tri Studničky) has burned down, Chata Kapitána Morávku (at Popradské Pleso) has been renamed Chata pri Popradskom Plese, and Poľana Kamzik (near Hrebienok) has been renamed Starolesnianska Poľana.

In Poland the refuges are usually known by a name that is shorter than that shown on maps, and some older maps may show names that are no longer used. The saddle that is known to local people as Raczkowa Przełęcz is shown on some maps as Gaborowa Przełęcz Wyżnia, with a note that the other name is incorrect.

We try to explain these situations in the text or gazetteers, where relevant, and hope that it will not be too confusing.

BORDER CONTROLS

In 2007 Poland and Slovakia became members of the Schengen Convention, which meant that they had to abolish border controls between the two countries. Now you can normally cross the border freely at all accessible points, including Rysy, where eagle-eyed guards once ensured that walkers returned they way they came. However, there may be times when guards or customs officials are required to set up temporary controls, so always take your passport if planning to cross the border.

See also Cross-border Walking on page 60.

SECTION 2
PREPARATION FOR WALKING

WHEN TO GO

Your decision may be affected by the weather – see page 28. For settled weather (though there is no guarantee) and to avoid crowds in the honeypots, the best time to go is between the end of August and early October. The peak period is from mid July to late August, when it is more difficult to find suitable accommodation, and the more popular walking routes and the honeypots are very busy. Whatever time you decide to go, book as far ahead as possible, as even at off-peak times a conference or other event may take up much of the accommodation.

OBTAINING INFORMATION

Postal and internet addresses, phone numbers and websites are given in this book so that you can obtain further information as required. The person who answers the phone may not speak English, and although German is widely spoken in Slovakia, it is not in Poland.

Phone numbers for places in Poland and Slovakia are those that you dial while in those countries. If dialling from outside, you need to prefix the local

The diesel train to Studený Potok at Tatranská Lomnica station, Slovakia

number with the international dialling code and remove its initial zero. The international dialling codes vary between countries, as follows.

To Poland from: UK, Irish Republic, Canada, New Zealand and Slovakia – 0048, Australia – 001148, Canada and USA – 01148, South Africa – 0948.

To Slovakia from: UK, Irish Republic, Canada, New Zealand and Slovakia – 00421, Australia – 0011421, Canada and USA – 011421, South Africa – 09421. If calling Slovakia from Poland, you dial 0, await a second tone, then 0421.

TRAVEL AND INSURANCE

Details of travel to and within Poland and Slovakia are given in Sections 3 and 4, for each country.

For either country, with rail services becoming ever faster in Europe, and if your finances and diary are reasonably elastic, you may wish to consider travelling all the way by train from the UK, perhaps with an overnight stop en route, or by using an overnight sleeper. If time is pressing, out by train, home by air, could be the answer. Details of international rail services can be obtained from several specialist travel agents – for a list of these in the UK, visit National Rail on http://bit.ly/dQQ8h8 or www.nationalrail.co.uk/stations_destinations/travel/travel_europe.html.

Travel insurance is vital. Although it is unlikely that you will need mountain rescue, there is a charge for this in Slovakia and you should check that your insurance covers it. If not, a policy is available at local tourist and mountain rescue information offices.

British and Irish citizens should obtain the Health Advice for Travellers document from a post office, or online through www.dh.gov.uk or www.oasis.gov.ie, and also the EHIC – European Health Insurance Card – details of which are explained in the leaflet or on those websites. This entitles citizens of EU countries to obtain reciprocal health benefits in other EU countries.

ACCOMMODATION

As you would expect in a holiday area that has been established for over two hundred years, there is plenty of accommodation in the High Tatras. There are at least ten thousand beds in hotels and pensions in the Slovak resorts, and a similar number in Zakopane and its outlying villages, making them the most important tourist areas in their respective countries.

During the communist era, virtually all the accommodation was owned either by government agencies, which limited the opportunities for commercial enterprise, or by trade unions for the exclusive use of their members. Nowadays the hotels and pensions are mostly privately owned. Some of the larger hotels are run by hotel chains, in particular Sorea in Slovakia, which is that country's largest hotel company. International hotel groups are also taking an interest in the Tatras – Best Western have already signed up a hotel in Tatranska Lomnica. Trade unions still own many of the establishments, but non-members are now welcome to stay.

There is a good choice of hotels and pensions in all categories up to four stars. At the time of writing there is one five-star hotel in Štrbské Pleso (Grand Hotel Kempinski High Tatras), and two in Zakopane (Hotel Litwor, Villa Marilor).

Hotels usually have a restaurant providing all meals, and sometimes a coffee shop or cafeteria where light meals and snacks are provided all day. Guest houses or pensions (*penzión* in Slovak, *pensjonat* in Polish) may provide bed and break-fast only, or half-pension (bed, breakfast and evening meal), but it is unusual for them to provide full-pension (including lunch).

Many experienced mountain walkers prefer to stay up in the mountains, as this saves considerable effort and allows a deeper exploration of the summits and higher routes (see 'Mountains Chalets or Refuges', page 51). There are mountain hotels at Popradské Pleso, Velické Pleso and Hrebienok on the Slovak side and at Kalatówki on the Polish side. They offer a higher standard of accommodation than the chalets or refuges.

There are several hostels in the Zakopane area but none on the Slovak side. Camping is only permitted at official campsites – there are just a few on either side, with varying facilities. The number of self-catering establishments is growing rapidly on both sides.

A growing trade in inexpensive private house accommodation is developing, especially in Zakopane, and this can be booked through local travel agencies. Note that meals (including breakfast) may not be served in these places. You can either eat at nearby hotels or restaurants, or at some places there is a kitchen available for the use of guests.

In Zakopane you will often see *pokoje* (room), *pokoje gościnne* (guest room) or *noclegi* (overnight accommodation) written on boards outside private houses. You may also see people standing at stations or beside the road, showing any of these words on scraps of cardboard. You can of course take up such offers at your own risk, but you should be aware that they are not controlled by any official body and there is no guarantee of standards or professionalism.

You can book direct, though you may find it more practical to book a package tour from your own country, or contact a travel agency located in the High Tatras, which should be well placed to find out which hotels have space available and are best suited to your requirements (they may charge a booking fee). Most tourist information offices provide a booking service. Details of local travel agencies are

Promenaders in Krupówki street in Zakopane

included in the 'Shopping and Local Services' information in Sections 3 and 4 for each country.

It is always advisable to book accommodation in advance if possible, but some travel agencies in the Tatras will do their best to find accommodation for tourists who arrive without a booking (see Appendix C for more details).

FITNESS

To get the most from any walking holiday, the fitter you are when you start, the better. Prepare yourself by doing some hard walking at home, preferably in mountain or hill country, or at the very least, tone up your muscles and flex your joints with stretching exercises. Remember, too, that you will probably be spending all or most of your time at a higher altitude than you are used to, and it may take a few days to adjust to this. There is less oxygen at high altitudes, and you may find yourself getting out of breath more quickly than you expected.

Plan your first few walks along the easier routes, leaving the tougher ones till later. As the latter are usually scenically more spectacular, this should also provide the added benefit of building up to a climax. If you find that you are having difficulty on the easier routes, you would be well advised not to tackle the harder ones.

Be prepared for an occasional 'bad day', when you find it hard to keep going up the steeper routes, though of course this will affect everyone differently. Local people say, 'Every third day will be a struggle. ' If this affects you, try one of the easier walks, or do some sightseeing, or explore the villages – there is plenty to keep you interested.

If there are children in your party, unless they have walked in high mountains before, you should plan to keep to the easier routes, to see how they adapt, before considering tackling any harder ones.

There is a good choice of alternative attractions in the Tatras for any members of your party who do not wish to tackle the mountains – see 'Diversions' in Sections 3 and 4 for each country. Some 'easy access' trails have been developed but they are quite steep in places.

CLOTHING AND EQUIPMENT

What you wear in the evening is best left to your own judgement, though formal clothes are rarely seen in the Tatras. Some guidance on your walking apparel may be helpful, however – to enjoy your holiday to the full, it is wise to take clothing that is both hard wearing and comfortable.

Modern clothing specially designed for outdoor activities can provide considerable advantages. For example, 'breathable' materials allow perspiration to escape while keeping rain out, though garments made from them are usually more expensive. Cheaper alternatives may be adequate if you are lucky with the weather, but you must decide whether it is worth spending the extra money for added protection. Study advertisements and articles in one of the walkers' magazines that are readily available in most newsagents, or on the internet, and ask for advice at outdoor equipment shops.

As your feet, naturally, are going to be the most important parts of your body on this holiday, let us start with **footwear** and work up. The section on Mountain Safety and Emergency Services (see page 54) outlines the reasons for taking walking boots, rather than trainers or walking shoes, though on some low-level walks the latter may be adequate. Lightweight walking boots may be suitable for most walking in the Tatras, but you should seek advice at an equipment shop. Whichever kind of footwear you have, make sure that it fits well and is well worn in, because nothing is more certain to spoil your holiday than new boots that have raised blisters by the end of the first day.

The composition of your **socks** will be a matter of trial and error. Some walkers manage with one thick pair in boots, others find two pairs (a thick pair on top of a thin one) necessary for comfort. Wool is generally most suitable for a thick pair, though thin cotton, silk or acrylic ones are often worn underneath.

Whether you should cover your **legs** (with trousers or breeches) or bare them (with shorts or skirt) is again up to your own inclination, but if you opt for the latter, be prepared to don waterproof trousers or breeches if it turns cold or windy, especially when stopping for an extended open-air break.

For your **upper half**, if possible wear something underneath your shirt that will 'wick' (carry away) the perspiration from your body, helping to keep your back dry under a rucksack. Whatever the weather down in the valley, always carry at least one warm pullover, and/or a fleece-lined jacket. When you stop, perspiring, for lunch on a high mountain pass or peak, wind whistling across your shoulders, you will need the extra layer. For the same reason, **hat** and **gloves** will be appreciated. When you are wet (from rain or perspiration), a spare T-shirt or shirt will be welcome when you stop for lunch, and a **sweatband** for your head or wrist may be useful.

Never tackle a mountain without **waterproof clothing,** carried in your ruck-sack. There is often some reluctance to don waterproofs, as condensation can make you as wet or wetter than rain, but as many modern waterproofs are breath-able, this should not be a problem. In the mountains you should carry a full set of waterproofs, ie trousers and a jacket with hood, or a hat. You may also find **gaiters** invaluable, as they help to keep water and snow out of your boots.

The most efficient way of carrying all your spare items is in a **rucksack**, as it leaves both hands free in situations when you need to hold on to something. A small 'day sack' will be adequate for most excursions into the mountains. The capacity of rucksacks is usually measured in litres – that is, the amount of water that can be poured inside – and those suitable for day trips are in the 20 to 35 litre range, with smaller ones available for children. Always put both straps over your

Looking towards Jahňací Štít from Široké Sedlo in the White Tatras (Green 5900, Slovakia) (photo: R Turnbull)

shoulders – you never know when you may need the full support of both hands and arms in an emergency.

Your choice of rucksack will depend on what you intend to put in it. The very least would include the items mentioned in the section on Mountain Safety and Emergency Services, ie spare clothing, waterproofs, water-bottle, first aid kit, map, compass, whistle and emergency food. Unless you are sure of eating at a mountain chalet, you may also wish to carry your lunch food, and perhaps a camera.

If you are planning to stay overnight in a mountain chalet, a larger rucksack may be needed, for toilet accessories and a sheet sleeping bag, and possibly more spare clothing.

On the waymarked routes no special **climbing gear** is needed, but if you go off these routes with a mountain guide you may need some form of harness, to be clipped on to some of the ironware encountered. This can be hired locally if necessary – your guide will advise. An **ice-axe** may be useful if you are visiting the Tatras in late autumn, winter or spring, as snow may then be encountered.

Those who feel uncomfortable on slippery surfaces may wish to take one or two **walking sticks** or **poles**, which may also be helpful at any time when descending. They are strongly recommended for anyone walking in the Tatras in late autumn, winter or spring, when snow may cover the routes, even at lower altitudes. Easily packed telescopic poles are available in outdoor equipment shops, but when flying you should pack them in your checked baggage as airlines will not normally allow them to be taken into the cabin.

A **torch** will be needed for a few waymarked routes in Poland, which descend into or through caves. In any case, it is a good idea to carry a small torch (with spare battery and bulb) in case you get benighted on tricky mountain paths – this is more likely in the late season (September/October) or in winter.

MAPS

No walker should venture into the mountains without a good walking map of the area. Even though 'tourist routes' in the Tatras are usually very well waymarked, it is possible to get lost or disorientated, or signs and waymarks can go missing, so a map is essential (it can be embarrassing to have to ask strangers to see theirs).

Always keep in contact with your map – in other words, whenever you reach a path junction, a chalet or other identifiable feature, identify your location on the map, then if you do get lost you should have some idea of where you are.

There are some excellent walking maps covering the High Tatras in Slovakia and Poland, at various scales, usually 1:25,000 (4cm = 1km, or approximately 2½in = 1 mile) and 1:50,000 (2cm = 1km, or approximately 1¼in = 1 mile).

Because of the way the border runs, most maps cover both sides to some extent. The names of most places in the mountains are slightly different in Polish and Slovak, but most maps show both versions, at least on or near the border. So if you plan to spend all or most of your time in one country, it will be best to obtain that country's maps, but they may be suitable for an occasional trip into the other country.

Try to buy at least one map before you go, so that you can familiarise with the area, and in conjunction with this book, plan your walks in advance. Most of the maps listed below can be bought at specialist map shops in other countries, or online, though this will probably be more expensive than buying them locally. There are many places in the Tatras where you can buy maps, including bookshops, hotels, street kiosks and tourist information offices.

Some of these maps have additional general information on the reverse, but usually in Slovak or Polish only (at the time of writing only one of the maps listed had a fully English version – 'Sygnatura: Tatraplan sheet 2502', see below). The key on nearly all other maps at least includes a translation of symbols into English, and it is possible that other fully English versions will become available – check when buying. (Some of the map text is tiny, so you may find a magnifying glass helpful – some compasses incorporate one.)

Note that some maps also show cross-country skiing and cycling routes, and may appear very similar to walking routes and educational trails. Check the symbols carefully in the key.

Several maps are published, at scales of around 1:300,000 to 1:800,000, of the whole of Slovakia or Poland, and may be useful for your journeys to and from the Tatras.

Below is a list of a selection of maps of the Tatras that were available in 2010. The name of the publisher precedes the map title, with English translation and scale in brackets. The size is shown in millimetres (width x height), and the approximate area covered is shown by reference to significant place names nearest to their southwest, southeast, northwest and northeast corners respectively.

Maps Showing the Full Tatras Range (Western, High, White)
CartoMedia: Praktyczny Atlas Tatr (1:25,000). A handy 144-page pocket atlas of the whole range of Western, High and White Tatras. 115 x 185mm. Additional information in Polish only but key to symbols has an English translation. Includes street maps of Zakopane, Štrbské Pleso, Nová Lesna, Starý Smokovec, Tatranská Lomnica, Tatranská Kotlina and Poprad at 1:15,000.

Starý Smokovec church , Slovakia

Sygnatura: Tatry w Całości (the Whole Tatras, 1:50,000) 1070 x 670mm. Covers the area between Bobrovec, Stará Lesná, Trstená and Czarna Góra. Reverse shows additional information in Polish only, and has a street map of Nowy Targ.

Eko-graf: Tatry Polskie i Słowackie (Polish and Slovak Tatras, 1:50,000) 980 x 480mm. Covers the area between Smrečany, Stará Lesná, Brestová and Ždiar. A compact map showing most of the entire range of the Western, High and White Tatras. The reverse shows additional information in Polish only, and has a street map of Zakopane at 1:20,000.

Sygnatura: Dookoła Tatr (Around the Tatras, 1:100,000) 970 x 670mm. Covers the area between Chopok, Spišská Nová Ves, Námestovo and Piwniczna Zdroj. Includes much of the Low Tatras and other nearby ranges. The reverse includes general information in Polish only, also street plans of Nowy Targ, Liptovský Mikuláš and Poprad.

Maps of the Slovak High Tatras
Sygnatura: Tatraplan sheet 2502 The High Tatras (1:25,000) 1320 x 890mm. English version covering High and White Tatras between Tri Studničky, Tatranská Kotlina, Nová Lesna and Tatranská Javorina. Reverse side has substantial information about the area in English and street plans of Štrbské Pleso, Starý Smokovec, Tatranská Lomnica and Nová Lesna.

VKÚ sheet 2: Vysoké Tatry (High Tatras, 1:25,000) 1210 x 765mm. Covers the area between Tri Studničky, Stará Lesná, Kuźnice and Ždiar. Printed one side only and sold in a plastic folder together with a booklet containing supplementary information (currently available in Slovak only) and a map measurer.

VKÚ sheet 113: Vysoké Tatry (High Tatras, 1:50,000) 580 x 1020mm. Covers the area between Važec, Poprad, Poronin and Veľká Franková. Printed one side only and sold in a plastic folder together with a booklet containing supplementary information (currently available in Slovak only) and a map measurer.

VKÚ: Ortofotomapa Vysoké Tatry (Orthophotographic Map of the High Tatras, 1:20,000) 1145 x 775mm. An unusual representation of the area based on satellite photography. Covers the area between Tri Studničky, Stará Lesná, Czarny Staw and Šalviový Prameň. Printed one side only. Includes panoramas of Tatras ranges from several angles.

43

Geodis: Vysoké Tatry Atlas Ortofotomáp (High Tatras Orthophotographic Atlas, 1:15,000) 128-page atlas based on satellite photogaphy. Covers the area between Hrádok, Stará Lesná, Kuźnice and Dolina Bachledova. Also contains 1:6000 scale photographic maps of the main resorts (Štrbské Pleso, Starý Smokovec and Tatranská Lomnica).

Shocart Active sheet 1097: Vysoké Tatry (High Tatras, 1:50,000). 655 x 945mm. Covers the area of Slovakia and Poland between Važec, Poprad, Szaflary and Spišská Stará Ves. Reverse side has information in Slovak only, plus key with English translation and a relief panorama of the Tatras.

Maps of the Polish Tatras
PPWK/Copernicus: Tatry Zachodnie (Western Tatras, 1:20,000) 875 x 600mm. Covers the area between Wołowiec, Kasprowy Wierch, Turek and Kuźnice. Reverse shows additional information in Polish only and panoramas of peaks from four viewpoints.

Sygnatura: Tatra National Park Tourist Map (1:25,000) 1190 x 815mm. Covers the area between Wałowiec, Morskie Oko, Witów and Bukowina Tatrzańska, including all of Zakopane and the Gubałówka ridge. Reverse shows additional information in Polish only, but includes information in English about geographical features, wildlife and mountain huts, panoramas of peaks from two viewpoints, and a town plan of Zakopane at 1:15,000.

Sygnatura: Tatry Wysokie Słowackie i Polskie (High Tatras of Slovakia and Poland, 1:25,000) 1190 x 815mm. Covers the area between Tri Studničky, Stará Lesná, Kuźnice and Ždiar. Reverse shows additional information in Polish only and a panorama of peaks.

Sygnatura: Tatry Zachodnie Słowackie i Polskie (Western Tatras of Slovakia and Poland, 1:25,000) 1190 x 815mm. Covers the area between Bobrovec, Tri Studničky, Habovka and Kuźnice. Reverse shows additional information in Polish only and a panorama of peaks.

Express Map: Supermapa Tatry (Tatras Supermap, 1:27,000) 1005 x 470mm. Covers the area between Wołowiec, Morskie Oko, Witów and Nowy Targ, divided between both sides. Waterproof and sectioned so that the map can be folded without damaging the creases. Also includes a street plan of Zakopane at 1:15,000.

Sygnatura: Tatry Polskie Kompaktowe (Polish Tatras Compact, 1:30,000) 935 x 610mm. Covers the area between Wołowiec, Morskie Oko, Witów and Bukowina Tatrzańska, including all of Zakopane and the Gubałówka ridge. Reverse shows additional information in Polish only.

Mapa Roku 3x1 Tatry Polskie (1:20,000) A pocket-size set of three maps in one folder, covering respectively the western, central and eastern regions of the Polish Tatras. Each map measures 675 x 480mm and the full area covered is between Wołowiec, Rysy, Siwa Polana and Łysa Polana. Includes a street plan of Zakopane.

Larger scale maps can be obtained locally of specific areas, such as **Orla Perć** and **Dolina Chochołowska**.

Street Plans
Some maps include street plans of the Tatras resorts as mentioned above. A wide selection of street plans of Zakopane can be bought there, and a street plan of Poprad can be bought at bookshops and tourist information offices in the Slovak resorts.

The authors are grateful to Stanfords for much of this information. Many of the maps shown can be obtained or ordered from their shops at 12 Long Acre, Covent Garden, London, WC2E 9LP (phone 020 7836 1321) or 29 Corn Street, Bristol, BS1 1HT (phone 0117 929 9966), or from their website www.stanfords.co.uk.

PATHS AND WAYMARKING

The Tatras are blessed with a dense network of well-maintained and waymarked walking routes – some 600km altogether. This is more than may appear likely from a glance at the map, but you should remember that in the mountains, paths twist and turn and rise and fall much more than in flatter terrain, and at high levels they frequently zigzag for quite long distances, the combined effect in some cases doubling the apparent length of a path.

You must keep to the waymarked routes, unless you are accompanied by a registered local mountain guide, and you are forbidden to take short cuts – if you are caught 'off-route' by a national park ranger, you are likely to be fined. This may annoy some walkers, but it is based on sound reasons, including protecting wildlife in the more sensitive areas, preventing erosion, or giving badly eroded areas a chance to recover (the Tatras, being the most accessible alpine mountains for a considerable section of the populations of Central and Eastern Europe, have suffered much overuse and erosion).

There are a few places where, though not actually permitted, it is accepted practice to go slightly off the waymarked path. These include the minor summits of Ostrva and Veľka Svišťovka along the Tatranská Magistrála in Slovakia, and of course places where picnic tables are provided away from the path.

For most walkers the waymarked routes will provide more than enough scope for their visit, and take them to some of the highest summits. More experienced mountain walkers can extend their range by engaging a local guide – see 'Mountain Guides', page 53. **In Poland, groups of more than ten people walking together are required to engage a mountain guide.**

Average **walking times** are indicated on signposts at each path junction, as well as on most maps, and they are also given in the lists of Suggested Routes and Path Descriptions later in this book. There may be slight variations between times shown in various sources. Time required for refreshment and other stops must be added, and you should allow plenty of extra time in case of unexpected delays.

As a rough guide, for every 300m (1000ft) of altitude, you can expect to take around an hour for the ascent, and 45 minutes for the descent, though on some routes descending is as tricky or strenuous as ascending, and therefore almost as time consuming. While paths are well constructed, the terrain is often steep and rocky, and you will need strong knees and ankles to stand up to the pounding they will receive on descents.

A typical Slovak High Tatras signpost, near Popradské Pleso

Unlike skiing, the **colours** that appear on waymarks have no bearing on the difficulty of any route – they have only been allocated by the authorities for ease of identification.

In Slovakia, four-digit **reference numbers** are used for administrative purposes by the national park authority, and appear on some maps, but do not appear on the waymarks themselves. However, they provide a useful means of reference in this book, so we have used them in the route descriptions. There is no equivalent numbering system in Poland, so the authors have devised their own numbering system (with three digits) for those routes. The corresponding numbers are shown on the maps on pages 2–3 and 4–5.

For more detailed information about the waymarking system in Slovakia and Poland, see 'Introduction to Walking...' in Sections 3 and 4.

Visitors to the national park area in Poland are charged a small **entry fee** – for more details, see 'Introduction to Walking...' in Section 4 (Poland).

On waymarked routes in both countries you will frequently encounter a variety of **green signs**, bearing text in either yellow (Slovakia) or white (Poland), always in the appropriate language, but usually with a translation into German, Russian or Hungarian, and occasionally English! They are invariably exhortations of a common-sense nature, concerning walkers' safety or the protection of the environment. They include, for example, 'Keep to the waymarked routes', 'No short cuts', 'Do not pick flowers or fruit', 'No camping or fires', 'No bathing in the tarns'.

Some short stretches of routes, described in this book as 'airy' or 'exposed' (steep ground with a long drop below), are protected by **fixed chains**, or sometimes wires of about 2cm diameter. You use them to haul yourself up – or lower yourself down, which is more difficult, as it is not so easy to see where to put your feet. The chains or wires are usually firmly attached to the rock, but you should test them first. For walkers who have yet to experience such situations, the anticipation is often worse than the actuality. Provided that you take care, and do not rush it, there is rarely cause for alarm, and there will be a thrill of achievement afterwards.

If there is a choice, you are advised to walk in the direction which will allow you to ascend, rather than descend, such sections. In either direction, you must always face the mountain, as this provides greater stability. Some busy routes with chains or wires have a one-way system, so that there is no conflict of interest between walkers travelling in opposite directions, and to reduce the risk of being hit by a rock dislodged by another walker.

Apart from the chains and wires, some routes involve short, steep stretches of **scrambling** – using hands as well as feet to get yourself up or down. Stretches involving fixed chains, wires or scrambling are clearly marked in this book, so if you do not like the sound of such activities, they can be avoided.

On routes needing a qualified mountain guide (also on the Orla Perć route in Poland), you are likely to encounter a **via ferrata**, an Italian term meaning 'iron way'. As well as chains or wires, this may involve ironware of a more exotic nature, such as fixed ladders and pegs, which you use to negotiate trickier sections in exposed situations. For walkers with a sense of adventure, confidence, a cool head and no great fear of heights, such routes represent the pinnacle of their experience.

In Slovakia the higher paths are closed during winter and spring (1 November to 15 June inclusive), partly because of danger from avalanches and partly due to consideration for wildlife, which may be hibernating or rearing their young.

In Poland there is no such formal closure, though walkers are expected to use their common sense and take notice of avalanche warnings posted at the kiosks where entry fees are collected. In this book we indicate whether for practical purposes each path is likely to be open or closed in winter and spring.

In both countries a considerable number of waymarked routes remain open in winter and spring – see Winter Walking, page 59. However, you should not use them if there is too much snow, making the waymarks invisible, or in fog. You can check the conditions at a tourist information or mountain rescue office.

Paths may be closed at other times for some other reason, such as emergency maintenance. In Slovakia you may see signs saying either *otvorená* (open) or *zatvorená* (closed) or *pozor lavíny* (beware avalanches). In Poland, *przejscie uzbronione* (no entry) or *uwaga lawiny* (beware avalanches).

REFRESHMENTS AND TOILETS

It is safe to drink **water** from taps in the Tatras villages and from the mountain chalets, although many people prefer to buy bottled water from shops or cafés. You can refill your water-bottles from springs (the water from some of these contains iron), and also from the higher tarns and streams in the mountains, provided that they are above the level of the mountain chalets. (It is not recommended to drink water from below this level, because there is a danger that it will have been contaminated by sewage from the huts.)

Ascending the chained approach to Priećne Sedlo (Yellow 8860, Slovakia) (photo: R Turnbull)

The source of 'Starý Smokovec Water'

You can buy food for **picnic lunches** in supermarkets and food shops, of which there are plenty – the word 'supermarket' is often used, otherwise look for *potraviny* (food shop) in Slovakia, or *sklep spożywczy* (grocer's shop) in Poland.

There is a wide choice of refreshment facilities in the main resorts (often in hotels), and most of the smaller resorts have at least one or two bars or cafés. In Slovakia the cafés may be called *kaviareň* (coffee shop) or *cukráreň* (confectioners), in Polish *kawiarnia* or *cukiernik* respectively; most sell mouthwatering cakes and a bewildering range of coffees and teas. The entries for the resorts in the Gazetteers indicate the availability of refreshment facilities.

Refreshments can be obtained at **mountain chalets** or **refuges** (see below).

Toilets are generally available where refreshments are provided, at main railway stations and at the top and bottom stations of mountain railways and cable-cars. In Poland, toilet cubicles are also provided at most starting points beside roads, and at some other points along the long valleys that lead into the mountains – they are indicated on most walking maps and in the route descriptions in this book.

See also Mountain Safety and Emergency Services, page 54, regarding emergency rations.

MOUNTAIN CHALETS OR REFUGES

In the mountains there is a network of establishments that provide refreshments and accommodation. In the Slovak High Tatras there are 11, called *chata* ('chalet', plural *chaty*), on the Polish side there are eight, called *schronisko* ('refuge', plural *schroniska*). English speakers sometimes refer to them as 'mountain huts', Slovaks happily refer in English to 'chalets', whereas Poles prefer to translate to 'refuge', as 'chalet' implies 'toilet' to them! In this book we use the preferred translation on each side of the border.

Four hotels are situated at a comparatively high altitude in the High Tatras. In Slovakia, they are Chata Popradské Pleso (1494m, one star) above Štrbské Pleso, Hotel Sliezsky Dom (1663m, three stars) above Tatranská Polianka and Horský Hotel Sorea Hrebienok (1263m, three stars) above Starý Smokovec. In Poland, Hotel Gorski Kalatówki (1198m) above Kuźnice is really a mountain refuge offering accommodation and facilities of a higher standard than the others.

The chalets or refuges are located in such strategic positions that you are unlikely to undertake a day's walk in the Tatras without passing by or close to one or more of them. They are usually in splendid, often spectacular situations – beside a tarn, in a remote valley or below a towering cliff face. Food and drink cost more than in the resorts, due to transportation costs, but prices are reasonable. If it is cold or wet outside, a steaming bowl of goulash soup, some sausages or a mug of delicious, spiced lemon tea, will soon warm you up.

Toilet facilities in the chalets or refuges may be rather primitive, and you may wish to carry a small supply of your own toilet paper, as it may have run out.

Starolesnianská Polana and Rainerova Chata on the Tatranská Magistrála, Slovakia

In Slovakia the chalets are privately owned and leased to individual wardens. Since the revolution in 1989, three have reverted to their original names, because new ones were given by the communist authorities against the wishes of local people. They are Zamkovského Chata (formerly Nálepkova Chata or Chata Kapitána Nálepku), Chata pri Zelenom Plese (formerly Brnčalova Chata), and Chata pri Popradskom Plese (formerly Chata Kapitána Morávku). Old maps may show their previous names. There is a proposal to rebuild a second chalet at Popradské Pleso, Majláthová Chata, which was destroyed some time ago. Chata Kapitána Rašu near Tri Studnički burned down in 1993 – there are no plans to replace it, but it may still be shown on some maps.

The Polish refuges and Hotel Górski Kalatówki are operated by PTTK (see Polish gazetteer). During the communist era the Polish refuges had particularly long and tongue-twisting names, usually in honour of some local dignitary. Very few people used these names, and most were referred to by a shorter, popular name, which is now shown on most maps (some older maps may show the longer names). The larger Polish refuges operate a system whereby you must first queue to order and pay for your food and hot drinks at a separate counter, then you are given a ticket which you take to the kitchen hatch. The problem is in knowing what you want to order, as the menu may be difficult to establish! Under this system, cold drinks and confectionery are sold at the cash counter.

All the chalets or refuges have a rubber stamp, which many walkers use to record their visit in a notebook. Some maps include spaces for these stamps beside a picture of the refuge. Those in Poland also have a visitors' book for you to sign.

Approaching Schronisko Pieciu Stawow beside Przedni Staw Polski (Blue 209, Poland) (photo: R. Turnbull)

It is well worth considering staying overnight at a refuge or chalet, or touring from one to another. Apart from saving the effort of climbing several hundred metres each day, there is a special atmosphere and camaraderie among the guests that cannot be experienced at the resort hotels.

Simple dormitory accommodation is offered, though some also have bedrooms available. Washing and toilet facilities may be quite basic, in some cases in an outhouse. The accommodation is inexpensive, but in great demand during the summer months, especially August, and you should book ahead if possible. There is a custom in the mountains that, in emergency, walkers arriving late without a booking are not turned away, for obvious reasons, but will be found space on the floor, on or under tables, or any space large enough for a human frame. Blankets are provided, but you will need to take a lightweight or sheet sleeping bag.

For further information about these places, see their respective entries in the gazetteers in Sections 3 and 4, and Appendix B (Accommodation).

MOUNTAIN GUIDES

In the Slovak High Tatras you will need a qualified mountain guide if you wish to explore excellent recognised routes away from the waymarked network. Routes needing a guide include the two highest Tatras summits, Gerlachovský Štít (2654m) and Lomnický Štít (2634m), and some exciting ridge walks. They are not included on the waymarked network, either because they are too difficult or dangerous to undertake without specialised local knowledge, or to restrict the number of walkers using them where excessive use will cause damage, or a combination of both.

All these routes are regularly used by permitted groups. If you try to follow them without a guide, you may put yourself at risk of an accident, and it is certain that you will be spotted by a helicopter patrol, or challenged and fined by a national park warden or a mountain guide.

All routes requiring a guide involve a fair amount of scrambling, and use of wires and other fixed apparatus in exposed situations, so they are all rated 'difficult' or 'strenuous' by our grading system (see page 64).

In the Polish Tatras it is not possible for guides to take you to summits that are off the waymarked routes, but **all groups of ten or more people wishing to walk on the waymarked routes must be accompanied by a mountain guide**.

Another reason for hiring a guide is to enable you to get away from the crowds if you are visiting in the high season (July and August). At this time you are advised to book your guides at the earliest opportunity (even before you go if possible), as they are in great demand. Of course, even on the waymarked routes you will benefit from having a local guide with you to provide local knowledge, not only of the locations but of flora and fauna.

In Slovakia the guides are provided by the mountain rescue service (Horská Služba), and you can book your guide at their office in Starý Smokovec. The situation is more complicated in Poland as there are four guide organisations. (A detailed explanation is shown on the Tatra Mountains website at http://bit.ly/i7tU6o or http://tatramountains.org and search for 'guides') but you can book a guide at the national park information centre by Rondo Jana Pawła II (the roundabout at the foot of the approach road to Kuźnice). In either country you can also book guides through some local travel agencies or hotel receptions.

> Although this book is not aimed at **mountain climbers**, it is as well to mention here that members of climbing clubs can walk off the waymarked routes, subject to certain criteria that should be checked with the relevant national park authority (see page 29) – TANAP in Slovakia (www.tanap.sk) or TPN in Poland (www.tpn.pl). Climbing is not permitted in certain areas.

MOUNTAIN SAFETY AND EMERGENCY SERVICES

Anyone who walks in mountainous areas should be aware of the possible dangers that lurk around the corner, though with proper precautions they are most unlikely to cause harm in normal circumstances. Thunderstorms, falling stones, falls resulting in injuries, and heart problems are the most usual. It should be stressed that, while accidents can happen to anyone at any time, those who are prepared for them and know what to do in the event of an emergency are less likely to suffer serious consequences as a result. Never say 'It won't happen to me'!

First and foremost, you must wear **suitable footwear**. **Waterproofs**, **spare clothing**, **hat**, **gloves**, **water-bottle**, **small first aid kit**, **map**, **compass**, **whistle** and **emergency food** complete your minimum preparations for safety and comfort in the mountains. They need not be heavy – modern equipment of this kind is usually compact and light. The Clothing and Equipment section describes some of these items more fully, and here are the reasons for wearing or carrying them.

Footwear In the mountains, both for your own sake and that of other walkers, you must always walk carefully. Good-quality walking boots with a deep tread almost force you to do so, as they grip the surface in a way that no ordinary shoes can. Walking boots protect your ankles from damage on rocks and hidden cracks – trainers and walking shoes do not.

Waterproofs and Spare Clothing Weather can change quickly in the mountains (see page 28). Cloudbursts and strong winds may catch you before you have time to reach shelter. In such conditions, without waterproofs and spare clothing, the danger of suffering from hypothermia is very real indeed. Carry them!

Even though you may become very warm and perspire profusely while climbing, when you reach the top you will stop to rest, admire the view or take refreshment. This is usually in a high position where the wind is at its strongest, so you quickly start to feel cold. An extra pullover or windproof jacket, hat and gloves will then be much appreciated. On the other hand, do not allow yourself to overheat while climbing – take off as many layers as will allow you to continue to walk in comfort (and decency).

Renáta Nárožná approaching Široké Sedlo in the White Tatras, with Spišská Magura in the background (Green 5900, Slovakia)

First Aid Kit If you suffer a fall, or cut yourself on rocks, it may take several hours to reach a place where first aid is available. A basic kit should contain a selection of plasters, antiseptic cream and a triangular bandage. Buy one that includes some instructions on what to do in common cases needing treatment. Optional extras may include a blister kit, something for insect bites, tick remover, insect repellent and sun-protection cream. Depending on your susceptibilities, you may also need sunglasses, skin cream and lip salve.

Your kit should also include an advice sheet. Although expert attention should always be obtained as quickly as possible if necessary, or you may have a qualified first aider in your party, some immediate guidance may be very welcome

Map and Compass While waymarking on most routes in the High Tatras is very good, when tired or in poor visibility you may become disorientated, or take a wrong turning, and then a map and compass will be of enormous help in deciding which way to go, or how to regain your intended route.

Mobile Phone More for summoning help in emergency than for chatting with family or friends from the mountain tops, which may be very expensive. Note that some parts of the Tatras do not currently receive a signal – some maps show mobile phone coverage (see Maps, page 40).

Whistle For attracting attention in emergency. If you cannot easily reach help, attract attention to your plight by giving the international distress call – six long blasts, repeated every minute. An answering series of three blasts means that your signal has been noticed, and help is on the way. A torch can perform the same function in the dark, using flashes instead of whistle blasts.

Emergency Food If you should suffer an accident, or become lost and dispirited, it will boost both your morale and physical strength to dig out that bar of chocolate, or packet of peanuts or raisins, when the nearest refreshment facilities may be several hours away.

Weather Forecast Each day, before you set out, get the weather forecast from your hotel reception, an information office or the mountain rescue service, and plan a route that takes the weather into account.

Remember the **wind chill factor**. The higher the wind speed, the more it cools the temperature, so that you may not only have to battle against the wind, but also wear more clothes to guard against the cold. The more effort you have to put into your walking, the greater the cooling effect. The actual fall in the temperature experienced varies, depending on the wind speed and the amount of effort being expended, but while walking at a steady pace it is approximately in the region of 1–3°C (2–6°F) for every kilometre per hour of wind speed. You are likely to notice the wind speed more as you climb, especially where there is no protection from trees.

Remember the **altitude factor** (also called the lapse rate). On top of the wind chill effect, the temperature drops as you climb, by about 1°C (2°F) for every 150m.

Thunderstorms When a thunderstorm threatens, do not go higher but descend straight away, especially if you are on or near a summit or ridge, as lightning tends to strike in such places. Do not take shelter under a tree or prominent rock, as these are also favourite targets of lightning. Get down into a valley, or find a chalet or refuge where you can sit out the storm.

Falling Stones or Rocks Take care, especially when walking or scrambling on a steep slope with loose rocks, that you do not dislodge one, and watch out for those dislodged by walkers higher up the slope. If you should set loose a rock that threatens to roll some way downhill, yell out a warning. In English one would shout 'below!' or 'look out!', but better in the Tatras is *pozor!* in Slovakia, or *uwaga!* (pronounced 'oovahga') in Polish. Or you could try the German *Achtung!*

Slippery Rocks and Paths In wet weather some kinds of moss- or lichen-bearing rock, and wooden rain channels or bridges, become slippery, and paths can turn into torrents. Some walkers find one or two walking sticks or poles helpful on steep or rough ground, though they can also get in the way when scrambling or using chains and other fixtures.

Leave Word of Your Proposed Route Do this with someone, such as the hotel reception, who will realise if you fail to return that something may have happened, and will know where the mountain rescue will need to look. Some hotels keep a walks book for this purpose. Obviously you should then stick to your proposed route, and report in when you return.

Know Your Limits If the weather should deteriorate, or you are finding the going too hard, do not be ashamed to turn back.

Walk in Company Try to avoid walking alone on the more remote and less popular routes. If you should fall and twist your ankle, the sooner you get help the better, and an uninjured companion will be able to reach it much more quickly. Ideally there should be at least three in your party, so that one can go for help while the other stays with the injured person. If you should suffer an accident

Descending the chains from Giewont
summit (Blue 206, Poland)

when on your own, other walkers are usually very willing to help, as no doubt you would help them if necessary.

Help! If an accident should happen, for which help is needed, keep calm. Use your mobile phone to summon help. If you do not have one, or there is no signal, in most parts of the High Tatras there is usually a mountain chalet or refuge nearby, which is linked by telephone or radio to the mountain rescue service. If you are closer to a village, find a telephone kiosk, hotel or shop. Contact the mountain rescue service directly by dialling 18300 in Slovakia or 0603 100 100 in Poland. Alternatively, you can dial the international emergency number 112, but it may take longer to get through to the mountain rescue service.

In Slovakia there is a charge if you have to bring out the mountain rescue service. If your travel insurance does not cover this, you may wish to take out a policy that can be bought at local tourist information offices. There is currently no charge in Poland, unless due to wilful negligence on your part, such as ignoring professional advice, in which case you will be expected to pay the full cost, or at least make a donation.

WINTER WALKING

In the Slovak Tatras the higher routes are closed in winter and spring (generally 1 November to 15 June), because of the dangers from snow and ice on steep slopes, and from avalanches, and to protect wildlife, which may be hibernating or rearing their young.

On the Polish side there is no formal ban on walking in the higher regions, but some routes are inaccessible in practice. You are expected to use your common sense and take notice of avalanche warnings.

The path descriptions for each country include an indication as to whether each is open or closed in winter and spring. In Slovakia, most walking maps also include a symbol to indicate that certain routes are closed in winter.

Substantial snowfalls may occur from November onwards, more unusually in September or October, and the lakes start to freeze over. The average winter temperature in the High Tatras resorts is around minus 5–6°C (22–24°F). However, most of the lower routes, up to the mountain chalets or refuges, remain open and well used – as do the chalets and refuges themselves for welcome refreshment. Provided that you are well prepared, walking through the snow in winter can be a delightful experience. You will probably find that others have gone before you, treading out a path in the snow. Most of the chalets and refuges are open all year round, so there will be ample opportunity for a hot drink or meal.

You should wear and carry everything that you would in summer, with the addition of **gaiters**, which stop snow and water from entering your boots. Remember especially to carry a **hat**, **gloves** and a spare **pullover** or **fibre-pile jacket**.

A phenomenon of autumn and winter weather in mountainous areas is that of **inversion**. On windless days the cold, heavy air streams down from the mountains into the plains, pushing the warmer air up into the mountains, where it may stay for several days. This can make the temperature in the mountains, up to an altitude of around 1800m, warmer than that in the plain by up to 10°C (18°F). This also results in a layer of cloud at the level where the cold and warm air mix, so that there is sun in the mountains when it is gloomy in the plain.

CROSS-BORDER WALKING

As described in Border Controls (page 33), restrictions on crossing the border between Poland and Slovakia have been lifted, and normally everyone can now pass freely, though there may be times when checks have to be made. Unrestricted crossing of this border has, in fact, been the norm throughout history, but in 1981 tensions between the two countries resulted in the establishment of strict controls. They were eased slightly in 2001, when walkers were allowed to cross at the summit of Rysy, then in 2007 both countries joined the Schengen Convention, which requires that there should be no border controls between its members.

   This means that there are now many places in the Tatras where walkers can, at least in theory, walk from one country to the other. In the High Tatras, as well as Rysy, they include (showing names in their Slovak and Polish forms) the main frontier point at Lysá Poľana/Łysa Polana, Hladké Sedlo/Gładka Przełęcz and Sedlo Chalubinského Vrata/Wrota Chałubińskiego. Those in the Western Tatras include Volovec/Wołowiec, Končista/Kończisty Wierch and Gáborovo Sedlo/ Gaborowa Przełęcz. Plus Suché Sedlo/Sucha Przełęcz, which lies in either the High Tatras (according to the Slovak view) or Western Tatras (according to the Poles).

   The magnificent ridge walk in the Western Tatras from Volovec/Wołowiec to Vyšné Hutianské Sedlo/Wyżnia Hucianska Przełęcz is accessible at ten points from one side or the other, but difficulty of access means that in practice it would be a two-day expedition requiring a long descent into a valley for overnight accommodation.

   Indeed, apart from Lysá Poľana/Łysa Polana, any cross-border walk involves a long day (possibly with a night at a refuge) and a fair amount of planning. The

*Approaching Wołowiec from the east
(Red 002, Poland) (photo: R Turnbull)*

crossing point at Rysy offers the most practical option. Even though it may be possible, you should not just turn up and decide on impulse to carry on across the border, otherwise you may find yourself with no means of getting back to your base and stranded overnight in the country for which you have no accommodation or currency. **Do not forget your passport.**

If undertaking a cross-border walk in early summer, or in autumn, check snow conditions on the far side with the mountain rescue service, as they may be different from those on your side. Further advice is given in the relevant walk descriptions for each country.

MOUNTAIN PHOTOGRAPHY

Neither of the authors is an expert on photography, but we gladly pass on some hints gleaned from friends who are, and hope that this may be helpful.

With traditional photography, shots taken in the mountains exaggerate the ultra-violet glare, giving a bluish effect. This can be overcome by fitting (preferably) an ultra-violet filter, otherwise a blue one will do. A filter of any kind will help to protect your lens from getting scratched. In winter a grey filter absorbs the extra light reflected from snow.

Two to three hours after noon is a period to avoid for photography – at this time the ultra-violet is at its strongest, and there is no shadow, so the picture lacks depth.

To avoid fuzzy or blurred pictures, either carry a lightweight tripod or monopod, or rest the camera on a rock for steadiness.

With digital photography, for most people it will be sufficient to point and shoot. Photographic computer programmes should make your pictures good enough at least for the post-holiday slide show.

More general tips: use a wide-angle lens for better panoramas; keep your camera in its case in case you slip; take close-ups of flowers and insects; use a zoom lens for wild animals at a distance; keep notes of what you take – you are sure to forget where you took some of your best shots.

HOW TO USE THIS GUIDE

Sections 3 and 4 describe the details relevant to walking in the Slovak High Tatras and the Polish Tatras respectively. Within each section, first comes some **later history**, then an **introduction to walking in the region**, followed by **route suggestions**, then **path descriptions**, tables of **selected timings** and **highest summits**, information on **travel**, **diversions**, **shopping** and **local services**, other **useful information,** and finally a **gazetteer** of places of interest. Section 5 consists of six appendices devoted to various aspects of travel and other useful information.

Some **route suggestions** are circular, others start and finish at different points. All the starting and finishing points are served by the very efficient local public transport system, so you can use any of these routes, wherever you are staying.

Detailed **path descriptions** are shown separately, taking advantage of the existing numbering scheme in the Slovak Tatras National Park area. This avoids tedious repetition within the route suggestions, and also allows you to string together your own routes if required. The four-figure path numbers are shown on the VKÚ maps at 1:25,000 and 1:50,000 scales, but not on other maps, nor on signposts along the routes.

There is no equivalent numbering on the Polish side, so we have taken the liberty of providing our own three-figure system there. Summary maps showing the route networks can be found on pages 2–3 and 4–5.

On both sides of the border, the first digit of the path number corresponds to the colour. So, as with the numbering followed by the official system in Slovakia, all the Red routes start with 0, Blue with 2, Green with 5 and Yellow with 8. There are no Black routes in Slovakia, but in our system the Polish ones start with 9.

The Slovak path-numbering system generally runs from west to east, and we generally follow the same principle in both the Slovak and Polish sections. The path descriptions are usually written in the uphill direction, so if you follow them downhill you will need to reverse the instructions. We have divided the longer paths into sections by suffixing A, B, C, etc., to the path numbers.

There are three routes in the High Tatras that must be followed in one direction only, in order to reduce conflict of interest at difficult sections. Two are in Slovakia (short sections of Yellow 8853 over Bystrá Lavká and 8860 over Priečne Sedlo), one in Poland (Red 009 Orla Perć). In the Polish Western Tatras a short section of Blue 206 is one way at the summit of Giewont. The walking maps have arrow symbols where one-way traffic applies.

Within the path descriptions, rather than interrupt the flow with notes on places of interest passed along the way, some of which occur on more than one route, such places are shown in **bold type**, and can be looked up in the gazetteer at the end of the section.

All the route suggestions and path descriptions give the following information at the beginning: **start/finish** points (or a general name) and main **points of interest**, **altitude range**, **grade** of walk (see page 64), approximate **distance**, **average gradient**, **height gain** and/or **loss**, average **walking time**, whether open in **winter/spring**.

All **distances** are approximate, and are only quoted as a rough guide. Distances are a poor guide in the mountains anyway, because of the effect steepness and roughness of terrain will have on your walking time. You should take more notice of the average walking times quoted.

Distances are given in kilometres (km) and metres (m). For a rough conversion, to convert kilometres into miles, divide by five then multiply by eight, or halve it then add 25%. To convert metres into yards, add 10%. Altitudes are given in metres – for a rough conversion into feet, multiply by three then add 10%. Some altitudes are estimated from map contours.

Average **gradients** are calculated from the height gain or loss, divided by the estimated distance, so are themselves a correspondingly rough guide to the steepness of each route.

For each route and section, an estimated **walking time** is shown in each direction, which generally corresponds to those shown on maps or signposts. They are usually on the generous side, and fit walkers may find that they can cover the distance in a shorter time. Walking times make no allowance for refreshment and other stops. It is not a good idea to make strenuous efforts to beat these times – much more enjoyment will result from taking your time and admiring the views and surroundings.

Within the longer path descriptions an idea of the time taken to cover each section is shown in italics at the end of the paragraph.

Every effort has been made to be accurate, but changes can take place, either through natural causes, such as landslides during the winter, or the Tatranská Bora (see page 72), or through human activity, such as forestry, removal or addition of a landmark, or human error!

GRADING OF WALKS

There are walks in the High Tatras to suit walkers of most degrees of capability, so the route suggestions later in this book are graded to help you choose. Inexperienced walkers should start with the easier routes, then if they can cope with those they may wish to try something harder, a grade at a time. Strong, experienced walkers should not ignore the easier routes – they may sometimes need an easy day, and sometimes the weather may restrict everyone to lower altitudes.

There is no official grading of waymarked routes in the High Tatras, so ours is necessarily arbitrary, and should be treated as a guide only. The path descriptions in Sections 3 and 4 give further information about specific stretches of route, including where you may expect to encounter scrambling or fixed wires.

Our grading is a quick guide to the terrain you may expect to encounter, though you should read the descriptive text as well before deciding whether it is suitable. You should also take into account the walking times shown for each route suggestion and path description. Do not overestimate your capability.

There are four grades.

- **Easy** Mostly on paths, tracks or forest roads up to an average gradient of about 10%. Can be undertaken in trainers or tough walking shoes.

- **Moderate** Mostly on steeper, rockier paths and tracks up to an average gradient of about 15%. No continuous scrambling or exposed situations, though there may be an occasional short section of this. No fixed chains. Walking boots strongly recommended.

- **Strenuous** Very steep and rocky paths above 15% average gradient, usually including substantial sections of scrambling and exposure, and at least one fixed chain. Walking boots essential. Most of the high summits and passes on the waymarked route network come within this grade.

- **Difficult** These routes can only be undertaken in the company of a qualified local mountain guide. Terrain as for 'Strenuous', but with more scrambling, fixed wires and other metal aids in exposed situations. Walking boots essential. The guide will advise if any other climbing equipment is necessary (this can be hired locally).

SECTION 3
THE SLOVAK HIGH AND WHITE TATRAS

Excavations of Žltá Stena (Yellow Wall) near Tatranská Polianka have revealed the existence of a major fortified habitation that was destroyed by fire. It occupies a strategic site commanding extensive views over the Podtatranská Kotlina, the huge basin between the High and Low Tatras. The fort appears to date from the Bronze Age, at about the beginning of the first millennium BC, when the area was populated by Celtic people.

The area was invaded and settled during the 9th and 8th centuries BC by successive waves of Slavonic people who are thought to have originated in what is now eastern Poland and Belarus. One of these waves consisted of the Slovaks and the closely related Slovenes – in Slovak the words for these are respectively Slovensko and Slovinsko – who settled the area between the Tatras and the Adriatic Sea.

Approaching the summit of Kriváň (Blue 2903) (photo: R Turnbull)

During the 9th century AD this area was part of the Greater Moravian Empire, which extended from what is now the Czech Republic to Rumania, Moravia being the eastern part of the Czech Republic around Brno. Excavations at Slavkov, on the southeastern slopes of the High Tatras between Poprad and Starý Smokovec, have revealed the existence during this period of a human settlement, which could have been a resting place of some importance on the overland trade route linking the Baltic and Mediterranean seas. At this time the mountains were generally feared, visited only by an occasional brave hunter.

At the end of the 9th century the Greater Moravian Empire was destroyed by the Magyars and associated tribes, who are thought to have originated in that part of Asia immediately to the east of the Urals. They established a new homeland in what is now Hungary, driving a wedge between the Slovaks and the Slovenes. Slovakia was devastated, and became part of the Hungarian domain, with Hungarian nobility owning the land that continued to be worked by Slav peasants.

During the early Middle Ages, tribes living around the Tatras had a variety of origins, including Slavic and Germanic. Over several centuries they merged into a distinctive culture, which became known as the Góral, meaning 'highlanders'. The culture persists today in the valleys around Ždiar in Slovakia and Zakopane in Poland, where the traditional costumes, cuisine, folklore and music can still be found.

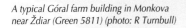

A typical Góral farm building in Monkova near Ždiar (Green 5811) (photo: R Turnbull)

The 13th century brought further invasion and terror, this time by the Tatars from Central Asia. They totally destroyed the Sub-Tatras Basin and surrounding areas in spring, with the result that the entire population either died of hunger through lack of crops, or sought refuge elsewhere. Travellers reported that they had walked through the area for days without seeing any sign of human life. To restore civilisation, King Bela IV of Hungary invited people from German-speaking lands, especially Saxony, to settle in the more low-lying areas. This included the plain to the south of the Tatras, known as Szepes in Hungarian. The new German inhabitants called it Zips, and to modern Slovaks it is Spiš.

On the walls of the nave of the Roman Catholic parish church in Poprad can be found a painting dating from the late 14th or early 15th century. It depicts the Tatras as the background of a Bible scene. Another pictorial record, dated 1475, shows Lomnický Štít, the second highest Tatra peak. It forms part of the coat of arms of the Berzevicky family from the village of Veľká Lomnica. The oldest plan of the Tatras forms part of a map of Hungary, dated 1556 and drawn by the Viennese historian Wolfgang Lazius.

During the 15th and 16th centuries there was continuous strife, caused by religious enmity (especially between the Hussites, followers of the Bohemian Jan Hus, and the Roman Catholic church), by various claimants to the Hungarian crown, and by pressure from refugees from the wars with the Ottoman Turks, especially from Wallachia (Southern Rumania). This forced many Slovaks to take refuge in the mountain valleys, eking out their existence by resorting to poaching and robbery.

These disturbances were subsiding by the 17th century, and at the same time people all over Europe began to take an interest in nature study, and in exploring mountainous areas. In 1615 the first recorded climb of a Tatra peak was undertaken, by a student called David Frölich from Kežmarok. It is not certain which peak was climbed, though it was probably Kežmarsky Štít, which is visible from Kežmarok.

By the early 18th century the Ottoman Turks had been expelled from central Europe, which became more settled under the domination of the Habsburg dynasty. Permanent settlements appeared in the foothills of the Tatras, and local people thoroughly explored the valleys and peaks, and established societies devoted to various aspects of their natural resources and culture.

Wealthier and more educated people from all over Europe began to travel around and explore the mountainous areas. The first ascents of Lomnický Štít, Jahňací Štít and Kriváň were made in 1793 by a Scottish physician and geographer, Robert Townson. He may have stayed at the chalet that was built in the same year on the southern slope of Slavkovský Štít, in a location that later developed into the resort of Starý Smokovec.

More exploration of the Tatras was carried out in 1813 by the Swedish botanist and natural historian, Göran Wahlenberg. His principal objective was the study of the flora, but his records also contain much about other branches of nature study, and served for many years as a valuable reference work for other explorers.

In 1843 the Irishman John Ball made the first recorded ascent of Ľadový Štít (he later became the first president of the London Alpine Club). In those days it took two days to climb the highest peaks, with much use of horses and mules. The intervening night was spent either in a hayloft, a cave or under an overhanging rock.

Until 1871 the Tatras remained a relative backwater for tourists, as it lay so far from the railways and main roads. In that year a railway line was completed from Ostrava to Košice, passing through Štrba and Poprad, making possible connections from Vienna, Prague and Berlin, and the Tatras tourist industry began to flourish.

Soon after this were founded the local associations that actively promoted walking and mountaineering in the Tatras. These included the Hungaro–Carpathian Association on the Slovak side, and the Towarzystwo Tatrzańskie (Tatras Society) on the Polish side. Their work included building and marking the paths, many of which are still used today, as well as organising the guiding and mountain rescue services, and starting the network of mountain chalets.

Although the First World War resulted in Slovakia being declared part of the new Republic of Czechoslovakia, the fighting did not affect the Tatras. However, the defeat of the Austro–Hungarian Empire in 1918 and the resurgence of the Slovak language resulted in German place names being rendered into Slovak, so Zips became Spiš, Kesmark became Kežmarok and Schmecks became Smokovec. Less obviously, Deutschendorf became Poprad. But Germanic influences can still be detected in the area, and some older people still have German as their mother tongue.

It was a very different story during the Second World War. In 1939 a puppet Slovak state was established under the Nazis, but with strong opposition in the form of local resistance units (partisans). This peaked at the end of 1944 and beginning of 1945, in what is now known as the Slovak National Uprising. There was fierce fighting in and around the Tatras villages, and in the valleys and forests, especially in the area around Podbanské. You may come across memorials at places where important battles took place.

In 1947 the High Tatras became a separate administrative region, called Vysoké Tatry. In 1999 it was awarded city status – though anywhere less like a city you are unlikely to find. To come right up to date, following the fall in 1989 of the communist regime in Czechoslovakia (the 'Velvet Revolution'), an amicable separation (the 'Velvet Divorce') into two independent states, the Czech and Slovak republics, took effect on 1 January 1993. On 1 May 2004, together with Poland and eight other countries, the Slovak Republic became a full member of the European Union. You should note that, although most English-speaking people refer informally to Slovakia, the official name of the country is the Slovak Republic.

WALKING

Nearly all the walking in Slovakia covered in this book takes place in the High Tatras (Vysoké Tatry). The Western Tatras (Zapadné Tatry), though providing extensive and delightful walking, are too remote and difficult of access to be of interest to people staying in the High Tatras resorts. Tourists are banned altogether from almost all of the White Tatras (Belianske Tatry), as well as from certain smaller areas in parts of the High Tatras not provided with waymarked routes – this is to protect the very fragile ecology, which has suffered from overuse in the past.

Six high summits on the Slovak side lie on the waymarked route network, and are therefore accessible without a guide. They are Kriváň, Kôprovský Štít, Rysy, Východná Vysoká, Slavkovský Štít and Jahňací Štít, all between 2200 and 2500m. Three other summits, though not particularly high, are easily accessible and provide fine views – they are Predné Solisko (2093m), Veľká Svišťovka (2037m) and Ostrva (1984m).

High passes on waymarked routes make a rewarding goal for a day's excursion – these include Sedielko (2372m), Priečne Sedlo (2352m), Prielom (2288m) and Poľský Hrebeň (2200m) in the High Tatras, and Široké Sedlo (1830m) in the White Tatras. Hladké Sedlo (1994m) on the border with Poland provides a magnificent view into the Valley of Five Polish Tarns but is difficult to reach from the Slovak resorts. High tarns and mountain chalets also make satisfying targets, and there are plenty of these between 1500 and 2000m.

The two highest summits, Gerlachovský Štít (2654m) and Lomnický Štít (2634m), and some exciting ridge walks, require a qualified mountain guide. It is easy to hire one for the day – see 'Mountain Guides', page 53.

See also Altitudes, page 21.

Waymarks In the Slovak High Tatras waymarks usually consist of three horizontal bands, the upper and lower ones being white, with the middle one either red, green, blue or yellow, to correspond with the colour shown for each route on the maps. There is just one exception: Green 5900 (White Tatras Traverse) has diagonal bands. At route starting points and junctions, the various waymarks (including

A typical Slovak High Tatras signpost, near Biela Voda (Yellow 8861)

an indication of walking times to major destinations) are attached to charming, picturesque and colourful rustic posts, made from fallen boughs to which a small red roof has been fixed. (You can ignore the frequent orange and black poles on the lower slopes and around the villages – they mark the location of gas mains.)

Educational Trails In the Slovak High Tatras, parts of some waymarked routes have been designated as *náučný chodník*, which literally means 'instructive trail' (as translated on some maps), but better known in English as 'educational trail'. Interpretation boards placed along the route describe matters of interest concerning flora, fauna, geology or history at that location. This applies to routes Red 0930B, Red 0930E and Green 5900. There is also a short, unwaymarked trail around the tarn of Skalnaté Pleso, and a heritage trail around Starý Smokovec.

Unfortunately the boards are currently in Slovak only, though translations into English were being considered at the time of writing – enquire at tourist information offices.

Cycle Routes Walkers should be aware that they will share some waymarked routes with cyclists, though much of the cycle route network is separate. Cyclists are asked to be in control at all times and give way to walkers, but beware of rogues! The terrain of most walking routes in the Tatras is too steep and rugged for even the hardiest of mountain bikes, so these shared routes are on the easier walking routes:

- Blue 2902A and Green 5802 from Podbanské up Kôprová Dolina
- Blue 2902B from Popradské Pleso station to tarn
- Green 5806A from Tatranská Polianka to Nižné Hagy
- Yellow 8851 from Podbanské up Tichá Dolina
- Yellow 8855 from Nižné Hagy to Vyšné Hagy
- Yellow 8861 from Biela Voda to Zelené Pleso.

The path beside Cesta Slobody (see page 93) is also shared. The service road from Starý Smokovec up to Hrebienok is a cycle route, as is the one from Tatranská Polianka up to Sliezsky Dom (parallel to Green 5806B and Yellow 8856). These service roads are not supposed to be used by walkers, but sometimes are.

Of course, some walkers may wish to try a bit of cycling for a change – bicycles can be hired locally (see page 164).

Terrain unsuitable for mountain bikes! – looking towards Lomnický Štít on the way down from Jahňací Štít (Yellow 8861) (photo: R Turnbull)

TATRANSKÁ BORA

At around 3.30pm on Friday 19 November 2004, without warning, a monstrous gale from the west tore up the Tatras slopes through the hamlet of Nadbanské, gathering speed as it crossed the shoulder to the south of Štrbské Pleso. Whipping through the forest-zone villages, including Smokovec and Tatranská Lomnica, and the mountain slopes around them, by the time this cataclysm reached Skalnaté Pleso its windspeed had been measured by the astronomical observatory there at almost 200kph (125mph) – way above hurricane force (130kph). Strong winds are not uncommon here, but the last time such a phenomenon had been recorded was in 1922. It is known as the Tatranská Bora, caused by a rare combination of climatic conditions, and the accepted wisdom is that it occurs only once a century – this one was early.

By 5.30pm the Bora had subsided after passing through Tatranská Kotlina, but during those two hours it left behind a scene of such horrendous devastation that nearly every tree in its path had been smashed down between the altitudes of 770m and 1250m. In fact more than half of the total forested area in Slovakia's Tatras National Park (24,000 of 46,000 hectares) had been totally or partially destroyed. In some places a lone spruce stood defiantly erect, or pathetically leaned eastwards at 45 degrees.

Mercifully there were no major human casualties on that traumatic evening, and surprisingly little structural damage. Even so, with deep snow, every road blocked, many bridges destroyed, telephone lines severed and mobile phone

Slavkovský Štít from Cesta Slobody, with one of the teams clearing up after the Tatranská Bora

relay masts out of action, it took two days for news of the disaster to reach the outside world. Movement within the area was almost impossible, and indeed dangerous – one person was killed by a falling tree on the following day.

Teams (such as the one in the photograph opposite) worked around the clock to remove trees and rootstocks, and for some time afterwards processions of lorries and trains were seen taking Tatras timber away to wherever a market for it could be found. It took seven months to fully restore the local train services.

Although the situation caused by the Bora itself turned out to be not as bad as originally feared, many more trees were later either destroyed by fire or infected by a species of bark beetle, which found the new microclimate very much to its liking. There was much debate about what should happen to land left bare of trees. Many thought that it should be left open, as some grand vistas had been opened up that were previously hidden by tree cover. There were even proposals for new golf courses. Eventually it was decided to replace most of the trees with a mixture of coniferous and deciduous varieties, and some 2.7 million had been replanted by 2010, though they will take 20 years to reach maturity. In some areas, such as Tichá Dolina and Kôprová Dolina, fallen trees have been left in place to create wildlife habitats, and these areas will be left to regenerate naturally.

There is a monument to the event in the centre of Starý Smokovec, and smaller memorials in the area record donations of replacement trees by various organisations, including one at Horný Smokovec for a donation made by Rotary International.

ROUTE SUGGESTIONS

Waymarked Network
Sections marked (★) include at least one fixed chain or wire, and/or some scrambling. All start and finish points are served by public transport.

For routes starting or finishing in Štrbské Pleso, see gazetteer (page 188) for a description of the route between station and tarn, where the waymarks start.

1 PODBANSKÉ – TICHÁ DOLINA – HLADKÉ SEDLO – KÔPROVÁ DOLINA – PODBANSKÉ (940m–1994m)

Grade The walking is moderate though the **distance** is strenuous

Distance 31.5km	**Average Gradient** 7%	**Height Gain** 1054m
Height Loss 1054m	**Time** 8h 00m	**Refreshments** Podbanské

Uses easy access routes, with short moderate ascents to Hladké Sedlo on the border, which has a magnificent view of the beautiful Valley of Five Polish Tarns. As a circular route it is best done in the direction described, providing a more direct return to Podbanské. Hladké Sedlo can be reached more easily by going in the opposite direction and returning by the same route, with an optional short diversion to Nižné Temnosmrečinské Pleso.

From Podbanské bus stop, follow these path sections:
Yellow 8851 11km N along Tichá Dolina to Rázcestie pod Tomanovou Dolinou
Red 0931 7km E to Sedlo Závory and Hladké Sedlo, returning to Sedlo Závory
Green 5801 2.5km S to Rázcestie pod Hlinskou Dolinou
Blue 2902A 6km SW to Rázcestie pod Grúnikom
Green 5802 3.5km W to Tichá
Yellow 8851 1.5km SW to Podbanské

2 ŠTRBSKÉ PLESO – JAMSKÉ PLESO – TRI STUDNIČKY – PODBANSKÉ (940m–1447m)

Grade Easy   **Distance** 13.5km   **Average Gradient** 5%
Height Gain 185m   **Height Loss** 600m   **Time** 3h 45m
Refreshments Štrbské Pleso, Podbanské

Štrbské Pleso – the tarn and hotels

A gentle introduction, or wet-weather walk, including the delightful Jamské Pleso tarn and fine views over the Sub-Tatras Basin.

From Štrbské Pleso station follow:
Red 0930F 4.5km NW to Jamské Pleso then 3.5km W to Tri Studničky
Red 0930G 5.5km W to Podbanské

3 ŠTRBSKÉ PLESO – KRIVÁŇ – TRI STUDNIČKY (1194m–2494m)

Grade Strenuous   **Distance** 12km   **Average Gradient** 20%
Height Gain 1139m   **Height Loss** 1300m   **Time** 6h 15m
Refreshments Štrbské Pleso

A well-used route with no fixed chain, but some scrambling, to one of the most popular summits – Kriváň, national symbol of Slovakia.

From Štrbské Pleso station follow:
Red 0930F 4.5km NW to Jamské Pleso (turn off shortly before lake)
Blue 2903 (★) 4km NW to Kriváň summit, and return to Rázcestie pod Kriváňom
Green 5803B 3.5km SW to Tri Studničky

4 ŠTRBSKÉ PLESO – KÔPROVSKY ŠTÍT – TRI STUDNIČKY (1194m–2363m)

Grade Strenuous   **Distance** 25km   **Average Gradient** 9%
Height Gain 1012m   **Height Loss** 1173m   **Time** 8h 30m
Refreshments Štrbské Pleso, Popradské Pleso

A less well-used route to a comparatively easy summit, with no chains or scrambling, and providing fine views over tarn-filled valleys. Popradské Pleso is the largest and deepest tarn in the Slovak Tatras.

From Štrbské Pleso station follow:
Red 0930E 4.5km N to Popradské Pleso
Blue 2902B 5km NW to Vyšné Kôprovské Sedlo
Red 0934 1km N to Kôprovsky Štít and return 1km to Vyšné Kôprovské Sedlo
Blue 2902A 13.5km SW to Tri Studničky

5 ŠTRBSKÉ PLESO – VODOPÁD SKOK – BYSTRÁ LÁVKA – VYŠNÉ WAHLENBERGOVO PLESO – ŠTRBSKÉ PLESO (1355m–2300m)

Grade Strenuous	**Distance** 14.5km	**Average Gradient** 15%
Height Gain 945m	**Height Loss** 945m	**Time** 6h 30m
Refreshments Štrbské Pleso, Chata pod Soliskom (on optional alternative only)		

A popular route, easily accessible from Štrbské Pleso, mostly above the tree-line, and with excellent views. The route is easy as far as the waterfall, but there is a fixed chain and some scrambling near the top. You must follow the route anticlockwise, as described, to avoid meeting oncoming walkers on the chain, and because if there is snow near the saddle the route is more difficult to find clockwise.

From Štrbské Pleso station follow:
Yellow 8853A 4.5km NW to Vodopád Skok and 2.5km further (★) to Bystrá Lávka
Yellow 8853B 1km SW to Vyšné Wahlenbergovo Pleso, 2.5km to junction Blue 2836B, 1.5km to junction Red 0930F
Red 0930F 2.5km SE to Štrbské Pleso

Optional Alternative Take Blue 2836B 1km SE to Chata pod Soliskom (some climbing), then either walk 3.5km down Blue 2836B to Štrbské Pleso or take chair-lift (total 15km or 11.5km).

6 ŠTRBSKÉ PLESO – CHATA POD SOLISKOM – PREDNÉ SOLISKO – CHATA POD SOLISKOM – FURKOTSKÁ DOLINA – ŠTRBSKÉ PLESO (1355m–2093m)

Grade Moderate	**Distance** 11.5km	**Average Gradient** 13%
Height Gain 738m	**Height Loss** 738m	**Time** 4h 15m
Refreshments Chata pod Soliskom, Štrbské Pleso		

Predné Solisko is a very popular minor summit, because it is just a short walk from the chair-lift, and provides good views over Štrbské Pleso.

From Štrbské Pleso station follow:
Blue 2836B 3.5km NW to Chata pod Soliskom (or take chair-lift)
Red 0935 1.5km N to Predné Solisko and return to Chata pod Soliskom
Blue 2836B 1km NW to Furkotská Dolina
Yellow 8853B 1.5km SE to junction Red 0930F
Red 0930F 2.5km SE to Štrbské Pleso

Optional Alternative From Chata pod Soliskom return on Blue 2836B to Štrbské Pleso – this has better views than 2836/8853/0930 (total 10km).

7 ŠTRBSKÉ PLESO – POPRADSKÉ PLESO – RYSY AND RETURN (1355m–2500m)

Grade Strenuous	**Distance** 18km	**Average Gradient** 15%
Height Gain 1145m	**Height Loss** 1145m	**Time** 9h 00m
Refreshments Štrbské Pleso, Popradské Pleso, Chata pod Rysmi		

One of the most popular routes, as Rysy is the highest summit on the waymarked route network, with fine views into Poland. You can save 15 minutes walking in each direction by starting instead at Popradské Pleso station and using Blue 2902B to and from the tarn. For a route suggestion that includes the Polish side of Rysy, see page 208.

From Štrbské Pleso station follow:
Red 0930E 4.5km N to Popradské Pleso
Blue 2902B 1.5km N to junction Red 0933
Red 0933 (★) 3km NE to Chata pod Rysmi and Rysy summit
Return by same route.

8 ŠTRBSKÉ PLESO – POPRADSKÉ PLESO – OSTRVA – BATIZOVSKÉ PLESO – SLIEZSKY DOM – STARÝ SMOKOVEC (1010m–1984m)

Grade Moderate	**Distance** 19km	**Average Gradient** 10%
Height Gain 571m	**Height Loss** 916m	**Time** 7h 00m
Refreshments Štrbské Pleso, Popradské Pleso, Sliezsky Dom, Starý Smokovec		

A route featuring one of the more dramatic sections of the Tatranská Magistrála (see page 93), with good views of the Sub-Tatras Basin. It can be followed in the reverse direction, but would then involve more climbing, unless you take the funicular to Hrebienok. For those wishing to return to Štrbské Pleso or Tatranská Lomnica, Green 5806B from Sliezsky Dom to Tatranská Polianka provides a quicker descent to the bus or train.

From Štrbské Pleso station follow:
Red 0930E 4.5km N to Popradské Pleso
Red 0930D 1.5km SE to Sedlo pod Ostrvou, then 3.5km E to junction Yellow
8855, then 1km NE to Batizovské Pleso and 1.5km SE to junction Yellow
8856, then 2km NE to Sliezsky Dom

The Hrebienok funicular

Green 5806B 0.5km SE to junction Yellow 8858
Yellow 8858 2km SE to junction Blue 2905 and 2.5km to Starý Smokovec

9 POPRADSKÉ PLESO STATION – POPRADSKÉ PLESO TARN – ŠTRBSKÉ PLESO (1250m–1494m)

Grade Easy	**Distance** 7.5km	**Average Gradient** 5%
Height Gain 244m	**Height Loss** 139m	**Time** 2h 15m
Refreshments Popradské Pleso, Štrbské Pleso		

An easy and popular short route to and from a beautiful tarn, passing the Dubček Stone, plus an opportunity to view the unique Symbolic Cemetery. In winter you will have to use Green 5805, as Red 0930E is closed because of avalanche danger.

From Popradské Pleso station (1km NE of Štrbské Pleso) follow:
Blue 2902B 3.5km N to Popradské Pleso tarn
Red 0930E 4km SW to Štrbské Pleso tarn

Optional Diversion On Yellow 8854 to Symbolický Cintorín (Symbolic Cemetery, small fee payable, closed 1 January to 15 June) adds 0.5km/15mins plus viewing time.

10 TATRANSKÁ POLIANKA – SLIEZSKY DOM – BATIZOVSKÉ PLESO – VYŠNÉ HÁGY (1010m–1879m)

Grade Moderate	**Distance** 13.5km	**Average Gradient** 12%
Height Gain 869m	**Height Loss** 794m	**Time** 6h 00m
Refreshments Tatranská Polianka, Sliezsky Dom, Vyšné Hagy		

This route used to be mostly in forest, but since the Tatranská Bora is now on open terrain nearly all the way, with grand views from the Tatranská Magistrála section (see page 93). Sliezsky Dom is one of the most scenic chalets in the High Tatras.

From Tatranská Polianka station follow:
Green 5806B 4.5km NW to Sliezsky Dom
Red 0930D 2km SW to junction Yellow 8856, then 1.5km NW to Batizovské Pleso, then 1km SW to junction Yellow 8855
Yellow 8855 4.5km S to Vyšné Hágy

11 TATRANSKÁ POLIANKA – SLIEZSKY DOM – STARÝ SMOKOVEC (1010m–1678m)

Grade Easy   **Distance** 11km   **Average Gradient** 12%
Height Gain 668m   **Height Loss** 668m   **Time** 4h 00m
Refreshments Tatranská Polianka, Sliezsky Dom, Starý Smokovec

Though the walking is generally easy, there are some steep sections, now mostly in open terrain. Sliezsky Dom is well situated on the beautiful small tarn of Velické Pleso.

From Tatranská Polianka station follow:
Green 5806B 5km NW to Sliezsky Dom
Green 5806B 0.5km SE to junction Yellow 8858
Yellow 8858 2km SE to junction Blue 2905 and 2.5km to Starý Smokovec

12 LYSÁ POĽANA – BIELOVODSKÁ DOLINA – POĽSKÝ HREBEŇ – SLIEZSKY DOM – TATRANSKÁ POLIANKA (970m–2200m)

Grade Moderate   **Distance** 23km   **Average Gradient** 11%
Height Gain 1230m   **Height Loss** 1190m   **Time** 9h 15m
Refreshments Lysá Poľana, Sliezsky Dom, Tatranská Polianka

This route can be followed in the reverse direction if preferred, providing less climbing, but the suggested direction allows a more gentle ascent, and gets the long bus journey out of the way in the morning.

From Lysá Poľana follow:
Blue 2907B 12km S to Litvorová Kotlina, then 2.5km SE to Litvorové Pleso, Zamrznuté Pleso and Poľský Hrebeň
Green 5806B 3.5km SE to Sliezsky Dom, and 5km SE to Tatranská Polianka.

Optional Alternative From Zamrznuté Pleso continue E on Blue 2907A to Prielom (★), 2km E to Zbojnícka Chata, and 5km SE to Starolesnianska Poľana, then on Green 5807 1.5km SE to Bilíkova Chata and Hrebienok. Same distance but grade 'Strenuous' – to be avoided if there is much snow, not recommended in the reverse direction.
Optional Extension To Východná Vysoká on Yellow 8857 adds 228m of ascent and 1h 15m.

13 STARÝ SMOKOVEC – HREBIENOK – VODOPÁD STUDENÉHO POTOKA – TATRANSKÁ LESNÁ (905m–1285m)

Grade Easy   **Distance** 7.5km   **Average Gradient** 9%
Height Gain 275m   **Height Loss** 380m   **Time** 2h 30m
Refreshments Starý Smokovec, Hrebienok, Tatranská Lesná (also Zamkovského Chata on optional extension)

A low-level walk mostly in forest, but providing excellent views of the Obrovský and Studený Potok cascades.

Starý Smokovec station

From Starý Smokovec (funicular station) follow:

Green 5807 2.5km NE to Hrebienok, 0.5km N to Bilíkova Chata/junction with
   Yellow 8859, and 0.5km to Vodopády Studeného Potoka; return 0.5km to
   Bilíkova Chata, then

Yellow 8859 3.5km SE to Tatranská Lesná

Optional Extensions

a) From Hrebienok, take Red 0930B 1.5km NW to Starolesnianska Poľana,
and 1.5km NE to Zamkovského Chata, passing Obrovský Vodopád; return to
Starolesnianska Poľana, then take Blue 2907A and Green 5807 1km to Bilíkova
Chata and Yellow 8859 3.5km to Tatranská Lesná (adds 1.5km).

b) From Tatranská Lesná follow footpath beside Cesta Slobody back to Starý
Smokovec (adds 3km).

Optional Alternative From Vodopády Studeného Potoka take Blue 2907A 6km E
to Tatranská Lomnica (adds 2km).

14 HREBIENOK – VELICKÉ PLESO – STARÝ SMOKOVEC (1010m–1687m)

Grade Easy to moderate	**Distance** 10.5km	**Average Gradient** 10%
Height Gain 402m	**Height Loss** 677m	**Time** 4h 00m
Refreshments Hrebienok, Sliezsky Dom, Starý Smokovec		

A route using the Tatranská Magistrála (see page 93) with good views over the
valley and up to the peaks. There is a short section of easy scrambling on Red
0930C, without much exposure.

Take funicular from Starý Smokovec N to Hrebienok, then follow:

Red 0930C 5.5km W to Velické Pleso/Sliezsky Dom

Green 5806B 0.75km SE to junction Yellow 8858

Yellow 8858 4km SE to Starý Smokovec

Optional Extension Green 5806B to Poľský Hrebeň and then Yellow 8857 to
Východna Vysoká (return same route) – adds 765m of ascent and 5 hours.

15 HREBIENOK – ZBOJNÍCKA CHATA – PRIELOM – POĽSKÝ HREBEŇ – SLIEZSKY DOM – TATRANSKÁ POLIANKA (1010m–2288m)

Grade Strenuous	**Distance** 17.5km	**Average Gradient** 15%
Height Gain 1003m	**Height Loss** 1278m	**Time** 8h 15m
Refreshments Hrebienok, Zbojnícka Chata, Sliezsky Dom, Tatranská Polianka		

The crossing of the Prielom saddle is one of the most exciting parts of the way-marked network, with fixed chains and exposed situations. The route is less strenuous in this direction, providing less height gain, but anyone feeling nervous about the descent from Prielom may find the opposite direction more comfortable. Prielom should be avoided when there is much snow, as it can then be dangerous.

Take funicular from Starý Smokovec N to Hrebienok, then follow:
Red 0930B 1.5km NW to Starolesnianska Poľana
Blue 2907A 5km NW to Zbojnícka Chata, and 2km W to Prielom (★)
Green 5806B (★) 0.5km SW to Poľský Hrebeň, 3.5km SE to Sliezsky Dom, and 5km SE to Tatranská Polianka

Optional Alternatives
a) From Hrebienok follow Green 5807 NW to Vodopády Studeného Potoka, then Blue 2907A as before – this makes little difference to the distance, adds a little climbing, and allows a view of the cascades.
b) From Sliezsky Dom follow Green 5806B and Yellow 8858 to Starý Smokovec (total 17km).
Optional Side Trip From Poľský Hrebeň on Yellow 8857 E to Východná Vysoká would add 1km, 228m of climbing and 1h 15m.

16 HREBIENOK – ZAMKOVSKÉHO CHATA – TÉRYHO CHATA – PRIEČNE SEDLO – ZBOJNÍCKA CHATA – HREBIENOK (1285m–2352m)

Grade Strenuous	**Distance** 18km	**Average Gradient** 15%
Height Gain 1067m	**Height Loss** 1067m	**Time** 8h 00m
Refreshments Hrebienok, Zamkovského Chata, Téryho Chata, Zbojnícka Chata		

A well-used route linking two popular chalets via an exciting saddle. The route must be followed in this direction, as there is one-way traffic on the chain at Priečne Sedlo.

Take funicular from Starý Smokovec N to Hrebienok, then follow:
Red 0930B 1.5km NW to Starolesnianska Poľana, and 1.5km NE to Zamkovského Chata
Green 5812A 3.5km NW to Téryho Chata
Yellow 8860 (★) 1.5km W to Priečne Sedlo, and 3.5km SW (★) to Zbojnícka Chata
Blue 2907A 5km SE to Starolesnianska Poľana
Red 0930B 1.5km SE to Hrebienok

17 HREBIENOK – ZAMKOVSKÉHO CHATA – TÉRYHO CHATA – SEDIELKO – JAVOROVÁ DOLINA – JAVORINA (1018m–2372m)

Grade Strenuous   **Distance** 20.5km   **Average Gradient** 12%
Height Gain 1087m   **Height Loss** 1354m   **Time** 7h 45m
Refreshments Hrebienok, Zamkovského Chata, Téryho Chata, Javorina

A testing route, which is not difficult, but includes some very steep sections. It is recommended in this direction to reduce the amount of ascent. Sedielko should be avoided if there is much snow, as it can then be dangerous.

Take the funicular from Starý Smokovec N to Hrebienok, then follow:
Red 0930B 1.5km NW to Starolesnianska Poľana, and 1.5km NE to Zamkovského Chata
Green 5812A 3.5km NW to Téryho Chata, and on 2km to Sedielko
Green 5812B 12km along Zadná Dolina and Javorová Dolina to Javorina

18 SKALNATÉ PLESO – ZAMKOVSKÉHO CHATA – HREBIENOK – STARÝ SMOKOVEC (1010m–1761m)

Grade Easy   **Distance** 6.5km   **Average Gradient** 11%
Height Gain Nil   **Height Loss** 751m   **Time** 2h 30m
Refreshments Skalnaté Pleso, Zamkovského Chata, Hrebienok, Starý Smokovec

Downhill nearly all the way, with some fine viewpoints and several refreshment opportunities. This section of the Tatranská Magistrála (see page 93) is an educational trail – the information boards are translated in the path description for Red 0930B.

With an early start you can include a side trip by cable-car from Skalnaté Pleso to the summit of Lomnický Štít, though you need to book in advance, as this is very popular. Note that the extension of Green 5808 from Skalnaté Pleso to Lomnické Sedlo, shown on older maps, is no longer accessible on the waymarked system.

Take the gondola lift from Tatranská Lomnica NW to Skalnaté Pleso then follow:
Red 0930B 2.5km SW to Zamkovského Chata, and a further 2km S to Hrebienok
Green 5807 (or funicular) 2km S to Starý Smokovec

Optional Side Trip Follow the educational trail around Skalnaté Pleso tarn, adding 1km and 20 minutes.

19 SKALNATÉ PLESO – VEĽKÁ SVIŠŤOVKA – ZELENÉ PLESO – VEĽKÉ BIELE PLESO – TATRANSKÁ LOMNICA (860m–2037m)

Grade Moderate (but with one short fixed chain)　　**Distance** 16.5km
Average Gradient 10%　　**Height Gain** 276m　　**Height Loss** 1177m
Time 6h 30m　　**Refreshments** Skalnaté Pleso, Zelené Pleso, Tatranské Matliare, Tatranská Lomnica

Using a section of the Tatranská Magistrála (see page 93), this popular route includes the minor summit of Veľká Svišťovka, with its outstanding views over the valleys and 'green lake', and of surrounding summits. The zigzag descent to Zelené Pleso includes a short section of fixed chain, with only minimal exposure.

Take the gondola lift from Tatranská Lomnica NW to Skalnaté Pleso then follow:
Red 0930A 2.5km N to Veľká Svišťovka, 2km NW (★) to Zelené Pleso, and 2km NE to Veľké Biele Pleso
Blue 2911A 4.5km SE to Šalviový Prameň and 2km further to junction with Yellow 8861, and 2km S to Tatranské Matliare (Metalurg/Hutník)
Yellow 8863 1.5km SW to Tatranská Lomnica

Optional Alternatives
a) From Zelené Pleso take Yellow 8861 3.5km E then SE to junction (Kovalčikova Poľana but not named on some maps), then Green 5809 1km S to junction, then Blue 2908 3.5km SW to Štart, then Green 5808 3km SE to Grandhotel Praha and 0.5km SW to Tatranská Lomnica (total 16km).
b) Taking Yellow 8861 from Šalviový Prameň to Biela Voda for the bus saves one hour, and you mostly follow the Kežmarská Biela Voda stream.
Optional Side Trip Follow the educational trail around Skalnaté Pleso tarn, adding 1km and 20 minutes.

20 TATRANSKÁ LOMNICA – ŠTART – ZELENÉ PLESO – VEĽKÉ BIELE PLESO – TATRANSKÁ KOTLINA (765m–1600m)

Grade Moderate　　**Distance** 23.5km　　**Average Gradient** 10%
Height Gain 740m　　**Height Loss** 835m　　**Time** 7h 00m
Refreshments Tatranská Lomnica, Zelené Pleso, Chata Plesnivec, Tatranská Kotlina

The beautiful Zelené Pleso and the haunting Veľké Biele Pleso are fine targets for this walk.

From Tatranská Lomnica railway station follow:
Green 5808 0.5km NE to Grandhotel Praha, then 3km NW to Štart
Blue 2908 3.5km NE to junction with Green 5809
Green 5809 1km N to junction with Yellow 8861
Yellow 8861 3.5km NW to Zelené Pleso
Red 0930A 2km NE to Veľké Biele Pleso
Green 5810 5km E to Chata Plesnivec, and 3km SE to junction with Blue 2909
Blue 2909 2km NE to Tatranská Kotlina

Optional Alternatives
a) Take the gondola-lift to the halfway point at Štart, saving nearly 300m of ascent.
b) From Veľké Biele Pleso use Blue 2911A/Yellow 8861 to Biela Voda for the bus, saving 1h 30m.

21 BIELA VODA – ZELENÉ PLESO – TATRANSKÁ LOMNICA (860m–1551m)

Grade Easy	**Distance** 16km	**Average Gradient** 8%
Height Gain 626m	**Height Loss** 691m	**Time** 5h 45m
Refreshments Chata pri Zelenom Plese, Tatranské Matliare, Tatranská Lomnica		

The quickest and easiest route to and from one of the most beautiful lakes in the Tatras.

From Biela Voda (bus, 2.5km NE of Tatranská Lomnica) follow:
Yellow 8861 3km NW to Šalviový Prameň, 4km NW to Zelené Pleso, 4km SE to Šalviový Prameň, and 1.5km SE to junction with Blue 2911A
Blue 2911A 2km S to Tatranské Matliare (Metalurg/Hutník)
Yellow 8863 1.5km SW to Tatranská Lomnica

22 BIELA VODA – ZELENÉ PLESO – KOLOVÉ SEDLO – JAHŇACÍ ŠTÍT AND RETURN (925m–2229m)

Grade Strenuous	**Distance** 19km	**Average Gradient** 15%
Height Gain 1304m	**Height Loss** 1304m	**Time** 9h 15m
Refreshments Zelené Pleso		

This route is not difficult (although there are chains at Kolové Sedlo), but provides outstanding views, including the 'green lake' and a full panorama of the White Tatras from Jahňací Štít.

Approaching the summit of Jahňací Štít (Yellow 8861) (photo: R Turnbull)

From Biela Voda (bus, 2.5km NE of Tatranská Lomnica) follow:
Yellow 8861 3km NW to Šalviový Prameň, 4km NW to Zelené Pleso, 2.5km NW to Kolové Sedlo (★) and Jahňací Štít; return by same route

23 BIELA VODA – KOPSKÉ SEDLO – JAVORINA (925m–1749m)

Grade Moderate	**Distance** 17.5km	**Average Gradient** 10%
Height Gain 824m	**Height Loss** 731m	**Time** 5h 45m

Refreshments Javorina (also Zelené Pleso on optional alternative)

This route provides opportunities to cross the range with no difficult sections, and to use one of the few paths that touch the White Tatras.

From Biela Voda (bus, 2.5km NE of Tatranská Lomnica) follow:
Yellow 8861 3km NW to Šalviový Prameň
Blue 2911A 4.5km NW to Veľké Biele Pleso, and 1.5km further to Kopské Sedlo
Blue 2911B 6km NW along Zadné Meďodoly to Pod Muráňom, and 2km further to Javorina (bus to Tatranská Lomnica)

Optional Alternative From Šalviový Prameň continue on Yellow 8861 4km NW to Zelené Pleso, then 2km NE on Red 0930A to Veľké Biele Pleso (adds 1.5km).

There are many other possibilities and variations using the waymarked network. Use the map on pages 2–3, together with your walking map, to devise your own routes. All the paths are described in Path Descriptions, page 93.

With a Guide

The following route suggestions all require the services of a mountain guide. They all include substantial sections off the waymarked routes, and nearly all involve to some extent a degree of exposure (in some cases very exposed), scrambling, and use of chains and other iron fixtures. **These routes should only be attempted by experienced mountain walkers**, with a good head for heights, who know that they can cope with such situations. Usually a very early start from the resort is necessary (around 5 or even 4am), to avoid the crowds on the mountain lifts, and to complete the ascent before the possibility of thunderstorms.

The times shown are for the guided section only – to these, in most cases, you must add the walks from and to the nearest resort (Selected Timings, page 146). There is a maximum of four or five walkers per guide, depending on the route and conditions.

A visitors book is kept at each summit.

24 SATAN (2422m)

Grade Strenuous	**Distance** 14km	**Average Gradient** 15%
Height Gain 1072m	**Height Loss** 1072m	**Time** 6h 00m
Refreshments Štrbské Pleso, Popradské Pleso		
Guide Meeting Point Štrbské Pleso		

One of the easiest guided routes, with no chains or scrambling.

From Štrbské Pleso you follow Yellow 8853A up Mlynická Dolina past Vodopád Skok, then about 1km further divert east to Nižne Kozie Pleso to use a rocky corridor to Satan's north summit. The return is by one of several routes eastward into Mengusovská Dolina, where you can go to either Popradské Pleso or Štrbské Pleso for refreshment.

25 VEĽKÝ MENGUSOVSKÝ ŠTÍT (2431m)

Grade Difficult	**Distance** 10km	**Average Gradient** 11%
Height Gain 937m	**Height Loss** 937m	**Time** 5h 30m
Refreshments Chata pri Popradskom Plese		
Guide Meeting Point Chata pri Popradskom Plese		

From Popradské Pleso you follow Blue 2902B to Veľké Hincovo Pleso, then you are on open rock all the way to the summit, with frequent use of harness and rope. From the summit there are beautiful views back over the Hincovo tarns and into Poland, including Morskie Oko.

26 VYSOKÁ (2547m)

Grade Difficult	**Distance** 16km	**Average** Gradient 14%
Height Gain 1100m	**Height Loss** 1100m	**Time** 7h 00m
Refreshments Popradské Pleso, Chata pod Rysmi		
Guide Meeting Point Popradské Pleso		

This is one of the most testing guided routes. Vysoká has two tops – the lower of these at 2526m is sometimes erroneously shown as the highest altitude. From here you have outstanding views over most of the High and White Tatras.

From Popradské Pleso the route goes immediately off the waymarked network northeast up Zlomisková Dolina, then shortly north up a side valley, over Dračie Sedlo (Dragon Pass, beside Zlomisková Veža). At the end of a long gully you come to a 40m wall with chains and rungs, after which it is just an easy 100m to the top. Your descent takes you further northwest along another gully to a natural rock arch and a ledge, which leads to Kohútik (Little Cock). A 50m chain takes you down to a path leading to Sedlo Váha on Red 0933, from where you can make an optional diversion to Rysy summit before descending to Chata pod Rysmi.

27 GÁNOK (2462m) AND VEĽKÝ GÁNOK (2459m)

Grade Difficult	**Distance** 12km	**Average Gradient** 11%
Height Gain 968m	**Height Loss** 968m	**Time** 5h 30m
Refreshments Chata pri Popradskom Plese		
Guide Meeting Point Chata pri Popradskom Plese		

(**Note** This peak is also known locally as Gánek, but usually shown as Gánok on maps. It is a Góral dialect word meaning 'verandah'.)

From Popradské Pleso you go very quickly off the waymarked trail, then it is nearly all the way on open rock to the summit, with frequent use of rope and harness. From the summit you should have a fine view of the Česká and Bielovodská valleys.

28 GERLACHOVSKÝ ŠTÍT (2654m)

Grade Difficult to very difficult, depending on conditions
Distance 15km　　　**Average Gradient** 22%　　　**Height Gain** 1655m
Height Loss 1655m　　　**Time** 7h 00m　　　**Refreshments** Sliezsky Dom
Guide Meeting Point Sliezsky Dom

A chance to stand at the highest point in the Carpathians! There are actually three peaks, and you can also climb Zadný (Hidden) Gerlachovský Štít, which is slightly lower, and has the added interest of bearing aircraft wreckage (see gazetteer).

From Sliezsky Dom you use an unwaymarked path northwestwards, which traverses beneath Kotlový Štít. You come to a gully with 100m of chains and rungs to reach a pass called Sedielko nad Kotlom (2450m), then traverse with great exposure over several gullies to another pass (Štrbina v Kotlovom, 2580m), finally ascending another gully to approach the summit from the east, with some scrambling. The descent is to the south, almost immediately using a 25m chain below the summit before following one of two gullies. These lead to a 200m section of chains and rungs, which brings you into Batizovská Dolina, then Batizovské Pleso on Red 0930A (Tatranská Magistrála). From here you can either return to Sliezsky Dom, or continue to Popradské Pleso and Štrbské Pleso, or descend directly to Vyšné Hágy.

29 BRADAVICA (2476m)

Grade Strenuous　　　**Distance** 12km　　　**Average Gradient** 14%
Height Gain 813m　　　**Height Loss** 813m　　　**Time** 6h 00m
Refreshments Sliezsky Dom
Guide Meeting Point Sliezsky Dom

No chains, but on one section you may have to be roped up. Bradavica has four summits, though it is usually the most southeasterly one that is ascended.

From Sliezsky Dom you ascend Velická Dolina on Green 5806B to Kvetnica. You then climb a gully for 150m to a minor summit called Rohatá Veža, and go through a natural rock arch. A very narrow path leads to a ridge, which is easily followed to the top. There are several descent possibilities, none of them very difficult.

30 ŠIROKÁ VEŽA (2461m)

Grade Strenuous   **Distance** 14km   **Average Gradient** 17%
Height Gain 1198m   **Height Loss** 1198m   **Time** 7h 00m
Refreshments Zamkovského Chata, Téryho Chata, Zbojnícka Chata
Guide Meeting Point Hrebienok or Skalnaté Pleso

This summit lies only a short distance off Yellow 8860, and would make a comparatively easy introduction to chains and scrambling under the watchful eyes of a guide, for those who feel a little nervous about the idea. There is a possibility that this summit may be added to the waymarked network.

From Hrebienok or Skalnaté Pleso, you follow Red 0930B to Zamkovského Chata, then Green 5812A to Téryho Chata, and Yellow 8860 to Priečne Sedlo, where the chains are encountered. From the saddle you divert up to Široká Veža, with some scrambling. The descent from Priečne Sedlo is on Yellow 8860 southwest to Zbojnícka Chata (more chains), then Blue 2907A southeast to Hrebienok.

31 PROSTREDNÝ HROT (2440m)

Grade Very difficult   **Distance** 14km   **Average Gradient** 17%
Height Gain 1177m   **Height Loss** 1177m   **Time** 7h 00m
Refreshments Hrebienok, Zamkovského Chata, Téryho Chata
Guide Meeting Point Hrebienok or Skalnaté Pleso

Though it has no chains, this route is very steep and exposed in places, but you are rewarded with outstanding views.

From Hrebienok or Skalnaté Pleso, as in route suggestion 28 to Téryho Chata. From there you ascend a steep gully southwest to Sedlo pod Prostredným Hrotom (Saddle below Prostredný Hrot), then follow a very narrow ridge to the summit. You can descend either by the same route, or continue south on an exposed zigzag path, where you may have to be roped up, into Veľká Studená Dolina for Blue 2907A to Hrebienok.

32 ĽADOVÝ ŠTÍT (2627m)

Grade Difficult   **Distance** 18km   **Average Gradient** 15%
Height Gain 1364m   **Height Loss** 1364m   **Time** 9h 00m
Refreshments Hrebienok, Zamkovského Chata, Téryho Chata
Guide Meeting Point Hrebienok or Skalnaté Pleso

In some references you may see the altitude of this peak as 2528m, which is wrong.

From Hrebienok or Skalnaté Pleso as in route suggestion 28 to Téryho Chata, then you divert from the waymarked route to pass the tarns at the head of Malá Studená Dolina, to ascend a steep zigzag path to Sedlo Ľadová Priehyba. You follow a very narrow ridge for 20 minutes – not difficult but very exposed in places, and you may have to be roped up – to the summit. To descend you continue a little further along the ridge to a section that is in effect a Grade 2 climb, where you are roped up for 100m. This leads to a gully, which you follow down to Sedielko and Green 5812A.

33 BARANIE ROHY (2526m)

Grade Difficult   **Distance** 17km   **Average Gradient** 15%
Height Gain 1263m   **Height Loss** 1263m   **Time** 8h 00m
Refreshments Hrebienok, Zamkovského Chata, Téryho Chata
Guide Meeting Point Hrebienok or Skalnaté Pleso

The ascent is not too difficult, but is exposed in places.

From Hrebienok or Skalnaté Pleso as in route suggestion 28 to Téryho Chata, then you go round the second of the Five Spiš Tarns and ascend a zigzag path to Baranie Sedlo. You follow a gully to the left, then ascend rock fields to the summit. The descent is by the same route. Alternatively, another route continues northeast into Veľká Zmrzlá Dolina and Zelené Pleso, but this adds 9km and 2h. This route as far as Baranie Sedlo used to be on the waymarked network, and at the time of writing there was a proposal to reopen it.

34 LOMNICKÝ ŠTÍT (2634m)

Grade Strenuous to very difficult   **Distance** 4km or 12km
Average Gradient 11%   **Height Gain** 442m   **Time** 2h 30m or 7h 00m
Refreshments Skalnaté Pleso, Lomnický Štít
Guide Meeting Point Tatranská Lomnica (cable-car station) or Skalnaté Pleso

Although Lomnický Štít is accessible by cable-car, you will have the satisfaction of reaching the second highest summit in the Tatras under your own power. **You must not attempt to undertake this route without a guide**, because it is difficult to find in places, and you could land yourself in trouble.

From Skalnaté Pleso you continue by chair-lift to Lomnické Sedlo (2190m), then walk up the ridge to the summit of Lomnicky Štít (1h 30m). It is mostly an easy scramble, but there are also some long fixed chains and a ladder to negotiate.

Alternatively, a very challenging route can be taken from Hrebienok via Bachledové Sedlo – this takes 6 hours, and involves a steep gully, an exposed ridge traverse, 200m of steep and exposed chains to another ridge, which is then easily followed to Lomnický Štít. The descent back to Lomnické Sedlo takes an hour, or you can take the cable-car direct to Skalnaté Pleso.

PATH DESCRIPTIONS

Cesta Slobody

Before we start on the paths themselves, a word about **Cesta Slobody** (Freedom Highway), as you may find it useful as a walking route to return to your accommodation, rather than take the train or bus. If you need a change from the mountains, or in bad weather, it could make an interesting easy walk in its own right, passing several places of interest.

The road is 68km long and connects Liptovský Hrádok with Kežmarok, passing through the Tatras resorts. It was so named in 1918 to celebrate the foundation of the then Czechoslovak Republic. It has been modernised from time to time, and you will come across old sections that have been bypassed and left for the use of local traffic, or sometimes just pedestrians and cyclists (Cesta Slobody is also a cycling route).

A hard-surfaced footway parallels Cesta Slobody for some 18km from Vyšné Hágy to Tatranské Matliare, via Nová Polianka, Tatranská Polianka, Tatranské Zruby, the Smokovec community, Tatranská Lesná and Tatranská Lomnica. While it is sometimes beside the traffic, it often meanders away from the road into the trees, or uses the old road before it was straightened.

Note Place names highlighted in **bold type** on the following pages can be looked up in the gazetteer, starting on page 170.

RED ROUTES

Note Red routes 0860 in the Western Tatras, and 0906 in the Spišská Magura, shown on some maps, are outside the scope of this book.

• 0930 TATRANSKÁ MAGISTRÁLA

This grand traverse provides an opportunity to feast your eyes on a whole variety of typical High Tatras scenes. Tatranská Magistrála means Tatras Highway, and is the only substantial red route in the Slovak High Tatras – all the others are short routes to summits. The Tatranská Magistrála parallels the main High

Tatras ridge on its south side, so when climbing from the resorts you are bound to cross it, and will recognise it by its white–red–white horizontally banded waymarks.

Fully opened in 1937, the Magistrála was the idea of the KČST (Klub Československých Turistov). Switchbacking along the southern slopes of the whole High Tatras range, Tatranská Magistrála now runs for 42km from Veľké Biele Pleso in the east, a tarn below the pass of Kopské Sedlo where the High Tatras give way to the White Tatras, to Podbanské, a village at the west end in the Western Tatras. On the way it passes other places that receive a mention in our gazetteer – Zelené Pleso, Skalnaté Pleso, Zamkovského Chata, Starolesnianska Poľana, Hrebienok, Velické Pleso, Batizovské Pleso, Popradské Pleso, Štrbské Pleso, Jamské Pleso, Tri Studničky.

Until 1978, when the White Tatras were put out of bounds to tourists, it continued on up to Kopské Sedlo and Hlúpy, then turned right to follow the ridge of the White Tatras to Skalné Vráta, before descending to finish at Tatranská Kotlina.

The route undulates considerably, alternatively dropping down into the valleys and rising up over passes and shoulders, so if you find it suits your plans better to walk from west to east, this may not make too much difference. Altitude ranges from 940m at Podbanské to 2020m at Sedlo pod Svišťovkou, a col close to the east end. At two points you come close to a minor summit – Ostrva (1984m) and Veľká Svištovka (2037m), both of which can be reached by a short diversion.

Much of the route passes through the forest belt, though some of this was destroyed by the Tatranská Bora (see page 72). There are frequent open areas providing some of the best views across the Sub-Tatras Basin to the Low Tatras. Sometimes, on rounding a bend, your breath will be taken away by the magnificent sight of a clear tarn reflecting in almost mirror perfection the backdrop of a craggy Tatra peak. Tarns are a regular feature – the route links 12, of varying sizes.

Separate sections of the Magistrála can be used to link routes from or to the resorts. While in general it offers fairly easy walking, there are several airy stretches across open rock, with some scrambling – these are pointed out in the relevant path description.

There is no lack of refreshment opportunities, as the Magistrála passes by or close to no fewer than six mountain chalets (Chata pri Zelenom Plese, Skalnatá Chata, Zamkovského Chata, Rainerova Chata, Bilíkova Chata and Chata pri Popradskom Plesom), as well as cafés at Skalnaté Pleso, Hrebienok and in the villages of Štrbské Pleso and Podbanské.

It is possible to do a tour along the whole route, though as this requires around 15 hours of actual walking, it is too much for one day, except in midsummer for

Rainerova Chata at Starolesnianská Poľana on the Tatranská Magistrála

exceptionally fit and experienced mountain walkers. It could be split into a tour of 2½ days, staying at chalets, subject to availability (advance booking is strongly advised), otherwise you can come down to a village for the overnight stop – easily done using the mountain lifts at Skalnaté Pleso (for Tatranská Lomnica) and Hrebienok (for Starý Smokovec).

Anyone wishing to follow the entire route will find it easier to start in the east where it is higher. A possible itinerary for such a tour, optionally with two overnight stops at Hrebienok or Starý Smokovec and Štrbské Pleso, would be:

Day 1 Bus to Biela Voda; walk to Veľké Biele Pleso to join Tatranská Magistrála to Hrebienok; funicular (or walk) down to Starý Smokovec (total walking time 6h 45m–7h 30m).

Day 2 Funicular to Hrebienok; Tatranská Magistrála to Štrbské Pleso (total walking time 7h 15m).

Day 3 Tatranská Magistrála to Podbanské (bus back to other resorts; total walking time 3h 45m).

Overnight accommodation, mostly dormitories only, may be available at (with approximate walking times from the previous place in hours and minutes): Chata pri Zelenom Plese (3h 15m from Biela Voda via Veľké Biele Pleso), Skalnatá Chata (limited, 2h 00m), Zamkovského Chata (0h 45m), Bilíkova Chata (0h 45m), Hrebienok (hotel, 0h 15m), Sliezsky Dom (2h 00m), Popradské Pleso (3h 30m), Štrbské Pleso (1h 00m) and Podbanské (3h 45m).

Because the Magistrála is so long, we have divided our route description into seven sections, each suffixed with a letter of the alphabet, as shown below.

0930A Veľké Biele Pleso–Skalnaté Pleso (for Tatranská Lomnica)
0930B Skalnaté Pleso–Hrebienok (for Starý Smokovec)
0930C Hrebienok–Sliezsky Dom
0930D Sliezsky Dom–Popradské Pleso
0930E Popradské Pleso–Štrbské Pleso
0930F Štrbské Pleso–Tri Studničky
0930G Tri Studničky–Podbanské

As the majority of walkers are unlikely to tackle the entire route, we describe each section in the **recommended** direction of walking, so not all are described east to west (eg 0930A).

• 0930A SKALNATÉ PLESO TO VEĽKÉ BIELE PLESO (1545m–2037m)

Grade Strenuous   **Distance** 6km   **Average Gradient** 15%
S–N Height Gain 361m/**Loss** 492m   **Time** 2h 30m
N–S Height Gain 492m/**Loss** 361m   **Time** 3h 00m
Winter/Spring Closed between Veľká Svišťovka and Zelené Pleso

The highest part of the Tatranská Magistrála, including one of the most beautiful tarns in the Tatras, Zelené Pleso. On a very short diversion, the minor summit Veľká Svišťovka can be included.

The map indicates that this part of the route should be done from north to south – this makes using the one short length of chain easier by ascending it, and if you thus feel more comfortable, you are advised to go north to south. However, this seems to be generally ignored, and the majority of walkers go south to north to reduce the climbing.

Approaching Veľká Švišťovka on the Tatranská Magistrála (photo: R Turnbull)

Most of this route is in open country with excellent views. It is very rocky – watch your step all the time! Some high parts are slightly exposed, and a short section through a gully is very steep and rocky, with fixed chains for support.

From **Skalnaté Pleso** gondola top station (1751m) go right to follow red waymarks. The path climbs steeply at first above the tarn, passing the observatory, then turns right to contour at around 1900m for some time, with excellent views down to Tatranská Lomnica and Tatranské Matliare, and over the Sub-Tatras Basin. After crossing a stream it starts to climb steeply again to Sedlo pod Svišťovkou (Saddle below Svišťovka, 2023m). The minor summit of **Veľká Svišťovka** (2037m) is but a short distance to the east, and while it is not strictly accessible to walkers, being off the waymarked route, everybody seems to go there! (*S–N 1h 75m, N–S 0h 50m.*)

From Sedlo pod Svišťovkou the path continues at first on a well-constructed but narrow ledge, with a long drop below. You pass a great lone slab of rock, which makes a good background for photographs, then descend a long series of zigzags down a steep shoulder, with the green tarn of Zelené Pleso providing a subtly changing backdrop at each turn. There is a slight sense of exposure at some of the turns, where care is needed on crumbly rock, and to spot the waymarks. You eventually come to a rocky gully, which requires a scramble, but with minimal exposure and fixed chains for support. Below this the path levels out through dwarf pine, and passes Čierne Pleso (Black Tarn) and another small tarn before reaching **Zelené Pleso** (1545m). (*S–N 0h 50m, N–S 1h 15m.*)

From Chata pri Zelenom Plese the route continues northeastwards, climbing gently through dwarf pine. Over to your right, you can clearly see the long zigzag path that brought you down from Svišťovka. You reach lonely Trojrohé Pleso (Three Horned Tarn), like a Scottish lochan, nestling in a hollow. Here you have a beautiful view of the White Tatras, with the triple-humped Košiare (2011m) prominent. Finally you cross a wooden bridge over a tinkling brook, Kežmarská Biela Voda (White Water of Kežmarok), to reach **Veľké Biele Pleso** (1620m). (*S–N 0h 30m, N–S 0h 30m.*)

• 0930B SKALNATÉ PLESO TO HREBIENOK (1285m–1761m)

Grade Moderate	**Distance** 4.5km	**Average Gradient** 11%
N–S Height Loss 476m	**Time** 1h 30m	**S–N Height Gain** 476m
Time 2h 00m	**Winter/Spring** Open	

This section is an educational trail (see page 70), enhanced by interpretation boards telling you something about the territory you are passing – all in Slovak! Help is at hand, though – a summarised translation of each board appears below. Before setting off from Skalnaté Pleso, you may wish to walk around the tarn, which has its own educational trail (no translation available) – this should take about 15–20 minutes.

From the exit at the top of the gondola-lift at **Skalnaté Pleso** (1761m, refreshments), go left for a few hundred metres to Skalnatá Chata (refreshments). Continue through open mountainside, passing Slnečná Vyhliadka (Sunny Viewpoint), where you can look out over Stará Lesná village, Poprad town and the Sub-Tatras Basin. You follow a narrow path, which at first contours at about 1700m, then drops steeply through trees after 2km and swings round to **Zamkovského Chata** (1475m, refreshments). Green 5812 joins here. (*N–S 0h 45m, S–N 1h 05m.*)

From the door of Zamkovského Chata follow the path ahead for 300m, dropping steeply to 1400m. The path then swings right to undulate at about this level, crossing bridges over two streams fairly close together – both are branches of Malý Studený Potok, the second the main one.

At the second bridge is **Obrovský Vodopád** (Giant's Waterfall). Shortly afterwards the path drops steeply again, gradually bears left, and crosses a larger stream, Veľký Studený Potok, joining Blue 2907. Continuing in broadly the same direction, you first come to **Starolesnianská Poľana** (refreshments), then progress downwards for a further 1km to reach the intersection with Yellow 8859 and **Hrebienok** (1285m, refreshments). (*N–S 0h 45m, S–N 0h 45m.*)

If you are starting from Hrebienok, the route to Skalnaté Pleso starts from behind the ski-slope control tower. The first 500m are described as an easy access trail but are very steep in places.

Here is a summary of what it says on the boards. (Some of the references to 'forest zone' may have been affected by the Tatranská Bora – see page 72.)

1) Skalnatá Chata stands at the site of the original shelter comprising a huge rock slab under which travellers could sleep. In 1877 the space was bricked up to provide more protection, and by 1918 this had been replaced by a concrete building. (Note that this board, which now states incorrectly that

the chalet is closed, as it was until recently, is located inside the entrance of Skalnatá Chata.)

2) You are crossing the ski-piste from Lomnické Sedlo to Štart – it is 2000m long, with a drop of 990m. This area offers good winter sports possibilities, and the most important ski events in the High Tatras are held here. The barriers you can see are a protection against avalanches. Remember that you can only walk on the waymarked paths – please do not walk on the ski-piste or other areas.

3) This area is inhabited by marmots – large brown rodents related to squirrels, but more like badgers in shape and size. They dig burrows in which they hibernate, can be identified by their piercing, bird-like cry, and can sometimes be seen basking on rocks in the sun. Chamois and the rare rock eagle may also be seen here.

4) This area, called Škaredý Žľab (Ugly Gully), is particularly avalanche-prone in winter, and you can easily identify several forms of erosion caused not only by them, but by the combination of wind, water and the sun's heat. There are over 300 regular avalanche lines in the High Tatras.

5) The vegetation here is mainly dwarf pine, which helps to stabilise the mountainside and prevent erosion. Much of the mountainside that is now pasture was formerly covered by dwarf pine. Other trees and plants in this area include limba-fir, rowan, bilberries, wild raspberries, juniper, gentian, broom, greater woodrush and smallreed.

6) This is called Slnečná Vyhliadka (Sunny Viewpoint) with good reason. You are standing at 1540m on the southern ridge that descends from Lomnický Štít, with an excellent view to the west of Veľká and Malá Studená Dolina (Great and Little Cold Valleys). The names hark back to the glacier that formed these valleys – at its greatest extent it was 220m thick and 9.8km long. As it receded, many tarns were formed. You are also at the upper limit of the pine forest zone – here the vegetation most commonly found is birch, rowan, willow and goat willow. To the south you can see the eastern part of the Low Tatras, whose highest summit, Kráľová Hoľa (King's Bare Hill, 1920m) can be identified by its transmitter mast.

7) We are passing the upper forest zone where the trees grow to 15m. They include pine, limba-fir, larch, birch and rowan. Also to be found are greater woodrush, black honeysuckle, wood sorrel, purple coltsfoot, broad buckler fern, ragwort and hawkweed.

8) There is an inversion of the usual vegetation zones here. The glacier gouged out the mountainside, leaving great rock walls. The rock was then split by frost and tumbled downhill, resulting in ground suitable for dwarf pine at a lower level than usual. Further up, a zone of ordinary pine can be found.

9) The two streams near here (Veľký and Malý Studený Potok – see number 6) originate from springs at 2128m and 2017m respectively. The main stream is 19km long and its water is very pure. Salmon, common and brook trout, and bullhead swim in it. The birds on the bank include the dipper and white wagtail.

• 0930C SLIEZSKY DOM TO HREBIENOK (1285m–1670m)

Grade Moderate (but with a short scramble)
Distance 7km	**Average Gradient** 6%
W–E Height Loss 385m	**Time** 1h 45m
E–W Height Gain 385m	**Time** 2h 00m

Winter/Spring Open (but a short section of scrambling requires care if icy)

This section, with exceptional views over to the Low Tatras, starts from outside Sliezsky Dom chalet (1670m, refreshments) beside **Velické Pleso**. At first you wind among scrub and rocks ahead for a few hundred metres, then turn right on a narrow path that climbs in 2km to 1700m at Slavkovské Pleso (marked on some maps as Slavkovské Plieska). The tarn lies a little to the left of the path, the minor peak immediately above is Senná Kopa (1848m), the great mass of **Slavkovský Štít** rears above that, and behind you is the Gerlach massif.

The path descends steadily for 3km to the junction with Blue 2906, and a further 1km to **Hrebienok** (1285m, refreshments). On the way you must negotiate a short, steep stretch of path that involves scrambling and is a little exposed in places. It is mostly downwards, so if you prefer to scramble up, follow this section E–W. There is a good view of the Smokovec villages and Poprad from here.

If starting from Hrebienok, take the path between the big Ski Club hut (with café and giant scoreboard) and a white building.

• 0930D SLIEZSKY DOM TO POPRADSKÉ PLESO (1494m–1966m)

Grade Strenuous	**Distance** 8.5km

Average Gradient 8% (but to Popradské Pleso is 29%)
E–W Height Gain 263m/**Loss** 432m	**Time** 3h 00m
W–E Height Gain 432m/**Loss** 263m	**Time** 3h 30m

Winter/Spring Closed (this sometimes applies in summer if there have been heavy snowfalls)

One of the tougher sections of the Tatranská Magistrála, especially if starting from Popradské Pleso. It is mostly above the tree-line, so you have constant views over the Sub-Tatras Basin, and you pass lonely Batizovské Pleso below Gerlachovský Štít. The minor summit Ostrva is easily reached on a short diversion.

From Sliezsky Dom (1670m, refreshments) by **Velické Pleso** the path contours at about 1650m through dwarf pine and rock, then descends a little to the junction with Yellow 8856 – named on the signpost as Rázcestie pod Suchým (Junction below Suchý Vrch) at 1720m. You then climb the shoulder of Suchý Vrch (Dry Hill), with views across the plain to Poprad, up to **Batizovské Pleso** at 1879m. (*E–W 1h 00m, W–E 1h 00m.*)

From there, you descend gently for 10 minutes to the junction with Yellow 8855 (Rázcestie pod Končistou) at 1850m, then follow a rocky, undulating path to windy Sedlo pod Ostrvou (Saddle below Ostrva, 1966m). (*E–W 1h 45m, W-E 1h 30m.*)

Although not on the waymarked network, most walkers make the short diversion to the summit of **Ostrva** (1984m), which is more sheltered.

The route continues on a long series of zigzags down to **Popradské Pleso** (1494m, refreshments). (*E–W 0h 30m, W–E 0h 45m.*)

• 0930E POPRADSKÉ PLESO TO ŠTRBSKÉ PLESO (1494m–1350m)

Grade Easy	**Distance** 4.5km	**Average Gradient** 4%
N–S Height Loss 139m	**Time** 1h 15m	
S–N Height Gain 139m	**Time** 1h 25m	
Winter/Spring Closed		

Starting from Chata pri Popradskom Plese (1494m, refreshments) at **Popradské Pleso**, go past the kiosks and ascend to the junction with Blue 2902B, then follow the red waymarks ahead. The path descends gently into the valley of **Mengusovská Dolina**, down which runs Hincov Potok, a trout stream feeding the Poprad river. You cross this on a wooden footbridge, from which a charming view extends upstream. The large numbers of boulders in this area are the result of frequent avalanches in winter – the reason for the closure of this path during that season. After climbing the southeastern slope of Patria as far as about 1500m, the path levels off and follows a ledge at this height for some time, with fine views across the valley. Soon after the path starts to descend, you reach Rázcestie nad Triganom (1499m), the junction with Green 5805. (*N–S 0h 30m, S–N 0h 40m.*)

*In Mengusovská Dolina, looking towards Kôprovský
Štít and Čubrina, near junction with Red 0930E
(Blue 2902B) (photo: R Turnbull)*

Descend steadily to a point just before the road near Hotel Patria. Instead of joining the road, look for an inconspicuous white–red–white Magistrála waymark in the trees on your right, marking a path that leads steeply down to cross a stream by a wooden footbridge. An information board tells you that dippers and woodpeckers may be seen in this area.

Now continue on to the main road, which you cross. Yellow 8853A joins here and runs together with the Magistrála beside **Štrbské Pleso** tarn (1350m). Turn left along the tarn shore for Štrbské Pleso village (refreshments). (*N–S 0h 45m, S–N 0h 45m.*)

See gazetteer (page 188) for directions on reaching the station from the tarn.

If starting from Štrbské Pleso, look for the instructional sign at the northeast corner of the tarn – the route to Popradské Pleso starts from here.

• 0930F ŠTRBSKÉ PLESO TO TRI STUDNIČKY (1350m–1140m)

Grade Easy	**Distance** 10km	**Average Gradient** 5%
E–W Height Gain 140m/**Loss** 350m		**Time** 2h 15m
W–E Height Gain 350m/**Loss** 140m		**Time** 2h 30m
Winter/Spring Open		

A gentle route, mostly in forest, but passing the delightful Jamské Pleso, and with some good views over the plain.

The Tatranská Magistrála skirts the southern side of the tarn at **Štrbské Pleso** (1350m, refreshments). Between the Kriváň and Solisko spa houses is a signpost, from which you follow the track with lamp-posts, rising into the forest. The waymarking is a little patchy along here – ignore the coloured spots, which indicate cross-country ski routes. At the fork of tracks, bear right, slightly uphill. At various track intersections, keep ahead.

After a little over 2km, mostly gently uphill, you pass the start of Yellow 8853B. The Magistrála now continues upwards as a rough, stony track for a further 2km to the junction with Blue 2903 and the tarn of **Jamské Pleso** (1447m). (*E–W 1h 00m, W–E 1h 00m.*)

The path contours beyond the tarn, initially on a narrow ledge, at around 1500m for 2km. Then you come to a fork of tracks – ignore the obvious one that goes ahead downhill and take the one that contours round to the right through woodland. It soon starts to drop steeply and in another 2km you reach the junction with Green 5803A.

Turn right, passing a monument to Kapitána Rašu – see gazetteer under **Tri Studničky** regarding this and the chalet that once stood here. The route now runs together with Green 5803 for several hundred metres, coming right down to the Cesta Slobody road at one point. Follow the old road for a few hundred metres to visit the charming rural hamlet of Tri Studničky (1140m). (*E–W 1h 15m, W–E 1h 30m.*)

• 0930G TRI STUDNIČKY TO PODBANSKÉ (1140m–940m)

Grade Easy	**Distance** 5km	**Average Gradient** 6%
E–W Height Gain 35m/**Loss** 235m		**Time** 1h 30m
W–E Height Gain 235m/**Loss** 35m		**Time** 2h 00m
Winter/Spring Open		

An easy route with some fine views of Kriváň, and of Bystrá, the highest Western Tatras peak. It used to be heavily forested but was badly affected by the Tatranská Bora (see page 72).

From **Tri Studničky** (1140m) follow the main track south for a short distance to the splendid 'hatstand' signpost, then take a path up to the right, following the white–red–white Magistrála waymarks. Climbing gently for 1.5km, to about 1175m, you eventually reach what used to be (until the Tatranská Bora) a forest road, which may not be marked on your map. Turn left down the road for 100m, then turn right on to a path. Unfortunately, when the forest road was built they omitted to repaint the waymarks at path junctions, but the magnificent view of **Kriváň** up the road is some compensation.

You soon join a track heading downhill, passing a wooden shelter with a picnic table in a clearing. In a short distance you join another forest road, then at a signpost beside another picnic table you turn right on to a track, with an enclosure nearby. After a few minutes, the track turns sharp left, then right at a loggers' clearing. Follow the track down to a meadow above the hamlet of **Nadbanské** (975m) and skirt the field to the road. This stretch is all well waymarked.

From Nadbanské you have a good view of two Western Tatras peaks – their highest, Bystrá (2248m), and Kotlová (1985m), and another sighting of Kriváň behind you. Turn right along the road through Nadbanské, then after bearing left in 100m turn right down a track to join the main road. Turn right on the path beside the road to cross the Belá river to **Podbanské** (940m, refreshments).

• 0931A POD TOMANOVOU TO TOMANOVSKÉ SEDLO (1150m–1686m)

This route, included in previous editions, has been closed for environmental reasons and is no longer on the waymarked network. It might still be shown on some maps.

• 0931 POD TOMANOVOU TO HLADKÉ SEDLO (1150m–1994m)

Grade Moderate	**Distance** 9km	**Average Gradient** 10%
W–E Height Gain 844m	**Time** 2h 30m	
E–W Height Loss 844m	**Time** 2h 00m	
Winter/Spring Closed		

The first 2km of the route runs together with Yellow 8851 on an asphalt road, as far as Rázcestie pod Kasprovým Vrchom. To your left are the rounded summits of the Červené Vrchy (Red Hills), the easternmost part of the Western Tatras, currently accessible only from Poland. From the junction the red route follows a track that is broad at first, then narrows as it climbs through meadows and thin forest into the upper part of Tichá Dolina (Zadná Tichá).

Now on your right you can see the bulk of Veľká Kopa (2052m) and its outlying minor summit, Magura (1901m) – these form part of a finger of the High Tatras called Liptovské Kopy (Stacks of Liptov). The main range of the High Tatras starts to your left, at **Laliové Sedlo**. The path becomes steeper, now through grass and rock, then swings left up to the broad saddle called Sedlo Závory (1679m), where it is joined by Green 5801.Now you have a fairly moderate climb for an hour or so to **Hladké Sedlo** (Smooth Saddle). From here you can see down into the beautiful **Dolina Pięciu Stawów Polskich** (Valley of Five Polish Tarns).

There was a proposal that this route should continue into Poland but at the time of writing this had not materialised. In any case it would be difficult to work it into a day trip from Podbanské to Zakopane and back, or vice versa. See page 60.

• 0932 POD TEMNOSMREČINSKOU TO NIŽNÉ TEMNOSMREČINSKÉ PLESO (1580m–1674m)

Grade Easy	**Distance** 1.5km	**Average Gradient** 7%
E–W Height Gain 94m	**Time** 1h 00m	
W–E Height Loss 94m	**Time** 0h 45m	
Winter/Spring Closed		

Easy walking through Temnosmrečinská Dolina to the tarn of the same name.

The path starts from the junction with Green 5801, properly called Rázcestie pod Temnosmrečinskou Dolinou, at about 1580m, here in forest. It very quickly reaches dwarf pine for the remainder of the climb to the lower of the two quite large tarns, **Nižné Temnosmrečinské Pleso** (1674m). The waymarked route ends on its north-western shore – you cannot continue to the higher tarn. Shortly before the tarn, you can see far below to your right the waterfall called Vajanského Vodopád.

• 0933 NAD ŽABÍM POTOKOM TO RYSY (1640m–2503m)

Grade Strenuous	**Distance** 4km	**Average Gradient** 23%
SW–NE Height Gain 863m	**Time** 2h 45m	
NE–SW Height Loss 863m	**Time** 2h 00m	
Winter/Spring Closed		

A popular route leading to Rysy, the highest summit on the waymarked route system, and so the highest one for which you do not have to be accompanied by a mountain guide. It is strenuous and includes a fixed chain section, but is not difficult.

From its junction with Blue 2902B, properly called Rázcestie nad Žabím Potokom (Junction above Frog Brook, 1640m), the path climbs steeply, and quickly leaves the dwarf pine. A long series of zigzags leads to the southernmost of the Žabie Plesá (Frogs Tarns, 1919m), then another set of zigzags, including a great, steep slab of bare rock with two fixed chains (one up, the other down). More zigzags lead to **Chata pod Rysmi** (2250m). (*SW–NE 2h 00m, NE–SW 1h 25m.*)

The final section takes you first in just 15 minutes to the saddle called Váha (Weight, 2337m) then on to the summit of **Rysy**. (0h 30m). There are actually two summits – one each in Slovakia (2503m) and Poland (2499m), and you can visit either or both of these. (*SW–NE 0h 45m, NE–SW 0h 35m.*)

Although it is possible to continue on into Poland, following our Polish route 012, it is not recommended in this direction, as you would then have to descend a steep and difficult section between here and Czarny Staw. See page 208 for a suggested route in the opposite direction from Poland into Slovakia, also Cross-border Walking, page 60.

• 0934 VYŠNÉ KÔPROVSKÉ SEDLO TO KÔPROVSKÝ ŠTÍT (2180m–2363m)

Grade Strenuous	**Distance** 1km	**Average Gradient** 19%
S–N Height Gain 187m	**Time** 1h 30m	
N–S Height Loss 187m	**Time** 1h 30m	
Winter/Spring Closed		

On Kôprovský Štít, looking towards Štrbský
Štít, Kriváň and Bystrá (Red 0934) (photo: R Turnbull)

Kôprovský Štít is a comparatively easy summit to reach, with no fixed chains, and good views over three valleys – southeastwards into Mengusovská Dolina and northwestwards into Temnosmrečinská Dolina, each with their tarns, and south-westwards into Hlinská Dolina.

• 0935 CHATA POD SOLISKOM TO PREDNÉ SOLISKO (1830m–2093m)

Grade Moderate	**Distance** 1.5km	**Average Gradient** 18%
S–N Height Gain 263m	**Time** 0h 45m	
N–S Height Loss 263m	**Time** 0h 30m	
Winter/Spring Closed		

Predné Solisko (2093m) is one of the easiest viewpoints to reach – especially if you use the chair-lift from Štrbské Pleso – so it can get crowded at peak times. The route, which starts at the back of **Chata pod Soliskom** (1830m, refreshments), is fairly steep, but boulders have been cleverly placed to provide steps for most of the way.

BLUE ROUTES

Note Blue routes 2807 and 2809 in the Spišská Magura, and 2901 in the Western Tatras, shown on some High Tatras maps, are outside the scope of this book.

• 2836A ŠTRBSKÉ PLESO TO ŠTRBA AND KOLESÁRKY (1320m–829m)

Grade Easy	**Distance** 21km	**Average Gradient** 2%
N–S Height Loss 491m	**Time** 1h 30m	
S–N Height Gain 491m	**Time** 1h 45m	
Winter/Spring Open		

A waymarked route that links the footpath networks of the High and Low Tatras, mostly on roads and beside the railway line. The upper part of this route, which used to be heavily forested, was badly affected by the Tatranská Bora (see page 72).

From **Štrbské Pleso** station (1320m, refreshments) go left past the Panoráma Hotel, where you join the track descending from the tarn. Turn left, downhill, and soon join the railway line as it passes under the road. Now you closely follow the line, crossing the road again, but at the next meeting with the road you turn left to cross the line and descend into the village of **Tatranská Štrba** (900m, refreshments). At the crossroads a branch leads off (right) to the station – called plain Štrba! It continues ahead down the road into the large villages of **Štrba** (829m, refreshments) and **Šuňava** (900m, refreshments), then follows a track to the hamlet of Kolesárky in the Low Tatras.

• 2836B ŠTRBSKÉ PLESO TO CHATA POD SOLISKOM AND FURKOTSKÁ DOLINA (1350m–1830m)

Grade Moderate	**Distance** 4km	**Average Gradient** 13%
SE–NW Height Gain 480m/**Loss** 30m		**Time** 1h 45m
NW–SE Height Gain 30m/**Loss** 480m		**Time** 1h 30m
Winter/Spring Closed		

A long, straight slog in the uphill direction, but this can be avoided by using the chair-lift, which starts beside the FIS Hotel at Štrbské Pleso tarn. If you decide to walk up, and need to make frequent stops to regain your breath, turn round for splendid views back over the tarn.

The route starts from Štrbské Pleso tarn, 1km north of the railway station – see gazetteer (page 188) for route instructions from station to tarn. A blue arrow indicates the point where the path leaves the northwest corner of the tarn. After 50m, turn left (not waymarked), and you shortly reach a large clearing to your right. In winter this is abuzz with skiers and spectators, for it is the main practice area for **Štrbské Pleso** (1350m), the busiest ski resort in the Slovak Tatras, and nearby are two ski-jumps. Unless you are a keen student of winter sports architecture and rusty wire, you can ignore these and follow the ski-tow pylons for a long, straight, hard climb to the broad, cleared ski-piste. You will either be encouraged or frustrated by the sight of **Chata pod Soliskom** (1830m, refreshments), which hovers endlessly above. (*SE–NW 1h 30m, SE–NW 1h 00m.*)

From the west end of the chalet buildings, follow the blue waymarks steeply downhill on a narrow, rocky path to Furkotská Dolina (1800m) and the junction with Yellow 8853. (*SE–NW 0h 15m, NW–SE 0h 30m.*)

- **2902A TRI STUDNIČKY TO VYŠNÉ KÔPROVSKÉ SEDLO (1140m–2180m)**

Grade Easy to Hlinská Dolina, moderate to Vyšné Kôprovské Sedlo
Distance 13km
Average Gradient 8% to Hlinská Dolina, 16% to Vyšné Kôprovské Sedlo
SW–NE Height Gain 1200m/**Loss** 160m   **Time** 5h 00m
NE–SW Height Loss 1200m/**Gain** 160m   **Time** 4h 15m
Winter/Spring Open to Rázcestie pod Grúnikom (junction with Green 5802)

The lower part of this route, which used to be heavily forested, was badly affected by the Tatranská Bora (see page 72).

The route starts to the left of the rustic buildings of **Tri Studničky** (1140m), at first through meadows. At about 1280m it crosses Veľká Pálenica, the foot of the shoulder that descends southwest from Kriváň via the minor summit of **Grúnik**. The path now descends on big zigzags to meet Green 5802 at a junction called Rázcestie pod Grúnikom (1120m), in the long valley called **Kôprová Dolina**. For the next 2km you gently climb an asphalt road, crossing and recrossing the brook (Kôprovský Potok) – there are picnic tables at several points. To the right you can see the impressive summit of **Kriváň**, to the left the lower but bulky massif of the Liptovské Kopy (Stacks of Liptov).

The road ends and you continue on a path through forest and meadows for 3km to the junction with Green 5801 (Rázcestie pod Hlinskou Dolinou) at just over 1400m. The route turns right, descending at first to cross Kôprovský Potok, then climbing Hlinská Dolina with Hlinský Potok to your right. You emerge from the forest into the dwarf pine, with the massif of Hrubé (Coarse) to the right. The path ascends several terraces through grass and rock, then steepens and zigzags to the saddle, Vyšné Kôprovské Sedlo (2180m).

• 2902B POPRADSKÉ PLESO STATION AND TARN TO VEĽKÉ HINCOVO PLESO – VYŠNÉ KÔPROVSKÉ SEDLO (1250m–2180m)

Grade Easy to Popradské Pleso tarn, moderate to Vyšné Kôprovské Sedlo
Distance 8.5km
Average Gradient 7% to Popradské Pleso, 14% to Vyšné Kôprovské Sedlo
S–N Height Gain 930m   **Time** 2h 30m
N–S Height Loss 930m   **Time** 2h 00m
Winter/Spring Open as far as Rázcestie nad Žabím Potokom (1km beyond Popradské Pleso)

The first section of this route is a long slog up the service road to Popradské Pleso, but it is well used by walkers and cyclists (it is an official cycle route) as the quickest way to reach the popular tarn, and beyond that (on paths mostly in dwarf pine and above the tree-line) the summit of Rysy.

Approaching Popradské Pleso from the Symbolic Cemetery approaching Blue 2902B (Yellow 8854)

Veľké Hincovo Pleso and Hincovo Sedlo (Blue 2902B)

From **Popradské Pleso** station (1250m, toilets beside car park attendant's cabin), turn right along the road (the old main road before the modern highway was built further south) for 150m to a left-hand bend, where the service road to the tarn goes right, past an electricity station. You follow this road all the way to the tarn, passing the **Dubček Stone**, and negotiating a considerable number of bends, and crossing the infant River Poprad, then the Krupá stream.

Before reaching the tarn, you meet the junction with Yellow 8854, which you can follow as an alternative route to the tarn via **Symbolický Cintorín** (small fee payable). Otherwise keep ahead on the blue route, shortly passing the junction with Green 5805 near the south end of the tarn. A little further on you cross the Tatranská Magistrála (Red 0930E), and you can turn right along it for the delights of **Popradské Pleso** (1494m) and its chalet. (*S–N 0h 50m, N–S 0h 40m.*)

The blue route continues ahead on a forest path, ascending gently, to emerge into the dwarf pine, then crosses a stream to Rázcestie nad Žabím Potokom (Junction above Frog Brook), where Red 0933 takes most of the walkers up to Rysy. Blue 2902B continues ahead in the dwarf pine, but soon comes to bare rock, which it climbs by means of short, steep zigzags. The path now ascends gently to the largest tarn in the Slovak Tatras, **Veľké Hincovo Pleso** (1946m). You can make this the goal of your walk, and although unwaymarked, you can follow the path that leads for 2.5km around the tarn. (*S–N 1h 00m, N–S 0h 50m.*)

If continuing on to Vyšné Kôprovské Sedlo (2180m), turn left just before the tarn, soon climbing steeply on more zigzags to the saddle. (*S–N 0h 40m, N–S 0h 30m.*)

• 2903 BIELY VÁH TO KRIVÁŇ (1200m–2494m)

Grade Strenuous	**Distance** 6.5km	**Average Gradient** 20%
SE–NW Height Gain 1294m	**Time** 4h 15m	
NW–SE Height Loss 1294m	**Time** 3h 30m	
Winter/Spring Open only as far as Red 0930 and Jamské Pleso		

A well-graded path to the summit that is Slovakia's national symbol, with no fixed chains and some scrambling. It passes the idyllic tarn Jamské Pleso.

The lower part of this route used to be heavily forested but was badly affected by the Tatranská Bora (see page 72).

The bus stop at Rázcestie Biely Váh (1200m, near the place called Na Striedku on the map) is the first one out of Štrbské Pleso in the direction of Podbanské and Liptovský Hrádok. Follow the blue waymarks, crossing first the junction with Green 5803, then a stream, which is the infant Biely (White) Váh – one of the two main contributors to Slovakia's longest river, the Váh. The other is the Čierny

(Black) Váh, which rises in the Low Tatras. Ascending its valley, you cross back over the stream then reach the junction with Red 0930. (*SE–NW 1h 15m, NW–SE 1h 00m.*)

To the left along the red route is **Jamské Pleso** (1447m) – well worth a 15-minute detour.

Continue climbing, now in forest, above the valley called **Važecká Dolina**, reaching the tree-line near the minor summit of Jamy (Pits, 1572m), which gives Jamské Pleso its name. You now begin the long ascent up the crest of a spur called Predný Handel, which leads first to the junction with Green 5803B (Rázcestie pod Kriváňom). (*SE–NW 2h 00m, NW–SE 1h 45m.*)

A short climb takes you to the ridge called Pavlov Chrbat, which you follow to the summit of **Kriváň** (2494m), with just a little scrambling. (*SE–NW 0h 45m, NW–SE 0h 30m.*)

• 2905 TATRANSKÉ ZRUBY TO POD SENNOU KOPOU (990m–1325m)

Grade Moderate	**Distance** 2.5km	**Average Gradient** 14%
SE–NW Height Gain 335m	**Time** 1h 00m	
NW–SE Height Loss 335m	**Time** 0h 45m	
Winter/Spring Open		

*A little-used route linking the village of **Tatranské Zruby** to Yellow 8858, and thereby to Sliezsky Dom. It is straight and steep, and used to be entirely in forest until the Tatranská Bora struck (see page 72).*

• 2906 STARÝ SMOKOVEC TO SLAVKOVSKÝ ŠTÍT (1010m–2452m)

Grade Moderate	**Distance** 8km	**Average Gradient** 18%
SE–NW Height Gain 1442m	**Time** 4h 45m	
NW–SE Height Loss 1442m	**Time** 3h 15m	
Winter/Spring Closed		

Slavkovský Štít, dominating Starý Smokovec, is an obvious early target for walkers staying there, with excellent views as a reward. Do not underestimate this route – though appearing fairly short and innocuous on the map, it is a long, hard climb. There are no difficult parts, although at one point a short, narrow ridge is slightly exposed. The lower part, which is still forested, can be avoided by taking the funicular to Hrebienok (refreshments), then using Red 0930C to the junction with Blue 2906. The upper part is either in dwarf pine or on open rock, with constant good views.

The route starts along a track to the left of the funicular station in **Starý Smokovec** (1010m) and follows the railway line for several hundred metres. It then bears left, away from the track, and soon joins the fence of a water-protection zone, which is fed by streams flowing from Päť Prameňou (Five Springs). Twisting and turning constantly, the path eventually reaches the junction with Red 0930C. (*SE–NW 1h 00m, NW–SE 0h 30m.*)

Continue ahead, following an earth-and-rock path that crosses the ski-pistes above **Hrebienok** (1285m) before reaching a rocky verandah (with iron railing) called Slavkovská Vyhliadka (1632m). From this exalted pulpit you can look out over the twin valleys of **Veľká** and **Malá Studená Dolina**. The highest summit in view is Lomnický Štít (2634m), easily identifiable with its meteorological station, while Prostredný Hrot (Middle Point, 2440m) pokes its head in on the left. (*SE–NW 0h 40m, NW–SE 0h 30m.*)

Now among dwarf pine, another 30-minute climb brings you to a second viewpoint, from where you can see the green roof of Zamkovského Chata to the right, and look back to Hrebienok. In 15–20 minutes you reach a narrow ledge above the dwarf pine, with a view over Smokovec and other nearby villages. Another 15–20 minutes brings you to a thin ridge, slightly exposed, with the Sub-Tatras Basin on your left and Veľká Studená Dolina on your right. Continue climbing for an hour or so to reach the outlying summit of Nos (Nose, 2283m), which lies up to your left and can be ascended quite easily. (*SE–NW 2h 05m, NW–SE 1h 35m.*)

Summon up your strength and push on to reach the summit of **Slavkovský Štít** (2452m). (*SE–NW 1h 00m, NW–SE 0h 40m.*)

2907A TATRANSKÁ LOMNICA TO PRIELOM (860m–2288m)

Grade Moderate to Zbojnícka Chata, strenuous to Prielom
Distance 14.5km
Average Gradient 9% to Zbojnícka Chata, 17% to Prielom
SE-NW Height Gain 1428m **Time** 5h 30m
NW-SE Height Loss 1428m **Time** 4h 35m
Winter/Spring Open only as far as Zbojnícka Chata

This is a fairly easy route as far as Zbojnícka Chata, though at one point there are two short scrambles with fixed chains. The passage over Prielom can be daunting in this direction, requiring an exposed descent using fixed chains. It is more easily tackled upwards, so would be better approached from the north (Blue 2907B) or on Green 5806 via Poľský Hrebeň. It is advisable to avoid this route altogether if wet, icy or under snow.

Vodopády Studeného Potoka (Blue 2907A)

The path starts near the Morava Hotel in **Tatranská Lomnica** (860m) – from the station, go past the shops then turn left, cross the main road and continue ahead up through the park. The route generally continues up the service road for Štart, but a path cuts out one long bend. On the fourth bend after rejoining the road, the route bears left, beneath the gondola cables and away from the road. Eventually, after climbing a long series of steep stone steps through forest and semi-open meadows, you cross a curving wooden bridge over Studený Potok (Cold Brook), which at this point cascades impressively for several hundred metres as **Vodopády Studeného Potoka**. *(SE–NW 1h 30m, NW–SE 1h 15m.)*

Continue upwards for 15 minutes to the junction with Green 5807, then on a broad path to **Starolesnianska Poľana** (1295m, refreshments at Rainerova Chata). A couple of minutes further on you cross the Tatranská Magistrála (Red 0930B). The path continues, rocky but quite gently graded, through the forest in Veľká Studená Dolina, one of the main valleys in the Slovak High Tatras. On reaching the dwarf pine, it crosses the brook then climbs steeply. Care is needed, using sharp boulders as steps to cross a stream, then a bridge across Veľký Studený Potok. The route then crosses an expanse of smooth rock, and two short scrambles with fixed chains are encountered. In the valley below lie two small tarns – Vareskové Pleso (Stirring Stick Tarn) and Dlhé Pleso (Long Tarn, one of two so called in the High Tatras). Another steep ascent brings you to **Zbojnícka Chata** (1960m, refreshments). *(SE–NW 2h 45m, NW–SE 2h 20m.)*

The path from the chalet starts fairly gently, but soon climbs steeply, becoming more so as you approach the saddle. A final push brings you to **Prielom** (2288m). *(SE–NW 1h 15m, NW–SE 1h 00m.)*

• 2907B LYSÁ POĽANA TO PRIELOM (970m–2288m)

Grade Easy to Kačacia Dolina, then strenuous to Prielom
Distance 15.5km   **Average Gradient** 3% to Kačacia Dolina, 28% to Prielom
N–S Height Gain 1318m   **Time** 5h 45m
S–N Height Loss 1318m   **Time** 5h 00m
Winter/Spring Open to Biela Voda

An easy route up Bielovodská Dolina leads through forest and flowery meadows, with several picnic spots and beautiful views of the peaks above, to some idyllic tarns at the foot of one of the most strenuous and formidable sections on the waymarked network – though this can be avoided by switching to Green 5806 via Poľský Hrebeň.

The upper part of this route is not recommended in icy conditions, or when under snow, as it can be very slippery.

At the saddle Prielom, looking towards Český Štít and Rysy (Blue 2907A/B) (photo: R Turnbull)

From the bus terminus at **Lysá Poľana** (970m, refreshments) walk towards the frontier station, but turn left shortly before reaching it, along a side road that leads for some distance along **Bielovodská Dolina** (White Water Valley). The Biela Voda river on your right forms the border with Poland for several kilometres, and the notices on its banks warn you not to attempt to swim across! After 3km or so you pass, lying away from the road, a large foresters' chalet (1020m), which is also a mountain rescue centre – there are some picnic tables and an ornamental water conduit. (*N–S 0h 45m, S–N 0h 45m.*)

A kilometre further on is another, smaller foresters' hut, also with a picnic table, and yet another kilometre brings you to a bridge over the river, where the border swings away to the southwest. The picnic table here is the most pleasantly situated one on this route. In 1500m you cross back to the east bank of the river – the picnic table on the far side has a roof. The forest road now gets rougher and narrower, but continues for some distance along the valley, climbing quite steeply for a while. Yet another picnic table is sited beneath the huge crag of Skorušniak on the far side of the valley. (*N–S 1h 30m, S–N 1h 25m.*)

At times as a narrow path, at others as a broader track, the route now climbs more steeply, twisting and turning through the forest, then passing through a brief zone of dwarf pine, until you climb above the tree-line to pass Litvorové Pleso (Angelica Tarn), lying a little below the path at 1860m. Some crags provide sheltered picnic spots beside the tarn. (*N–S 1h 45m, S–N 1h 30m.*)

Zamrznuté Pleso (2013m, Frozen Tarn) is passed on the way to Rázcestie pod Poľským Hrebeňom (Junction below Poľský Hrebeň). (*N–S 0h 45m, S–N 0h 35m.*)

You now have the option of turning right on Green 5806 for the easier route over Poľský Hrebeň. If you choose **Prielom** (2288m), be prepared for a strenuous and exposed climb using a series of fixed chains. (*N–S 1h 00m, S–N 0h 45m.*)

- ### 2908 ŠTART TO SKALNATÉ PLESO (1140m–1761m)

Grade Easy	**Distance** 8.5km	**Average Gradient** 8%
SE–NW Height Gain 621m	**Time** 3h 00m	
NW–SE Height Loss 621m	**Time** 2h 15m	
Winter/Spring Open only to Sedlo pod Malou Svišťovkou		

From **Štart** (1140m), the middle station of the gondola-lift from Tatranská Lomnica, go to your right along the path that is level at first, then alternately rises, falls and contours round the east side of the minor summit (not visible through the forest) of Malá Svišťovka (1561m). Some 15 minutes after the junction with Green 5809 (Poľana pod Malou Svišťovkou, 1310m), the path swings sharply left and climbs quite steeply to the saddle Sedlo pod Malou Svišťovkou (1521m), where you emerge into dwarf pine. The route now goes up to the right, and you cross a stream on a wooden bridge before climbing steadily, still in dwarf pine, to **Skalnaté Pleso** (1761m, refreshments).

• 2909 KEŽMARSKÉ ŽĽABY TO TATRANSKÁ KOTLINA (920m–765m)

Grade Easy	**Distance** 5km	**Average Gradient** 4%
SE–NW Height Gain 20m/**Loss** 155m		**Time** 1h 30m
NW–SE Height Gain 155m/**Loss** 20m		**Time** 1h 30m
Winter/Spring Open		

A short route through the forest linking the villages of Kežmarské Žľaby and Tatranská Kotlina. It also provides an alternative starting or finishing point for those wishing to walk to Chata Plesnivec and Veľké Biele Pleso

From the bus stop at **Kežmarské Žľaby** (920m) follow the blue waymarked track beside the holiday centre for a few hundred metres until you reach an asphalt road. Turn right along this, passing a reservoir. The road becomes a track, passing the junction with Yellow 8864, and eventually you reach the junction Rázcestie Čierna Voda (910m), where you join Green 5810 for the descent into **Tatranská Kotlina** (765m, refreshments).

• 2911A TATRANSKÉ MATLIARE TO KOPSKÉ SEDLO (885m–1749m)

Grade Easy to moderate	**Distance** 9.5km	**Average Gradient** 9%
SE–NW Height Gain 864m	**Time** 3h 45m	
NW–SE Height Loss 864m	**Time** 2h 45m	
Winter/Spring Open as far as Veľké Biele Pleso only		

This route leads to two very attractive spots at the meeting point of the High and White Tatras – the tarn, Veľké Biele Pleso, and the saddle, Kopské Sedlo. It is one of the four routes that cross the main High Tatras range, continuing as Blue 2911B, below.
    The lower part of this route used to be heavily forested but was badly affected by the Tatranská Bora (see page 72).

From the sanatorium in **Tatranské Matliare** (885m) follow the asphalt side road to a number of holiday centres, including Metalurg and Hutník (refreshments), where Yellow 8863 joins from the left. It continues to climb, crossing several

A 'hatstand signpost' at Kopské Sedlo
in the White Tatras (Blue 2911A)

streams, until it joins the forest road bringing Yellow 8861 from Biela Voda. (*SE–NW 1h 00m, NW–SE 0h 40m.*)

The two routes share the forest road for a while, climbing quite steeply close to the fast-flowing Biela Voda Kežmarská (Kežmarok White Water) and crossing it at one point, until Šalviový Prameň (Sage Spring, 1200m) is reached. There is a covered picnic table here. (*SE–NW 0h 30m, NW–SE 0h 20m.*)

50m further on, the routes part – Blue 2911 leaves the forest road to take a broad track off to the right, among spruce and bilberries, leading to another covered picnic table. It then follows a steep and stony path, sometimes beside Biela Voda Kežmarská, crossing it from time to time on wooden bridges. There are some very pretty spots along here, some with a good view back to the forested saddleback hill called Stežky (1529m). Eventually you reach the dwarf pine zone, then **Vel'ké Biele Pleso** (1620m), with the High Tatras to your left and the White Tatras to your right. (*SE–NW 1h 40m, NW–SE 1h 15m.*)

From Vel'ké Biele Pleso, the path gradually becomes steeper, with some treacherous loose earth and rock near the top, to reach **Kopské Sedlo** (1749m). (*SE–NW 0h 35m, NW–SE 0h 30m.*)

• 2911B JAVORINA TO KOPSKÉ SEDLO (1018m–1749m)

Grade Moderate	**Distance** 8km
Average Gradient 9% (11% Pod Muráňom to Kopské Sedlo)	
NW–SE Height Gain 731m	**Time** 3h 00m
SE–NW Height Loss 731m	**Time** 2h 30m
Winter/Spring Open to Pod Muráňom	

This is one of just four waymarked routes that touch the White Tatras, albeit only the foothills, providing a unique opportunity to see the special plant-life of that area. Most of the route is in open country, with good views and easy gradient, though it climbs quite steeply through the forested section. There are picnic tables at frequent intervals, including several covered ones. Most of this route (from Pod Muráňom upwards) is closed from 1 November to 15 June inclusive.

From the road junction at **Javorina** (1018m, refreshments, shown as Tatranská Javorina on some maps) follow the minor road south beside the Javorinka river, together with Green 5812. Beyond the south end of the village, a dirt road leads in 10 minutes to the foresters' hut at Kubalová. Bear left here (another forest road leads off to the right). Soon the great, isolated slab of Muráň (1890m), westernmost of the White Tatras peaks, towers ahead like a mini-Matterhorn. Then you see the pass of Kolové Sedlo, separating Jahňací Štít (on its left, 2229m) and Zmrzlá Veža (2310m). You pass on your right a water-treatment station, just before the path junction (Rázcestie pod Muráňom) with picnic tables, where the blue and green routes separate. (*NW–SE 0h 35m, SE–NW 0h 35m.*)

Blue 2911 turns left across the Javorinka river, still on a dirt road as far as **Pod Muráňom** (1090m). A stone track leads between meadows for several hundred metres, then climbs into the forest, shortly reaching a loggers' clearing with a covered picnic table. The forested hills to your right are Veľký and Malý Baboš; the evenly shaped peak to their left is Svišťovky, beyond which is Jahňací Štít. Curving round to the right is the valley of Javorová Dolina. At a track junction by a stream, take the left fork (covered picnic tables) and enter the ravine of Zadné Meďodoly (Rear Coppermines) below the hill called Bránka (Little Gate). In another 15 minutes fork left, and in 20 minutes cross the stream to a small clearing (picnic tables), where a spring provides an opportunity to refill your bottle. (*NW–SE 0h 55m, S–NW 0h 45m.*)

You shortly reach more open country in the foothills of the White Tatras, with a clear view of the great whaleback of **Havran** (Raven, 2152m) ahead, flanked by Nový Vrch (1999m) on its left and **Ždiarska Vidla** (2146m) on its right. In July and August these meadows are ablaze with plants typical of alpine limestone terrain, such as edelweiss and gentian. You climb steadily, maybe escorted by tortoise-shell butterflies and flying beetles, on a narrow and stony path, sometimes crossing the remains of last winter's avalanches. Ahead, you see for the first time your target – Kopské Sedlo – while to your right the brook Meďodolský Potok tinkles through open grassland below. The path is not too steep, and requires little effort to reach **Kopské Sedlo** (1749m). (*NW–SE 1h 30m, SE–NW 1h 10m.*)

GREEN ROUTES

Note Green 5706 and 5707 in the Spišská Magura, and 5732 in the Low Tatras, shown on some High Tatras maps, are outside the scope of this book.

• 5801 POD HLINSKOU DOLINOU TO SEDLO ZÁVORY (1410m–1879m)

Grade Strenuous	**Distance** 2km	**Average Gradient** 24%
S–N Height Gain 469m	**Time** 1h 30m	
N–S Height Loss 584m	**Time** 1h 15m	
Winter/Spring Closed		

A short route linking the valleys of Kôprova Dolina and Ticha Dolina.

From the junction with Blue 2902A (Rázcestie pod Hlinskou Dolinou, 1410m), the path climbs through forest to the junction with Red 0932 (Rázcestie pod Temnosmrečinskou Dolinou). Here you turn left to climb steeply, at first through forest, but quickly emerging into the dwarf pine, up the valley of Kobylia Dolina. Near the top, now among rocks, you pass a tarn on your right (Kobylie Pleso). The path continues steadily up to Sedlo Závory (1879m), a minor saddle, where it joins Red 0931.

· 5802 TICHÁ TO POD GRÚNIKOM (980m–1115m)

Grade Easy   **Distance** 4km   **Average Gradient** 4%
W–E Height Gain 135m   **Time** 0h 45m
E–W Height Loss 135m   **Time** 0h 45m
Winter/Spring Open

*This is actually a level, asphalt road beside the south bank of Kôprovský Potok,
linking Yellow 8851 at Tichá with Blue 2902A at Rázcestie pod Grúnikom. It is
also an official cycle route.*

· 5803A ŠTRBSKÉ PLESO TO TRI STUDNIČKY (1350m–1140m)

Grade Easy   **Distance** 9km   **Average Gradient** 3%
SE–NW Height Loss 210m   **Time** 2h 15m
NW–SE Height Gain 210m   **Time** 2h 30m
Winter/Spring Open

*A gentle route through the former forest and meadows, running parallel to (and
sometimes beside) the Cesta Slobody road. It used to be heavily forested, but was
badly affected by the Tatranská Bora (see page 72).*

See gazetteer (page 188) for a route description from station to tarn in **Štrbské
Pleso** (1350m). From the Solisko sanatorium at the southwest corner of the tarn,
turn left a little to enter the forest. The route then runs mostly slightly downhill
or level, with an occasional short climb, all the way to Tri Studničky. You cross
several streams, and about halfway along is the junction with Blue 2903. Later
on you pass a monument to Kapitána Rašu – see gazetteer under **Tri Studničky**
regarding this and the chalet that once stood here.

· 5803B TRI STUDNIČKY TO POD KRIVÁŇOM (1140m–2190m)

Grade Strenuous   **Distance** 4.5km   **Average Gradient** 30%
SW–NE Height Gain 1060m   **Time** 2h 00m
NE–SW Height Loss 1060m   **Time** 1h 30m
Winter/Spring Closed

An alternative route to or from Krivaň, which is steeper than Blue 2903.

Štrbské Pleso – the tarn, looking towards Kriváň and Hrubý Vrch (Green 5803A) (photo: R Turnbull)

From **Tri Studničky** (1140m) at the junction with Blue 2902, take the right-hand path, which at first gently climbs a valley. It then gets steeper through forest to a series of zigzags leading to the grassy minor summit of **Grúnik** (1576m) on the southwest shoulder of Kriváň. The route then climbs the shoulder, called Priehyba, at first through dwarf pine then on bare rock, and crosses a gully (Krivánsky Žľab) to meet Blue 2903 below **Kriváň** at Rázcestie pod Kriváňom (2190m).

5805 NAD TRIGANOM TO POPRADSKÉ PLESO (1440m–1499m)

Grade Easy	**Distance** 2.5km	**Average** Gradient 4%
S–N Height Loss 40m/**Gain** 54m		**Time** 0h 45m
N–S Height Loss 54m/**Gain** 40m		**Time** 0h 45m
Winter/Spring Open		

This route comes into its own in winter, when the parallel Red 0930E is closed. However, in spring it tends to get very wet, so at that time people wishing to reach Popradské Pleso tarn use Blue 2902 from Popradské Pleso station.

From Rázcestie nad Triganom (1499m), the junction with Red 0930E (1480m), the path descends steeply to Hincov Potok (1440m), crosses it, then rises steeply again to the junction with the asphalt service road (Blue 2902). Cross this and descend to **Popradské Pleso** tarn (1494m). Here you can either turn left along the shore to Chata pri Popradské Pleso (refreshments), or right for Yellow 8854 to **Symbolický Cintorín**.

• 5806A NIŽNÉ HÁGY TO TATRANSKÁ POLIANKA (910m–1010m)

Grade Easy   **Distance** 5km   **Average Gradient** 2%
SW–NE Height Gain 100m   **Time** 1h 15m
NE–SW Height Loss 100m   **Time** 1h 00m
Winter/Spring Open

This gentle path used to be heavily forested but was badly affected by the Tatranská Bora (see page 72). It is also an official cycle route.

From the bus stop at **Nižné Hágy** (910m) walk north along the road for 100m, then turn right to follow the waymarks through the forest on a good path. After descending to cross a stream, you climb again to a junction of forest roads – ignore these and bear right on a level grass path. In 10 minutes you start climbing quite steeply to meet the Cesta Slobody road at Danielov Dom (1000m). Cross over then turn right on a pavement beside the road. The new road now crosses a stream on a viaduct, but you follow the old road into **Tatranská Polianka** (1010m, refreshments).

• 5806B TATRANSKÁ POLIANKA TO POĽSKÝ HREBEŇ (1010m–2200m)

Grade Moderate to strenuous   **Distance** 8.5km   **Average Gradient** 14%
SE–NW Height Gain 1190m   **Time** 4h 00m
NW–SE Height Loss 1190m   **Time** 3h 30m
Winter/Spring Open only as far as Velické Pleso

The lower part of this route was deforested by the Tatranská Bora (see page 72), but higher up it is in forest and dwarf pine as far as Sliezsky Dom, then above the tree-line to the saddle of Poľský Hrebeň, passing two tarns. It becomes very steep as you approach the saddle, with a fixed chain section on bare rock – best avoided in wet or icy conditions, or when under snow. The route runs parallel to and sometimes crosses the service road for Sliezsky Dom, which is also an official cycle route.

From **Tatranská Polianka** station (1010m) cross the main road (Cesta Slobody) and go right a short distance to the parade of shops. Turn left here up a side road, which is the service road to Sliezsky Dom. It first passes to your left the Dr Guhra sanatorium for respiratory ailments. Then, some way further up, the waymarked route starts to make a number of short cuts on steep paths, avoiding the road's hairpin bends. A long, road-avoiding stretch brings you to the junction with Yellow 8856, below Veľký Krížny Kopec (Big Cross Hill). (*SE–NW 1h 00m, NW–SE 0h 50m.*)

The yellow route continues along the road, but for Green 5806 keep ahead on the footpath, beside Velický Potok, climbing steeply through forest until the dwarf pine is reached, then the junction with Yellow 8858. A little way beyond this is Sliezsky Dom (1678m, refreshments) beside **Velické Pleso** tarn, and the junction with Red 0930C/D. (*SE–NW 1h 00m, NW–SE 0h 50m.*)

Continue beside the tarn, at the north end of which is a cascade. You climb beside it on a zigzag path, known locally as Večný Dážď (Eternal Rain) from the spray. With Velické Potok to your left, the path now climbs steeply in two great stages up Kvetnica (Flower Valley – and it is a good place for flowers), to reach Dlhé Pleso (Long Tarn, 1929m – one of two with this name in the High Tatras). Continuing up to **Poľský Hrebeň** (2200m), you must negotiate a 50m fixed chain. (*SE–NW 1h 45m, NW–SE 1h 30m.*)

The route actually continues a little way beyond the saddle, dropping steadily in a short distance to the junction with Blue 2907 (Rázcestie pod Poľským Hrebeňom, 2100m). (*SE–NW 0h 15m, NW–SE 0h 15m.*)

• 5807 STARÝ SMOKOVEC TO VODOPÁDY STUDENÉHO POTOKA (1010m–1285m)

Grade Easy	**Distance** 3.5km	**Average Gradient** 9%
S–N Height Gain 285m/**Loss** 30m		**Time** 1h 00m
N–S Height Gain 30m/**Loss** 285m		**Time** 0h 45m
Winter/Spring Open		

The whole of this route runs as a broad, well-defined path through the forest zone, though most of the lower part was deforested by the Taranská Bora (see page 72). It is not much used in the uphill direction, as the funicular can be used to save climbing. It is often used downhill when the trains are crowded.

The route starts to the right of the funicular station in **Starý Smokovec** (1010m) then runs between the track and the service road all the way to **Hrebienok** (1285m, refreshments). From time to time it joins the road. (*S–N 0h 45m, N–S 0h 30m.*)

From Hrebienok, the path descends in 10 minutes to **Bilíkova Chata** (1255m, refreshments), then continues level for a while and climbs in 5 minutes to meet Blue 2907, which joins from the right. For the best view of the cascades (**Vodopády Studeného Potoka**), walk a short distance down Blue 2907 to the bridge (1265m). (*S–N 0h 15m, N–S 0h 15m.*)

• 5808 TATRANSKÁ LOMNICA TO SKALNATÉ PLESO (860m–1761m)

Grade Moderate	**Distance** 6km	**Average Gradient** 15%
SE–NW Height Gain 901m	**Time** 2h 00m	
NW–SE Height Loss 901m	**Time** 1h 30m	
Winter/Spring Open		

The lower part of this route is in the forest zone, though much of it was deforested by the Tatranská Bora (see page 72). It gets steeper as you climb into the sembra pine.

On some older maps the route is shown in two separate sections – from Tatranská Lomnica to Štart and from Skalnaté Pleso to Lomnické Sedlo, with the section from Štart to Skalnaté Pleso missing. The upper section to Lomnické Sedlo has since been closed to walkers, unless accompanied by a mountain guide (see With a Guide, page 88), while the 'missing' section has been reinstated.

The route starts beside Grandhotel Praha on the north side of **Tatranská Lomnica** (860m) and winds its way up to Štart (1140m), closely following the line of the former cable-car to Skalnaté Pleso, which was decommissioned in 1996. Above Štart, however, you cross and recross the gondola-lift all the way to **Skalnaté Pleso** (1761m, refreshments).

• 5809 POĽANA POD MALOU SVIŠŤOVKOU TO KOVALČIKOVÁ POĽANA(1310m–1240m)

Grade Easy	**Distance** 1km	**Average Gradient** 7%
S–N Height Loss 70m	**Time** 0h 05m	
N–S Height Gain 70m	**Time** 0h 10m	
Winter/Spring Open		

A short route through the forest west of Šalviový Prameň, whose start and finish points may not be named on your map. It links Blue 2908 at Poľana pod Malou Svišťovkou (1310m) to Yellow 8861 at Kovalčiková Poľana (1240m).

• 5810 TATRANSKÁ KOTLINA TO VEĽKÉ BIELE PLESO (765m–1600m)

Grade Moderate	**Distance** 10km	**Average Gradient** 9%
E–W Height Gain 835m	**Time** 3h 30m	
W–E Height Loss 835m	**Time** 3h 00m	
Winter/Spring Open to Chata Plesnivec only		

Though mainly in forest, this route is of particular interest as one of the few that touch the White Tatras, on their southern slopes, with occasional good views. It also passes Chata Plesnivec, the only chalet in the White Tatras. It is less visited than those further west, and passes through bear territory! The first 2km are shared with Blue 2909, with seats at frequent intervals.

From the bus stop at the southeast end of **Tatranská Kotlina** (765m), you follow a hard-surfaced road, passing a mountain rescue centre (with picnic table) soon after the start. Near a custard-and-rust-coloured hacienda-style building, turn left along a path through trees to reach a forest road, with a black-painted sign-holder, and bear left along it. There has been some tree felling in this area, and some of the waymarks may have disappeared – if in doubt, use your compass to follow bearing 225 as closely as possible. The forest road eventually reaches the point where the blue and green routes separate, called Rázcestie Čierna Voda (Black Water Junction). (*E–W 0h 30m, W–E 0h 30m.*)

Turn right along a narrow earth path, which climbs steadily through the forest, now with green waymarks only. Eventually it levels out and follows the contours, and comes to a series of zigzags at the top of which is **Chata Plesnivec** (1340m, Edelweiss Chalet, refreshments), the junction with Yellow 8864, and a good view down Dolina Siedmich Prameňov (Seven Springs Valley). (*E–W 1h 15m, W–E 1h 00m.*)

From Plesnivec the route continues to the left and soon climbs steeply up a shoulder, then crosses the valley. You come to a ledge, where the path undulates for a while, with a fine view at one point down the valley and across the Sub-Tatras Plain. It then descends quite steeply for 100m or so, before climbing again to reach a broad, semi-open ledge with grass and dwarf pine. You are now at the east end of the White Tatras, with a good view to the southeast of the forested, rounded minor summit of Stežky (1529m). (*E–W 0h 40m, W–E 0h 30m.*)

The route follows the ledge for several hundred metres, then re-enters the forest, where an unmarked track joins from the left. Leaving the forest again, and still climbing, you pass through a zone of dwarf pine and rowan, to the foot of **Predné Meďodoly** (Front Coppermines). There is a picnic table at the top of the shoulder. After descending the far side of the moraine, the path crosses a wooden bridge over Napájadlový Potok (Trough Brook), which is often dry in summer and autumn, then gently ascends to **Veľké Biele Pleso** (1600m). (*E–W 1h 05m, W–E 1h 00m.*)

• 5811 ŽDIAR AND MONKOVÁ DOLINA (896m–1140m)

Grade Easy	**Distance** 3.5km	**Average Gradient** 7%
E–W Height Gain 244m	**Time** 1h 00m	
W–E Height Loss 244m	**Time** 0h 45m	
Winter/Spring Open		

This low-level route, linking two points along the road to Lysá Poľana, provides access to the only one that crosses the White Tatras. It follows the Biela river, in a valley that is called either Monková Dolina or Dolina Bielej. Buses from Tatranská Lomnica to Lysá Poľana stop at either end of the route.

The route starts from the south side of the main road in **Ždiar** (896m, refreshments), by a dilapidated building that used to be a trade union centre. It follows a tarmac lane for 1km beside the Biela river, passing some very attractive farm buildings, then goes left along a footpath into the forest. Soon you see the large Hotel Magura to your right, across a meadow. A little further on you reach a wooden hut, where fees used to be collected for walkers crossing the White Tatras on Green 5900, which leads off to the left from here (there is no longer a charge).

Keep ahead, climbing steadily and veering round to the right, with the wooded hill called Plošové Turne above. Eventually you reach Ždiar's ski terrain (Strednica). A final steep climb up a grassy slope takes you past the pylons of a ski-tow back to the main road.

(This route continues on the far side of the road into the foothills of the Spišská Magura range, linking with routes that are outside the scope of this book.)

• 5812A ZAMKOVSKÉHO CHATA TO SEDIELKO (1475m–2372m)

Grade Strenuous	**Distance** 5.5km	**Average Gradient** 17%
SE–NW Height Gain 897m	**Time** 3h 30m	
NW–SE Height Loss 897m	**Time** 3h 00m	
Winter/Spring Open as far as Téryho Chata		

A very well-used route through one of the prettiest valleys in the Tatras, also linking two popular chalets. Together with Green 5812B, it is one of just three routes that cross the main High Tatras ridge. Sedielko, a pass on the main ridge of the High Tatras, is dangerous if there is much snow.

Zamkovského Chata (Green 5812A)

From **Zamkovského Chata** (1475m, refreshments) you climb Malá Studená Dolina, at first in the forest, but soon coming to the dwarf pine and a rock face called Vielký Hank (Great Slope), which you climb on steep zigzags, passing a yellow wall which is very popular with climbers. The path then turns right to Malý Hank (Little Slope), with more zigzags, to reach **Téryho Chata** (2013m, refreshments), in its idyllic location beside Päť Spišských Plies (Five Spiš Tarns). The route continues, now together with Yellow 8860 for a while, on stony ground to cross a stream and go round the rock wall. At the parting with the yellow route, take the right-hand path up a small grassy kettle (the geological type), passing **Modré Pleso** (Blue Tarn), the highest tarn in all of the Tatras at 2192m, then steeply on rock to the saddle of **Sedielko** (2372m) – see Green 5812B.

• 5812B JAVORINA TO SEDIELKO (1018m–2372m)

Grade Moderate to Žabie Javorové Pleso, strenuous to Sedielko
Average Gradient 9% to Žabie Javorové Pleso, 25% to Sedielko
Distance 12km
N–S Height Gain 1354m   **Time** 5h 00m
S–N Height Loss 1354m   **Time** 4h 15m
Winter/Spring Open only to Rázcestie pod Muráňom

This route provides easy walking, for the most part, up Javorová Dolina (Maple Valley) and beside the Javorinka river, with good views of the high peaks above, although it gets much steeper towards the top. The first 2km are shared with Blue 2911B.

The route starts from **Javorina** (1018m, refreshments, shown as Tatranská Javorina on some maps) up **Javorová Dolina**. See Blue 2911B for a description as far as Rázcestie pod Muráňom, where that route leads off to the left. Keep ahead along the forest road for another kilometre or so, then the valley starts to climb quite steeply, and the road becomes a track, passing through forest and meadows. In 3km, still climbing steeply, you reach the dwarf pine and have a great view of the long ridge leading up to Javorový Štít. The path crosses the infant Javorinka river, now in the upper part of the valley, which is called Zadná Dolina, and climbs to a grassy terrace. At the head of the valley is Žabie Javorové Pleso (Frog Maple Tarn, 1886m), after which the path zigzags steeply to **Sedielko** (2372m) – see Green 5812A.

5900 WHITE TATRAS TRAVERSE (935m–1934m)

Grade Strenuous	**Distance** 4km	**Average Gradient** 24%
N–S Height Gain 900m/**Loss** 81m		**Time** 3h 00m
One-way traffic (N–S only)		**Winter/Spring** Closed

After a 15-year closure for ecological reasons, this route was reopened in 1993 – see the paragraph on the White Tatras, page 20. It is very steep in places, with some scrambling, but not difficult, although in wet weather it can be quite slippery on the limestone. For this reason it is recommended that you walk from north to south, thereby tackling the steepest parts uphill, which is safer when wet.

Note that the waymarks differ slightly, in that the white–green–white bands are diagonal. No official number has been allocated, so to fit in with our system we call it 5900.

From the junction with Green 5811, beside Beliansky Potok (935m), you are accompanied by Rigľový or Rigeľský Potok, the stream that occupies the valley called Monková Dolina (Rigľanská Dolina on some maps), as you climb steeply to the top of the pine forest. (*N–S 2h 00m.*)

Now in dwarf pine, stop and turn round occasionally for magnificent views down the valley and across to the lower parallel range called Spišská Magura. In clear weather you should also be able to see the ranges beyond, in Poland, which are called Zamagurze Spiskie and Pieniny Spiskie. Several seats and picnic tables are strategically located for a much-needed breather. Eventually you reach **Široké Sedlo** (Dry Saddle, 1826m), a splendid viewpoint, both north to the Spišska Magura and south into the High Tatras, with Jahňací Štít prominent. (*N–S 0h 30m.*)

Renáta admiring the view of the Spišská Magura from Rigľanská Dolina in the White Tatras (Green 5900)

A sign makes clear that you cannot continue along the path to the right, so continue to the left, a little higher, to reach another saddle, Vyšné Kopské Sedlo (1934m), the highest point of this route. It lies below Hlúpy (Stupid), the third highest peak of the White Tatras at 2061m. From here you can see the eastern part of the White Tatras. Heading south, you descend to **Kopské Sedlo** (1750m), where you join Blue 2911. *(N–S 0h 30m.)*

YELLOW ROUTES

Note Yellow 8712 in the Spišská Magura, shown on some High Tatras maps, is outside the scope of this book.

• 8851 PODBANSKÉ TO SUCHÉ SEDLO (940m–1985m)

> **Grade** Easy to Rázcestie pTD, moderate to Suché Sedlo
> **Distance** 16km
> **Average Gradient** 2% to Rázcestie pTD, 14% to Suché Sedlo
> **SW–NE Height Gain** 40m   **Time** 5h 15m
> **NE–SW Height Loss** 40m   **Time** 4h 30m
> **Winter/Spring** Open only as far as Tichá

This is one of the most remote routes in the High Tatras. It is mostly on an asphalt road, and is an official cycle route, but you are rewarded with beautiful views of

133

mountains in both the High and Western Tatras. Although, according to the map, the valley of Tichá Dolina lies in the Western Tatras (Západné Tatry), it is locally considered to belong to the High Tatras. This route does in fact lead almost to the high saddle, Ľaliové Sedlo, which is generally accepted (in Slovakia at least) as the point where High meets Western Tatras.

From the car park at **Podbanské** (940m) cross the bridge over the Belá river, then turn left along an asphalt road leading to Horáreň (mountain lodge) Tichá, and the junction with Blue 5802. On the opposite side of the river is Grand Hotel Permon, formerly a trade union holiday centre. At Tichá (980m) you are almost surrounded by mountains, with Kriváň dominant to the east. To the west are the first peaks of the Western Tatras. (*SW–NE 0h 30m, NE–SW 0h 30m.*)

The road is virtually flat, and after Tichá, where it bears left into Tichá Dolina, you hardly notice the gentle ascent. A beautiful panorama unfolds, with the rounded peaks of the **Červené Vrchy** (Red Hills) ahead – also in the Western Tatras. At Rázcestie pod Tomanovou Dolinou (1150m) you join Red 0931, and the two routes coincide for the next 2km. (*SW–NE 2h 30m, NW–SE 2h 30m.*)

At the next junction, Rázcestie pod Kasprovým Vrchom, the asphalt finishes and the routes part. (*SW–NE 0h 30m, NE–SW 0h 30m.*)

Yellow 8851 goes left across a meadow, then into the forest, and starts to climb steeply, including a long zigzag section towards the summit of Beskyd (2012m). Just short of it, the path bears left and heads for Suché Sedlo (Dry Saddle, 1985m). Regrettably it is dry in every sense, as the facilities within a stone's throw at the top of the cable-car at Kasprowy Wierch, just in Poland, are currently out of bounds to those on the Slovak side (but see Cross-border Walking, page 60). (*SW–NE 1h 45m, NE–SW 1h 00m.*)

• 8853A ŠTRBSKÉ PLESO TO SKOK AND BYSTRÁ LÁVKA (1350m–2300m)

Grade Moderate to Vodopád Skok, strenuous to Bystrá Lávka and Vyšné Wahlenbergovo Pleso (chains) **Distance** 7km
Average Gradient 12% to Vodopád Skok, 31% to Bystrá Lávka, 17% to Vyšné Wahlenbergovo Pleso
SE–NW Height Gain 950m/**Loss** 155m
NW–SE Height Gain 155m/**Loss** 950m
Time 3h 30m to Bystrá Lávka, 4h 00m to Vyšné Wahlenbergovo Pleso
Winter/Spring Open only as far as Vodopád Skok

Vodopád Skok, one of the most impressive cascades in the High Tatras, is one of the features of this route, which continues on to Bystrá Lávka, one of its highest

Vodopád Skok (Yellow 8853A) (photo: R Turnbull)

saddles. In winter and spring, the route is open from Štrbské Pleso as far as Skok, but the upper part is closed. There are two stretches of chains beyond Skok, and if there is much snow the upper part can be dangerous. If you start up the chained section to Bystrá Lávka you must continue on to Yellow 8853B, as you are not allowed to descend it. If you do not wish to tackle the chains, you must return the way you came along Yellow 8853A.

135

See gazetteer (page 188) for route instructions from station to tarn in **Štrbské Pleso** (1350m). Turn right along the east side of the tarn to the halfway point, then turn off to pass a *rašelinisko* (peat bog nature reserve) and turn left along a road, passing Hotel FIS. This shortly finishes, and you continue ahead on a path that climbs through forest then dwarf pine, with some zigzags, and views down into **Mlynická Dolina**. After the dwarf pine you soon come to the impressive waterfall Vodopád **Skok** (1700m). (*SE–NW 1h 15m, NW–SE 1h 00m.*)

Above Skok you encounter the first chains, and a small tarn called Pleso nad Skokom. Higher up you pass through a cluster of small tarns, then another series of steep zigzags leads to a traverse across a gully, with more chains, and on up to **Bystrá Lávka** (Sharp Notch, 2300m). There are many loose rocks here, so you must walk with great care. From the saddle there are excellent views of the surrounding peaks, valleys and tarns. (*SE–NW 2h 15m.*)

The route continues beyond Bystrá Lávka down to meet Yellow 8853B at Vyšné Wahlenbergovo Pleso.

• 8853B FURKOTSKÁ DOLINA TO VYŠNÉ WAHLENBERGOVO PLESO (1475m–2145m)

Grade Strenuous	**Distance** 3km	**Average Gradient** 23%
SE–NW Height Gain 670m	**Time** 2h 40m	
NW–SE Height Loss 670m	**Time** 1h 55m	
Winter/Spring Closed		

This route is exceptionally steep in places, but leads up the pretty valley of Furkotská Dolina, with its tarns named after the Swedish botanist, Göran Wahlenberg. The route up to Bystrá Lávka is not accessible from this direction.

From the junction with Red 0930F at the foot of Furkotská Dolina (1475m), follow the yellow waymarks, at first on an earthy, gently graded path through the forest, but soon becoming ever steeper and rockier as it reaches the dwarf pine. Here it comes close to Furkotský Potok, and this is followed to the junction with Blue 2836B – this is the point referred to as Furkotská Dolina on signposts, at 1710m. Looking back you have a fine vista over the Sub-Tatras Basin, with the villages of Tatranská Štrba and Štrba in clear view. (*SE–NW 0h 45m, NW–SE 0h 35m.*)

The path continues steeply in dwarf pine, but now leaving Furkotský Potok far below, and eventually climbs sharply the moraine of **Nižné Wahlenbergovo Pleso** (2053m), which you pass on its right. (*SE–NW 1h 15m, NW–SE 0h 50m.*)

A second steep moraine leads in 30 minutes to **Vyšné Wahlenbergovo Pleso** (2145m).

8854 SYMBOLICKÝ CINTORÍN (THE SYMBOLIC CEMETERY) (1494m–1525m)

Grade Moderate	**Distance** 1.5km	**Average Gradient** 5%
S–N Height Gain 25m/**Loss** 31m		**Time** 0h 30m
N–S Height Gain 31m/**Loss** 25m		**Time** 0h 30m
Winter/Spring Normally open 16 June to 31 December		

A fascinating loop providing an alternative route to Popradské Pleso. Despite the low average gradient, it is very steep in places, and there are even chains at one point.

From the junction with Blue 2902B at 1500m, the path descends a little to cross the infant river Poprad, then soon climbs quite steeply. There is a very steep section with chains just before you reach **Symbolický Cintorín** (Symbolic Cemetery), and the path through the cemetery itself is quite steep in places, reaching 1525m. At the chapel you are asked to contribute a small amount towards upkeep of the cemetery. The path descends back over the river to Popradské Pleso (1494m) to follow its western shore for 500m to Chata pri Popradskom Plese (refreshments).

In the Symbolic Cemetery (Yellow 8854) (photo: R Turnbull)

Chata pri Popradskom Plese (Yellow 8854 and Red 0930E)

- ## 8855 NIŽNÉ HÁGY TO BATIZOVSKÉ PLESO (910m–1879m)

Grade Moderate	**Distance** 7km	**Average Gradient** 14%
S–N Height Gain 969m	**Time** 3h 15m	
N–S Height Loss 969m	**Time** 2h 45m	
Winter/Spring Open		

A steep path providing a link from the train station at Vyšné Hágy to the Tatranská Magistrála. It actually starts lower down at Nižné Hágy, and used to be heavily forested until the Tatranská Bora in 2004 (see page 72).

From the forest lodge at **Nižné Hágy** (910m), opposite Green 5806A, you go left along an asphalt road past some apartment houses, then ascend past more apartments, still on the road, until you reach Cesta Slobody (Freedom Highway) at **Vyšné Hágy** station (1085m). Follow the old road to the left for a short distance, then turn right to cross the railway line near a forest lodge. You climb through the forest, with the stream called Malý Šum to your right, to reach a meadow with a spring and picnic tables. The path now steepens, and eventually you cross a stream to reach the dwarf pine. Then keep on up to the Tatranská Magistrála (Red 0930D), which you can follow for some 500m to **Batizovské Pleso** (1879m).

- ## 8856 PRI VELICKOM MOSTE TO POD SUCHÝM VRCHOM (1250m–1720m)

Grade Moderate	**Distance** 4km	**Average Gradient** 12%
SE–NW Height Gain 470m	**Time** 1h 15m	
NW–SE Height Loss 470m	**Time** 1h 00m	
Winter/Spring Open		

An alternative route to the Tatranská Magistrála from Tatranská Polianka. It provides a short cut avoiding Sliezsky Dom, whose service road (also an official cycle route) is followed for much of this route.

The route starts from Green 5806 at a roofed picnic table at 1250m, where it crosses the service road to Sliezsky Dom beside Velicky Potok, and below Veľký Krížny Kopec (Big Cross Hill). This point is known as Rázcestie pri Velickom Moste (Junction at the Bridge over Velicky Brook). It uses the service road for almost 2km, until a very sharp right-hand hairpin bend is reached in 30 minutes. Leaving the road on a rocky path to the left, it soon leaves the forest zone and enters the dwarf pine, with good views down to the plain. Climbing steadily, you reach the junction with Red 0930D at Rázcestie pod Suchým Vrchom (Junction below Dry Hill) at 1720m.

• 8857 POĽSKÝ HREBEŇ TO VÝCHODNÁ VYSOKÁ (2200m–2428m)

Grade Moderate	**Distance** 1km	**Average Gradient** 23%
W–E Height Gain 220m	**Time** 0h 45m	
E–W Height Loss 228m	**Time** 0h 30m	
Winter/Spring Closed		

A very steep, but short and not difficult route, leading to a popular viewpoint at the heart of the High Tatras.

The route starts from Green 5806B at the saddle **Poľský Hrebeň** (2200m). There is a series of short and steep zigzags, then you traverse a terrace to reach the summit of **Východná Vysoká** (2428m).

• 8858 STARÝ SMOKOVEC TO NA VELICKEJ POĽANE (1010m–1560m)

Grade Moderate	**Distance** 4.5km	**Average Gradient** 10%
SE–NW Height Gain 450m	**Time** 2h 15m	
NW–SE Height Loss 450m	**Time** 1h 45m	
Add 15 minutes to these times for Sliezsky Dom		
Winter/Spring Open		

A useful route linking Starý Smokovec with Sliezsky Dom on Velické Pleso. It used to be heavily forested but was badly affected by the Tatranská Bora (see page 72).

The route starts 200m east of the funicular station along the back road in **Starý Smokovec** (1010m) close to Hotel Bystrina. It climbs steadily through the forest, crossing the ski-lift track and several streams, to meet Blue 2905 coming from Tatranské Zruby at Rázcestie pod Sennou Kopou (Junction below Senna Stack, 1325m). It then steepens into the dwarf pine, and joins Green 5806B at Rázcestie nad Velickej Polane (Junction below Velické Meadow, 1560m), 500m south of **Velické Pleso** and Sliezsky Dom (refreshments).

• 8859 TATRANSKÁ LESNÁ TO PRI VODOPÁDOCH STUDENÉHO POTOKA (905m–1255m)

Grade Easy	**Distance** 3.5km	**Average Gradient** 10%
SE–NW Height Gain 350m	**Time** 1h 30m	
NW–SE Height Loss 350m	**Time** 1h 15m	

Add 15 minutes to these times for Bilíkova Chata or Hrebienok

Winter/Spring Open

A romantic route through the forest between the railway line and the beautiful cascades called Vodopády Studeného Potoka. It provides a useful link to Hrebienok and Bilíkova Chata.

The path starts opposite the station at **Tatranská Lesná** (905m), climbing quite steeply at first, while the brook called Studený Potok twists and tinkles below to your right. The path levels out where it runs beside the brook, then climbs steeply again, finally passing the cascades of **Vodopády Studeného Potoka** to join Green 5807 at a point called, naturally, Rázcestie pri Vodopádoch Studeného Potoka (Junction at Cold Brook Cascades, 1255m). Refreshments are quite near at hand at **Bilíkova Chata,** 15 minutes' level walk to your left along Green 5807.

• 8860 TÉRYHO CHATA TO PRIEČNE SEDLO AND ZBOJNÍCKA CHATA (1960m–2352m)

Grade Strenuous	**Distance** 5km
Average Gradient 23% to Priečne Sedlo, 11% to Zbojnícka Chata	
NE–SW Height Gain 339m/**Loss** 392m	**Time** 3h 00m
Winter/Spring Closed	

Note: This route can only be followed in one direction (NE–SW)

A popular but demanding route, always above the tree-line, crossing the saddle of Priečne Sedlo. There are excellent views all the time, especially from the saddle. The approach is very steep, with a long stretch of fixed chains in three separate sections. At weekends in high season there are often queues for these. The one-way system is partly to avoid congestion on the chains, and so that you ascend them, rather than descend, which would be very difficult.

From **Téryho Chata** (2013m, refreshments), the route starts by sharing with Green 5812A for 1.5km. It then turns left to climb steeply to **Priečne Sedlo** (2352m), tackling the chains as you approach the top. (*NE–SW 1h 30m.*)

Ascending the chained approach to Priečne Sedlo (Yellow 8860)

Descending from the saddle, you pass several tarns, including one of the largest in this group, Sivé Pleso (Grey Tarn). After crossing Veľký Studený Potok (Great Cold Brook) you climb again briefly to join Blue 2907A at **Zbojnícka Chata** (1960m, refreshments). (*NE–SW 1h 30m.*)

• 8861 BIELA VODA TO JAHŇACÍ ŠTÍT (925m–2229m)

Grade Easy (to Zelené Pleso), strenuous to Jahňací Štít
Distance 9.5km   **Average Gradient** 9% to Zelené Pleso, 27% to Jahňací Štít
SE–NW Height Gain 1304m   **Time** 5h 00m
NW–SE Height Loss 1304m   **Time** 4h 15m
Winter/Spring Open only as far as Zelené Pleso

A route of two moods – one gentle and full of anticipation, mostly in the forest, to the beautiful emerald tarn of Zelené Pleso, one stern as you leave the tarn, mostly on open rock, to face the stiff climb to Jahňací Štít. The upper section includes some short fixed chains in an exposed situation.

As Zelené Pleso is one of the loveliest spots in the High Tatras, with a welcoming chalet, the lower part of this route is well used – even in winter – both by cross-country skiers and local people going to skate on the tarn. It is also an official cycle route.

From the bus stop and car park at **Biela Voda** (925m, no refreshments) follow the dirt road up through the forest to the junction with Blue 2911A, which it joins for a while. (*SE–NW 0h 30m, NW–SE 0h 25m.*)

The road continues, still in the forest, crossing the Biela Voda Kežmarská river, to Šalviový Prameň (1200m), where the two routes part company. (*SE–NW 0h 30m, NW–SE 0h 25m.*)

Yellow 8861 stays on the dirt road, which shortly turns left to recross the river. Now with the river on your right, in 10 minutes you reach the junction with Green 5809 (Kovalčiková Poľana, 1240m) and continue climbing steadily through the forest, eventually reaching the dwarf pine, having turned left out of the main valley into Dolina Zeleného Plesa. The river is replaced on your right by the brook, Zelený Potok, which naturally leads you unerringly to **Zelené Pleso** and its chalet (1545m, refreshments). (*SE–NW 2h 30m, NW–SE 2h 10m.*)

Leaving the chalet, you start to climb steeply behind it on a narrow path, at first continuing among dwarf pine. You reach Červená Dolina (Red Valley), which has several small tarns, including Červené Pleso (Red Tarn), the largest. After skirting its southern shore you continue climbing with Jastrabia Veža (Hawk Tower) to your left. At the valley head you use several short lengths of fixed chain

Looking towards Kolový Štít on the way down from Jahňací Štít (Yellow 8861) (photo: R Turnbull)

to surmount the wall. You follow a ridge to the saddle Kolové Sedlo (2118m), then cross a sequence of ribs and gullies to the summit of **Jahňací Štít** (2229m). (*SE–NW 1h 30m, NW–SE 1h 15m.*)

• 8862 TATRANSKÁ KOTLINA TO BELIANSKA JASKYŇA (765m–855m)

Grade Easy	**Distance** 1.5km	**Average Gradient** 6%
E–W Height Gain 90m	**Time** 0h 20m	
W–E Height Loss 90m	**Time** 0h 15m	
Winter/Spring Open		

*A short but steep access route to the fascinating cave of **Belianska Jaskyňa** (855m). It starts from the back of the car park at the north end of **Tatranská Kotlina** (765m, refreshments).*

• 8863 TATRANSKÁ LOMNICA TO TATRANSKÁ MATLIARE (900m–910m)

Grade Easy	**Distance** 1km	**Average Gradient** 1%
SW–NE Height Gain 10m	**Time** 0h 20m	
NE–SW Height Loss 10m	**Time** 0h 20m	
Winter/Spring Open		

*A short route providing a useful link between **Tatranská Lomnica** (by Grandhotel Praha, 900m) and Blue 2911A just outside **Tatranské Matliare** (910m) by the Metalurg/Hutník holiday centre. It used to be heavily forested but was badly affected by the Tatranská Bora (see page 72).*

• 8864 DOLINA SIEDMICH PRAMEŇ (900m–1240m)

Grade Moderate	**Distance** 3km	**Average Gradient** 11%
SE–NW Height Gain 340m	**Time** 1h 30m	
NW–SE Height Loss 340m	**Time** 1h 20m	
Winter/Spring Open		

This route was until recently the private service track for goods to Chata Plesnivec during its period as a national park research centre. It is accessible from either Kežmarské Žľaby or Tatranská Kotlina along Blue 2909, and provides an opportunity for a circular walk to Chata Plesnivec when combined with Green 5810.

From Blue 2909 at Veľke Stádla the route goes immediately into the narrow Dolina Siedmich Prameň (Seven Springs Valley), closely following Milý Potok (Pleasant Brook), and crossing it several times. The gradient is fairly moderate at first, but steepens when you reach the point where the valley divides and you take the right-hand branch, now following Hlboký Potok (Deep Brook). The path becomes very steep as you approach **Chata Plesnivec** (Edelweiss Chalet, 1240m, refreshments), passing close to the Seven Springs.

SELECTED TIMINGS

This section provides a quick-reference, rough guide to selected walking times. Taken from a variety of sources, they are approximate – always allow extra time for your journey, in case of unforeseen difficulties. **By adding together the various sections, these tables can be used to compute the total times for your own routes**.

Of course, people walk at differing speeds. On your first day of walking, you can compare your own times with those shown to get an idea of whether you are faster or slower. This is only for your information – there is no point in racing the signposts!

Note Velické Pleso is usually referred to as Sliezsky Dom, the mountain cha-let there.

Remember that routes beginning with 0 = Red, 2 = Blue, 5 = Green, 8 = Yellow

From/to	Time	Via routes
BATIZOVSKÉ PLESO to:		
Hrebienok	3h 00m	0930D/C
Popradské Pleso	2h 15m	0930D
Sliezsky Dom	1h 15m	0930D
Tatranská Polianka	2h 00m	0930D, 8856, 5806B
Vyšné Hágy	1h 30m	0930D, 8855
BIELA VODA to:		
Jahňací Štít	5h 15m	8861
Veľké Biele Pleso	2h 45m	8861, 2911A
Zelené Pleso	2h 45m	8861
BYSTRÁ LÁVKA to:		
Chata pod Soliskom	2h 15m	8853B, 2836B
Štrbské Pleso	3h 00m	8853B, 0930F
CHATA POD RYSMI to:		
Popradské Pleso	2h 00m	0933, 2902B
Rysy	1h 00m	0933
Sedlo Váha	0h 15m	0933
Štrbské Pleso	3h 00m	0933, 2902B, 0930E

CHATA POD SOLISKOM to:

Bystrá Lávka	2h 45m	2836B, 8853B
Nižné Wahlenbergovo Pleso	1h 30m	2836B, 8853B
Predné Solisko	0h 45m	0935
Štrbské Pleso	1h 15m	2836B

FURKOTSKÁ DOLINA to:

Bystrá Lávka	2h 30m	8853B
Chata pod Soliskom	0h 30m	2836B
Nižné Wahlenbergovo Pleso	1h 15m	8853B
Štrbské Pleso	1h 15m	8853B, 0930F

HREBIENOK to:

Bilíkova Chata	0h 05m	5807
Skalnaté Pleso	2h 00m	0930B
Slavkovský Štít	4h 00m	0930C, 2906
Sliezsky Dom	2h 00m	0930C
Starolesnianska Poľana	0h 15m	0930B
Starolesnianska Poľana	0h 20m	5807
Starý Smokovec	0h 45m	5807
Tatranská Lesná	1h 30m	5807, 8859
Tatranská Lomnica	1h 45m	5807, 2907A
Zamkovského Chata	0h 45m	0930B
Zbojnícka Chata	2h 45m	0930B, 2907A

JAMSKÉ PLESO to:

Kriváň	3h 30m	2903
Biely Váh	0h 45m	2903
Štrbské Pleso	1h 00m	0930F
Tri Studničky	1h 30m	0930F

JAVORINA to:

Hrebienok	8h 45m	5812B/A, 0930B
Kopské Sedlo	3h 00m	2911B
Sedielko	5h 15m	5812B
Starý Smokovec	9h 30m	5812B/A, 0930B, 5807
Tatranská Lomnica	6h 30m	2911B/A, 8863
Téryho Chata	6h 15m	5812B/A
Veľké Biele Pleso	3h 30m	2911B/A

KEŽMARSKÉ ŽĽABY to:

Plesnivec	2h 30m	2909, 5810 or 8864
Tatranská Kotlina	1h 30m	2909
Veľké Biele Pleso	3h 00m	2909, 5910

KOPSKÉ SEDLO to:

Javorina	2h 30m	2911B
Skalnaté Pleso	3h 00m	2911A, 0930A
Veľké Biele Pleso	0h 30m	2911A
Zelené Pleso	1h 00m	2911A, 0930A

LYSÁ POĽANA to:

Hrebienok	8h 45m	2907B/A, 5807
Poľský Hrebeň	5h 15m	2907B, 5806B
Prielom	5h 45m	2907B
Sliezsky Dom	7h 00m	2907B, 5806B
Starý Smokovec	9h 30m	2907B/A, 5807
Tatranská Lomnica	10h 00m	2907B/A

PLESNIVEC to:

Kežmarské Žľaby	2h 30m	5810 or 8864, 2909
Tatranská Kotlina	2h 00m	5810
Veľké Biele Pleso	1h 30m	5810

POD MURÁŇOM to:

Javorina	0h 45m	2911B/5812B
Kopské Sedlo	2h 15m	2911B
Sedielko	4h 30m	5812B
Tatranská Lomnica	5h 45m	2911B/A, 8863
Téryho Chata	5h 45m	5812B/A
Veľké Biele Pleso	2h 45m	2911B/A

PODBANSKÉ to:

Hladké Sedlo	5h 30m	8851, 0931
Kriváň	4h 00m	0930G, 5803B
Štrbské Pleso	3h 45m	0930G/F, 5803A
Štrbské Pleso	4h 00m	0930G/F
Suché Sedlo	5h 30m	8851
Tri Studničky	1h 30m	0930G

POĽSKÝ HREBEŇ to:

Sliezsky Dom	1h 45m	5806B

POPRADSKÉ PLESO (tarn) to:

Kôprovské Sedlo	2h 15m	2902B
Popradské Pleso (station)	0h 50m	2902B
Rysy	3h 15m	2902B, 0933
Sliezsky Dom	3h 30m	0930D
Štrbské Pleso	1h 15m	0930E
Veľké Hincovo Pleso	1h 30m	2902B

POPRADSKÉ PLESO (station) to:

Popradské Pleso (tarn)	1h 00m	2902B
Rysy	4h 15m	2902B, 0933
Veľké Hincovo Pleso	2h 30m	2902B

PRIELOM to:

Poľský Hrebeň	1h 00m	2907B, 5806B

RÁZCESTIE BIELA VODA (junction 2911/8861) to:

Biela Voda	0h 30m	8861
Jahňací Štít	4h 00m	8861
Kopské Sedlo	2h 45m	2911A
Tatranské Matliare	0h 45m	2911A
Veľké Biele Pleso	2h 15m	2911A
Zelené Pleso	1h 30m	8861

RÁZCESTIE ČIERNA VODA (junction 2909/5810) to:

Kežmarské Žľaby	1h 00m	2909
Plesnivec	1h 30m	5810
Tatranská Kotlina	0h 30m	2909/5810
Veľké Biele Pleso	3h 00m	5810

RÁZCESTIE NA MAGISTRÁLE (junction 0930C/2906) to:

Hrebienok	0h 15m	0930C
Slavkovský Štít	4h 15m	2906
Sliezsky Dom	1h 45m	0930C
Starý Smokovec	0h 30m	2906

RÁZCESTIE NA VELICKEJ POLANE (junction 5806B/8856) to:

Batizovské Pleso	1h 30m	8856B, 0930D
Sliezsky Dom	1h 00m	5806B
Tatranská Polianka	0h 30m	5806B

RÁZCESTIE NAD TRIGANOM (junction 0930/5805) to:

Popradské Pleso	0h 30m	0930E
Popradské Pleso	0h 45m	5805
Rysy	3h 45m	0930E, 2902B, 0933
Štrbské Pleso	0h 30m	0930E
Veľké Hincovo Pleso	2h 00m	0930E, 2902B

RÁZCESTIE POD FURKOTSKOU DOLINOU (junction 0930F/8853B) to:

Bystrá Lávka	3h 15m	8853B
Jamské Pleso	0h 30m	0930F
Kriváň	3h 00m	0930F, 2903
Podbanské	3h 15m	0930F/G
Štrbské Pleso	0h 30m	0930F
Tri Studničky	1h 45m	0930F
Vyšné Wahlenbergovo Pleso	2h 30m	8853B

RÁZCESTIE POD KONČISTOU (junction 0930D/8855) to:

Batizovské Pleso	0h 15m	0930D
Sliezsky Dom	1h 15m	0930D
Vyšné Hágy	1h 15m	8855

RÁZCESTIE POD SUCHÝM VRCHOM (junction 0930D/8856) to:

Batizovské Pleso	0h 30m	0930D
Hrebienok	2h 30m	0930D
Popradské Pleso	3h 00m	0930D
Sliezsky Dom	0h 30m	0930D
Tatranská Polianka	1h 30m	8856, 5806B

RÁZCESTIE POD POĽSKÝM HREBEŇOM (junction 2907B/5806B) to:

Kačacia Dolina	1h 15m	2907B
Lysá Poľana	4h 15m	2907B
Poľský Hrebeň	0h 15m	5806B
Prielom	0h 45m	2907B
Sliezsky Dom	1h 00m	5806B
Zbojnícka Chata	1h 45m	2907B/A

RÁZCESTIE PRI VODOPÁDOCH STUDENÉHO POTOKA (junction 2907A/5807) to:

Bilíkova Chata	0h 15m	5807
Hrebienok	0h 20m	5807
Starolesnianska Poľana	0h 15m	2907A
Starý Smokovec	1h 00m	5807
Tatranská Lesná	1h 30m	5807, 8859
Tatranská Lomnica	1h 30m	2907A
Téryho Chata	2h 45m	2907A, 0930B, 5812A
Zbojnícka Chata	2h 45m	2907A

ŠALVIOVÝ PRAMEŇ to:

Biela Voda	1h 00m	8861
Jahňací Štít	3h 30m	8861
Kopské Sedlo	2h 15m	2911A
Tatranská Lomnica	1h 30m	2911A, 8863
Veľké Biele Pleso	1h 45m	2911A
Zelené Pleso	1h 45m	8861

SKALNATÉ PLESO to:

Hrebienok	1h 30m	0930B
Obrovsky Vodopád	1h 00m	0930B
Šalviový Prameň	1h 30m	2908, 5809, 8861
Štart	1h 30m	5808
Štart	2h 15m	2908
Sedlo pod Malou Svišťovkou	0h 30m	2908
Tatranská Lomnica	2h 15m	5808
Veľká Svišťovka	1h 15m	0930A
Zelené Pleso	2h 15m	0930A

SLIEZSKY DOM to:

Batizovské Pleso	1h 15m	0930D
Hrebienok	2h 00m	0930C
Poľský Hrebeň	2h 00m	5806B
Starý Smokovec	2h 00m	5806B, 8858
Tatranská Polianka	1h 30m	5806B
Vyšné Hágy	3h 00m	0930D, 8855

STAROLESNIANSKA POĽANA to:

Hrebienok	0h 25m	2907A, 5807
Lysá Poľana	8h 30m	2907A/B
Obrovský Vodopád	0h 20m	2907A, 0930B
Prielom	3h 45m	2907A
Skalnaté Pleso	1h 45m	0930B
Tatranská Lomnica	1h 30m	2907A
Téryho Chata	2h 30m	0930B, 5812A
Zbojnícka Chata	2h 30m	2907A

ŠTART to:

Šalviový Prameň	1h 30m	2908, 5809, 8861
Skalnaté Pleso	2h 00m	5808
Skalnaté Pleso	3h 00m	2908
Tatranská Lomnica	0h 30m	5808
Zelené Pleso	2h 30m	2908, 5809, 8861

STARÝ SMOKOVEC to:

Bilíkova Chata	0h 50m	5807
Hrebienok	0h 45m	5807
Slavkovský Štít	5h 00m	2906
Sliezsky Dom	2h 30m	8858, 5806B

ŠTRBSKÉ PLESO (tarn★) to:

Bystrá Lávka	3h 20m	8853A
Jamské Pleso	1h 00m	0930F
Junction 0930F/8853B	0h 30m	0930F
Kôprovský Štít	4h 15m	0930E, 2902B, 0934
Kriváň	3h 30m	0930F, 2903
Podbanské	3h 45m	0930F/G
Podbanské	3h 45m	5803A, 0930G
Popradské Pleso	1h 05m	0930E
Rysy	4h 20m	0930E, 2902B, 0933
Sliezsky Dom	4h 35m	0930E/D
Tri Studničky	2h 15m	0930F or 5803A
Veľké Hincovo Pleso	2h 35m	0930E, 2902B
Vodopád Skok	1h 20m	8853A
Vyšné Kôprovské Sedlo	3h 45m	0930E, 2902B

★From Štrbské Pleso station add five minutes

TATRANSKÁ KOTLINA to:

Belianska Jaskyňa	0h 40m	8862
Kežmarské Žľaby	1h 30m	2909
Plesnivec	2h 00m	5810
Veľké Biele Pleso	3h 30m	5810

TATRANSKÁ LESNÁ to:

Bilíkova Chata	1h 45m	8859
Hrebienok	2h 15m	8859, 5807
Starolesnianska Poľana	2h 00m	8859, 5807

TATRANSKÁ LOMNICA to:

Bilíkova Chata	2h 00m	2907A, 5807
Hrebienok	2h 15m	2907A, 5807
Javorina	6h 30m	8863, 2911A/B
Kopské Sedlo	4h 00m	8863, 2911A
Šalviový Prameň	2h 00m	8863, 2911A
Skalnaté Pleso	2h 45m	5808
Starolesnianska Poľana	2h 00m	2907A
Štart	0h 45m	5808
Zamkovského Chata	2h 30m	2907A, 0930B
Zbojnícka Chata	4h 00m	2907A
Zelené Pleso	3h 30m	8863, 2911A, 8861

TATRANSKÁ POLIANKA to:

Batizovské Pleso	3h 00m	5806B, 8856, 0930D
Lysá Poľana	8h 30m	5806B, 2907B
Nižné Hágy	1h 00m	5806A
Poľský Hrebeň	4h 00m	5806B
Sliezsky Dom	2h 00m	5806B
Štôla	1h 15m	5806A

TATRANSKÉ MATLIARE to:

Kopské Sedlo	3h 45m	2911A
Šalviový Prameň	1h 30m	2911A
Veľké Biele Pleso	3h 15m	2911A
Zelené Pleso	3h 15m	2911A, 8861

TATRANSKÉ ZRUBY to:

Sliezsky Dom	2h 15m	2905, 8858, 5806B

TÉRYHO CHATA to:

Hrebienok	1h 45m	5812A, 0930B
Javorina	5h 30m	5812A/B
Priečne Sedlo	1h 30m	8860
Sedielko	1h 30m	5812A
Starý Smokovec	2h 15m	5812A, 0930B, 5807
Zamkovského Chata	1h 00m	5812A
Zbojnícka Chata	3h 00m	8860

TRI STUDNIČKY to:

Hladké Sedlo	4h 30m	2902A, 5801, 0931
Kriváň	2h 30m	5803B
Nižné Temnosmrečinské Pleso	4h 15m	2902A, 5801, 0932
Podbanské	1h 30m	0930G
Štrbské Pleso	2h 15m	5803A
Štrbské Pleso	2h 30m	0930F

VELICKE PLESO – see Sliezsky Dom

VEĽKÉ BIELE PLESO to:

Biela Voda	2h 00m	2911A, 8861
Javorina	2h 30m	2911A/B
Kopské Sedlo	0h 30m	2911A
Skalnaté Pleso	2h 30m	0930A
Tatranská Kotlina	3h 30m	5810
Tatranské Matliare	2h 15m	2911A
Zelené Pleso	0h 30m	0930A

VYŠNÉ HÁGY to:

Batizovské Pleso	2h 30m	8855
Popradské Pleso	4h 30m	8855, 0930D
Sliezsky Dom	3h 30m	8855, 0930D

ZAMKOVSKÉHO CHATA to:

Hrebienok	0h 45m	0930B
Javorina	7h 15m	5812A/B

Sedielko	3h 15m	5812A
Skalnaté Pleso	1h 00m	0930B
Starolesnianska Poľana	0h 30m	0930B
Starý Smokovec	1h 15m	0930B, 5807
Téryho Chata	1h 45m	5812A

ZBOJNÍCKA CHATA to:

Hrebienok	2h 30m	2907A, 0930B
Kačacia Dolina	3h 00m	2907A/B
Lysá Poľana	6h 00m	2907A/B
Starolesnianska Poľana	2h 30m	2907A
Poľský Hrebeň	2h 15m	2907A, 5806B
Prielom	1h 15m	2907A
Tatranská Lomnica	4h 00m	2907A

ZELENÉ PLESO to:

Biela Voda	2h 30m	8861
Jahňací Štít	2h 30m	8861
Kopské Sedlo	1h 00m	0930A, 2911A
Skalnaté Pleso	2h 00m	0930A
Tatranské Lomnica	3h 00m	8861, 2911A, 8863
Veľká Svišťovka	1h 15m	0930A
Veľké Biele Pleso	0h 30m	0930A

HIGHEST SUMMITS (ABOVE 2300m)

See also Altitudes, page 21.

The translations are in some cases very rough. Many summits are simply named after the nearest villages in the plain below.

Note Gerlachovská Veža, here shown separately, is generally regarded as part of Gerlachovský Štít and not counted in the order of peaks.

★ = shared with Poland
+ = accessible to walkers
G = accessible to walkers with a qualified mountain guide
C = accessible by cable-car

Summit	Translation	Height
Gerlachovský Štít (G)	Gerlachov Peak	2654m
Gerlachovská Veža	Gerlachov Tower	2642m
Lomnický Štít (G) (C)	Lomnica Peak	2634m
Zadný Gerlach	Hinder Gerlach	2630m
Ľadový Štít (G)	Icy Peak	2627m
Pyšný Štít	Haughty Peak	2623m
Lavinový Štít	Avalanche Peak	2606m
Malý Ľadový Štít	Little Icy Peak	2602m
Kotlový Štít	Kettle Peak	2601m
Kežmarský Štít	Kežmarok Peak	2558m
Vysoká (G)	High	2547m
Končistá	The One at the End	2535m
Baranie Rohy (G)	Ram's Horns	2526m
Ťažký Štít	Difficult Peak	2500m
Rysy ★+	Gashes	2499m
Kriváň +	The Crooked One	2494m
Spišský Štít	Spis Peak	2481m
Bradavica (G)	Wart	2476m
Snehový Štít	Snow Peak	2465m
Široká Veža (G)	Broad Tower	2461m
Gánok (G)	Verandah	2459m
Batizovský Štít	Batizovce Peak	2456m

Slavkovský Štít +	Slavkov Peak	2452m
Prostredný Hrot (G)	Middle Sharp	2440m
Veľký Mengusovský Štít (G) ★	Great Mengusovce Peak	2438m
Čierny Štít	Black Peak	2434m
Kvetnicová Veža	Flowerpot Tower	2433m
Hrubý Vrch	Rough Hill	2428m
Východná Vysoká +	East High	2428m
Zlobivá	The Infuriating One	2426m
Litvorový Štít	Litvorov Peak	2423m
Satan (G)	Satan	2422m
Kolový Štít	Stake Peak	2418m
Javorový Štít	Maple Peak	2417m
Huncovský Štít	Huncovce Peak	2415m
Furkotský Štít	Furkotský Peak	2405m
Veľké Solisko	Big Sun Point	2404m
Východný Mengusovský Štít ★	East Mengusovce Peak	2398m
Popradský Ľadový Štít	Poprad Icy Peak	2396m
Štrbský Štít	Strba Peak	2395m
Prostredný Mengusovský Štít ★	Middle Mengusovce Peak	2393m
Svišťový Štít	Marmot Peak	2382m
Zadná Bašta	Hinder Lookout	2380m
Čubrina ★	(No translation)	2378m
Divá Veža	Wild Tower	2376m
Veľká Ľadová Veža	Great Icy Tower	2376m
Predná Bašta	Front Lookout	2366m
Kôprovský Štít +	Dill Peak	2363m
Východná	The Eastern One	2356m
Kôpky	Little Stack	2354m
Slavkovská Kopa	Slavkov Stack	2346m
Žabia Veža	Frog Tower	2340m
Malý Kriváň	Little Crooked One	2334m
Hlinská Veža	Earthy Tower	2330m
Velický Štít	Velický Peak	2320m
Veľká Granátova Veža	Great Garnet Tower	2313m
Zmrzlá Veža	Frozen Tower	2310m
Štrbské Solisko	Strba Sun Point	2302m
Svinica ★+	Porcine	2300m

TRAVEL

Public Transport To and From the Slovak High Tatras

For contact details of the operators mentioned, see Appendix C, Useful Addresses. All times and distances shown below are approximate.

The region has its own airport, located 4km northwest of the centre of Poprad. It is usually marked on maps as Letisko (Airport) Poprad–Tatry. In timetables it may be either Poprad–Tatry, Tatry–Poprad, or even Poprad–Zakopane, and has the somewhat unflattering international airport code TAT.

The airport is very convenient for the High Tatras, being just 10km from Starý Smokovec, 16km from Tatranská Lomnica, and 27km from Štrbské Pleso. By car or taxi this should take between 10 and 30 minutes, or you can take a short bus or taxi ride to Poprad railway station, then the Tatras Electric Railway. In spring 2011, Czech Airlines (020 7365 9189, www.czechairlines.co.uk) started a service from Prague to Poprad. They do not currently serve UK airports so travellers from the UK would still have to book connecting flights to Prague.

The nearest airport with international services from other European airports is Kraków in Poland, from where trains and buses go to Zakopane, then bus from there to the Slovak side. Kraków may be more convenient anyway if you intend to visit both Polish and Slovak Tatras. There is a limited number of flights to Košice, further east, from where trains go to Poprad.

Alternatively you can travel via Bratislava, the capital of Slovakia, which is 350km from the High Tatras resorts. With funding from various sources, including the

The electric train to Starý Smokovec at Tatranská Lomnica station

European Union, its city centre has become a very attractive place to spend a night or two en route to or from the Tatras. Its airport (also known as Letisko MR Štefánika after the Slovak co-founder of Czechoslovakia) is linked with a growing number of international destinations, including London Luton (EasyJet) and London Stansted (RyanAir).

A much wider network of international flights serves Vienna, whose airport has a direct bus connection with Bratislava, a distance of just 42km.

There are InterCity train services to Poprad from Bratislava (4 hours), Vienna (5½ hours) or Košice (1 hour). Bratislava and Vienna airports have direct bus services to Bratislava's main railway station (you must buy a ticket from the machine beside the bus stop before boarding). A train service links Poprad with most of the High Tatras resorts.

The InterCity trains are comfortable, and the journey from Bratislava is very pleasant, following the valley of Slovakia's longest river, the Vah, beside lakes and between wooded hillsides that become ever higher and grander as you approach the Tatras. High above, castles cling precariously to rocky outcrops – the one at Trenčin is really spectacular. With the Western Tatras to your left and the Low Tatras to your right, magnificent, broad-shouldered Kriváň, the national symbol of Slovakia, is your first glimpse of the High Tatras peaks.

If you are staying in Štrbské Pleso, you may find it more convenient to travel by train to the main line station called Štrba (actually at Tatranská Štrba), then take the rack railway to Štrsbké Pleso. However, as the InterCity trains do not stop there, you would have to take a slower train or change en route.

Details of train services in Slovakia can be obtained from the website of ŽSR (Železnice Slovenskej Republiky/Slovak Railways) at www.zsr.sk.

Long-distance buses serve Poprad from Bratislava, Brno, Budapest, Prague, Zakopane, Hamburg and Düsseldorf. Eurolines (www.eurolines.com) has direct coach services from London to Bratislava, Budapest and Prague. A direct bus service operated by Strama (www.strama.eu) links Zakopane with Łysa Polana/Lýsá Poľana, Ždiar, Tatranská Lomnica, Starý Smokovec and Poprad.

Public Transport Within the Slovak High Tatras

An electric railway along the foot of the mountains links Poprad with Tatranská Lomnica, Starý Smokovec and Štrbské Pleso. It is known as TEŽ, which stands for Tatranské Electricke Železnice (Tatras Electric Railway), although the vehicles are sometimes referred to as trams rather than trains. A Swiss-built fleet was introduced in 2004. There are stations at all the villages and hamlets along the line, and most of these are starting points for walking routes into the mountains.

An electric rack railway links Štrbské Pleso with the main line station called Štrba, which (confusingly) is actually at a separate village called Tatranská Štrba – but note that there is also a halt for local trains at Štrba itself!

A diesel-hauled service links Tatranská Lomnica with a station called Studený Potok (close to Veľká Lomnica) on the line from Poprad to Kežmarok.

Times of services are displayed at all the railway stations, and can be obtained from tourist information offices. They are usually shown as a list of departure times for the various destinations, though full railway timetables are displayed at main stations – some are on drums, which you roll by hand. Some services are qualified by notes referring to operational limitations, such as weekdays only – at present these are shown in Slovak only.

Train tickets must be bought before boarding, either at machines or ticket offices at stations, or at post offices, tourist information offices and selected shops. They must be stamped on boarding in a stamping-machine. You can buy tickets for a single journey, or a block covering eight sections. Most journeys cover more than one section, as explained on the reverse of the ticket. There is a proposal to introduce season tickets.

Bus services run parallel to the railway lines, and some of these continue to the more remote High Tatras villages of Tatranská Kotlina, Ždiar and Javorina, as well as Lysá Poľana on the border with Poland, and infrequently to Podbanské in the Western Tatras. Bus fares are paid to the driver on boarding. Departure times are shown at bus stations and at bus stops.

Taxis are readily available throughout the High Tatras resorts.

Mountain Transport

Mountain lifts of various kinds provide a means of avoiding some of the hard work of climbing through the forest zone. There may be queues at peak times, especially in good weather.

From Štrbské Pleso a chair-lift operates to Chata pod Soliskom, from 08.30 to 16.00 daily (journey time 20 minutes).

From Starý Smokovec a funicular railway runs for nearly 2km up to Hrebienok, from 07.30 to 19.00 daily – except on alternate Mondays, when it starts at 09.00 (journey time 7 minutes).

From Tatranská Lomnica a 4-seater gondola-lift climbs 4km to Skalnaté Pleso, from 07.00 to 18.00 daily (journey time 15 minutes). There is a halfway station, confusingly called Štart – if you are continuing to the top, you stay in your gondola as it clatters through the points, but you can alight or board there if you wish (there are no facilities). Note that the chair-lift shown on some maps starting beside Grandhotel Praha no longer operates.

From Skalnaté Pleso a cable-car to Lomnický Štít operates all year from 08.00 to 18.00. Although you cannot walk down from the top without a guide, it is very popular because of the magnificent views, and you are only allowed to stay for 35 minutes. It is advisable to book in advance. Rather awkwardly, this can only

Skalnaté Pleso and its observatory on the Tatranská Magistrála

be done at the cable-car's bottom station at Skalnaté Pleso, although you can do this by phone, or ask your hotel reception to do it for you, checking the weather forecast at the same time. The phone numbers are 052 4467 884 for general information, or 052 4467 412 to book the cable-car.

Also from Skalnaté Pleso, a chair-lift operates in summer only to Lomnické Sedlo from 08.00 to 18.00 daily (journey time 9 minutes). Again, this is normally only for the views and a kiosk, as it is only possible to walk a short distance at the top without a guide.

Special offers may be available covering several lifts – you should enquire at a tourist information office or at a mountain lift ticket office.

In very bad weather the mountain lifts may have to suspend operations. At the end of the summer and winter seasons, usually in November and April/May, they may close for 2–3 weeks for maintenance.

By Car

Approaching from western Europe, you should head for Prague or Bratislava. From Prague, motorways run eastwards to Brno or Olomouc, then a main road takes you further east to Trenčín in Slovakia. From Bratislava, a motorway goes to just before Žilina, about halfway to the High Tatras. A motorway is planned to eventually go through to Poprad, but meanwhile you must use a single-carriageway main road, turning off at Tatranská Štrba for Štrbské Pleso, or at Poprad for Starý Smokovec or Tatranská Lomnica.

Lomnický Štít from Cesta Slobody, showing the effects of the Tatranská Bora

Approaching from Poland, you should head first for Kraków, then southeast to Nowy Targ and on to cross into Slovakia at Jurgów or Lysá Poľana (Łysa Polana in Polish). From there it is a short drive to Tatranská Kotlina, where you turn right along Cesta Slobody (Freedom Highway), which links all the High Tatras resorts.

Cars can be rented in Poprad (see Shopping and Local Services, page 166).

Private vehicles are banned at all times from side roads leading up into the mountains. They may only be parked in the official car parks, shown on the maps, where a charge is made from July to September and during the Christmas and Easter periods. Most hotels and pensions provide free parking for their guests.

Passports and Visas

Slovakia and Poland are now both members of the Schengen Convention, in which all countries share the same passport and visa requirements, but you are advised to check the latest situation with your travel agent, airline or a consulate of Slovakia or Poland.

All visitors to the Schengen Convention countries need a valid full passport or European Union identity card. Nationals of most English-speaking countries do not need a visa for stays of up to 90 days. Nationals of other countries may need a visa, obtainable in advance from a consulate of any Schengen country including Slovakia and Poland.

DIVERSIONS

If some members of your party do not wish to walk, or need a change from walking, or have enough energy left for night life, here are some suggestions. You can get more details from your hotel reception, or tourist information offices in the High Tatras.

Special offers may be available at some of the establishments mentioned – check with your hotel reception or at local tourist information offices.

Sightseeing Excursions
* Raft sailing on the River Dunajec, beside the border with Poland to the northeast. Includes lunch and a visit to Červený Kláštor – the Red Monastery.
* Low Tatras. You can visit the spectacular Demänovské limestone caves, and take a chair-lift to the summit of Chopok (2024m), one of the highest in the range. Lunch is included.
* Tour of Spiš. You will often see this word included in place names to the east and southeast of the High Tatras. It refers to an ancient Germanic people, of which there are many traces in the architecture and culture of this region. Lunch is included.
* Tour into Poland, including Zakopane (see gazetteer, page 305) and Nowy Targ, which has an interesting market on Thursdays.
* Sightseeing flights from Poprad–Tatry Airport – a splendid way to admire the High Tatras in good weather.

You can easily visit Poprad and Kežmarok (see gazetteer, pages 182 and 176) by public transport.

Art Gallery
Galleria Villa Flóra, Starý Smokovec.

Museums
* Tatranská Lomnica: TANAP (National Park) Museum.
* Ždiar: Museum of Folk Architecture.
* Poprad: Podtatranské Muzeum.
* Kežmarok: Castle Museum.
* Prybilina: Museum of Liptov villages (open air).
* Levoča: Spiš Museum in the town hall.
* Spišsky Hrad: Castle Museum.

Sports
Bobsleigh Tatrabob, Tatranská Lomnica. Open all year, 680m long with 45m descent.

Cycle/Mountain Bike Hire Sportcentrum, Horný Smokovec; Tatrasport Adam & Andreas, Starý Smokovec; Penzión Slalom, Tatranská Lomnica. Details of cycle routes in the High Tatras can be obtained from tourist information offices and from the TANAP information centre in Tatranská Lomnica.

Fitness and Aquatic Centres (including Sauna) Podbanské: Grand Hotel Permon; Štrbské Pleso: Hotel Borovica, Hotel FIS, Hotel Patria; Gerlachov: Hotel Hubert; Starý Smokovec: Grand Hotel, Hotel Bellevue; Tatranská Lomnica: Grand Hotel Praha, Hotel Slovan, Hotel Uran, Hotel Odborar.

Golf Bestvina Golf Academy at the 27-hole Black Stork Golf Course near Veľká Lomnica. Equipment can be hired.

Minigolf Tatranská Lomnica.

Horse Carriage Rides JMG Travel, Štrbské Pleso. Destinations include Popradské Pleso.

Horse Riding Hotel Hubert, Gerlachov; TKPK (Tatras Horse Friends Club), Tatranské Matliare.

Swimming Pools Aquacity at Poprad is a modern complex of indoor and outdoor thermally heated pools, as well as flume, saunas, restaurant, café, bar and minigolf. Website www.aquacity.sk. AquaPark Tatralandia offers all this and more on a larger scale but is further away at Liptovský Mikuláš (60km from Starý Smokovec). Website www.tatralandia.sk.

The following hotels in the High Tatras have small indoor swimming pools: Hotel Patria, Štrbské Pleso; Grandhotel and Hotel Smokovec, Starý Smokovec; Hotel Bellevue, Horný Smokovec; Hotels Titris Odborár and Urán, Tatranská Lomnica.

Tennis Štrbské Pleso; Tatranská Lomnica.

Ten-pin Bowling Hotel Atrium, Nový Smokovec.

Adrenalin Parks (obstacle courses up high in the trees) Štrbské Pleso, Tatranská Kotlina.

Dining with Entertainment
In most cases this is provided at a *koliba* (literally 'chalet') where live folk music is performed in the evening.
Štrbské Pleso: 2 kolibas.
Starý Smokovec: Zbojnícka Koliba (gipsy music).
Starý Smokovec: Slovak Restaurant (live folk music).
Stará Lesná: Zbojnícka Koliba (gipsy music).
Tatranská Lomnica: Zbojnícka Koliba (gipsy music).

Night Clubs
Štrbské Pleso: Vatra Bar, Hotel Patria.
Starý Smokovec: Crystal Bar, Grandhotel.
Stará Lesná: Night Club, Hotel Horizont.

Cinemas
Cinema Tatry, Tatranská Lomnica; Kino Tatran, Poprad.

SHOPPING AND LOCAL SERVICES

The following is a summary of facilities available in the High Tatras area. Many shops will show outside the English word for the service offered, but we give the Slovak equivalent in brackets in case of need. Some shops may have English speakers, and German is widely understood, but a Slovak dictionary or phrasebook may be helpful.

Generally, shops and supermarkets are open Mondays to Fridays from 8am to 12 noon, and from 2pm to 6pm; Saturdays from 8am to 1pm. Some shops in the resorts open longer hours and on Sundays.

Poprad has a wide range of shops for all general purposes.

Tourist Information
There is a tourist office for the whole High Tatras region, based in Starý Smokovec: phone 052 442 5230; e-mail zcr@tatryinfo.sk; website www.tatryinfo.eu (the official site of the High Tatras) or www.vysoketatry.com (a privately run site).

Also resort tourist information offices at:
Štrbské Pleso (phone 052 449 2391, e-mail strbskepleso@tatryinfo.eu)
Starý Smokovec (phone 052 442 3440, e-mail smokovec@tatryinfo.eu)
Tatranská Lomnica (phone 052 446 8119, e-mail lomnica@tatryinfo.eu)
Poprad (phone 092 721 700, e-mail poprad@tatryinfo.eu)
Bratislava (phone 07 544 33 715, e-mail info@bkis.sk, www.bratislava.sk)

Books and Maps
There are bookshops (books is *knihy*) that also sell maps (*mapy*) in Štrbské Pleso, Tatranská Lomnica and Poprad. Maps are also sold at tourist information offices, souvenir shops and some hotels.

Car Rental
Hertz Slovakia. By advance arrangement, vehicles based at Košice can be delivered to Poprad–Tatry Airport (phone 055 789 6041). Poprad: Argus Rentals (www.argusrentals.com).

Car Repair/Service Stations
Poprad: Autonova (phone 052 788 6771).

Currency Exchange
All hotels and travel agencies offer currency exchange facilities (*zmenáreň*). There are banks at Tatranská Lomnica and Poprad, and autocash machines in most of the larger resorts.

Filling Stations
There are filling stations (*čerpacia stanica*) at Tatranská Strba, Novy Smokovec and Ždiar, as well as 24-hour filling stations in Poprad.

Internet Cafés *(Internetová Kaviareň)*
Starý Smokovec – Fun Travel (phone 052 442 2093).
Starý Smokovec – Tourist Information Office.
Tatranská Lomnica – Café Townson (phone 052 478 2731).

Mountain Guides *(Horský Vodca)*
Horská Služba, Starý Smokovec (phone 052 442 2855 or 2761, e-mail spolok@sinet.sk, www.tatraguide.sk).

Pharmacies *(Lekáreň)*
In Štrbské Pleso, Starý Smokovec, Tatranská Lomnica and Poprad.

Post Offices *(Pošta)*
Štrbské Pleso: turn right outside the railway station for 50m.
Starý Smokovec: turn left outside the railway station for 50m.
Tatranská Lomnica: turn right outside the station for 100m.
Ždiar: on the main road near the filling station.

Shopping Malls
At Poprad.

Sport/Equipment Shops
There are many in all the main resorts including:
Horný Smokovec: Športcentrum Galfy (www.galfy.sk).
Starý Smokovec: Tatrasport Adam (phone 052 442 5241, e-mail tatrasport@tatry.net).

Supermarkets/Foodshops *(Potraviny)*
There are plenty of food shops in the villages, as well as small supermarkets in the larger resorts – they are open daily (Sundays to 1pm). The Tesco on the outskirts of Poprad is open '24/7' (24 hours a day, seven days a week).

Tatras National Park (TANAP, Tatranský Národný Park)
TANAP's main information office is located at its museum in Tatranská Lomnica (phone 052 446 7951, e-mail tanap@tanap.org, website www.tanap.org). TANAP also has small information offices at Štrbské Pleso and Tatranská Štrba.

Taxis
Taxis *(taxi)* can be arranged through your hotel reception, or phone:
0905 552 672, 0903 907 427, or 0903 123 124.

Travel Agencies *(Cestovná Kancelária)*
Usual opening hours are Monday to Friday 9am to 5pm, Saturday 9am to 12 noon.
Štrbské Pleso: JMG (phone 052 449 2582, www.jmg.sk).
Starý Smokovec: T-Ski Travel (phone 052 442 3200, www.slovakiatravel.sk).
Poprad: Satur (phone 052 772 1740, www.satur.sk).

OTHER USEFUL INFORMATION

Here are some more little snippets of information that do not fit in under any of the foregoing headings.

Cost of Living
Public transport and food are reasonably priced. Hotel accommodation is quite moderately priced. Clothes and luxury goods are not such good value.

Currency
Slovakia joined the Eurozone on 1 January 2009, so euro (€) are now used throughout the country, and may be accepted at some tourist-oriented shops and businesses in Poland.

Electricity
220 volts. Two-pin plugs are used – you may need an adaptor.

Meals
Food and drink in cafés and restaurants in the High Tatras resorts are reasonably priced. Prices in the mountain chalets are higher, due to additional transportation costs.

Meat tends to be quite spicy. Vegetarian food is becoming more widely available, but may consist of just pizzas, cheese and egg dishes. Specialities of the region include *oštiepok* and *bryndza* (both sheep's-milk cheese), *bryndzové halušky* (sheep's-milk cheese noodles), *zemiaková placka* (potato pancakes) and *Slovenská pochútka* (Slovak titbits – pies filled with spiced pork or beef and onions).

News
English language newspapers are currently not normally available in the High Tatras. You can keep in touch online at an internet café (see above) through http://news.bbc.co.uk. The BBC World Service may be obtainable on various radio frequencies (details on www.bbc.co.uk/worldservice). Radio Tatras International's FM broadcasts were not operating at the time of writing but they continue to provide an online English language news service at www.rti.fm.

Phoning Home from Slovakia
Dial 00 then the following prefixes – Australia 61, New Zealand 64, South Africa 27, UK 44, Irish Republic 353, USA/Canada 1 – then the area code, then the individual number. Note that for UK numbers you must omit the area code's initial 0. If you wish to use your mobile phone abroad, you should contact your

service provider beforehand as special 'roaming' arrangements may need to be made to ensure that it will work.

Public Holidays

January 1	New Year's Day and Slovak Republic Establishment Day
January 6	Epiphany
Variable	Good Friday, Easter Day and Easter Monday
May 1	Labour Day
May 8	Liberation Day
July 5	St Cyril and St Methodius Day
August 29	Slovak National Uprising Anniversary
September 1	Constitution Day
September 15	Our Lady of Sorrows Day
November 1	All Saints Day
November 17	Freedom and Democracy Day
December 24–26	Christmas Eve, Christmas Day and Boxing Day

Široká Veža from the Tatranská Magistrála at Hrebienok

Tipping

At your discretion, a small tip may be given for good service to waiters, bartenders, taxi drivers, receptionists, room-cleaning staff and hairdressers. The generally accepted amount is 5%. In a restaurant, the range is 10 cents to €2.

Toilets

Men – *muži* or *páni*
Women – *ženy* or *dámy*
There is sometimes a guardian who collects a nominal charge.

GAZETTEER

Baranie Rohy (Ram's Horns, 2526m) A distinctive peak, very popular with climbers, to the north of Téryho Chata in Malá Studená Dolina. Once on the way-marked-path network, at the time of writing it was only accessible with a guide, but there was a proposal to reopen the route at least as far as Baranie Sedlo, the saddle below the summit.

Batizovce (750m) A large village in the Sub-Tatras Basin southwest of Starý Smokovec. It was founded by a nobleman called Botyz or Batiz, who was granted the land in 1264 by King Bela IV of Hungary. There are two manor houses and two churches (one Catholic, one evangelical).

Batizovské Pleso (Batizovce Tarn, 1879m) A pretty tarn north of Vyšné Hágy, surrounded by some of the highest Tatra summits: Končistá (2535m), Batizovský Štít (2456m), Gerlachovský Štít (2654m) and Kotlový Štít (2601m).

Belianska Jaskyňa (White Cave, 885m) A large limestone cave above Tatranská Kotlina in the White Tatras, of which about 1km is open all year round to the public – the only publicly accessible one in the Slovak High, White or Western Tatras. It is one of 12 state-owned show caves in Slovakia – details online at www.ssj.sk.

The entrance is at 885m, and you descend 112m to 773m. Discovered in the 1880s, this was one of the first caves to be electrically lit, in 1896, and the lighting certainly enhances the stalactites and other limestone formations. Guided tours take place daily except Mondays, they last about an hour, and you should allow 20 minutes on foot each way from the village.

Belianska Kopa (1832m) A minor summit above Kopské Sedlo, northwest of Tatranská Lomnica between the High and White Tatras. It used to be a much-used sheep pasture, before livestock was banned from the national park.

Biela Voda (White Water, 920m) The starting point of Yellow 8861 on Cesta Slobody (Freedom Highway) northeast of Tatranská Lomnica. This location is not named as such on some maps, but is close to Kyslý Prameň (Sour Spring). There is a bus stop and car park but no other facilities.

Bielovodská Dolina The longest valley (10km) on the north side of the Slovak High Tatras, and one of the prettiest in the area, falling through many terraces. It is named after the river called Biela Voda (White Water), which for much of its length forms the border with Poland, with the customs post of Lysá Poľana on its banks.

Bilíkova Chata (Bilík Chalet, 1255m, phone 052 442 2439 www.bilikovachata.sk) A very popular chalet north of Starý Smokovec, from which it is easily accessible, either on foot or with the funicular. Originally a simple hut, built in 1875, it was enlarged and rebuilt in 1934, and then operated as a mountain resort called Studenopotocké Kúpele for some years. After the Second World War it was renamed after Captain Pavel Bilík of the Starý Smokovec border patrol, who was executed at Kežmarok by the Nazis in 1944. Now privately owned, the chalet was refurbished in 1993 and has 32 beds.

Bradavica (Wart, 2476m) A peak to the northwest of Starý Smokovec that is clearly visible from Veľká Studená Dolina, and accessible to walkers with a guide.

Brnčalova Chata – see Zelené Pleso.

Bystrá Lávka (Sharp Notch, 2300m). A pass northwest of Štrbské Pleso, connecting the Mlynická and Furkotská valleys. The slightly higher Bystré Sedlo to its north until recently used for Yellow 8853 but had to be closed to walkers due to erosion.

Červené Vrchy (Red Peaks, in Polish Czerwone Wierchy) The name reflects the autumnal colour of the grass that covers this range of rounded summits. They lie at the east end of the Western Tatras, rising above Tichá Dolina to the north of Podbanské. In the past they attracted shepherds, whose flocks were banned from the national park area in the 1950s, and miners who were unsuccessful in their attempts to find copper.

Česká Dolina (Czech Valley) has recently resumed its original name, Ťažká Dolina (Difficult Valley). The pronunciation of 'Česká' and 'Ťažká' is very similar, hence the confusion, and you may see either version on maps. It is a hanging valley above the south end of the long Bielovodská Dolina, on the north side of the High Tatras, and it contains two small tarns (Ťažké Pleso and Zmrzlé Pleso). Though inaccessible to walkers it can be viewed from the saddle called Váha on the way to Rysy.

Chata Kapitána Morávku – see Popradské Pleso.

Chata Kapitána Nálepku – see Zamkovského Chata.

Chata Kapitána Rašu – see Tri Studničky.

Chata Plesnivec (Edelweiss Chalet, 1350m, mobile phone 090 525 6722) The only chalet in the White Tatras, indeed the only inhabited building there. The first inhabitant on this site, during the 18th century, was an Austrian gold prospector called Drechsler, who lived in a simple shed. In 1932 this was replaced by a private cottage, which after the Second World War was opened to the public as a chalet. In 1955 it was closed for use as a research base by the national park, but reopened to the public in 1997. It has a dormitory with 20 beds.

Chata pod Rysmi (Chalet below Rysy, 2250m, phone 052 442 2314 www.chatapodrysmi.sk) The highest chalet in the Tatras, in a superb position 250m below Rysy summit. Built in 1932 and owned by KST (Klub Slovenských Turistov), it is open to walkers from 16 June to 31 October only, but also in winter to climbers and mountain skiers in good snow conditions. Accommodation for those wishing to stay the night is provided in one dormitory with 14 beds.

The chalet has been damaged by avalanches several times in recent years, and was being rebuilt at the time of writing. It used to have one of the largest karabiners (an item of climbing equipment) in the world, at about 60cm long, suspended from the eaves outside.

Chata pod Soliskom (1830m, Chalet below Solisko, mobile phone 090 794 9442 www.chatasolisko.sk) A very popular chalet northwest of Štrbské Pleso, from which it is easily reached by chair-lift. It is the starting point for the short climb to Predné Solisko. There is also a café called Bivák Club in the chair-lift building, and both are heaving with skiers in winter, as this is the top of the main ski slope at Štrbské Pleso.

Chata pri Zelenom Plese – see Zelené Pleso

Čierny Štít (Black Peak, 2434m) A triangular peak north of Starý Smokovec, rising from three valleys – Čierna Javorová Dolina, Veľká Zmrzlá Dolina and Malá Zmrzlá Dolina. Its south wall is very popular with climbers.

Dolný Smokovec (890m) A large but attractive village 2km southeast of Starý Smokovec, quietly situated away from the main roads. Its name means Lower Smokovec, from *dolina* (valley). It has a supermarket and several restaurants. The pretty wooden church was built at the beginning of the 20th century, and there is also a large children's sanatorium for the treatment of tuberculosis and other respiratory diseases. The village has two stops on the railway from Poprad to Starý Smokovec – Dolný Smokovec and Pod Lesom.

Dubček Stone This massive, natural granite slab has been adopted by the Slovaks as a memorial to Alexander Dubček (1921–92), who is regarded as the hero of the Prague Spring of 1968. For a short interval during the years of communist repression, he achieved worldwide fame as the leader of liberal opposition to the hardliners. After being elected as First Secretary – equivalent to prime minister – he placed liberal communists in leading state posts, began to pursue a foreign policy that was independent of the USSR, and promised a gradual democratisation of political life. All this alarmed the Soviets, and the Warsaw Pact countries invaded Czechoslovakia, arresting Dubček and other leaders. He was eventually forced to resign and spent two decades in the political wilderness. Then, after the Velvet Revolution of 1989, he was unanimously elected Speaker of the Czechoslovak parliament, and by the time of his death had become a highly respected figure and an icon of Slovak independence.

Encian – see Skalnaté Pleso

Furkotský Štít (2405m) A triangular peak at the head of Furkotská Dolina, and above Bystré Sedlo, northeast of Štrbské Pleso. Immediately below, to the south, is the tarn called Vyšné Wahlenbergovo Pleso, whose slopes in previous centuries were visited by poachers and miners. The first tourist to reach the summit was a Pole, Kazimir Przerwa-Tetmajer, in 1890. More recently the summit has been used as a measuring point by army cartographers.

Ganek (2459m, also called Ganok) A group of three summits southeast of Rysy – easily visible from the saddle called Váha. It is well known to climbers for its gallery.

Gerlachov (791m) A village in the Sub-Tatras Basin southwest of Starý Smokovec. Founded in the late 13th century by a merchant called Gerlach, it became a centre for the distillation of sembra oil, once used in spa treatments but now banned. In 1876 the village was destroyed by fire. It is now a typical agricultural village, and has an evangelical church.

Gerlachovský Štít (Gerlachov Peak, 2654m) The highest mountain in the High Tatras, Slovakia and the whole Carpathian range, it is also the highest point in Europe north of the Alps. For long a target of hunters and botanists, its first known ascent was made by Johan Still in 1874. The peak is now accessible to walkers only if accompanied by a local mountain guide. The secondary summit, Zadný (Back) Gerlachovský Štít (2606m), carries the remains of a military aircraft, which crashed in 1944 killing all the crew. They are buried at Gerlachov and there is a memorial to them in the Symbolický Cintorín (qv).

Grúnik (1576m) A minor summit on an outcrop on the southwestern slope of Kriváň. During the Second World War it held a partisan bunker, and in January 1945 was the site of a major battle. The bunker has been reconstructed as a memorial, and can be visited from Green 5803, although it is difficult to find.

Havran (Raven, 2152m) The highest summit of the White Tatras.

Hladké Sedlo (Smooth Saddle, 1993m) A pass on the border with Poland, northwest of Štrbské Sedlo. From here you can look out over the upper part of the beautiful Dolina Pięciu Stawów Polskich (Valley of Five Polish Tarns). The first recorded visit was in 1827 by Albrecht von Sydow.

Hlúpy (Stupid, 2061m) A broad, grassy summit in the centre of the White Tatras. It is not accessible to walkers, but Green 5900 passes beneath it.

Horný Smokovec (950m) The upper and newest part of Smokovec (*horný* from *hora*, meaning mountain). Refreshments are available in the *denný bar* of Hotel Poľana, and in the Hotel Bellevue and Hotel Panda. The sanatorium is for children with respiratory ailments. Buses and trains from Starý Smokovec to Tatranská Lomnica call at the village's two stops – Horný Smokovec and Pekná Vyhliadka (Pretty View).

Hrebienok (Little Crest, 1285m) A collection of buildings on a short ridge above Starý Smokovec. It is a major starting point for walkers, lying at the top of the funicular from Starý Smokovec, which was completed in 1908. The station building has a café and toilets and there is another café in Horský Hotel Sorea Hrebienok. The service road doubles as a scooter run in summer and a toboggan run in winter (equipment can be hired). A plaque here commemorates the visit by HM Queen Elizabeth II on 28 October 2008. In winter this whole area is bristling with skiers. Bílíkova Chata (see above) is just a few minutes' walk away.

Huncovský Štít (2415m) A peak to the east of Lomnický Štít, visible from Skalnaté Pleso. It is thought to be one of the first Tatras summits to be climbed, during the 17th century. The name comes from the village in whose parish the peak used to lie – Huncovce, near Kežmarok.

Jahňací Štít (Lamb Peak, 2229m) The easternmost peak in the High Tatras, first climbed by the Scotsman Robert Townson in 1793.

Jamské Pleso (1447m) An idyllically located tarn on the Tatranská Magistrála, northwest of Štrbské Pleso. There are fine views both down over the plain and up to the peaks from the scattering of picnic tables among the scrub. The minor peak to the northwest is called Jamy (Pits, 1572m), from which the lake takes its name. To the north Sedielková Kopa (Little Saddle Stack, 2062m) can be seen. On the east side of the tarn once stood Nedobrého Chata, built in 1936 by Gustav Nedobrý, but burned down in 1943 during the partisan uprising.

Jastrabia Veža (Hawk Tower, 2139m) This is the great, dark-grey crag that soars above Zelené Pleso (qv). It is also known as Karbunkulová Veža (Emerald Tower) for its part in the legend of how Zelené Pleso got its name.

Javorina (1018m – shown on some maps as Tatranská Javorina) A quiet village at the west end of the White Tatras, beside the Javorinka river, named after the village. Both take their name from Javorová Dolina (see below). Javorina lies 2.5km east of the Polish border, and was one of the earliest settlements in the Tatras, having been established in 1759 for the mining of iron ore. In the village centre are a post office and two churches, and in the churchyard of the wooden church is the grave of Jaroslav Votruba, a notable painter of Tatras scenes.

The wooden church and a hunting lodge, also of wood, near the Hotel Kolowrat, were once part of the estate of the Prussian nobleman Kristián Kraft Hohenlohe. During the 19th century he bought the whole of Javorina parish and developed it into his conception of a forest village. He built the church and lodge, and tried to set up a nature reserve with animals from other countries, but they could not survive in the different environment. In 1936 the estate was returned to the state.

Refreshments can be obtained 500m north of the village at the modernistic Hotel Kolowrat, which lies at the spot marked as Pri Bránke on the map. Buses to Lysá Poľana from Poprad, Starý Smokovec and Tatranská Lomnica stop at Javorina.

Javorová Dolina (Maple Valley) A quiet valley, 8km long, running south from Javorina. From the 16th century until the 1950s it was sheep-rearing country. During the 18th century it was the scene of frantic activity, as prospectors came to hunt a rumoured source of cinnabar (an ore containing mercury), which turned out to be false. The Hohenlohe estate (see Javorina) brought tourists to the valley in the 19th century.

Javorový Štít (Maple Peak, 2417m) A steep-sided pinnacle of a peak at the head of Javorová Dolina, northwest of Starý Smokovec. It was first climbed by Antonia and Karl Englisch, together with their local guide Jan Hunsdörfer, in 1897.

Kačacia Dolina (Duck Valley) The upper part of Bielovodská Dolina, lying just off the waymarked network, because Blue 2907 turns off before reaching this area. It lies at the top of a moraine, which also holds in the tarn of Kačacie Pleso. A stream falls from the tarn as a waterfall – Hviezdoslavov Vodopád, named after the 19th-century Slovak poet known simply as Hviezdoslav, which roughly translated means 'star worshipper'. His real name was Pavol Országh. According to a local legend, the valley is the home of a very special duck, which each Midsummer's Day lays a golden egg at the foot of the waterfall, then spends the rest of the year in the mountains. More prosaically, the tarn does attract a large migrant duck population.

Kežmarok A historic small town near the east end of the High Tatras, just off most walking maps, about 13km southeast of Tatranská Lomnica. It is easily accessible direct by bus from all the Tatras villages, or by train from Starý Smokovec via Poprad, or from Tatranská Lomnica via Studený Potok. The imposing castle is open on the hour for guided tours, and contains a museum dedicated to artisan activities. The town hall has a Renaissance bell tower, and there is a small cultural museum. The old wooden Lutheran church, built in 1717 without any help from metal (even nails were avoided), was restored during the 1990s. A modern Protestant one in oriental style can also be visited.

Kežmarská Chata See Veľké Biele Pleso.

Kežmarské Žľaby (Kežmarok Gullies, 920m) A hamlet on Cesta Slobody (Freedom Highway). There is a field study centre for children, but no facilities for walkers.

Kežmarský Štít (Kežmarok Peak, 2558m) The tenth highest summit in the High Tatras, adjoining Lomnický Štít. Its first recorded ascent was in 1615, by David Frölich from Kežmarok.

Končistá (2535m) One of the more prominent Tatras peaks, as seen from the Sub-Tatras Basin. It lies above Batizovské Pleso, northeast of Štrbské Pleso, and the name is a dialect word meaning 'end' (of the range).

Kôprová Dolina (Dill Valley) One of the longest Tatras valleys, at 11km, running northeastwards from Podbanské in the western part of the High Tatras. It was visited during the 15th and 16th centuries by miners from Liptov seeking gold and antimony, and later by hunters and shepherds. During the early part of the 20th century there was a chalet here called Vatra (bonfire).

Kôprovský Štít (Dill Peak, 2367m) One of the easier peaks in the Tatras, though it requires a lengthy approach. It lies north of Štrbské Pleso, close to the border with Poland, and has beautiful views over three valleys, two of them lake filled.

Kopské Sedlo (Stack Saddle, 1749m) The 'official meeting point' of the High and White Tatras, and therefore the easternmost point of the High Tatras. There are actually two saddles here – the northernmost is the higher one. Together they cover a broad, grassy expanse where three valleys meet – Zadné Meďodoly, Predné Meďodoly and Dolina Bielych Plies. This area was once the location of some unsuccessful copper mines.

Kopské Sedlo is one of the best viewpoints in the Tatras, reached by easy routes, yet the distance from the nearest transport ensures that it rarely gets crowded. If not too windy it makes a great picnic spot, and there is a table at the lower, southernmost saddle, which also has an excellent view down Dolina Bielych Plies to the Sub-Tatras Basin. Three White Tatras peaks are visible from here are – Havran (2152m), Hlúpy (2061m), and Košiare (2011m) with its three distinctive humps. Close by, to the southeast, with a green, rounded summit, is Belianská Kopa (1832m). To the south is Kežmarský Štít (2558m), and to the southwest, with its lone pinnacle, is Jahňací Štít (2229m).

Kotlový Štít (2601m) The peak that hides Gerlachovský Štít from the Sub-Tatras Basin. It is the ninth highest in the Tatras.

Kriváň (the Crooked One, 2494m) Though only 15th in the overall 'peaking order', this is the second highest summit on the Tatras waymarked network. The distinctive and imposing curved shape that gave rise to its name is best seen from Podbanské and Pribylina (a village to the southwest of Podbanské on the way to Liptovské Hrádok). This peculiarity proved irresistible to early climbers, who included the Scotsman Robert Townson in 1793 (the first recorded ascent), the Swedish naturalist Göran Wahlenberg in 1813, and King Friedrich August II of Saxony in 1840. Kriváň has become the national symbol of Slovakia, because it can be seen from such a great distance. In 1841 a pilgrimage to the summit by Slovak writers and poets took place, and since 1955 this has been commemorated with an annual pilgrimage at the end of August.

Ľadový Štít (Icy Peak, 2627m) The fourth highest summit in the High Tatras, it dominates the head of Malá Studená Dolina behind Téryho Chata, northwest of Starý Smokovec. The first recorded climb was by the Irishman John Ball in 1843.

Ľaliové Sedlo (Lily Saddle, 1947m) The official meeting point (according to the Slovaks, but not the Poles) of High and Western Tatras, therefore the westernmost point of the High Tatras. It lies north of Tri Studničky, on the border between Slovakia and Poland. Though on one of the waymarked routes in Poland (where it is known simply as Liliowe, and the altitude is given as 1952m), at the time of writing it is accessible to walkers from Slovakia only if accompanied by a mountain guide, using an unwaymarked path that starts from Sedlo Závory.

Litvorová Dolina (Angelica Valley – marked on maps as Litvorová Kotlina) Once a popular sheep pasture, this high valley and its tarn are now much visited by walkers crossing the saddles of Polský Hrebeň and Prielom.

Lomnické Sedlo (Lomnica Saddle, 2189m) An easily visited saddle at the top of the chair-lift from Skalnaté Pleso, northwest of Tatranská Lomnica. There are spectacular views over the Sub-Tatras Basin and over the Päť Spišských Plies (Five Spiš Tarns). A formerly waymarked path to it, shown on older maps (an extension of Green 5808), is no longer accessible to walkers, as it has been obliterated by the popular ski slope that descends from here.

Lomnický Štít (Lomnica Peak, 2634m) The second highest summit in the Tatras, whose first recorded ascent was by the Scotsman Robert Townson on 17 August 1793 with two local hunters as his guides. However, it is believed that an ascent was made some years earlier by a local shoemaker, Štefan Fábry. At that time it was thought by the local Spiš people to be the highest Tatras peak, and they called it Dedko (grandfather), while its slightly lower neighbour, Kežmarský Štít, was Babka (grandmother). Since 1940 it has been served by cable-car from Skalnaté Pleso (see Mountain Transport, page 160) and is accessible on foot only if accompanied by a local mountain guide. At the summit are a café, a refreshment kiosk and an astronomical and meteorological station of the Slovak Academy of Science.

Lučivná (799m) A village and climatic spa in the Sub-Tatras Basin, lying midway between Štrba and Svit.

Lysá Poľana (Bald Meadow, 970m) A small settlement that developed around the customs post on the border with Poland, beside the river called Biela Voda in Slovak or Białka in Polish (both mean or imply White Water). In Poland its name is written Łysa Polana, with a slightly different pronunciation. On the Slovak side of the border are a large car park and couple of shops selling souvenirs and alcohol, while there are toilets and another car park on the Polish side. Buses come from Poprad, Starý Smokovec and Tatranská Lomnica in Slovakia, and from Zakopane in Poland. On the Slovak side, the bus stop is in the car park opposite the buffet. On the Polish side, buses stop beside the border post en route between Zakopane and Poľana Palenica (shown as Palenica Białczańska on some maps).

Malá Studená Dolina (Little Cold Valley) A comparatively short (4km) but much visited valley in the central High Tatras, north of Starý Smokovec. There are two popular chalets – Zamkovského Chata at the foot, and Téryho Chata at the head – and the upper part contains the Päť Spišských Plies (Five Spiš Tarns).

Matejovce – see Poprad.

Mengusovce (810m) A village southwest of Starý Smokovec, with fine views of the High Tatras. It was founded in the 13th century as part of the estate of the neighbouring village of Batizovce. The village has an attractive Roman Catholic church.

Mengusovská Dolina A much-used valley climbing northwards from Štrbské Pleso, past the popular tarn of Popradské Pleso, towards Veľké Hincovo Pleso (qv) and Rysy summit.

Mlynica (688m) A small village in the Sub-Tatras Basin, lying between Tatranská Lomnica and Poprad. Founded in the 13th century by immigrants from Saxony, it became the first protestant village in the Spiš region. It has two churches now, one Catholic (dating from the 13th century), the other evangelical (19th century). In the second half of the 19th century it provided many mountain guides for excursions into the Tatras. Mlynica is also the name of the stream that flows through Štrbské Pleso to join the River Poprad at Svit.

Mlynická Dolina The 6km long valley in which Štrbské Pleso lies. In its upper part can be found the beautiful Skok waterfall and a large number of small tarns. Now popular ski terrain in winter, it was formerly much used for sheep grazing.

Modré Pleso (Blue Tarn, 2190m) The highest tarn in the Slovak High Tatras, it lies just below the saddle called Sedielko, at the head of Malá Studená Dolina to the north of Starý Smokovec.

Nadbanské (970m) Normally a peaceful hamlet lying just to the east of Podbanské, at the foot of the west slope of Kriváň, this was where the Tatranská Bora first struck in November 2004 (see page 72). Its name means 'above the mine' (compare Podbanské), and derives from the copper mines that existed here until the 19th century. There are no facilities here for walkers.

Nálepkova Chata – see Zamkovského Chata.

Nižné Hágy (910m) (Lower Hágy) A hamlet between Vyšné Hágy and Stôla, served by the bus from Štrbské Pleso to Poprad via Svit.

Nižné Rakytovské Pleso (Low Rakytov Tarn, 1323m) The lowest tarn in the Slovak High Tatras, situated 2km west of Štrbské Pleso – it is the larger of the two tarns shown there.

Nižné Temnosmrečinské Pleso (Lower Spruce Tarn, 1674m) A large and pretty tarn at the end of the waymarked path along Kôprová Dolina, northwest of Štrbské Pleso.

Nižné Wahlenbergovo Pleso (Lower Wahlenberg Tarn, 2053m) A tarn passed on the waymarked route along Furkotská Dolina, northwest of Štrbské Pleso.

Nová Lesná (New Forest, 746m) A village lying a little to the east of the main road between Starý Smokovec and Poprad, with panoramic views of the High Tatras. It has for many years been the home of leading Tatras guides, including Jan Still, one of the first people to reach the summit of Gerlachovský Štít.

Nová Polianka (New Polianka, 1000m) A hamlet on Cesta Slobody (Freedom Highway) between Starý Smokovec and Štrbské Pleso. Walkers can slake their thirst in the bar of the Vojenský Ústav Dýchacich Chorob (Military Institute for Respiratory Ailments).

Nový Smokovec (New Smokovec, 1000m) The western part of the Smokovec community. Nový Smokovec was established in the second half of the 19th century by the physician Dr Mikulás Szontagh. One of the pensions here, Villa Dr Szontagh, doubled as his home and a sanatorium for his richest patients. The buildings called Palace Grand and Branisko are sanatoria-hotels. You cannot help but notice the hulking great sanatorium called Royal Palace, looming up behind the railway station. Built in 1925, it had in its heyday a worldwide reputation for luxury. Of more modest proportions, but almost as noticeable, is the circular Hotel Atrium. Nearby is Hotel MS-70 (closed at time of writing), which was built as the press centre for the World Nordic Ski Championships in 1970. In winter the terrain above Nový Smokovec, called Jakubková Lúka (Jacob's Meadow), is alive with downhill skiers. At the west end of the resort is an estate called Sibír, with its own railway station and some pensions – it means Siberia!

Nové Štrbské Pleso (New Štrba Tarn, 1305m) This small, artificial tarn was created in the late 19th century out of the swamp that previously occupied the land southeast of Štrbské Pleso. There are several hotels, including one (Hotel Baník) beside the lake where refreshments can be obtained.

Obrovský Vodopád (Giant's Waterfall, 1400m) The bridge over Malý Studený Potok (Little Cold Brook) provides an excellent view of the waterfall. Until the late 19th century a smugglers' path led from here into Poland. Note how the trees nearby cling almost impossibly to the rock face.

Ostrva (1984m) A minor summit dominating Popradské Pleso, from which Red 0930 zigzags up the north slope to a saddle below the summit at 1962m. The broad summit itself, though not on the waymarked route, is easily accessible to and generally visited by walkers for the panoramic views.

Päť Spišských Plies (Five Spiš Tarns) A group of small and pretty tarns at the head of Malá Studená Dolina, to the north of Starý Smokovec. They are best viewed from the saddle called Sedielko. Nearby is the chalet Téryho Chata.

Pekná Vyhliadka – see Horný Smokovec.

Plesnivec – see Chata Plesnivec.

Pod Muráňom (Below Muráň, 1100m) A forester's house and mountain rescue centre near the foot of Javorová Dolina, 2km southeast of Javorina. Muráň is the distinctive slab of a mountain, the westernmost summit of the White Tatras, that rears above the farm.

Podbanské (Below the Mine, 940m) A quiet village at the foot of Kôprová Dolina between the High and Western Tatras. Nowadays left in peace from main road traffic by a bypass, it has a relaxed atmosphere, though a series of battles of the Slovak National Uprising were fought here during 1944–5. In the village centre refreshments can be obtained at Krčma pod Kriváňom (Tavern below Kriváň), and there is a grocery (*potraviny*). Refreshments and meals can also be obtained at Hotel Kriváň – from the village centre take the path up the hill behind Krčma pod Kriváňom.

Just 1000m up the valley is Grand Hotel Permon, reached on its own service road from the village (separate from the track used by Yellow 8851). It was built during the communist era as a trade union holiday centre, and has a large indoor swimming pool, conference facilities and a truly grand view of Kriváň.

Buses from Štrbské Pleso to Liptovský Hrádok go via Podbanské – the bus stops are 50m south of the main road junction. No timetable is displayed by the stops, but you can get them from the reception desk at Hotel Kriváň, nearby. There is a car park by the main road junction.

Podspády (Underslope, 912m) A quiet village on the Javorinka river on the north side of the White Tatras, 5km from the Polish border. There is a small supermarket at the village centre. Buses from Poprad to Lysá Poľana stop at Podspády, and go via Starý Smokovec and Tatranská Lomnica.

Poľana Kamzík – see Starolesnianska Poľana.

Poľský Hrebeň (Polish Ridge, 2200m) A saddle on the main ridge of the High Tatras, northwest of Starý Smokovec, linking the valleys Velická Dolina and Bielovodská Dolina. Its name may come from past use by, depending on your source of information, shepherds or smugglers from Poland.

Poprad (672m) The main commercial centre for the Tatras region, with a population of around 55,000, it is a busy town with a pleasantly pedestrianised central area of shops and restaurants. The town grew up around a number of villages after the opening of the railway to Košice in 1871. It has never had any historical significance, but there is a historic old quarter called Spišská Sobota (qv) and the town is home to one of Slovakia's leading ice-hockey teams. The suburbs of Veľká, Matejovce and Stráže pod Tatrami, formerly separate villages, are also worth exploring.

Among the buildings of interest are the Renaissance bell tower, the Gothic church of Svätý Juraja (St George), and the Sub-Tatras Museum. Another good reason for a visit is the stunning view of the whole High Tatras range from various points in the town, including the airport (which was funded by Bata, the famous shoe manufacturer). There are frequent train and bus connections to and from all the main Tatras resorts in Slovakia – the trains to Starý Smokovec and Štrbské Pleso leave from the high-level part of the railway station.

Popradské Pleso (Poprad Tarn, 1494m) A large tarn that is the popular target of an easy stroll from Štrbské Pleso. It has long been on the tourist trail, with a first recorded mention by the local naturalist, David Frölich, during the first half of the 17th century. There is now a railway station named after it, though this is an hour away on foot – see Blue 2902. The tarn is in a beautiful setting beneath the towering summit of Ostrva, but the collection of refreshments kiosks and the throng of customers on the west shore may be a detraction for some. It is sometimes called Malé Rybie Pleso (Little Fish Tarn).

The Poprad river, which issues from the tarn, flows through the town of the same name, then continues through Poland to join the Dunajec and then the Vistula into the Baltic Sea. All the streams further west feed the Váh, a tributary of the Danube, which of course flows to the Black Sea.

On the west shore of the tarn is one of the most visited chalets in the Slovak High Tatras, developed from a log cabin built in 1879. During the late 19th and early 20th centuries, it suffered the fate of being burned down or pulled down, then rebuilt, several times. For a while it was run as a mountain hotel called Chata Kapitána Morávku, after Captain Štefan Morávek, who was killed in 1945 while leading a Slovak partisan reconnaissance patrol. Now calling itself Horský Hotel Popradské Pleso (phone 910 948160, www.popradskepleso.sk), it provides meals and refreshments all year round, and can accommodate about 120 people in simple bedrooms and small dormitories.

A second chalet was under construction at the time of writing, to be called Majláthova Chata. This was the name of the original chalet, after Vojtech Majláth, President of the Hungarian Carpathian Union.

Predné Meďodoly (Front Copper Mines) A gently sloping valley between the High and White Tatras, for long it was an idyllic sheep pasture, but during the 17th and 18th centuries both this and Zadné Meďodoly (Back Copper Mines) became the scene of unsuccessful copper-mining activities.

Predné Solisko (Front Solisko, 2093m) A minor summit which, being one of the easiest high viewpoints to reach in the High Tatras, with the help of the chair-lift, tends to get very busy. There are three higher summits – Štrbské Solisko (2302m) can be seen looking northwest from Predné Solisko, Malé Solisko (2334) and Veľké Solisko (2404m) are out of sight beyond Štrbské Solisko, and to the south is a splendid view over Štrbské Pleso to the Sub-Tatras Basin. Other summits in view are: Satan (bearing 20, 2422m), Patria (bearing 85, 2203m), Kriváň (bearing 290, 2494m) and Krátka (bearing 300, 2370m).

Priečne Sedlo (Transverse Saddle, 2352m) A deep saddle between Široká Veža and Priečna Veža, northwest of Starý Smokovec. It is well used, being on a popular route between the valleys of Malá and Veľká Studená Dolina. From here can be seen the summits of Slavkovský Štít and Bradavica, and there are fine views over the two valleys with their chalets (Zbojnícka Chata and Téryho Chata).

Prielom (Crack, 2288m) An aptly named pass, literally a crack in the mountains, to the northwest of Starý Smokovec. It is difficult to negotiate, with steep drops and fixed chains on both sides.

Prostredný Hrot (Middle Edge, 2440m) This summit north of Starý Smokovec, above Téryho Chata, is off the waymarked network, but can be visited with a mountain guide. It is not difficult to reach, and has a magnificent view over the Sub-Tatras Basin.

Rainerova Chata – see Starolesnianska Poľana.

Rysy (Gashes, 2500m) On the border between Poland and Slovakia, this popular summit is the highest in Poland, the highest in Slovakia on the waymarked network, and therefore the highest point in the High Tatras that can be reached without a mountain guide. There are actually two summits, shown on the map as 2503.0m on the Slovak side and 2498.7m on the Polish side. For the origin of the name, see the gazetteer in Section 4 on Poland. Vladimir Ilyich Lenin is supposed to have climbed Rysy, and there used to be a plaque to record this feat, but it has now been removed, and there seems to be some doubt about the veracity of the story.

Sedielko (Little Saddle, 2372m) This is the highest saddle on the waymarked route network in the Tatras. It lies to the north of Starý Smokovec and has good views over the Päť Skišských Plies (Five Spiš Tarns) and Zadná Dolina, the upper part of Javorová Dolina.

Sibír – see Nový Smokovec.

Široké Sedlo (Wide Saddle, 1830m) The central saddle of the White Tatras range, situated between the peaks of Ždiarska Vidla (Ždiar's Pitchfork, 2146m) and Hlúpy (Stupid, 2061m), it lies on the one accessible walking route across the White Tatras. Southwards from here you have a marvellous view of the easternmost peaks of the High Tatras, dominated by Jahňací Štít in the foreground and Lomnický Štít in the background. Northeast lies the village of Ždiar, with the Spišská Magura range behind it. Beyond, in good weather, you can see the Pieniny mountains in Poland.

Skalnatá Chata (Rocky Chalet, 1725m) A mountain chalet just a few hundred metres south of the gondola-lift top station at Skalnaté Pleso, on the Tatranská Magistrála. Refreshments are available and there is also a small dormitory with four beds (phone 052 446 7075). It lies on the site of one of the very first 'refuges' in the High Tatras, consisting of an overhanging rock called Ohnisko (Fireplace). Eventually a simple chalet was built in 1914, and this has been rebuilt several times. At the time of writing the warden was Ladislav (Laco) Kulanga, who holds several records for carrying on his back the heaviest weight of goods to various chalets, said to be equivalent to a family of two adults and two children!

Skalnaté Pleso (Rocky Tarn, 1751m) A small but well-visited tarn beside the top station of the gondola-lift from Tatranská Lomnica, which is a little higher at 1761m. The bottom stations of the chair-lift and cable-car to Lomnické Sedlo and Lomnický Štít respectively are also located here (see Mountain Transport, page 160). The huge and rather ugly top station contains a restaurant, a café and toilets. The observatory and other buildings above the far side of the tarn belong to the Slovak Academy of Science, and 18 new comets have been discovered from there – so far. Some maps show the nearby building Encian (Gentian) at this location – it was once a mountain hotel, but was closed at the time of writing. There is an educational trail around the lake (see page 70).

Skok (more properly Vodopád Skok, Jump Waterfall, 1780m) An impressive waterfall in Mlynická Dolina, north of Štrbské Pleso, from some parts of which it is visible. Nearby is a tarn called Pleso Nad Skokom (Tarn above Skok).

Slavkovský Štít (Slavkov Peak, 2452m) The fourth highest peak on the waymarked route network in the Slovak High Tatras, named after the village of Slavkov near Poprad. A major earthquake several thousand years ago (see also Vodopády Studeného Potoka) is thought to have dislodged the top of Slavkovský Štít, which until then was probably the highest in the Tatras. This was the target of one of the earliest recorded ascents in the High Tatras, by Juraj Buchholz in 1664.

From the summit there is a grandstand view over the Sub-Tatras Basin, while other major peaks in sight are: Gerlachovský Štít (bearing 265, 2654m), Bradavica (bearing 280, 2476m), Javorový Štít (bearing 335, 2417m), Široká Veža (due north, 2461m), Prostredný Hrot (bearing 15, 2440m), Lomnický Štít (bearing 30, 2634m).

Sliezsky Dom – see Velické Pleso.

Spišská Sobota (680m) Now one of the oldest parts of Poprad, this was once the wealthiest town in the Sub-Tatras Basin in its own right, until the rise of Poprad itself in the late 19th century. It is well worth a visit from your Tatras resort, having been very sympathetically restored, with a central square around which are many glorious buildings, including the Gothic church of Svätý Juraja (St George), Renaissance houses and memorials galore. Some of the buildings now house restaurants serving traditional food.

Stará Lesná (Old Forest, 740m) A one-street village south of Tatranská Lomnica, at its north end are Hotel Horizont (restaurant) and Hotel Ceva (snack bar, coffee shop and swimming pool). The church dates from the 13th century, but was rebuilt in the Baroque style in the 18th century. Some buses from Tatranská Lomnica to Kežmarok go via Stará Lesná.

Starolesnianska Poľana (Old Forest Meadow, 1295m, formerly Poľana Kamzík) A clearing a little to the north of Hrebienok, which was the site of the first mountain chalet in the Slovak Tatras. Called Rainerova Chata, it was built in 1863 by Ján Juraj Rainer, who developed the spa at Starý Smokovec. It burned down and was replaced in 1884 by Chata Kamzík (Chamois Chalet), but that was closed in the 1970s when its sewage started to cause hygiene problems for the villages below. The raised foundations remain, and provide a popular picnic site in a sunny location. A simple, small-scale version of the original chalet, also called Rainerova Chata, was erected amongst the foundations in 1980 to serve as a shelter. Then in 1998 it was upgraded to provide a limited range of refreshments, postcards, souvenirs and information. It also contains a small exhibition on the history of mountain porters and equipment. It does not offer overnight accommodation. This well-wooded area abounds in limba-fir, rowan and bilberries.

Štart (1120m) The middle station of the gondola-lift from Tatranská Lomnica to Skalnaté Pleso. There are no facilities here for walkers.

Starý Smokovec (Old Smokovec, 1010m) The administrative centre of the whole High Tatras region, which has been elevated to the status of City of Vysoké Tatry. It is joined to Nový Smokovec and Horný Smokovec (qqv) to form the community that you will sometimes see written as Smokovce (the plural form). Hiding away off the main roads 1.5km to the southwest is the separate village of Dolný Smokovec (qv). You can understand why this location was chosen as a recuperation centre – there is a healthy, clean feeling about the place, imbued by the scent of pine trees.

Starý Smokovec is the oldest resort in the High Tatras, established in 1793. At that time, being in the German-speaking province of Zips in the Austrian Empire, it was called Schmecks, which is colloquial German for 'tastes good' (referring to the spa water), and eventually this became Smokovec in Slovak. One of the oldest and most attractive remaining buildings from that period is Villa Flora, on the main road, built in 1839. Nearby Villa Alica was recently restored by Norwegian interests.

In the northeastern corner of the village is the original spring that led to the establishment of Starý Smokovec as a spa. At the time of writing it was a simple affair, consisting of a small circular stone structure where anyone could fill up their own bottles for free. This laid-back state of affairs may not last much longer. The water, known as *kyselka*, contains iron and has an unusual and slightly acidic taste that is quite refreshing. It occurs in several places in the Carpathians, and elsewhere is bottled and sold commercially.

In the lower part of the village is Hotel Smokovec, regarded as the community's central point. The busy station regularly sees three trains on adjacent platforms – once passengers have alighted or changed trains they set off almost simultaneously for either Poprad, Tatranská Lomnica or Štrbské Pleso. Close by you will find the post office, supermarket and other shops, restaurants, bars, and the Policlinic (health centre).

In the upper part is the imposing Grand Hotel, built in 1904. Nearby are the Catholic church (1894) and the bottom station of the funicular to Hrebienok (qv).

A pleasant tree-lined pedestrian thoroughfare (unnamed) leads westwards to Nový Smokovec, passing the huge Palace spa-sanatorium. Many of the large buildings that look like hotels in Starý Smokovec are actually spas.

There is an educational trail around the village, with seven panels, but they are in Slovak only, and at the time of writing no English translation was available.

Stôla (860m) A typical old village of the Sub-Tatras Basin, lying just off the road from Vyšné Hágy to Mengusovce, it was once a centre of manufacture of sembra pine oil, used in local sanatoria. The heart of the village, with its church, lies on a side road to the west of the main road. There is a post office, small general store, buffet, and a sanatorium. Buses from Štrbské Pleso to Poprad via Svit stop at Stôla.

Štrba (827m) A large village in the Sub-Tatras Basin, founded in the 13th century, it developed following the building of the railway line to Košice, and was especially noted as a base for carriage drivers.

Štrbské Pleso (Štrba Tarn, 1320m–1355m) A sprawling mountain resort, the highest community in Slovakia, established in 1873 beside the tarn above the town of Štrba, hence the name. Most facilities of use to walkers are grouped around the railway station – supermarket, open-air market and refreshments (*denný bar*, kiosks, and restaurants). The split-level station also contains toilets, a spacious waiting room and left luggage facilities. Most of the buildings in the resort are modern – some unfortunately rather too functional in design. At the north end of the village are the Patria and FIS Hotels, near the ski slopes. A side road near Hotel Patria leads to a long, cream-coloured building, which used to be a sanatorium but in 2009 became the Grand Hotel Kempinski High Tatras, currently the only five-star establishment in the area.

Štrbské Pleso is served by train from Poprad and Starý Smokovec, by rack railway from Tatranská Štrba, and by bus from Poprad, Starý Smokovec, Podbanské and other places in Slovakia. Private vehicles are banned from the village, and there is a car park on the approach road from Cesta Slobody (Freedom Highway) and another at the railway station.

This is Slovakia's leading winter sports resort – the World Nordic Championships were held here in 1970. The main ski facilities, dominated by two ski-jumps, are located on the north side of the tarn.

Note To reach the tarn from the railway/bus station, go to the right of the supermarket then climb the steps leading up to a road, which you cross, and continue ahead for 50m to the tarn. To reach the station from the southeast corner of the tarn, go to the left of a white electricity sub-station, cross the road then go down the steps.

A footpath completely encircles the tarn itself (1350m), which contains several rare species of fish. It passes a monument to Maša Haľamová (1908–1995), a renowned Slovak poet who lived here for many years. There are good views here – to one side, over the tarn towards Vysoká and its neighbouring peaks, to the other over the plain of Liptovská Kotlina. On the western shore is a small peninsula, where seats provide a pleasant resting place, and on which is located a memorial (inscribed *čest ich pamiatke*, meaning 'in their memory') to the Slovak national heroes Jan Rašo (killed 26 September 1944) and Štefan Morávka (killed 14 January 1945), after whom two nearby mountain chalets were formerly named.

See also Nové Štrbské Pleso.

Studený Potok (Cold Stream) One of the main streams in the High Tatras, it is formed by its tributaries where they merge on leaving the valleys of Malá Studená Dolina and Veľká Studená Dolina. The stream flows southeast to join the River Poprad at Veľká Lomnica, where the railway station is also called Studený Potok, and the line from Tatranská Lomnica meets the one from Poprad to Kežmarok and beyond.

Svinica (Porcine, 2300m) The westernmost peak in the High Tatras, lying on the border with Poland.

Svit (717m) A small industrial town in the Sub-Tatras Basin to the south of Starý Smokovec, it was created in 1936 by the world-famous Czech shoe manufacturers Bata, and its name comes from the initials of the factory complex – Slovenská Viskozová Továreň (Slovak Viscose Factory).

Symbolický Cintorín (Symbolic Cemetery, 1540m) A memorial near the tarn called Popradské Pleso to those who gave their lives in the mountains. No one is buried here – there are just plaques and crosses, often decorated with flowers. There is a small chapel with a single bell inscribed in Slovak, 'In memory of the dead, a warning to the living. ' The 'cemetery', started in 1936, was the idea of Otakar Štafl, a painter of the Prague Academy, who was also for a while the manager of the chalet at Popradské Pleso. It is normally closed from 1 January to 15 June for reasons of nature conservation, and in any case its steep paths can be treacherous when icy. At the end of September each year the cemetery is the scene of the Mountain Rescue Service Day ceremony, in honour of the people who perform this valuable task. A small charge is payable at the chapel.

Tatranská Javorina – see Javorina.

Tatranská Kotlina (Tatras Basin, 760m–765m) A resort at the east end of the White Tatras, established in 1881. On the south side of the road in the village centre is a modern complex containing a supermarket, post office and café, serving a large spa. Nearby are a coffee bar (Kaviareň Čarda), and the hotel and conference centre Pavilón Fontána. At the north end of the village, at the foot of the path leading to Belianska Jaskyňa (qv), is a car park, buffet and small store. 1km south, at the main road junction, is Penzión Limba, which has a restaurant. The Tatranská Bora (see page 72) blew itself out here after causing such havoc in November 2004.

Tatranská Lesná (905m) A small holiday resort on the railway between Starý Smokovec and Tatranská Lomnica. Refreshments can be obtained at two guest houses that were formerly trade union holiday centres – Penzión Erika and Penzión Karpatia. There is no car park.

Tatranská Lomnica (850m–860m) A spacious village, one of the largest resorts in the High Tatras, with many facilities and excellent transport connections. It was established in 1893 with the construction of the Hotel Lomnica, near the station. This handsome building is in typical Tatras style, but at the time of writing closed and in a sad state of disrepair.

The resort has developed around a central park on the hillside. The hotels Grandhotel Praha, Horec (Gentian) and Slovan are on the upper side of the park, others (Slovakia and Titris Odborár) are near the railway/bus stations on the lower side. The large, modern Hotel Morava on the upper side of the park is also a trade union holiday centre. There is a large residential development of private apartments on the west side of the village.

Tatranská Lomnica is a winter sports resort – lifts take skiers up to 2190m at Lomnické Sedlo. A more recent addition to the facilities is Tatrabob, an all-year-round bobsleigh run – a lift takes you to the top, then you launch yourself down the run, which winds down the hillside for 680m, with a drop of 45m.

At the east end is the TANAP (National Park) Museum, with an interesting display of Tatras wildlife, and an excellent audio-visual show once or twice daily, with an English commentary. Nearby is the Tatra Nature Exhibition with an interesting botanical garden. The village offers a good choice of refreshment facilities. The railway station is the terminus of branch lines from Starý Smokovec and from Studený Potok station at Veľká Lomnica. House martins that nest in the station buildings provide endless entertainment with their dazzling displays of precision flying. Buses link the village with all parts of the High Tatras, Poprad, Kežmarok and many other nearby towns in Slovakia. There are two car parks on the west side of the village.

Tatranská Polianka (1005m–1010m) A small spa resort 3km southwest of Starý Smokovec, founded in 1885, in its early days it became a leading ski resort, and the first international race took place here, but there are now no ski facilities left. There is a small supermarket at the village centre, buses and trains between Starý Smokovec and Štrbské Pleso stop here, and there is a car park.

Tatranská Štrba (827m) A village to the south of Štrbské Pleso, which has developed around its station (called plain Štrba) on the main line from Bratislava to Košice – this is in fact the highest main-line railway station in Slovakia. A rack railway connection to Štrbské Pleso itself also starts here. In the village is Tatranský Lieskovec (Tatras Hazelnut), a complex of apartments for people working in the High Tatras resorts.

Tatranské Matliare (885m) A small but long-established holiday resort northeast of Tatranská Lomnica, with a couple of trade union holiday centres, Hutník I and II, where refreshments can be obtained. The former luxury Hotel Esplanade is now an army health centre, also offering accommodation and refreshments to the public. The novelist Franz Kafka was a patient here. Buses from Starý Smokovec and Tatranská Lomnica to Lysá Poľana stop here.

Tatranské Zruby (Tatras Log Cabins, 990m) Since 1923 a rest centre for the military southwest of Nový Smokovec, but tourists are welcome at its Koliba bar. Buses and trains between Starý Smokovec and Štrbské Pleso stop here. There is no car park.

Ťažká Dolina – see Česká Dolina.

Téryho Chata (Téry's Chalet, 2015m, phone 052 442 5245, open all year) An isolated chalet at the head of Malá Studená Dolina, near Päť Spišských Plies (Five Spiš Tarns). Built in 1899, it was named after Dr Edmund Téry (1856–1917), a Hungarian physician, mountaineer and pioneer of tourism development in the Tatras. The chalet is now owned by KST (Klub Slovenských Turystov/Slovak Touring Club) and has 24 beds in dormitories.

Tri Studničky (Three Little Wells, 1180m) A charming and peaceful rural hamlet, built on a slope in the foothills of Kriváň, well away from the main road. TANAP (the national park authority) has a base here. Close by to the south is a splendid example of a typical Tatras 'hatstand' signpost. There are no facilities for walkers in the hamlet.

One kilometre south is a monument (*pomník*) to Captain Jan Rašo, a partisan who was killed during a battle of the Slovak National Uprising on 26 September 1944. A mountain chalet nearby called Važecka Chata was burned down during the battle. It was replaced by one called Chata Kapitána Rašu, in his memory, but that too burned down in 1993, and there are no plans to replace it.

Važec (792m) A village in the Liptov Basin southwest of Štrbské Pleso, from which it can be reached by train or bus. Founded in the 13th century, it was rebuilt in 1931 after being destroyed by fire. On the southwest side of the village is Važecká Jaskyňa, a 400m long limestone cave, which is open to the public.

Važecká Dolina A valley on the south side of Kriváň, once a popular walking route to the summit (the uncoloured path can still be seen on the map), but now a strict nature reserve.

Velické Pleso (1663m). A quietly situated tarn at the foot of Gerlachovský Štít. At its south end is Sliezsky Dom (Silesian House, 1670m, phone 091 188 2879, e-mail recepcia@sliezskydom.sk, website www.sliezskydom.sk), a spacious three-star mountain hotel providing meals and refreshments all year round, as well as 130 beds in bedrooms and a dormitory. The present building, opened in 1968, has several predecessors – the first, built in 1874, was destroyed by an avalanche. The name comes from the Silesian section of the Hungarian Carpathian Association, which built one of the early chalets.

Veľká Lomnica (639m) A large village in the Sub-Tatras Basin to the southeast of Tatranská Lomnica. It is one of the oldest settlements in the area, having been established by a Slavonic tribe in the seventh century on the site of a Neolithic settlement. Its railway station is called Studený Potok (qv).

Veľká Studená Dolina (Great Cold Valley) One of the most visited valleys in the High Tatras, 5.5km long, close to the north of Starý Smokovec. Hrebienok, the upper terminus of the funicular, lies above its southern slopes. The broad head of the valley contains no less than 27 small tarns, at the centre of which lies the popular chalet Zbojnícka Chata. Until 1901, when it was acquired by the state, the valley belonged to the parish of Stará Lesná.

Veľká Svišťovka (Great Little Marmot, 2037m) A fairly easily accessible minor summit at the east end of the High Tatras, with fine views of the White Tatras, across the Sub-Tatras Basin, and down to Zelené Pleso. The distinctive summit on bearing 35 is Bujačí Vrch (Bull Hill, 1946m), the easternmost of the White Tatras. On bearing 310 is Jahňací Štít (2229m) in the High Tatras.

Veľké Biele Pleso (Great White Tarn, 1612m) A magical, yet rather melancholy, spot on the way to Kopské Sedlo, north of Tatranská Lomnica. The largest of several small tarns in Dolina Bielych Plies (White Tarns Valley), it is a splendid place for a picnic, with several tables, and a view up to the pass of Kopské Sedlo

(1749m) and the minor summit of Belianská Kopa (White Stack, 1832m). Some of the tables have been placed near the foundations of the former Kežmarská Chata (Kežmarok Chalet), which was dismantled when the White Tatras were closed to visitors in 1978. Between the two world wars it was used as an army training centre, but the foundations and some piles of bricks are all that remain.

Veľké Hincovo Pleso (1946m) The largest and deepest tarn in the Slovak High Tatras, lying close to the border with Poland at the foot of Kôprovský Štít, north of Štrbské Pleso. It covers about 20 hectares, is 53m deep, and contains 4 million cubic metres of water.

Veľký Slavkov (677m) A large village in the Sub-Tatras Basin, lying a little to the east of the main road from Poprad to Starý Smokovec. It was established by Germanic people in the 13th century, and its Gothic church dates from this period. There is also an evangelical church of the 18th century.

Veľký Studený Potok (Great Cold Stream) It is the tradition that, if you like it here, and throw a coin from the footbridge into the brook, you will return! The coins are collected to help with chalet maintenance, if possible before the spring, otherwise the torrent of meltwater carries the coins to an unknown fate further downstream. The bridge is located on Red 0930B, a few minutes' walk beyond Starolesnianska Poľana north of Starý Smokovec. For most of the year the water here is very blue, clear and soft – this is because of its purity, coming from granite rock with no mineral salts, but in May and early June melted snow turns it to a blue-grey foam.

Vodopády Studeného Potoka (Cold Stream Waterfalls) A pretty series of cascades at the confluence of the two streams that form Studený Potok, to the north of Starý Smokovec. Two minutes' walk along Red 0930B from here, towards Hrebienok, you can see a large, flat and rocky open area, which until thousands of years ago was the bed of a lake, until a violent earthquake removed the moraine that dammed it, allowing the water to escape (see also Slavkovský Štít).

Východná Vysoká (Eastern Tall One, 2428m) The fourth highest summit on the waymarked route network in Slovakia, with excellent views. It lies above the saddle called Poľský Hrebeň, northwest of Starý Smokovec.

Vyšné Hágy (Upper Hágy, 1085m–1125m) A settlement to the east of Štrbské Pleso, consisting almost entirely of an extensive sanatorium complex that specialises in the cure of tuberculosis and respiratory ailments. It can be the starting point for walks, but there are no facilities for walkers. Buses and trains between Štrbské Pleso and Starý Smokovec stop here, as do buses from Štrbské Pleso to Poprad via Štôla. There are several car parks along Cesta Slobody (Freedom Highway) on the west side of the village.

Vyšné Wahlenbergovo Pleso (Upper Wahlenberg Tarn, 2157m) The second highest tarn in the Slovak High Tatras, northwest of Štrbské Pleso, it is named after Göran Wahlenberg (1780–1851), a Swedish naturalist who explored the High Tatras and described its plantlife in his book *Flora Karpatorum Principalium.*

Vysoká (Tall One, 2560m) One of the most imposing mountains in the High Tatras, with its twin peaks, it is eminently visible to the northeast from Štrbské Pleso. The first recorded ascent was in 1874, by the Hungarian Mor Dechy, accompanied by local guides.

Žabí Kôň (Frog Horse, 2291m) A relatively low peak on the west side of Rysy, but locally famous as the place where climbers take their 'graduation test', as it is a notoriously difficult climb.

Zamkovského Chata (Zamkovský Chalet, 1475m, phone 052 442 2636, e-mail zamka@zamka.sk, website www.zamka.sk) A very popular chalet, offering refreshment and accommodation (25 beds in small dormitories) all year round. It is situated above Malý Studený Potok to the north of Starý Smokovec, within easy reach of the funicular at Hrebienok. It was built in 1943 and named after Štefan Zamkovský (1908–61), a well-known Tatras mountaineer and guide. After the Second World War it was renamed Nálepkova Chata, or Chata Kapitána Nálepku, after Captain Ján Nálepka, who came from this area but was killed in battle in Russia in 1943. In 1991 it was returned to the Zamkovský family and reverted to the original name, although they have now sold it to private owners.

Zbojnícka Chata (Highwayman's Chalet, 1960m, mobile phone 0903 638000 www.zbojnickachata.sk) An isolated chalet in a lake-filled hanging valley above the head of Veľká Studená Dolina, northwest of Starý Smokovec. It takes its name from a nearby minor peak called Zbojnícky Chrbát (Highwayman's Back). The original chalet, constructed in 1907, was substantially rebuilt in 1984. It burned down in 1998 and was rebuilt in 2000 following an international appeal for funds, which received strong support in Britain. Now owned by KST, it offers refreshments all year round (including a delicious, spiced lemon tea) and accommodation for 16 people in a single dormitory.

Ždiar (896m) A large village on the east side of the White Tatras that straggles for several kilometres along the southern slopes of the Spišská Magura hills. It has many attractive shuttered wooden houses in the style of the Góral (mountain) people, who also inhabit the neighbouring region in Poland. There is a museum here called Ždiarsky Dom, devoted to the architecture and lifestyle of the Góral people, as well as a supermarket, small store, several restaurants, a hotel and many pensions.

Ždiarska Vidla (Ždiar's Pitchfork, 2146m) The second highest summit in the White Tatras.

Zelené Pleso (Green Tarn, 1545m) One of the loveliest places in the High Tatras, this is a popular resort for walkers and cyclists, and with local people, who come here to skate on the ice in late autumn. The water is actually green because of the way the light is affected by the mountains rising on three sides, but the legend is more romantic. A princess, it seems, fell asleep beside the tarn. She wore a ring containing a huge emerald, which caught the eye of a hawk. This felonous bird, perched on the great crag on the north side of the tarn, swooped down, removed the jewel and returned to its perch, but on the way dropped the emerald into the tarn. It could not be recovered, and the water turned green. The crag is called Jastrabia Veža, which means Hawk Tower.

Chata pri Zelenom Plese (Chalet at Green Tarn, 1551m, phone 0903 467 420, e-mail zelenepleso@zelenepleso.sk, www.zelenepleso.sk) is one of the most spectacularly situated chalets in the High Tatras. The original chalet here was built in 1897, replacing an earlier one on the south side of the tarn, and renovated in 1924. It had been called Chata pri Zelenom Plese, but after the Second World War was renamed Brnčalova Chata, in memory of Albert Brnčal, a celebrated mountaineer, teacher and Slovak nationalist who was killed in an accident at nearby Jastrabie Sedlo. The original name was resumed in 1991. Owned by KST, it offers refreshments, as well as 56 beds in dormitories, though you may need to book well in advance for these.

SECTION 4
THE POLISH TATRAS

LATER HISTORY

The plains and valleys on the north side of the Tatras (the region now called Podhale, meaning 'beneath the mountain meadows'), remained relatively uninhabited, at least as far as any recorded history is concerned, until the 13th century, when the earliest known settlement was established at Nowy Targ. It seems that the mountains were too much of a barrier to be surmounted by people living to the south, while those to the north relied too much on sea trade to venture so far from the Baltic Sea and the navigable rivers that feed it.

By this time, since about the mid 10th century, Poland had become recognised as an entity, with the Polish language becoming distinct from other Slavic tongues. Subsequent invasions reduced and even destroyed it as an independent state for many years. A golden age for Poland existed during the 16th century, and the First Polish Republic founded in 1569 lasted for 200 years.

Zakopane, first mentioned in a document signed by King Stefan Batory in 1578, may date from the 15th century. On some early maps it was shown as Zakopana. There are several competing explanations of the name's origin. The most likely seems to be from *za kopane*, literally meaning 'beyond the clearing' – and there is a place called Kopane on the slopes of the Gubałówka ridge. Others claim it means 'buried' or 'hidden' – a reference to the area's isolation from the rest of Poland at that time, or that it comes from *za kopanie* (By the Place Where Oats are Grown) – at that time it was a small farming settlement.

As in the Slovak Tatras, several tribes of varying origins, including Slavic and Germanic people, merged over several centuries into a distinctive culture, which became known as Góral, which means 'highlander'. The culture persists today in the area around Zakopane, and to a lesser extent around Ždiar in Slovakia, where the traditional costumes, cuisine, folklore and music can still be found.

In 1766 a foundry was established at Kuźnice ('smithy' in Polish) immediately to the south of Zakopane, using iron ore mined in the Tatras. It closed down in 1878, but the great waterwheel from that period still remains, close to the cablecar station.

In 1769 Poland ceased to exist as a state, as it was partitioned between Prussia, Russia and Austria–Hungary. Podhale then became a province of the Austro–Hungarian Empire, and was called Galizien in German. Austro–Hungarian rule was considered to be quite lenient, and the Polish language was allowed to continue in use.

At this time Zakopane became isolated from the rest of Poland. By the mid 19th century its different culture, dialect and beautiful scenery attracted intellectuals from all over Europe. Some buildings in the street in Zakopane called Kościeliska date from this period, as does the Old Church (Stary Kościół) of circa 1846.

Before the advent of accurate maps the exact line of national borders was in many places a vague notion in the minds of civil servants, and travellers in the 18th century were able to roam much of Europe with little hindrance and no need for passports. Thus the earliest recorded ascents of the Polish Tatras peaks were by people whose names we have already encountered in the Slovak section – in 1793 by the Scottish physician Robert Townson, and in 1843 by the Irishman John Bull, both accompanied by local hunters. Other summits were first climbed by local explorers, such as David Frölich, in the early 19th century.

At that time the Tatras were generally considered, abroad, to be part of Hungary, and Townson's illustrated book *Travels in Hungary,* published in 1797, became one of the classic works about these mountains.

A long-running border dispute between Galizien and its neighbouring Austro–Hungarian province of Zips (Spiš in Slovak), to the south, lasted 150 years, from around 1750 to 1902, and was eventually settled in court in favour of Galizien – see the gazetteer entry for Morskie Oko.

The greatest spur to the development of Podhale came with the railway line from Kraków to Zakopane, opened in 1899. Until then it took two days to cover this journey using horse-drawn vehicles. Thereafter, Zakopane quickly developed as a popular health resort.

Poland regained its independence in 1918 after the First World War, and the Second Polish Republic was established in 1921, but lasted just 18 years, until the Nazis invaded Poland in 1939. After the Second World War Poland became virtually a satellite of the Soviet Union. The rise of the Solidarity movement in the 1980s eventually led to the overthrow of the communist regime in 1989 and the establishment of the Third Polish Republic.

In 1999 Poland joined the NATO alliance, and in May 2004, together with Slovakia and eight other countries, it became a full member of the European Union. Although the country is fast catching up economically with other EU countries, rural areas are still quite underdeveloped, and you may see horse-drawn farm carts on country lanes.

Pope John Paul II

Karol Wojtyla was born near Kraków in 1920, and as a young man was a keen mountain walker, skier and footballer. He was ordained a priest in 1946 and quickly worked his way up the ranks, becoming Archbishop of Kraków in 1964, and created a cardinal in 1967. He was appointed Pope in 1978, and when he died in 2005 had become one of the longest-serving pontiffs, at 27 years.

He frequently visited the Tatras before his accession, and managed two visits during his papacy. As well as several churches in and around Zakopane, these included diversions into the mountain valleys – in June 1983, to Siwa Poľana and Dolina Chochołowska, and in June 1997 to Klastor SS Albertynek and Kasprowy Wierch. There are memorials or plaques at these places to mark his visit.

The Pope's route from Nowy Targ to Zakopane in 1997, along country lanes, was commemorated by naming it Droga Papieska (the Pope's Road), and a memorial to this event on the route north of Zakopane is passed by three of the routes described in the walks section – Red 014, Green 507 and Yellow 809.

WALKING

Zakopane, the main base in the Polish Tatras, is well located for exploration of both the Western and High Tatras on their Polish sides, so we cover both in this book. The town actually lies in the foothills of the Western Tatras. The High Tatras are within easy reach, but to explore the main part of the range you really first need to take a bus, taxi or cable-car.

There are fewer summits than in Slovakia, and they are not so high, though Rysy on the border can also be reached from Poland, and at 2500m is the country's highest peak. But the lakes are bigger than in Slovakia, there are excellent views of Slovakia's mountains, and Orla Perć (Eagle Edge), linking several high peaks, is the most challenging ridge route accessible without a guide in the High Tatras.

As the area available for walking in the Polish Tatras is smaller than the Slovak equivalent, and Poland has a much larger population, popular routes and honeypots tend to get more crowded on this side. In particular, Kuźnice, Kasprowy Wierch, Morskie Oko, Dolina Kościeliska and Giewont can get very busy, especially at peak periods. You may prefer to avoid them, at least at weekends, or try to get there early.

All of Poland's highest summits are to be found here in the Tatras, and most are accessible without a guide, being well waymarked. As well as Rysy, Świnica (2301m), Kozi Wierch (2291m), Granaty (2235m), Szpiglasowy Wierch (2172m) and Kościelec (2155m) all provide rewarding targets for experienced walkers, and several high passes can be reached, such as Mięguszowiecka Przełęcz (2307m), Zawrat (2158m), Krzyżne (2113m) and Wrota Chałubińskiego (2022m).

Orla Perć – approaching Świnica from the east (Red 009B) (photo: R Turnbull)

Giewont, a Western Tatras peak known as the the 'sleeping giant', though of relatively low altitude by Tatras standards, will provide a fairly challenging test early in your holiday, with some scrambling and fixed chains. It has two peaks at 1894m and 1728m and is eminently visible from Zakopane. Only the higher peak, with its enormous iron cross, is accessible.

Some fine ridge walking is easily accessible in the Western Tatras from Zakopane. A splendid 8km walk, not too difficult, runs along the frontier ridge through the Czerwone Wierchy (Red Hills). Despite the relaxation of border controls, in practice this route is only accessible from the Polish side. From Ciemniak in the west to Kasprowy Wierch in the east, it switchbacks between 1800m and 2100m, with outstanding views into both Poland and Slovakia.

Waymarks in the Polish Tatras are similar to those on the Slovak side, ie two white bands sandwiching a third band of the route's colour as shown on the map. A difference from Slovakia, though, is the use of spots of the appropriate colour on a white background to mark each end of the route.

An avalanche warning system operates, with notices posted at entry points to the national park: 1 = low, 2 = moderate, 3 = considerable, 4 = high, 5 = very high. This is only likely to affect those visiting in winter or early spring, but you are strongly advised to stay out of any affected area.

The method of showing the names of some geographical features on Polish maps is inconsistent and confusing. For example, what is written as Strążyska Polana on some maps will appear on others (and in this book) as Polana Strążyska, or Kościeliska Dolina as Dolina Kościeliska – for a full explanation, see Place Names, page 31.

See also Altitudes, page 21.

Descending the chains from Giewont summit (Blue 206)

Entry Fees

A small fee is collected at huts placed at entry points to the national park on waymarked walking routes. Reduced rates are available for passes covering 2, 3, 4 and 7 days.

Some visitors, especially those from Britain, may find this system irksome and contrary to their tradition of free entry to national parks. However, it is the accepted practice in Poland and some other countries, the charge is very small, and the amounts collected are used to maintain and improve the paths and facilities – which include toilets at many starting points. Please do not try to evade payment.

ROUTE SUGGESTIONS

Sections marked (★) indicate that there is a fixed chain or wire to be negotiated.

1 SIWA POLANA – SCHRONISKO CHOCHOŁOWSKA – WOŁOWIEC AND RETURN (907m–2063m)

Grade Easy to Schronisko Chochołowska, moderate to Wołowiec
Distance 20km
Average Gradient 4% to Schronisko Chochołowska, 17% to Wołowiec
Height Gain 1156m   **Height Loss** 1156m   **Time** 6h 45m
Refreshments Siwa Polana, Schronisko Chochołowska

Being comparatively remote from Zakopane, Dolina Chochołowska is a quiet valley. It is also very pretty, and from Wołowiec you have fine views into Slovakia.

Approaching Wołowiec from the north (Blue 200) (photo: R Turnbull)

The last 500m to Wołowiec summit are on a blue route coming from Slovakia. You can use this, but remember that you are not allowed to descend into Slovakia at present (but see Cross-border Walking, page 60).

From Siwa Polana (bus from Zakopane, or park in car park) follow:
Green 500A to Schronisko Chochołowska and (as Green 500B) on to Wołowiec, and return. Optional horse-drawn taxi or road train on lower part of the route.

2 POLANA HUCISKA – WOŁOWIEC – STAROROBOCIAŃSKY WIERCH – POLANA HUCISKA (982m–2176m)

Grade Strenuous	**Distance** 28km	**Average Gradient** 13%
Height Gain 1822m	**Height Loss** 1822m	**Time** 10h 00m
Refreshments Schronisko Chochołowska		

An arduous route, suitable only for walkers with stamina, visiting four summits, but with no difficult walking. You will be rewarded with one of the finest ridge walks in the Tatras, with views into Poland and Slovakia.

From Polana Huciska (horse-drawn taxi or road train from Siwa Polana) follow:
Green 500A/B to Schronisko Chochołowska and Wołowiec (see route suggestion number 1 regarding the final section to Wołowiec summit)
Red 002 to Raczkowa Przełęcz
Green 503 to Siwa Przełęcz
Black 902 to Leśniczówka Chochołowska
Green 500A to Polana Huciska

3 KIRY – DOLINA KOŚCIELISKA – SCHRONISKO ORNAK AND RETURN (927m–1100m)

Grade Easy	**Distance** 12km	**Average Gradient** 3%
Height Gain 173m	**Height Loss** 173m	**Time** 2h 30m
Refreshments Schronisko Ornak, Kiry		

A pleasant and easy stroll, and because of that, and its proximity to Zakopane, usually busy. There are several options for side trips to caves and waterfalls.

From Kiry (bus from Zakopane, or park in car park) follow:
Green 504A to Schronisko Ornak and return. Optional horse-drawn taxi on lower
part of the route.

4 BUŃDÓWKI – DOLINA STRĄŻYSKA – SARNIA SKAŁA – DOLINA BIAŁEGO – ZAKOPANE (830m–1377m)

Grade Moderate	**Distance** 13km	**Average Gradient** 9%
Height Gain 547m	**Height Loss** 547m	**Time** 4h 00m
Refreshments Buńdówki, Polana Strążyska, Zakopane		

A good short route to test your legs, mostly in forest, but with a good view over
Zakopane from Sarnia Skała.

From Buńdówki (southwest part of Zakopane) follow:
Red 008 to Polana Strążyska
Black 901C to Czerwona Przełęcz and Białe; short diversion to Sarnia Skała
Yellow 807 to Zakopane

5 KUŹNICE – GIEWONT – BUŃDÓWKI (830m–1894m)

Grade Strenuous	**Distance** 15.5km	**Average Gradient** 13%
Height Gain 880m	**Height Loss** 1065m	**Time** 6h 30m
Refreshments Kuźnice, Schronisko Kalatówki; Schronisko Kondratowa; Polana Strążyska; Buńdówki		

There are no difficulties on this route until the final ascent to Giewont, though it
is very steep in places. Those unwilling to tackle the fixed chains to and from the
summit can wait at the foot. Splendid views from Giewont over Zakopane and
Podhale, though the summit is likely to be crowded.

From Kuźnice (bus or horse-drawn taxi from Zakopane) follow:
Blue 206 (★) to Kalatówki, Kondratowa and Giewont
Red 008 (★) to Przełęcz w Grzybowcu, Polana Strążyska and Buńdówki

6 KASPROWY WIERCH – KOŚCIELEC – KUŹNICE (1025m–2155m)

Grade Moderate to strenuous	**Distance** 13.5km	**Average Gradient** 15%
Height Gain 486m	**Height Loss** 1456m	**Time** 4h 30m
Refreshments Kasprowy Wierch, Schronisko Murowaniec, Kuźnice		

*Near Kondracka Przełęcz
below Giewont (Blue 206)*

A route with some testing sections, especially on the ascent c
has fixed chains and some exposed sections – those wishing t
wait at Karb. Most of it is downward and above the tree-line, \
from Kościelec of the Orla Perć summits.

From Kasprowy Wierch cable-car station go southeast 300m to Sucha Przełęcz, then follow:
Yellow 812A to foot of chair-lift
Black 908 to Zielony Staw
Blue 208 to Karb
Black 909 (★) to Kościelec and return to Karb
Green 514 to Czarny Staw Gąsienicowy
Blue 207B to Schronisko Murowaniec and
Blue 207A to Kuźnice

Optional Alternative Instead of Blue 207A, the final descent from Murowaniec to Kuźnice can be made on Yellow 810, mostly among meadows rather than in forest.

7 KASPROWY WIERCH – ORLA PERĆ – KUŹNICE (1025m–2301m)

Grade Difficult	**Distance** 20km	**Average Gradient** 15%
Height Gain 977m	**Height Loss** 1917m	**Time** 11h 30m★
Refreshments Kasprowy Wierch, Schronisko Murowaniec, Kuźnice		

The most exciting route in the Polish Tatras, with spectacular, constantly changing views. Suitable only for more experienced mountain walkers with lots of stamina and a good head for heights. There are at least a dozen ups and as many downs, mostly quite short, but with frequent fixed chains, scrambling and exposure.

★To avoid such a long day, you would be well advised to consider spending a night or two at Schronisko Murowaniec, then use Black 908 to Świnica.

From Kasprowy Wierch cable-car station go southeast 300m to Sucha Przełęcz, then follow:
Red 009A (★) to Świnica and
Red 009B along Orla Perć to Krzyżne
Yellow 812C/B to Schronisko Murowaniec
Blue 207A to Kuźnice

SPROWY WIERCH – SKRAJNY GRANAT – KUŹNICE (1025m–2225m)

Grade Strenuous   **Distance** 15.5km   **Average Gradient** 16%
Height Gain 771m   **Height Loss** 1743m   **Time** 6h 00m
Refreshments Kasprowy Wierch, Schronisko Murowaniec, Kuźnice

An opportunity to sample Orla Perć without having to face the more exact-ing sections of that route, and passing the large and beautiful tarn Czarny Staw Gąsienicowy. There is one short fixed chain on the final approach to Skrajny Granat, where it is also very steep.

From Kasprowy Wierch cable-car station go southeast 300m to Sucha Przełęcz, then follow:
Yellow 812A to Schronisko Murowaniec
Blue 207B to Czarny Staw Gąsienicowy
Yellow 813 (★) to Skrajny Granat and return to Czarny Staw Gąsienicowy
Blue 207B to Schronisko Murowaniec and Blue 207A to Kuźnice

9 KASPROWY WIERCH – ŚWINICA – POLANA PALENICA (984m–2301m)

Grade Strenuous   **Distance** 15km   **Average Gradient** 13%
Height Gain 428m   **Height Loss** 1425m   **Time** 5h 30m
Refreshments Kasprowy Wierch, Polana Palenica, also Schronisko Pięciu Stawów 10 minutes off route

A chance to sample the comparatively easy section of Orla Perć between Świnica and Zawrat. It is not difficult, but steep and exposed in places. On the descent to Polana Palenica you pass Wielki Staw Polski, the largest tarn in the Tatras, and two picturesque waterfalls.

From Kasprowy Wierch cable-car station go southeast 300m to Sucha Przełęcz, then follow:
Red 009A to Świnica and
Red 009B to Zawrat
Blue 209 to Wielki Staw Polski (optional diversion to Schronisko Pięciu Stawów)
Green 516 to Wodogrzmoty Mickiewicza
Red 011 or horse-drawn bus to Polana Palenica (bus to Zakopane)

*Looking towards Krzyżne
from Wielki Staw Polski
(Blue 209) (photo: R Turnbull)*

10 POLANA PALENICA – VALLEY OF FIVE POLISH TARNS – SZPIGLASOWA PRZEŁĘCZ – MORSKIE OKO – POLANA PALENICA (984m–2110m)

Grade Strenuous   **Distance** 21km
Average Gradient 4% on road sections, 20% on paths
Height Gain 1124m   **Height Loss** 1124m   **Time** 7h 15m
Refreshments Morskie Oko, Polana Palenica, also Schronisko Pięciu Stawów 10 minutes off route

This route ascends one of the most beautiful valleys in the Tatras – the Valley of Five Polish Tarns, passing two of its tarns and two picturesque waterfalls – and climbs to a spectacular viewpoint in the High Tatras. It is not particularly difficult, though there is one fixed chain approaching Szpiglasowa Przełęcz. Much of it is on traffic-free roads, but horse-drawn buses are available.

From Polana Palenica (bus from Zakopane, or park car park) follow:
Red 011 (or horse-drawn bus) to Wodogrzmoty Mickiewicza
Green 516 to Wielki Staw Polski (optional diversion to Schronisko Pięciu Stawów)
Blue 209 and
Yellow 814 (★) to Szpiglasowa Przełęcz and on to Morskie Oko
Red 011 (or horse-drawn bus) to Wodogrzmoty Mickiewicza and Polana Palenica
Optional Side Trip Yellow 814 to Szpiglasowy Wierch adds 20 minutes.

11 POLANA PALENICA – RYSY AND RETURN BY SAME ROUTE (OR CONTINUE INTO SLOVAKIA) (984m–2500m)

Grade Strenuous   **Distance** 28km
Average Gradient 4% on road sections, 22% on paths
Height Gain 1509m   **Height Loss** 1509m   **Time** 10h 45m
Refreshments Polana Palenica, Morskie Oko

This is the least strenuous way to reach Poland's highest summit, especially if you take the horse-drawn bus for the first and last 7km along the road. Because of Rysy, and the presence of the beautiful tarn Morskie Oko with its popular refuge, this is one of the busiest routes in the Polish Tatras. Red 012 includes a very difficult stretch that can feel very exposed on the descent.

From Polana Palenica (bus from Zakopane, car park) follow:
Red 011 (or horse-drawn bus) to Wodogrzmoty Mickiewicza and Morskie Oko
Red 012 to Rysy
Return by the same route.

You can if you wish continue into Slovakia, following route suggestion number 7 in the Slovak section of this book, finishing at either Štrbské Pleso or Popradské Pleso Station. This would make the total distance 23km, the height loss 1144m, and the total time approximately 9h 30m. Or you could stay at a Slovak mountain chalet (Chata pod Rysmi or Chata pri Popradskom Plese). You should of course ensure that you can either stay the night at one of these places, by booking in advance, or have time to take public transport or a taxi back to Poland.

    If you are making a cross-border expedition, it is better to do it as described above, rather than from Slovakia into Poland, so that you ascend the difficult stretch on Red 012, which would be very difficult on the descent.

    See also Cross-Border Walking on page 60.

12 ZAKOPANE HORSESHOE AND GUBAŁÓWKA RIDGE (830m

Grade Easy   **Distance** 4km to 17km
Average Gradient 4% to 14%
Height Gain 287m–460m   **Height Loss** 287m–460m
Time 1h 00m to 4h 30m
Refreshments Harenda, Gubałówka, Zakopane

We have coined the term Zakopane Horseshoe for this little-used route, as it describes such a shape while following two ridges to the east and north of the town. It provides a pleasant change from the mountains, with mostly easy walking and fine views, but there are some steep sections. The longest and steepest ascent can be avoided by taking the funicular or chair-lift from Zakopane to Gubałówka, then following the route as described below in reverse.

The following combination is suggested, to give, at 17km, a full day's walking, though there are several short-cut possibilities, with public transport back to Zakopane at all three intermediate locations shown below.

From Zakopane follow:
Yellow 808 to Harenda
Yellow 809 to Eliaszówka and Gubałówka

Return to Zakopane by any of routes Blue 203, Yellow 806 or Black 906, or by mountain lift.

PATH DESCRIPTIONS

Note Place names highlighted in **bold type** on the following pages can be looked up in the Gazetteer starting on page 290.

RED ROUTES

• 001 POLANA TRZYDNIÓWKA TO TRZYDNIOWIAŃSKI WIERCH AND SCHRONISKO CHOCHOŁOWSKA (1081m–1758m)

Grade Moderate   **Distance** 8km   **Average Gradient** 16%
E–W Height Gain 725m/**Loss** 658m   **Time** 4h 05m
W–E Height Gain 658m/**Loss** 725m   **Time** 4h 00m
Winter/Spring Closed

*A long, horseshoe-shaped route in the foothills of the Western Tatras that can
be undertaken as a half-day circular route from Schronisko Chochołowska, taking horse-drawn transport (or hired cycle) there. The route lies mainly in forest,
but comes into the open at Trzydniowiański Wierch (1758m), where there are
good views of the great Długi Upłaz (Long Ridge) to the south. This route is little
used, and some parts, especially in the dwarf pine, can be overgrown. It provides
access to Długi Upłaz via Green 502*

Both ends of the route join different points along Green 500A in **Dolina
Chochołowska**. Approaching from the north, you reach the first point 10 minutes
after passing through the gorge called Wyżnia Chochołowska Brama, at Polana
Trzydniówka. The route at first climbs the dry gully Krowieniec to reach the spur
Kulawiec, then you follow this all the way, passing out of the forest into dwarf
pine then open rock, to reach Trzydniowiański Wierch at 1758m. (*E–W 2h 15m,
W–E 1h 45m.*)

Here is the junction with Green 502. Red 001 continues by descending steeply for several hundred metres along a rib, then turns left to cross and
recross a gully before re-entering the forest. A stream is crossed before reaching a
meadow with shepherds' huts, Jarząbcze Szałasiska (1265m), which was reached
by Pope John Paul II during a visit here in 1983 (see page 198). (*E–W 1h 10m,
W–E 1h 40m.*)

Now sharing with Yellow 801, follow the brook, Jarząbczy Potok, all the way
down to Dolina Chochołowska and the junction with Green 500A. The red waymarks continue left along the service road to Schronisko Chochołowska. (*E–W 0h
40m, W–E 0h 50m.*)

• 002 DŁUGI UPŁAZ (THE LONG RIDGE) (1831m–2176m)

Grade Strenuous   **Distance** 7.5km   **Average Gradient** 20%
E–W Height Gain 810m/**Loss** 706m   **Time** 3h 35m
W–E Height Gain 706m/**Loss** 810m   **Time** 3h 40m
Winter/Spring Closed

*This excellent ridge walk along the border with Slovakia provides some of the
finest views in the whole of the Tatras. It takes in four summits, including one of
the highest in the Western Tatras, Starorobociański Wierch. The walking is not
difficult, but being remote from roads and transport requires a long approach
and descent to make a tough day – or you could consider staying overnight at
Schronisko Ornak and/or Schronisko Chochołowska. It is best approached from
the east, as this involves a more gradual ascent.*

Although the ridge walk continues eastwards for 2km to Błyszcz and Pyszniańska Przełęcz, with routes descending into Slovakia, at present this is in effect a dead end for people approaching from Poland (but see Cross-border Walking, page 60). Indeed, some parts of the route are well inside Slovakia, and there are links from that side at four more points. As they are in the Western Tatras, they are not covered in the Slovak section of this book.

Green 503 brings you to the saddle **Raczkowa Przełęcz** (1959m). Turn left if you wish to make the side-trip to Błyszcz (2159m), just a stone's throw from Bystrá (2248m) in Slovakia, the highest summit of the Western Tatras. The round trip will add about 80 minutes to your walk. Along the way you pass the saddle Bystry Karb (1953m), to which a route comes up from Slovakia, but remember that you cannot go down it at present.

Otherwise turn right to follow Red 002, and start switchbacking with a long climb along the ridge to the summit of Starorobociański Wierch (2176m). In Slovakia this is known locally – and more conveniently – as Klin (Wedge). Keep on down to the saddle Starorobociańska Przełęcz (1975m) and rise again to Kończysty Wierch (End Hill, 2002m), the junction with Green 502. (*E–W 0h 75m, W–E 0h 70m.*)

After Jarząbcza Przełęcz (Rowan Pass, 1954m) comes the longest climb on the route, to Jarząbczy Wierch (Rowan Peak, 2137m). (*E–W 0h 40m, W–E 0h 30m.*)

A path from Slovakia joins here, and keeps very steep, zigzag company with the Polish one for part of the way to Niska Przełęcz (Low Saddle), which is the lowest point of the route at 1831m. The summit of Łopata (Spade) is inaccessible to walkers, and to bypass it you must enter Slovakia (legally) for 300m to reach Dziurawa Przełęcz (Pockmarked Saddle, 1836m). Finally you climb to Wołowiec (2063m) to meet Blue 200. (*E–W 1h 45m, W–E 1h 45m.*)

• 003 POLANA PISANA TO JASKINIA MYLNA (1018m–1250m)

Grade Moderate	**Distance** 1km	**Average Gradient** 20%
N–S Height Gain 232m	**Time** 1h 00m	
S–N Height Loss 232m	**Time** 1h 00m	
Winter/Spring Normally open		

A short but fascinating diversion off Green 504A, not marked on our diagrammatic map. It descends Jaskinia Mylna (Confusing Cave), discovered in 1887. You can make short diversions to two smaller caves along the route, though these require an extra 15–25 minutes each. Be prepared to get wet and dirty, and each person must carry a torch with spare battery and bulb. There is one-way traffic, from south to north.

Polana Pisana can be reached from Kiry along **Dolina Kościeliska** on foot (Green 504A) or by horse-drawn taxi (*dorożka*). The entrance is from the south end of the route, near the great cliff called Skała Pisana. Having turned right from the valley, you soon pass Black 904, a very short dead-end route to another explorable cave, Jaskinia Raptawicka. The small cave Jama Obłaskowa can also be visited.

You arrive at the cave entrance (*wejście*) and begin your passage through Jaskinia Mylna. The route inside is waymarked, and there are two scrambly sections, one with a fixed chain, the other with an iron railing. The floor is very rough, so you must watch your step. As you leave the exit (*wyjście*) there is a beautiful view along Dolina Kościeliska.

• 004 POLANA CUDAKOWA TO CIEMNIAK (952m–2096m)

Grade Strenuous	**Distance** 5km	**Average Gradient** 22%
NW–SE Height Gain 1144m		**Time** 4h 00m
SE–NW Height Loss 1144m		**Time** 3h 00m
Winter/Spring Normally open		

A useful access route to the Czerwone Wierchy ridge. Though mostly very steep and in forest, the walking is not difficult and there are some good views.

The route is approached from **Kiry** on Green 504A (or you can take a horse-drawn taxi). From Polana Cudakowa (952m) you immediately start climbing steeply up a ridge (Adamica) to the meadow Polana Upłaz (1300m). (*1h 15m up, 0h 55m down.*)

More forest brings you to another meadow that steeply ascends a ridge to a great rock called Piec (1460m), above which you can see **Giewont** to your left. The route continues very steeply through dwarf pine, then comes into the open below Przełącka przy Kopie (Little Saddle by the Stacks). Skirting the summit of Chuda Turnia (Thin Cliff), you come to Chuda Przełącka (Thin Saddle) at 1850m. (*1h 55m up, 1h 25m down.*)

Here is the junction with Green 505, which contours round to your right. A final push up Red 004 on Twardy Grzbiet (Hard Crest) brings you to the summit of Ciemniak (2096m) and the junction with Red 007. (*0h 50m up, 0h 40m down.*)

• 005 NĘDZÓWKA TO PRZYSŁOP MIĘTUSI (952m–1189m)

Grade Moderate	**Distance** 4km	**Average Gradient** 12%
NW–SE Height Gain 319m/**Loss** 82m		**Time** 1h 30m
SE–NW Height Gain 82m/**Loss** 319m		**Time** 1h 15m
Winter/Spring Normally open		

This mostly forested route starts from the **Nędzówka** bus stops on the main road running westwards out of Zakopane. First follow a farm track, opposite the junction with a side road, then after 300m turn right along a forest road. In another 300m turn left up a gully (Staników Żleb) where the path is usually wet. Climb steadily, passing through a meadow, to the broad saddle Wyżnie Stanikowe Siodło (1271m) below the minor summit of Hruby Regiel. (*NW–SE 1h 00m, SE–NW 0h 40m.*)

Descend a little, then follow a ridge at about 1260m for 300m, and descend further to Przysłop Miętusi (1189m), a saddle well known for its beautiful views of the **Czerwone Wierchy**. Here is the junction with Black 901B and Blue 202. (*NW–SE 0h 30, SE–NW 0h 35m.*)

• 006 WYŻNIA TOMANOWA POLANA TO TOMANOWA PRZEŁĘCZ (1476m–1686m)

Grade Moderate	**Distance** 1.5km	**Average Gradient** 14%
W–E Height Gain 210m	**Time** 0h 35m	
E–W Height Loss 210m	**Time** 0h 25m	
Winter/Spring Closed		

Some of the Western Tatras summits, as seen from Dolina Tomanowa (Red 006) (photo: R Turnbull)

This short route leads to one of the lowest passes on the main ridge of the Western Tatras, Tomanowa Przełęcz (1686m), once much used by traders and afflicted with robbers. The path continues into Slovakia, though for the present you must return the way you came (but see Cross-border Walking, page 60).

From Green 505 at the east end of Wyżnia Tomanowa Polana (Upper Tomanowa Meadow, 1476m) the path immediately enters the forest, but soon comes into dwarf pine, and finishes on a scree slope leading to Tomanowa Przełęcz (1686m).

• 007 KASPROWY WIERCH TO CIEMNIAK (1987m–2122m)

Grade Moderate	**Distance** 9km	**Average Gradient** 11%	
E–W Height Gain 551m/**Loss** 444m		**Time** 3h 00m	
W–E Height Gain 444m/**Loss** 551m		**Time** 3h 05m	
Winter/Spring Closed			

A splendid and comparatively easy switchback of a ridge walk, much of it on grass, and quickly accessible via the chair-lift from Kuźnice to Kasprowy Wierch. For the whole length you have extensive panoramic views into Poland and Slovakia. The route follows the border between the two countries, marked by short white posts with red tops.

Several routes come up from the Polish side, offering alternative descents, but the Slovak side is extremely steep, and no routes venture up from there. You are strongly advised not to attempt this route in mist or bad light, as there are places where a few steps in the wrong direction could lead to a dangerous fall.

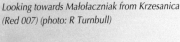

Looking towards Małołaczniak from Krzesanica (Red 007) (photo: R Turnbull)

From the top of the cable-car at **Kasprowy Wierch** (1987m) descend south on Yellow 812A for 250m to Sucha Przełęcz (1950m) to join Red 007. This heads west, descending to Goryczkowa Przełęcz nad Zakosy (1816m). You then face a series of climbs up rounded summits that increase in height as you progress westwards. The first three are quite gentle – Pośredni Wierch Goryczkowy (1874m), Goryczkowa Czuba (1913m) and Suchy Wierch Kondracki (1890m) – then you descend to the saddle of Przełęcz pod Kondracką Kopa, where Green 508 joins. (*E–W 1h 20m, W–E 1h 40m.*)

The next three summits are Kopa Kondracka (2005m, Yellow 805), Małołaczniak (2096m, Blue 202) and Krzesanica (2122m). On the final stretch to Ciemniak (2096m) you must particularly watch out for a sudden vertiginous drop at the edge of the grass. Red 004 and Green 505 lead down from here. (*E–W 1h 30m, W–E 1h 25.*)

• 008 BUŃDÓWKI TO WYŻNIA KONDRACKA PRZEŁĘCZ (WKP) (FOR GIEWONT) (898m–1780m)

Grade Easy to Polana Strążyska, strenuous to WKP
Distance 6.5km **Average Gradient** 6% to Polana Strążyska, 16% to WKP
N–S Height Gain 882m **Time** 3h 00m
S–N Height Loss 882m **Time** 2h 20m
Winter/Spring Closed

Though a much frequented route, the ascent is very steep and tiring, so it is more often used for the descent from Zakopane's 'mascot' peak of Giewont. It is mostly in forest as far as the west end of the Giewont massif, then in the open all the way to WKP – the pass just below the summit.

From **Buńdówki** (900m, refreshments) the route ascends **Dolina Strążyska**, frequently crossing its stream, Strążyski Potok, to Polana Strążyska (1042m, refreshments). (*0h 40m up, 0h 35m down.*)

Here you join Black 901B and share its path up through forest for the next 1.5km to the saddle Przełęcz w Grzybowcu (1311m). You also share some of the path with a stream, making it slippery, so care is needed, especially if descending. (*0h 50m up, 0h 35m down.*)

The black route now descends westwards, but Red 008 climbs southeastwards to a spur called Grzybowiec, which it follows, now with the summit of Giewont ahead. The path leaves the forest to skirt the rocky western slope of Mały (Little) Giewont to Siodlo (Little Saddle) – effectively a notch in the rock – with a beautiful view down **Dolina Małej Łąki**. Now the path steepens considerably to reach the saddle Wyżnia Kondracka Przełęcz (1780m) and Blue 206, which will take you to the summit of Giewont. (*1h 30m up, 1h 10m down.*)

• 009A KASPROWY WIERCH TO ŚWINICA (1987m–2301m)

Grade Strenuous	**Distance** 3.5km	**Average Gradient** 18%
NW–SE Height Gain 474m/**Loss** 160m		**Time** 2h 00m
SE–NW Height Gain 160m/**Loss** 474m		**Time** 1h 30m
Winter/Spring Closed		

Much used as an access route to Orla Perć, this is a fine ridge walk in its own right, effectively a continuation of Red 007. There is little difficulty except on the final ascent to Świnica. You should have splendid views in one direction over the tarns of Gąsienicowa Dolina in Poland, and in the other towards Kriváň in Slovakia.

Looking down on Zadni Staw Polski, and up to Hrubý Vrch in Slovakia, from Świnica (Red 009A/B) (photo: R Turnbull)

From the cable-car station at **Kasprowy Wierch** (1987m) follow Yellow 812A south for 250m to Sucha Przełęcz (1950m), a five-way junction. The yellow route descends leftwards into Dolina Gąsienicowa, while Slovakia's Yellow 8851, currently inaccessible from Poland, bears down to the right into Ticha Dolina (but see Cross-border Walking, page 60). Following the ridge, Red 007 comes along from behind, and Red 009 takes over as it continues up to the summit of Beskid (2012m), the first of four summits. At the next saddle, **Liliowe** (1952m), Green 511 comes up from the Polish side. (*NW–SE 0h 25m, SE–NW 0h 15m.*)

With little effort, two more summits (Skrajna Turnia at 2096m and Pośrednia Turnia at 2128m) are surmounted on the way to Świnicka Przełęcz (2051m), where Black 908 joins by yet another route from Dolina Gąsienicowa. (*NW–SE 0h 30m, SE–NW 0h 25m.*)

Now the going gets tougher, steeper and more exposed on the way to Świnica (2301m). (*NW–SE 1h 00m, SE–NW 0h 45m.*)

• 009B ORLA PERĆ (EAGLE EDGE) (2065m–2301m)

Grade Strenuous	**Distance** 5.5km	**Average Gradient** 20%
SW–NE Height Gain 439m/**Loss** 627m		**Time** 7h 50m
NE–SW Height Gain 627m/**Loss** 439m		**Time** 8h 20m
Winter/Spring Closed		

The zenith of the Polish Tatras for adventurous mountain walkers with a head for heights, a cool temperament, and who can cope with exposure. It includes most of **Orla Perć** *(Eagle Edge) between Świnica and Krzyżne and takes in a dozen summits. You are always above 2000m, with magnificent views all the way, dominated by tarns on either side – Czarny Staw Gąsienicowy to the north, and the Five Polish Tarns to the south.*

The section from Zawrat to Kozia Przełęcz is now one-way in that direction (west-east) and there may be a ranger controlling access.

At the saddle called Zawrat, a sign warns that you follow this route at your own risk! It is very exposed and worn, with many fixed chains and railings. There is an escape route here, should this put you off, and five more along the way.

The easiest way to reach Orla Perć is by cable-car to Kasprowy Wierch and Red 009A to Świnica.

From Świnica (2301m) you follow a rocky and tortuous path along the southern side of the ridge, gradually descending, with some exposure and negotiating two *kominy* (chimneys – wide cracks that are just about wide enough for your

Orla Perć – near Kozia Przełecz (Red 009B) (photo: R Turnbull)

body). Then comes a short climb to the saddle Zawrat (2159m, junction with Blue 207B/209). (*SW–NE 0h 50m, NE–SW 1h 00m.*)

You then walk along the ridge itself (here called Zmarzłe Czuby and Kozie Czuby), or just off it, to the summits of Mali Kozi Wierch (2228m) and Kozi Wierch (2291m), taking in several saddles including Kozia Przełęcz (2137m, junction with Yellow 814). Black 913 comes up to Kozi Wierch from the south. (*SW–NE 3h 10m, NE–SW 3h 10m.*)

The route continues along the south side of the ridge, close to the 2200m contour, with Przedni Staw dominating the view below, to the saddle Przełącka nad Buczynową Dolinka (2225m), another fine viewpoint. You descend a little down Żleb Kulczyńskiego (Kulczyński Gully), passing the junction with Black 912. (*SW–NE 0h 45m, NE–SW 0h 50m.*)

Having been heading generally eastwards until this point, you now turn northwards via another chimney, gradually regaining the ridge, where Green 515 comes up from Zmarzły Staw. The **Granaty** ridge is then closely followed, taking in the summits of Zadni (Inner, 2240m), Pośredni (Middle, 2234m) and Skrajny (Outer, 2225m) Granat, where Yellow 813 provides the last opportunity for an escape from Orla Perć, should you need it. (*SW–NE 0h 50m, NE–SW 0h 50m.*)

Heading eastwards once more, you stay on or close to the ridge, with one major diversion down to Buczynowa Turniczka (2065m), an outstanding viewpoint above Dolina Roztoki and some of the Five Polish Tarns. The route finishes at the saddle Krzyżne (2112m), the junction with Yellow 812B to the north and Yellow 812C to the south. (*SW–NE 2h 15m, NE–SW 2h 30m.*)

Orla Perć continues eastwards along the Wołoszyn massif, but this section is now closed to walkers.

• 010 TOPOROWA CYRHLA TO WAKSMUNDZKA ROWIEŃ AND WODOGRZMOTY MICKIEWICZA (992m–1405m)

Grade Easy	**Distance** 14km	**Average Gradient** 7%	
NW–SE Height Gain 500m/**Loss** 400m		**Time** 4h 10m	
SE–NW Height Gain 400m/**Loss** 500m		**Time** 3h 35m	
Winter/Spring Open			

A long but easy route, mostly in forest, with an occasional open meadow. Toporowa Cyrhla is served by bus from Zakopane and has no official car park, but there is space for a few cars.

The route starts about 100m back towards Zakopane from the bus stop in **Toporowa Cyrhla** (992m). You climb gently into the forest, sharing the path with Green 512 for the first 1.5km. At a fork the green route continues ahead while Red 010 bears left and continues climbing in forest. You contour to the right above Dolina Suchej Wody, crossing the brook Sucha Woda to a point called Psia Trawka (1188m) on the service road for Schronisko Murowaniec (Black 910). There is a covered picnic table here. *(1h 15m NW–SE, 1h 00m SE–NW.)*

Red 010 continues up a track opposite, gently climbing for 3km through forest. It levels out at a large meadow, Polana Waksmundzka, then climbs a little further to a smaller one, Waksmundzka Rowień (1405m), the highest point of this route, where you briefly share with Green 513. *(1h 00m NW–SE, 0h 50m SE–NW.)*

The path now descends comparatively steeply into **Dolina Waksmundzka**, and crosses its stream at about 1240m. Tread carefully – this is adder territory! The route climbs again, quite steeply at one point, to cross the shoulder of Wyżnia Kopka (Upper Stack). The path descends to the meadow Polana pod Wołoszynem (1250m), at the far side of which is the junction with Black 915. *(NW–SE 0h 50m, SE–NW 1h 00m.)*

The path rises a little then starts to descend, becoming steeper as it continues, and crossing a stream at one point. When you reach the road (**Droga Oswalda Balzera**), which is our Red 011, you can either turn left for 2.5km to the bus stop and car park at **Polana Palenica** (refreshments), or right for 500m to **Wodogrzmoty Mickiewicza** (1100m), a picturesque waterfall at the junction with Green 516. *(NW–SE 0h 35m, SE–NW 0h 45m.)*

If going SE–NW from Wodogrzmoty Mickiewicza, after walking 500m you must look carefully for some narrow steps which may be overgrown and easily missed. You may more easily spot the red waymarks on the trees on the slope above.

• 011 POLANA PALENICA TO MORSKIE OKO (990m–1406m)

Grade Easy   **Distance** 9km   **Average Gradient** 5%
N–S Height Gain 416m   **Time** 2h 35m
S–N Height Loss 416m   **Time** 2h 10m
Winter/Spring Normally open only as far as Włosienica

The lower section of this route, from Polana Palenica to the junction with Red 010, is not coloured on the map, nor is it waymarked, but is included here for convenience. It is one of the busiest routes on the network, as it leads to Morskie Oko, acknowledged as the most beautiful lake in Poland, and is the main approach route to Poland's highest point, Rysy. The route is mostly on hard-surfaced road, though not without interest, and there are short cuts on footpaths through some of the hairpin bends.

A bus service operates from Zakopane to Polana Palenica, which has a car park, refreshment kiosks and toilets. A horse-drawn bus goes from there to Włosienica, taking 80 minutes up and 45 down. It used to be possible to take motorised buses and cars as far as Włosienica, but subsidence has resulted in closure of the road. There are no plans to re-open it to general traffic in the foreseeable future.

From **Polana Palenica** follow the road, **Droga Oswalda Balzera**, up Dolina Białki (White Valley), whose river Białka flows well away to the left. After 1.5km you pass the little farm of Niżnia Polana pod Wołoszynem (1010m, Lower Meadow below Wołoszyn) below to your left. Another 1km or so, passing a cascading stream on your right, brings you to the junction with Red 010. (*N–S 0h 40m, S–N 0h 35m.*)

You soon come to two wooden chalets – a depot of the Nowy Targ Region Public Roads Department – then you can hear the crashing waters of **Wodogrzmoty Mickiewicza** (1100m), which you reach in another few hundred metres. You cross the bridge to the junctions with Green 516 and Green 517 – the latter providing an opportunity to divert to Schronisko Roztoki for a refreshment break. Continue up the road, with the forested summit called Roztoka Czuba (1426m) to your right. A long series of hairpin bends is avoided by a short-cut path, then you rejoin the road as it climbs the valley of **Dolina Rybiego Potoku**, with Rybi Potok (Fish Brook) below, to **Włosienica** (1315m, refreshments). (*N–S 1h 20m, S–N 1h 10m.*)

A little further up, to your right in the forest, is the **Szałasiska** campsite. The forest now starts to thin out, with more meadows, and you come to the junction with Blue 209 shortly before reaching **Morskie Oko** (1406m, refreshments). (*N–S 0h 35m, S–N 0h 25m.*)

You can if you wish extend your walk by making a circuit of the tarn, which takes about half an hour.

• 012 MORSKIE OKO TO RYSY (1406m–2499m)

Grade Strenuous	**Distance** 5km	**Average Gradient** 22%
NW–SE Height Gain 1093m	**Time** 4h 05m	
SE–NW Height Loss 1093m	**Time** 3h 05m	
Winter/Spring Closed		

One of the most popular and scenic routes in the Polish Tatras, linking the country's most beautiful lake with its highest summit. You can save some energy by taking the horse-drawn bus along most of the long approach road from Polana Palenica to Włosienica (Red 011).

The summit is accessible from both sides of the border, and gets very crowded, so you are advised to make an early start to beat the 'rush hour'. If you wish to continue into Slovakia, see route suggestion number 11 and Cross-border Walking, page 60.

From **Schronisko Morskie Oko** (1406m) you can follow either shore of the tarn, but the left-hand side is slightly shorter. At the far end the red route zigzags up the moraine to reach **Czarny Staw pod Rysami** (1583m). (*NW–SE 0h 45–50m, SE–NW 0h 35–40m.*)

Keep to the left shore of the tarn then climb again, more and more steeply, to the summit of Rysy. The final section is extremely strenuous, quite exposed in places and requires great care on the descent. (*NW–SE 3h 20m, SE–NW 2h 30m.*)

There are actually two summits – the one on the Polish side of the border is 2499m, the Slovak one 2503m.

• 013 DOLINA ZA MNICHEM TO WROTA CHAŁUBIŃSKIEGO (1788m–2022m)

Grade Strenuous	**Distance** 1.5km	**Average Gradient** 16%
NE–SW Height Gain 237m	**Time** 1h 00m	
SW–NE Height Loss 237m	**Time** 0h 45m	
Winter/Spring Closed		

A short side trip from Yellow 814 to a border saddle with fine views of Morskie Oko and the Temnosmrečinske tarns in Slovakia. You are on open rock all the way, and pass between a number of very small tarns.

• 014 THE CHOCHOŁÓW UPRISING TRAIL: PORONIN – GUBAŁÓWKA – CHOCHOŁÓW (732m–1120m)

Grade Easy	**Distance** 21km	**Average Gradient** 3–4%
E–W Height Gain 388m/**Loss** 360m		**Time** 6h 00m
W–E Height Gain 360m/**Loss** 388m		**Time** 6h 00m
Winter/Spring Open		

This easy trail (Szlak imienia Powstania Chochołowskiego in Polish) passes through typical Podhale scenery in the low hills to the north of Zakopane. It was created in the 1950s in commemoration of the Chochołów Uprising of 1840, when just six people from the village of that name held out for two days against the Austrian army. The times shown above are as quoted on maps, though fast walkers should complete it in considerably less time, and could walk the whole trail in one day (morning up, afternoon down) using buses from Zakopane. Going west–east involves slightly less ascent.

An even easier option would be to divide it into two sections, generally along a ridge or downhill, by taking the cable-car, chair-lift or funicular from Zakopane to the highest point at about 1120m at **Gubałówka** or **Pałkówka**, then buses back to Zakopane from the far ends. One day would go west for 12km to **Chochołów**, mostly through fields, passing the tops of Tominów Wierch (1019m) and Ostrysz (1023m). The second day would go generally northeast for 9km along quiet lanes (**Droga Papieska** and Rafaczańska Grapa) and tracks to Poronin.

The trail is actually part of a much longer one that continues eastwards from Poronin through the village of Bukowina Tatrzańska to the hills of Zamagurze Spiskie and Pieniny Spiskie, then further to the Pieniny National Park, one of Poland's most visited tourist regions.

Chochołów is worth visiting in its own right (see gazetteer). From there or Poronin, buses will bring you back to Zakopane.

BLUE ROUTES

• 200 GRZEŚ TO WOŁOWIEC (1653m–2064m)

Grade Easy to moderate	**Distance** 4km	**Average Gradient** 10%
N–S Height Gain 411m	**Time** 1h 45m	
S–N Height Loss 411m	**Time** 1h 30m	
Winter/Spring Closed		

Grassy and rounded, this is a comparatively easy ridge route along the border, with fine views, and includes the saddle Łuczniańska Prełęcz (1602m) and the minor summit of Rakoń (1879m). It can be approached from the north via Yellow 800, or from the south via Green 500B or Red 002. Although there are routes into Slovakia at each end, at the time of writing it was not permitted to continue there – but see Cross-border Walking, page 60.

· 201 STARE KOŚCIELISKA TO POLANA NA STOŁACH (971m–1417m)

Grade Moderate   **Distance** 2km   **Average Gradient** 18%
NE–SW Height Gain 446m   **Time** 0h 45m
SW–NE Height Loss 446m   **Time** 0h 35m
Winter/Spring Normally open

A little-used and peaceful dead end, mostly in forest but grassy at the top, from where there are good views of the Czerwone Wierchy. Polana na Stołach has a collection of disused but attractive shepherds' huts. The route starts from the south end of Stare Kościeliska, off Green 504A, then snakes its way up through the forest.

· 202 GRONIK TO MAŁOŁACZNIAK (938m–2096m)

Grade Easy to Przysłop Miętusi, strenuous to Małołaczniak
Distance 8km   **Average Gradient** 9% to Miętusi Przysłop, 18% to Małołaczniak
N–S Height Gain 1158m   **Time** 4h 00m
S–N Height Loss 1158m   **Time** 3h 00m
Winter/Spring Closed

*A popular route providing a direct ascent from the outskirts of Zakopane to the **Czerwone Wierchy**. It is in forest for two-thirds of the way, though there are good views of the mountains and over Dolina Miętusia from Przysłop Miętusi. The last third is on open rock, climbing steeply to Małołaczniak on the Slovak border, with a tricky section including a fixed chain. Gronik is served by buses from Zakopane, and has a car park, cafés and toilets.*

From the bus stop at **Gronik**, go back towards Zakopane for 200m then turn right up a lane leading to the car park. Together with Yellow 805, the blue route steadily climbs a track for 1.5km. The routes divide at the end of the track, with Blue 202 taking a path to the right. It climbs more steeply now to the little grassy saddle Przysłop Miętusi (1189m), converging with Red 005 and Black 901B. (*N–S 1h 00m, S–N 0h 45m.*)

Blue 202 turns left and contours through forest and meadow for 1km. Now the climbing begins in earnest, at first in forest, then on open rock. The going gets harder as you climb a gully called Kobylarzowy Żleb, and includes a fixed chain, and there is an exposed section where care is needed, especially if descending. The final stretch to the summit of Małołączniak (2096m) gets a little easier, and you are rewarded with fine views into Ticha Dolina in Slovakia. Red 007 provides the link here, either eastwards to the cable-car at Kasprowy Wierch, or westwards to Ciemniak. (*N–S 3h 00m, S–N 2h 15m.*)

• 203 ZAKOPANE TO PAŁKÓWKA AND GUBAŁÓWKA (850m–1123m)

Grade Moderate   **Distance** 5km
Average Gradient 10% to Pająkówka, 2% to Gubałówka
S–N Height Gain 290m/**Loss** 40m **Time** 0h 30m
N–S Height Gain 40m/**Loss** 290m **Time** 0h 20m
Winter/Spring Open

A route through forest and across ski slopes to or from Gubałówka, on the ridge to the north of Zakopane, with great views of the High Tatras. The route is steep in places, and can be difficult to find on either side of the ski slopes. Buses and mountain lifts link Zakopane with Pałkówka and Gubałówka.

From Zakopane, the route starts up the lane called Szymaszkowa, to the right of the car parks of Hotel Mercure Kasprowy.

If starting from **Gubałówka**, follow the **Droga Papieska** road, together with Red 014 and Black 906, west along the ridge to the T-junction at **Pałkówka** where you turn left then right along a lane.

• 204 ZAKOPANE TO NOWE BYSTRE (820m–1065m)

Grade Easy to moderate   **Distance** 5km   **Average Gradient** 10%
S–N Height Gain 245m/**Loss** 204m   **Time** 2h 00m
N–S Height Gain 204m/**Loss** 245m   **Time** 1h 55m
Winter/Spring Open

A comparatively easy route into the farmland north of Zakopane. The southern part climbs quite steeply through woods and ski slopes, but this can be avoided by taking the bus or funicular from Zakopane to Gubałówka. A better option may be bus to Nowe Bystre and walk back to Zakopane. Waymarking is patchy.

From the funicular bottom station in Zakopane, take the path to the right then turn left up a lane to climb steeply through woods and ski slopes. At the top, turn left to a lane and follow this to the **Droga Papieska**. (*S–N 1h 15m, N–S 1h 00m.*)

Cross over and follow a track through forest, descending steadily to a meadow at Piszczorówka. Turn right and follow the lane to Nowe Bystre, from where buses go to Zakopane. (*S–N 0h 45m, N–S 0h 55m.*)

205 ZAKOPANE TO KUŹNICE (900m–1025m)

Grade Easy	**Distance** 2km	**Average Gradient** 6%
N–S Height Gain 125m	**Time** 0h 30m	
S–N Height Loss 125m	**Time** 0h 30m	
Winter/Spring Open		

Although actually the road from Zakopane to Kuźnice, it is an official and well-used walking route, and there are several points of interest. According to Zakopane town maps, the waymarking starts in the town centre and follows Krupówki, Władysława Zamoyskiego and Titusa Chałubińskiego streets up to Rondo Kuźnickie (Kuźnice Roundabout). However, you would be hard pressed to spot any waymarks there, and in any case people approach the roundabout from all directions, depending on where they are staying. Therefore our description starts at the roundabout, beside which is a national park information centre.

Although closed to private vehicles, the road up from the roundabout is used by fast and frequent buses and taxis – so take care. For a quieter alternative to the lower part of the route as far as Kuźnicka, see Green 509.

From Rondo Kuźnickie (900m) walk up the pavement on the right-hand side of the road called Aleja Przewodników Tatrzańskich (Tatras Guide Avenue). Horse-drawn cabs (*dorożki*) wait for customers on the left-hand side – you may prefer to hire one, at least on the uphill journey. The lower part of the road runs between sections of fenced-off forest to the small settlement of **Murowanica** (990m), passing the handsome, traditional, Zakopane-style Klasztor Księżówka (Duke's Monastery). Green 501 (Droga pod Reglami) comes in from the right here, and Green 509 to Nosal starts on the left at the road junction.

Soon afterwards are the meadows of Kuźnicka (Little Kuźnice) – the slope to the right is a practice ski area in winter. The unusual memorial on your right, inscribed 'Ofiarom Zbrodni Hitlerówskiej' ('To the victims of the crimes of Hitler'), consists of artillery and a fixed ladder and was created by local sculptor Władysław Hasior. Opposite is the Zakopane office of the Polish border guards.

Where the road swings right you should cross and keep ahead to **Kuźnice** (1025m).

The Hasior war memorial on the road to Kuźnice (Blue 205)

• 206 KUŹNICE TO GIEWONT (1025m–1894m)

Grade Moderate to Polana Kondratowa, strenuous to Giewont
Distance 8km   **Average Gradient** 7% to Polana Kondratowa, 19% to Giewont
NE–SW Height Gain 869m   **Time** 3h 15m
SW–NE Height Loss 869m   **Time** 2h 30m
Winter/Spring Normally open only as far as Polana Kondratowa

A well-used route up the valleys of Dolina Bystrej and Dolina Kondratowa to two popular refuges and Giewont, the Sleeping Giant, the nearest and most distinctive mountain as seen from Zakopane. Much of it is in forest, but there are extensive sections through meadows and dwarf pine. The final ascent to the summit involves some scrambling and fixed chains, but you are rewarded with outstanding views all around – of the Western Tatras to the south, over Zakopane and Podhale to the north, and down the valleys to east and west.

The route passes the convent of Klasztor Albertynek. Nuns from here, and monks from the nearby monastery of Klasztor Albertynow, follow this route to pay their respects to Giewont's summit cross. They can be very fit, and may pass you at speed!

You are strongly advised to arrive at the summit as early as possible, to beat the crowds and avoid any threatening thunderstorm.

From **Kuźnice** (1025m, refreshments), in company with Black 901C, climb the steep, cobbled road called Droga Brata Alberta (Brother Albert Way), close to the cable-car wires. The Bystra stream occupies the valley of **Dolina Bystrej** down to your left. You soon reach **Klasztor Albertynek** (1100m) where Yellow 815 to **Klasztor Albertynow** (not shown on our map) leads off to the right. Just beyond this point is the hut where national park entry fees are collected – its location enables visitors to the religious establishments to avoid payment. (*NE–SW 0h 20m, SW–NE 0h 15m.*)

In 50m the blue route divides to go either above or below Polana Kalatówki. The right fork, continuing up the cobbled road with a better view, leads in 15 minutes to **Hotel Gorski Kalatówki** (1198m, refreshments), where Black 901C strikes off to the right. The left fork bypasses the hotel, saving 5 minutes or so. The two routes reunite 1km further up the valley. (*NE–SW 0h 30m, SW–NE 0h 25 m.*)

The route now turns up a path to the right and undulates for a while before bearing right up the side valley, Dolina Kondratowa, to join a broad stone track by a picnic table, where you turn right. A sign indicates that the route to the left is 'no entry'. (If walking SW–NE, watch out for the path which bears left off the main track beyond the picnic table.) The track leads out of the forest to the meadows

227

A nun from Klasztor Albertynek admires the view
from Giewont summit (Blue 206)

of Polana Kondratowa, the junction with Green 508 and **Schronisko Kondratowa** (1333m, refreshments). (*NE–SW 0h 40m, SW–NE 0h 30m.*)

Blue 206 continues up the valley, gently at first, with scattered clumps of dwarf pine and, in summer, a profusion of red admiral butterflies. Visible below is the green route, making for Kopa Kondracka. After a while the gradient increases, quite steeply in places, and for some metres care is needed where a stream shares the path, making it slippery. Eventually you reach Przełęcz Kondracka (1725m) and the junction with Yellow 805. A sign here uses the word *przełom*, meaning a gap created by constant erosion by a stream. (*NE–SW 1h 15m, SW–NE 1h 00m.*)

Away to the right now is the summit of Giewont with its tall iron cross. Blue 206 turns right, up the southern shoulder of Giewont, to a ledge where Red 008 comes up from the left. With all these junctions of busy routes, it can get very crowded in this area, and it has been known for an opportunistic canned-drinks seller to station himself here.

Continue on a rocky path, which gets steeper as you approach the summit, to the point where you are scrambling, with the help of fixed chains. There may be rangers controlling numbers at the usually very crowded summit, and you may be asked to limit your time there. You have to keep a careful eye out for the waymarks, because the path divides halfway up to provide a one-way system to and from the summit of **Giewont** – watch for the arrow keeping ascending walkers to the right. Do not attempt to use the left-hand route because you may cause problems for those coming down. The summit, dominated by the great iron cross, is rocky and windy, with a vertiginous drop to the north, but it is a popular picnic spot and you may have to squeeze yourself into any space you can find. To leave the summit you must follow the arrows that start at its west end. (*NE–SW 0h 30m, SW–NE 0h 20m.*)

207A KUŹNICE TO SCHRONISKO MUROWANIEC (1025m–1500m)

Grade Easy to moderate	**Distance** 5.5km	**Average Gradient** 8%
NW–SE Height Gain 475m	**Time** 2h 10m	
SE–NW Height Loss 475m	**Time** 1h 40m	
Winter/Spring Normally open only as far as Schronisko Murowaniec		

A picturesque route leading mostly through dwarf pine and above the tree-line to the pleasantly situated refuge at Murowaniec.

From **Kuźnice** (1025m), go east to cross a bridge over the Bystra stream, beside a small tarn, together with Green 509 and Yellow 810. The yellow immediately turns right, while the blue and green bear left up a track. In 10 minutes the blue

On Skupniów Upłaz en route to Schronisko Murowaniec (Blue 207A)

turns right to climb steeply through forest for another 20 minutes to an eroded bluff. Here you look out over **Dolina Bystrej** towards Polana Kalatówki and its mountain hotel beneath Giewont – a spiked summit from this angle. You can repeat this a little further on by diverting a little to your right at Boczań (1208m). (*NW–SE 0h 30m, SE–NW 0h 20m.*)

The path now climbs through forest and storm-swept trees on the crest of the northern spur of Kasprowy Wierch, and eventually emerges into the open on an eroded, rocky slope called Skupniów Upłaz. You have superb views of Nosal, Zakopane and the countryside beyond as you climb to Przełęcz między Kopami (Saddle Between the Stacks, 1499m) and the junction with Yellow 810. The stacks in question are the minor summits of Mała and Wielka Królowa Kopa, which are inaccessible to walkers. (*NW–SE 1h 15m, SE–NW 0h 55m.*)

The path continues on the level for a while, passing a vantage point with a picnic table, then descends gently through a collection of summer huts, including Betlejema (Bethlehem), a bothy belonging to the PTTK, and a weather station. Where the path divides, bear left to reach **Schronisko Murowaniec** (1500m, refreshments). Green 812, Black 908 and Black 910 also come here. (*NW–SE 0h 25m, SE–NW 0h 25m.*)

• 207B SCHRONISKO MUROWANIEC TO ZAWRAT (1500m–2158m)

Grade Moderate to Czarny Staw, strenuous to Zawrat
Distance 4.5km   **Average Gradient** 9% to Czarny Staw, 18% to Zawrat
NW–SE Height Gain 658m   **Time** 2h 35m
SE–NW Height Loss 658m   **Time** 1h 55m
Winter/Spring Normally open only as far as Schronisko Murowaniec

Relatively easy walking as far as the northernmost of three tarns called Czarny Staw (Black Tarn), after which it becomes very steep on the way to the high saddle

Approaching Zawrat (Blue 207B)
(photo: R Turnbull)

Zawrat on Orla Perć, with scrambling and several fixed chains. The lower part of the route is very popular, as can be judged by its eroded condition in some parts.

From the main entrance of **Schronisko Murowaniec** (1500m, refreshments) turn right, then in 100m bear left, now in dwarf pine. The path climbs gently to reach Pomnik Karłowicza, a monument to Mieczysław Karłowicz, a composer and pioneer skier who was killed by an avalanche here in 1909 at the tragically young age of 32. It continues up the valley of Czarny Potok (Black Brook) to a moraine, which you climb steeply to the large tarn **Czarny Staw Gąsienicowy** (to distinguish it from two others with the same name) (1637m). Green 514 goes off to the right here. (*NW–SE 0h 35m, SE–NW 0h 25m.*)

Many walkers turn back here, but Blue 207B continues along the tarn's left-hand shore, passing the junction with Yellow 813. It then climbs steadily to a rock face below Zawrat, where Green 515 and Yellow 814 turn off to the left. The character of this route now changes dramatically as it climbs very steeply above Zmarzły Staw (Frozen Tarn), with scrambling and exposed situations, and there can be danger from falling rocks. There are three stretches of fixed chain as you approach Zawrat (2158m). (*NW–SE 2h 00m, SE–NW 1h 30m.*)

You are now on the famous **Orla Perć** (Eagle Edge, Red 009B), on which you can turn right for the cable-car at Kasprowy Wierch. Do not turn left unless you are a very experienced and confident mountain walker. Blue 209 comes up to the saddle from the south.

• 208 CZERWONE STAWKI TO KARB (1698m–1853m)

Grade Moderate	**Distance** 1.5km	**Average Gradient** 12%
W–E Height Gain 155m	**Time** 0h 30m	
E–W Height Loss 155m	**Time** 0h 20m	
Winter/Spring Closed		

A useful link route, entirely above the tree-line, with splendid views over several small tarns.

From Czerwone Stawki (1698m, Little Red Tarn) on Black 908, the path climbs steadily, above the south side of the tarn Kurtkowiec, noted for containing the highest island in Poland at 1688m. The path steepens as it follows a stream, and zigzags above Długi Staw (Long Tarn) as it approaches the saddle Karb (1853m), where it joins Black 909 and Green 514.

209 MORSKIE OKO TO VALLEY OF FIVE POLISH TARNS AND ZAWRAT (1406m–2158m)

Grade Moderate to strenuous	**Distance** 10km	**Average Gradient** 8%
SE–NW Height Gain 891m/**Loss** 139m		**Time** 3h 50m
NW–SE Height Loss 891m/**Gain** 139m		**Time** 3h 10m
Winter/Spring Closed		

A switchback route with great views, passing through dwarf pine and above the tree-line. It climbs over two shoulders, then finally ascends the lovely Valley of Five Polish Tarns – you see all of them – to Zawrat, a high saddle on Orla Perć. It is quite tricky in places, with some scrambling and fixed chains.

From **Schronisko Morskie Oko** (1406m, refreshments) walk north for 400m along the road, together with Red 011. As you reach some small tarns on your right, look out for blue waymarks on your left. These indicate your path, which climbs steeply through dwarf pine. You must take care, as the rocks are uneven underfoot, and some low branches may catch your head. At two points you cross a landslip, the result of avalanches, requiring a scramble across loose rock, with fixed chains for support. The gradient becomes gentler as you approach Kepa (1683m), off to the right, and the saddle Wolarnia (1700m), with fine views of **Rysy** and over **Dolina Rybiego Potoku**. (*SE–NW 0h 50m, NW–SE 0h 40m.*)

Continue around the shoulder Opalone (Sunburned), then descend into Świstówka Roztocka, a boulder-filled hanging valley that was once the bed of a tarn, until its moraine was breached. Climb again, now on the dip slope of Świstowa Czuba (1763m). The view onwards of three of the Five Polish Tarns is breathtaking. A side path leads to the sheer north face, though you are strongly recommended not to follow it – take note of one of the few signs in English, 'Attention: do not walk – life threat'! (*SE–NW 0h 30m, NW–SE 0h 25m.*)

The path down from Świstowa Czuba is quite steep – if you are coming in the opposite direction, considerably steeper than it looks from the tarn. A short climb up its moraine leads to **Schronisko Pięciu Stawów** (refreshments) at Prezdni Staw Polski (Front Polish Tarn, 1672m) and the junction with Black 914. (*SE–NW 0h 40m, NW–SE 0h 35m.*)

Passing to the west of Przedni Staw, on a fairly level path, you come in quick succession to Mały Staw Polski (Little Polish Tarn), above which is a bothy belonging to PTTK, and **Wielki Staw Polski** (Big Polish Tarn, 1664m). Shortly before the latter, a path to your right (not waymarked but well used) provides a short cut to Green 516 and the **Siklawa** waterfall. Close by is the junction with Yellow 812C. (*SE–NW 0h 10m, NW–SE 0h 10m.*)

Above Wielki Staw the path is at first comparatively easy, climbing steadily in open terrain and passing the junction with Black 913 and Yellow 814. It then steepens considerably, with zigzags, to a spur. You follow this, with views of Czarny Staw Polski (Black Polish Tarn) and Zadni Staw Polski (Back Polish Tarn), to Zawrat. You also see a number of small tarns that do not count in the valley title. (*SE–NW 1h 40m, NW–SE 1h 20m.*)

You are now on the famous **Orla Perć** (Eagle Edge, Red 009B), on which you can turn left for the cable-car at Kasprowy Wierch. Do not turn right unless you are a very experienced and confident mountain walker. Blue 207B comes up to the saddle from the north.

· 210 ZAZADNIA POLANA TO POLANA PALENICA (944m–1210m)

Grade Easy to moderate **Distance** 6km	**Average Gradient** 8%
N–S Height Gain 266m/**Loss** 226m	**Time** 1h 55m
S–N Height Gain 226m/**Loss** 266m	**Time** 1h 45m
Winter/Spring Open	

This route goes mainly through the forest, passing the charming little monastery at Wiktorówki, and the open, grassy expanse of Rusinowa Polana. Take a bus from Zakopane to Zazadnia, where buses terminate, then walk 750m south along the road to the meadow called Zazadnia Polana. Buses run from Polana Palenica back to Zakopane. There is a small car park at the start of the route.

From Zazadnia Polana (940m), climb Dolina Filipka on the track that serves the chapel at Wiktorówki. It undulates across several brooks that flow into the main stream, Filipczański Potok. After a while the track climbs more steeply, bearing left into Dolina Złota (Golden Valley), with Złoty Potok (Golden Brook) on your left. Approaching the head of this valley, and climbing ever more steeply, the blue route leaves the track to follow a path up to the right, behind the isolated monastery at **Wiktorówki** (1140m). You can continue along the track if you wish to visit the monastery, and there is a short cut at the back to take you back to the route. (*N–S 1h 05m, S–N 0h 50m.*)

Continuing your ascent, in 10 minutes you reach **Rusinowa Polana** (1210m) and the junction with Green 513. Keep ahead on a track that contours through the meadows at the foot of a steep hill, and passes between a number of shepherds' huts. Bear right, still in the meadows, to reach the junction with Black 915. The black route continues ahead, while the blue one goes left into the forest, just before the end of the meadows. It descends quite steeply, sometimes using flights of wooden steps, into **Dolina Waksmundzka**, whose brook guides you for most of the rest of the way, but finally the path bears left across a meadow to **Polana Palenica** (984m, refreshments), and the junction with Red 011. (*N–S 0h 50m, S–N 0h 55m.*)

GREEN ROUTES

Note When reading maps, be careful not to confuse the green waymarked routes (shown by broken lines) with nature reserve borders (marked by unbroken green lines with lateral spurs).

• 500A SIWA POLANA TO SCHRONISKO CHOCHOŁOWSKA (907m–1148m)

Grade Easy	**Distance** 7km	**Average Gradient** 3%
NE–SW Height Gain 241m	**Time** 2h 05m	
SW–NE Height Loss 241m	**Time** 1h 45m	
Winter/Spring Open		

The valley of Dolina Chochołowska is one of the prettiest in the Tatras, and offers pleasant walking. The route follows the service road to Schronisko Chochołowska and has little motorised traffic – only authorised service vehicles may use it.

It is a well-used cycle route – indeed, you can hire bikes for one-way use to avoid some walking. There are three points where you can pick up or drop off – Siwa Polana, Polana pod Jaworki (for Black 901A) and Zawiesista (for Yellow 802 and Black 902).

Buses serve Siwa Polana from Zakopane, and there is a car park. To save time and energy, at least in one direction, you can take either the little road train from Siwa Polana to Polana Huciska (3km), or a dorożka (horse-drawn taxi) from Siwa Polana nearly all the way to Schronisko Chochołowska.

From **Siwa Polana** (907m, refreshments) follow the service road southwestwards as it gently ascends the well-wooded valley of **Dolina Chochołowska**, keeping close to the left bank of its main stream, Chochołowska Potok, and crossing brooks issuing from side valleys. A stone memorial marks the spot where Pope John Paul II's helicopter landed during his visit in 1983. In 15 minutes you pass the junction with Green 501 at the little meadow Merkusia Polanka. In another 40 minutes you come to the much larger meadows of Polana Huciska, where there are picnic tables and where sheep graze. Soon after that is the junction with Black 901A, then Leśniczówka (Forester's Lodge) Chochołowska, which used to be a refuge. Ahead now rises a wooded and rounded minor summit called Wielki Kopieniec. A long side valley called Starorobociańska Dolina comes in here, bringing Yellow 802 and Black 902, and there are picnic tables near the bridge over its stream. (*NE–SW 1h 25m, SW–NE 1h 15m.*)

In 15 minutes you pass the first junction with Red 001, then cross to the right bank of the main stream to reach the expansive, sloping pastures of Polana Chochołowska, where cattle and sheep graze. Passing between farm huts, you come to the junction with Szlak Papieski Biały Żolty (the Pope's White and Gold Trail – see page 250), bringing with it Yellow 801 and Red 001 again on its horseshoe course. You come to the point where horse-drawn taxis turn around, because the road rises more steeply now as it carries all three routes through bends to **Schronisko Chochołowska** (1148m, refreshments). (*NE–SW 0h 40m, SW–NE 0h 30m.*)

• 500B SCHRONISKO CHOCHOŁOWSKA TO WOŁOWIEC (1148m–2064m)

Grade Strenuous	**Distance** 8km	**Average Gradient** 18%
NE–SW Height Gain 916m	**Time** 2h 05m	
SW–NE Height Loss 916m	**Time** 1h 45m	
Winter/Spring Closed		

A well-used route providing access to the Western Tatras summits.

From **Schronisko Chochołoska** (1148m, refreshments) go down to the horse-drawn taxi terminus and follow the path heading off to the right into the forested valley Wyżnia (Upper) Chochołowska Dolina. It is fairly level at first, but after 1km starts to climb steeply, with the brook Wyżni Chochołowski Potok down to your left. The forest thins out, then you come to dwarf pine and eventually open rock on a zigzag path to the top of the ridge, which is also the border with Slovakia, at an unnamed point around 1890m. (*NE–SW 2h 30m, SW–NE 2h 00m.*)

The green waymarks finish here, but you can follow Blue 200 either left for a short but steep climb to the summit of Wołowiec (2064m), or right for an easy ridge walk back to Schronisko Chochołowska via Rakoń and Grześ.

• 501 DROGA POD REGLAMI (897m–1000m)

Grade Easy	**Distance** 13km	**Average Gradient** 2%
W–E Height Gain 123m/**Loss** 110m	**Time** 3h 30m	
E–W Height Gain 110m/**Loss** 123m	**Time** 3h 30m	
Winter/Spring Open		

One of two long, parallel routes (see also Black 901 Sciezka nad Reglami) that run along the foothills of the Western Tatras above Zakopane. Regle means 'forest zone', and Droga pod Reglami means Route below the Regle. It undulates between 897m and 1000m, from Merkusia Polanka in the west to Murowanica in the east. Most of the route is a track or quiet lane, but at Kiry you must walk beside the road for 1km. It is also an official cycle route in summer, and a cross-country ski track in winter.

The route could be completed in half a day by taking the bus from Zakopane to Siwa Polana, which is 1km from Merkusia Polanka, and walking back to Zakopane from Murowanica (1–2km). There are opportunities for refreshment at Kiry, Gronik and Buńdówki, and toilet cubicles at several points where other routes start.

The west and east ends of the route are quite gently graded, but the central section between Kiry and Gronik is steeper.

There are two optional short side trips, to Dolina za Bramka (Green 506) and Dziura (Black 907).

The west end of the route, from Merkusia Polanka to Kiry, has green way-marks, so we include it here, but the remainder has no waymarks.

• 502 TRZYDNIOWIAŃSKI WIERCH TO KOŃCZYSTY WIERCH (1758m–2002m)

Grade Moderate	**Distance** 2km	**Average Gradient** 13%
N–S Height Gain 244m	**Time** 1h 00m	
S–N Height Loss 244m	**Time** 0h 45m	
Winter/Spring Closed		

A grassy ridge providing a short link between Trzydniowiański Wierch (1758m), the highest point of Red 001, and Kończysty Wierch (2002m) on Red 002, and the border with Slovakia. It is quite steep in places, but not difficult, and there are good views into the valleys on either side. The waymarked route passes below the minor summit of Czubik (1846m), but walkers can use an alternative higher route that crosses the summit.

• 503 IWANIACKA PRZEŁĘCZ TO RACZKOWA PRZEŁĘCZ (1459m–1959m)

Grade Easy to moderate	**Distance** 5km	**Average Gradient** 15%
N–S Height Gain 634m/**Loss** 134m	**Time** 2h 35m	
S–N Height Loss 634m/**Gain** 134m	**Time** 2h 15m	
Winter/Spring Closed		

A pleasant, grassy walk along the Ornak ridge, but with some rocky patches. Once you have got the initial climb in forest out of the way, it is fairly easy going in the open, with views of the main border ridge ahead and into the valleys on either side.

From Yellow 802 at Iwaniacka Przełęcz (1459m) you climb steeply, at first in forest then dwarf pine, to Suchy Wierch Ornaczański (1832m), then follow the open, undulating ridge at about this height for most of the way. You take in several saddles and minor summits, including Ornak at 1854m. Black 902 comes up to Siwa Przełęcz (1812m), the final saddle, then the gradient steepens a little to Raczkowa Przełęcz (1959m) on Red 002. (*N–S 2h 35m, S–N 2h 15m.*)

A route from Slovakia (not covered in this book) comes up to this point, but for the time being you are not allowed to continue there (see Cross-border Walking, page 60).

504A KIRY TO SCHRONISKO ORNAK (927m–1108m)

Grade Easy	**Distance** 6.5km	**Average Gradient** 3%
N–S Height Gain 181m	**Time** 1h 30m	
S–N Height Loss 181m	**Time** 1h 20m	
Winter/Spring Normally open		

The most popular route in the Polish Tatras, being an easily accessible and gently graded stroll on a broad road through forest and sheep-grazing meadows along the pretty valley of **Dolina Kościeliska**. *It leads to Schronisko Ornak, an attractively situated refuge, with several short side trips to caves along the way. The route follows, and often crosses, the Kościeliski stream, and more streams flow in from side valleys. Aim to start early, and avoid the weekend if possible.*

The starting point at Kiry can be reached by bus from Zakopane, and has a car park, refreshments and toilets. Horse-drawn taxis (dorożki) ply between Kiry and Polana Pisana – they may save energy, but not much time.

As you set off from **Kiry** (927m, refreshments) through the broad meadows of Wyżnia Miętusia Kira, you pass a foresters' lodge on your right, while to your left rises the rocky spire of Czerwony Gronik, a minor summit at 1248m. Roe deer graze here, and may scurry away as you approach. After 20 minutes or so you enter the forest, passing the junction with Red 004, and join Black 901 for a short stretch before it bears off to the right.

Shortly after the second junction you reach Stare (Old) Kościeliska, the original settlement, where mining once took place. Here is the tiny rustic Kaplica

Zbójnicka – the Highwaymen's Chapel – where it is the custom to throw coins to protect yourself from their attentions! At the far end of the meadow is Ośrodek Hutniczy, an old forge – testimony to the mining of iron ore hereabouts during the 19th century. Blue 201 starts off to the right here, or you can make a short diversion to the Mroźna cave on Black 903 (not shown on our map). (*N–S 0h 35m, S–N 0h 30m.*)

In 25 minutes you reach **Polana Pisana** (1018m, toilets), the terminus for horse-drawn taxis and a popular picnic spot. Side trips to several caves are possible here – to Jaskinia Mylna and Jaskinia Raptawicka on Red 003, and to Smocza Jama on Yellow 803 (neither is shown on our map). The route now climbs more steeply to the meadows of Polana Smytnia, shortly after which is the junction with Green 505 and Black 905, and the welcome refuge **Schronisko Ornak** at Mala Polanka Ornaczanska (1108m). Yellow 802 starts a little further along the track. (*N–S 0h 55m, S–N 0h 50m.*)

• 504B KIRY (927m) TO PAŁKÓWKA (1129m)

Grade Easy	**Distance** 6km	**Average Gradient** 4%
SW–NE Height Gain 220m/**Loss** 25m		**Time** 1h 45m
NE–SW Height Loss 220m/**Gain** 25m		**Time** 1h 25m
Winter/Spring Open		

A route climbing the hillside west of Kościelisko, following quiet lanes and tracks, to the Gubałówka ridge, with good views of the Tatras as you approach the top. The lower section is also a cycle route. The starting point at Kiry can be reached by bus from Zakopane, and has a car park. Or, to save climbing, you could take a mountain lift to Gubałówka then walk down.

From **Kiry** (927m, refreshments) follow the lane northwards past the Hotel Halit, with the Kirowa Woda (Kiry Water) river on the left. You shortly pass the Góralskie Chatki (Highland Hut) campsite and rise through a forested section. A sports centre heralds a stretch through outlying settlements of Kościelisko, where you cross the Antalowski brook and keep ahead along a track, now climbing steadily. Keep ahead at the road in Rysulówka, and again in 500m along a major road. In 150m bear right on to a track and follow it up the hillside with good views of the Tatras. The route bears right around the head of a valley to the top of the Butorowy Wierch chair-lift, where you turn left along a lane, in company with Blue 203, to join the Gubałówka ridge at Pałkówka (1129m).

You can return to Zakopane on Blue 203, Yellow 806 or Black 906, or by bus or mountain lift from various points along the ridge.

• 505 SCHRONISKO ORNAK TO CEMNIAK (1108m–2096m)

Grade Moderate to strenuous	**Distance** 6km	**Average Gradient** 13%
W–E Height Gain 988m	**Time** 4h 20m	
E–W Height Loss 988m	**Time** 3h 25m	
Winter/Spring Normally open		

This Z-shaped route passes through remote terrain in and above the forest, which is a favourite hibernation area for bears – do not come here alone in autumn! The going is generally not difficult, but there is one very steep section.

From **Schronisko Ornak** (1108m, refreshments) go northwards a little, passing the junction with Black 905, then turn right off the main track. You climb the valley of **Dolina Tomanowa** in forest, with its brook below to your right. As you approach the valley head, the forest thins and you climb steeply to the junction with Red 006. (*W–E 1h 30m, E–W 1h 10m.*)

Turn left and continue climbing for a while before contouring round into Czerwony Żleb (Red Gully). Now the path climbs very steeply among dwarf pine, and you pass the remains of a furnace, bearing testimony to the iron ore that was mined here in the early 19th century. After rounding the rocky western shoulder of Ciemniak, you descend for a while, then contour to Chuda Przełączka (Narrow Minisaddle). (*W–E 2h 00m, E–W 1h 35m.*)

You are joined by Red 004, which you can follow back to Dolina Kościeliska, for the final push to the summit of Ciemniak (2096m). (*W–E 0h 50m, E–W 0h 40m.*)

• 506 DOLINA ZA BRAMKA (919m–989m)

Grade Easy	**Distance** 2km	**Average Gradient** 7%
NE–SW Height Gain 130m	**Time** 0h 25m	
SW–NE Height Loss 130m	**Time** 0h 20m	
Winter/Spring Normally open		

A short diversion off Green 501 up Dolina za Bramka (Valley Beyond the Little Gate), which is very picturesque, with several waterfalls, and noted for its dolomitic rocks. Because of that, and its proximity to Zakopane, this route can get very busy at times.

• 507 ZAKOPANE TO SZAFLARY (640m–1018m)

Grade Easy	**Distance** 18km	**Average Gradient** 8%
S–N Height Gain 219m/**Loss** 69m		**Time** 4h 30m
N–S Height Gain 69m/**Loss** 219m		**Time** 4h 45m
Winter/Spring Normally open		

Part of a 50km route linking Zakopane with Dursztyn in the Pieniny Spiskie hills to the northeast. Combining the Droga Papieska with the Szlak Gotycki (Gothic Trail), this route follows tracks and quiet lanes through villages on an open ridge, providing a fascinating glimpse into the rural life of Podhale. The whole trail, much of it a cycle route, can be found on the Sygnatura 1:100,000 scale map Dookoła Tatr. It is described here as far as Szaflary, from where buses return to Zakopane.

The start is on the northeastern outskirts of Zakopane, in a district called Szymony, which can be reached by bus towards Poronin – alight at the stop called Kasprowicza.

Turn left along Szpitalna street, which shortly crosses Zakopane's river, Zakopianka, and climbs to two large sanatoria. After a long, right-hand bend, where the road divides, take a path to the left, which climbs steeply up the hillside, short-cutting a zigzag track. At the top turn left along a lane called Rafaczańska Grapa, joining Red 014 and Yellow 809, with beautiful views of the Tatras. This leads to a road junction at Eliaszówka (1018m), the highest point of the route, where the routes diverge. Here is a memorial to a visit by Pope John Paul II in 1997 – see page 198. (*S–N 0h 50m, N–S 0h 40m.*)

Green 507 now heads northwards along the **Droga Papieska**, on an open ridge at around 950m, following lanes through the villages of Ząb and Czierwienne. It now gradually descends northeastwards on tracks and lanes through Skrzypne and Maruszyna to Szaflary. (*S–N 3h 40m, N–S 4h 05m.*)

• 508 SCHRONISKO KONDRATOWA TO PRZEŁĘCZ POD KONDRACKĄ KOPĄ (1333m–1863m)

Grade Moderate	**Distance** 3km	**Average Gradient** 18%
NE–SW Height Gain 530m	**Time** 1h 30m	
SW–NE Height Loss 530m	**Time** 1h 10m	
Winter/Spring Closed		

A pleasant, open route ascending the upper part of Dolina Kondratowa to the Czierwone Wierchy (Red Peaks), on the ridge that forms the border with Slovakia.

Schronisko Kondratowa (Blue 206/Green 508)

From **Schronisko Kondratowa** (1333m, refreshments) on Blue 206 follow the route with green waymarks along the valley bottom in front of the refuge. It runs level for some time, then starts to climb steeply on stepped boulders, zig-zagging as it gets higher, to reach the border ridge and Red 007 at Przełęcz pod Kondracką Kopą (Pass below Kondracka Stack, 1863m). The red-topped white posts here mark the actual border.

• 509 NOSAL (940m–1206m)

Grade Moderate	**Distance** 4km	**Average Gradient** 12%
N–S Height Gain 266m/**Loss** 181m		**Time** 1h 10m
S–N Height Gain 181m/**Loss** 266m		**Time** 1h 05m
Winter/Spring Normally open		

A scenic, semi-circular link between Zakopane and Kuźnice via Nosal, a minor summit overlooking the town. Being so easily accessible, and with fine views, it gets very busy. Parts of the route are very steep and rocky, involving short scrambles. Most of it is in forest, though there are good views from the summit over Zakopane and Kuźnice.

The green waymarks start at Murowanica, where buses stop en route to Kuźnice, on Blue 205. However, another approach route from Zakopane avoids this busy road and can provide a pleasant alternative on foot to or from Kuźnice.

Approaching from the town centre, on reaching Kuźnickie Rondo turn left along Droga na Bystre for 100m. Just past the filling station, turn right up a lane called Bulwary Słowackiego (Slovak Boulevard), which closely follows the Bystra stream. When the lane ends, keep ahead on a path and up steps, cross a road and still keep ahead to the national park hut, where entrance fees are collected.

For Kuźnice, keep on past the hut and a small tarn (a former millpond providing a popular relaxation spot) to join the road, where you turn left. For Nosal, turn left at the hut.

Kuźnice from Nosal (Green 509)

If starting from Murowanica, go sharp left down Mieczysława Karłowicza street for a short distance, then turn right across the Bystrej stream on a footbridge. Turn right to the national park hut.

Soon after the hut the path starts climbing steeply and relentlessly, with steps and short scrambles, to the summit of Nosal (1206m). You pass several rocky outcrops with vertiginous drops – they make good rest stops with fine views over Kuźnice and up Dolina Bystrej. (*N–S 0h 40m, S–N 0h 30m.*)

The first 20m down from the summit are very steep, then it is an easy descent on a rocky path in forest. The path levels out at Nosalowa Przełęcz (1103m), where Yellow 811 goes off to the left. It contours round two gullies, and is joined by Blue 207 for the final descent to **Kuźnice** (1025m, refreshments), which you approach across another former millpond. (*N–S 0h 30m, S–N 0h 35m.*)

• 510 KUŹNICE TO KASPROWY WIERCH (1025m–1987m)

Grade Moderate	**Distance** 8km	**Average Gradient** 13%
N–S Height Gain 962m	**Time** 3h 45m	
S–N Height Loss 962m	**Time** 2h 55m	
Winter/Spring Closed		

*A monotonous, twisting and rather pointless route, leading from **Kuźnice** to the summit of **Kasprowy Wierch**, as does the cable-car that plies tauntingly up and down overhead. It is mostly in forest, though at the halfway stage (Myślenickie Turnie, 1360m) there is a view down the cable-car wires towards Kuźnice.*

To add to the frustration, there are no refreshment or toilet facilities at the halfway station, but you can if you feel so inclined give up and take the cable-car for the rest of the way. Above the halfway point you are mostly climbing grassy ski slopes among the dwarf pine.

This route may be useful if you arrive on foot at Kasprowy Wierch without a booking on the cable-car, then you may prefer to walk down rather than queue.

• 511 SUCHA DOLINA STAWIAŃSKA TO LILIOWE (1685m–1952m)

Grade Strenuous	**Distance** 1.5km	**Average Gradient** 17%
N–S Height Gain 267m	**Time** 1h 10m	
S–N Height Loss 267m	**Time** 0h 50m	
Winter/Spring Closed		

*An alternative route for walkers from **Schronisko Murowaniec** aiming for the border ridge. Entirely on open, bare rock, it is steep but not difficult.*

• 512 TOPOROWA CYRHLA TO WIELKI KOPIENIEC AND JASZCZURÓWKA (894m–1328m)

Grade Moderate	**Distance** 7km	**Average Gradient** 11%
E–W Height Gain 328m/**Loss** 428m		**Time** 1h 55m★
W–E Height Gain 428m/**Loss** 328		**Time** 2h 05m★
★Add 40 minutes for the summit.		
Winter/Spring Open		

A horseshoe-shaped route, mostly in forest but with some good views, linking two points on the road east of Zakopane with the minor summit of Wielki Kopieniec or its adjoining meadow. It is probably best to start from Toporowa Cyrhla, as this involves less climbing. However, if you prefer to ascend the summit's very steep south side, you should start from Jaszczurówka.

At Toporowa Cyrhla the bus stop is in the village, 200m northeast of the starting point. There is no official car park, only space for a few cars. At Jaszczurówka the bus stop is close to the finishing point, but the car park is 250m away, opposite the famous wooden chapel.

From **Toporowa Cyrhla** (992m, refreshments), in company with Red 010, the route gently ascends through fields to enter the forest, where you pay your entry fee. Halfway up, the red route branches off to the left, then the going gets steeper as you approach Polana Kopieniec, where you have a choice. (*E–W 0h 40m, W–E 0h 30m.*)

The easy way continues through the long, broad meadow, with its sheep and picturesque huts. Alternatively, for the minor summit Wielki Kopieniec (1328m), take a zigzag path to your right, to reach the top in about 25 minutes and enjoy the fine view of the High Tatras. Take care on the descent, as it is very steep, to rejoin the main route at the south end of the meadow.

After steeply descending a forested combe, the route crosses a broad stream, then clips the corner of another meadow, Polana Olczyska, which has several picnic tables and where Yellow 811 comes in from the left. Continue down the valley to **Jaszczurówka** (refreshments). (*E–W 1h 15m, W–E 1h 35m, plus 40 minutes for the summit.*)

• 513 WIERCH PORONIEC TO GĘSIA SZYJA AND SCHRONISKO MUROWANIEC (1101m–1560m)

Grade Moderate (but with some strenuous sections)
Distance 14km   **Average Gradient** 5%
NE–SW Height Gain 664m/**Loss** 265m   **Time** 4h 15m
SW–NE Height Gain 265m/**Loss** 664m   **Time** 3h 55m
Winter/Spring Normally open

*Though mainly in forested foothills, this switchback route encounters open mead-
ows and fine viewpoints, including Gęsia Szyja, possibly the best outlook from
any minor summit in the Tatras.*

*Buses from Zakopane to Łysa Polana stop at Wierch Poroniec. The car park
is 250m south of the bus stop, and has a separate access to the route. There are
refreshment kiosks and toilets at the car park.*

From Wierch Poroniec (1101m) the path gently ascends a broad track called
Siedlarska Droga (Seven Forests Way), passing Goły Wierch (Bare Hill). A right
fork leads to **Rusinowa Polana** (1210m) and the junction with Blue 210. A
10-minute detour to the right down the blue route is well worth considering,
to visit the forest monastery of **Wiktorówki**. (*NE–SW 1h 00m, SW–NE 0h 50m.*)

You now face a fearsome climb up the long, very steeply sloping meadow,
passing an icon, but with fine views along Dolina Białki. The slope continues into the trees, and can be muddy and slippery after wet weather – care is
needed if descending. A broad grass track leads through the forest, and soon
narrows to become an earth-and-root path, climbing to the ridge of a shoulder
that leads in 30 minutes to **Gęsia Szyja** (1490m), an even finer lookout, with
views in all directions. The route now descends first to a little saddle called
Waksmundzki Przysłop (1443m), then to a clearing called Waksmundzka
Rowień (1413m), where the route is briefly shared with Red 010. (*NE–SW 1h
00m, SW–NE 0h 50m.*)

Continue down through the pastures of Polana Waksmundzka (1390m) with
its shepherds' huts, then climb and descend once more to Polana Pańszczyca
(1400m). There is now a long section of steady climbing up **Dolina Pańszczyca**,
crossing first a side stream, then the main brook (Pańszczycki Potok), soon after
which is the junction with Black 911. (*NE–SW 1h 15m, SW–NE 1h 05m.*)

The going gets easier now, as you contour round the northern shoulder of
Granaty, called Wolarczyska, the highest part of this route at about 1560m.
A long descent into **Dolina Suchej Wody** (Dry Water Valley) takes you across
its brook (Sucha Woda) to a final short climb, together with Yellow 812B to

Schronisko Murowaniec (1500m, refreshments) and the junction with Blue 207 and Black 910. (*NE–SW 1h 00m, SW–NE 1h 10m.*)

• 514 CZARNY STAW GĄSIENICOWY TO KARB (1624m–1853m)

Grade Strenuous	**Distance** 0.75km	**Average Gradient** 31%
NE–SW Height Gain 229m	**Time** 0h 35m	
SW–NE Height Loss 229m	**Time** 0h 25m	
Winter/Spring Closed		

A short but very steep route with outstanding views, providing a link to the saddle Karb. It is a stiff, rocky climb, with a short, slightly airy section, but not difficult.

From Blue 207B at the northwest corner of **Czarny Staw Gąsienicowy** (1624m), climb steeply and steadily southwest, away from the lake, on a zigzag path leading to the ridge Mały Kościelec (1863m). The route continues to the left along the ridge to the saddle Karb (1853m). This bit is slightly exposed at one point, but with excellent views on both sides down to the lakes. From here you can either continue climbing to Kościelec on Black 909, or head back down towards Murowaniec on Blue 208.

• 515 ZMARZŁY STAW TO ZADNI GRANAT (1766m–2240m)

Grade Strenuous	**Distance** 1km	**Average Gradient** 46%
W–E Height Gain 474m	**Time** 1h 55m	
E–W Height Loss 474m	**Time** 1h 30m	
Winter/Spring Closed		

*An access route to **Granaty**, the central peaks of **Orla Perć**. It is very steep, especially lower down, but not difficult, and all on open rock.*

Green 515 sets off with Yellow 814 from their junction with Blue 207 at a rock face below Zawrat. They pass Zmarzły Staw (Grey Tarn) then split after 50 minutes. Green 515 goes left, passing the junction with Black 912 in a further 20 minutes, then continues its zigzag course up to Zadni Granat.

• 516 WODOGRZMOTY MICKIEWICZA TO WIELKI STAW POLSKI (1100m–1664m)

Grade Moderate	**Distance** 6.5km	**Average Gradient** 10%
NE–SW Height Gain 564m	**Time** 2h 15m	
SW–NE Height Loss 564m	**Time** 1h 45m	
Winter/Spring Closed		

A popular route up the forested Dolina Roztoki, leading to the beautiful Dolina Pięciu Stawów Polskich (Valley of Five Polish Tarns), and passing the impressive Siklawa waterfall. The starting point can be reached by horse-drawn bus or on foot from Polana Palenica.

From **Wodogrzmoty Mickiewicza** (1100m, toilets) at the west end (nearest the cascades) of what used to be a car park, the route starts steeply up stone cobbles for some metres, then bears left up even steeper stone steps – these can be avoided by using a track to the right, which shortly rejoins the waymarked route. You descend a little to join Roztoka Potok, a brook that is soon crossed on a wooden bridge. An undulating path continues up the valley to Nowa Roztoka, a wooden shelter beside a glade frequented by jays.

Roztoka Potok now divides into several streams, which you cross on a series of wooden bridges – if the first is flooded, use a smaller one a little way upstream. After this the waymarked path takes a sharp right fork and starts to climb steeply. In 15 minutes you come to the dwarf pine zone and have a view of the mountains above, while the gnarled crags of Świstowa Czuba rise to your left. In another 20 minutes you reach the junction with Black 914, which provides a shorter but steeper route to Schronisko Pięciu Stawów. (*NE–SW 1h 30m, SW–NE 1h 10m.*)

You pass under the wires of the goods lift serving the refuge, then another 25 minutes' climbing brings the reward of a most impressive sight, the waterfall **Siklawa** (1580m), where two narrow falls at the top merge into a wide one at the foot. The path zigzags up beside the falls, passing unofficial, unwaymarked side paths that are used as short cuts to the refuge. You soon reach **Wielki Staw Polski** (1664m) and the junction with Blue 209. (*NE–SW 0h 45m, SW–NE 0h 35m.*)

517 WODOGRZMOTY MICKIEWICZA TO SCHRONISKO STARA ROZTOKA (1031m–1100m)

Grade Easy	Distance 0.75km	Average Gradient 9%
W–E Height Loss 69m	Time 0h 10m	
E–W Height Gain 69m	Time 0h 15m	
Winter/Spring Open		

*An easy stroll down to the attractively situated refuge **Schronisko Roztoka** (1031m), starting from the east end (furthest from the cascades) of the former car park at **Wodogrzmoty Mickiewicza** (1100m). It is a dead end at present, as the track shown on the map running north from the refuge to Polana Palenica is not currently accessible to walkers.*

518 CZARNY STAW POD RYSAMI TO POD CHLOPKIEM (1583m–2307m)

Grade Strenuous	Distance 1.75km	Average Gradient 42%
N–S Height Gain 724m	Time 2h 55m	
S–N Height Loss 724m	Time 2h 20m	
Winter/Spring Closed		

A very steep serpentine of a route, always zigzagging on open rocky terrain, to one of the highest accessible saddles in the Polish Tatras, situated among its highest peaks. There are two scrambles with fixed chains.

The route starts from Red 012 at **Czarny Staw pod Rysami** (1583m) and at first climbs southwest into a kettle (the geological type) called Mięguszowiecki Kocioł. It swings southeast towards the minor summit of Kazalnica, below whose rock face the fixed chains are encountered. Heading southwest again, still furiously zigzagging, the saddle shown on the map as Mięguszowiecka Przełęcz pod Chlopkiem is reached at 2307m. Mercifully, it is known by locals simply as Pod Chlopkiem.

Here, on the border with Slovakia, you are among the five highest summits in Poland. Just southeast of the saddle is Mięguszowiecki Szczyt Czarny (2410m, Black Mengusovce Peak) – locals call it Chlopek (Little Peasant) – the fourth highest summit in the Polish High Tatras. Beyond that is Rysy, the highest at 2499m. To the northwest is the fifth highest, Pośredni Mięguszowiecki Szczyt (2393m, Middle Mengusovce Peak), with the main Mięguszowiecki Szczyt (2438m, second highest) beyond that.

800 SCHRONISKO CHOCHOŁOWSKA TO GRZEŚ (1148m–1653m)

Grade Strenuous	**Distance** 3km	**Average Gradient** 17%
F–W Height Gain 505m	**Time** 1h 45m	
W–E Height Loss 505m	**Time** 1h 15m	
Winter/Spring Closed		

A quick and relatively easy way up to the border ridge from Schronisko Chochołowska – especially if you take the horse-drawn taxi or a rented cycle part way to the refuge. It is mostly in forest, quite steep in places, with zigzags.

From Green 500A near Schronisko Chochołowska (1148m, refreshments) take the path from the second bend that climbs into the forest beside the Bobrowiecki brook. Near the top it bends left to climb out of the gully, while Black 916 leads ahead to Bobrowiecka Przełęcz, recently reopened to walkers. The forest clears a little, allowing a good view down Dolina Chochołowska, then the path swings right and climbs more steeply to the border ridge. You must turn left here, as the route going right into Slovakia is also currently inaccessible to walkers from Poland – but see Cross-border Walking, page 60. Yellow 800 finishes at the minor summit, Grześ (1653m, confusingly also known as Kończiste in Poland, while in Slovak it is Lúčne), another fine viewpoint, but you can continue along the ridge on Blue 200.

801 THE POPE'S WHITE AND GOLD TRAIL: SCHRONISKO CHOCHOŁOWSKA TO JARZĄBCZE SZAŁASISKA (1148m–1265m)

Grade Easy	**Distance** 2.5km	**Average Gradient** 5%
N–S Height Gain 117m	**Time** 0h 50m	
S–N Height Loss 117m	**Time** 0h 40m	
Winter/Spring Open		

This route is Szlak Papieski Biało-Złoty (the Pope's White and Gold Trail), created to commemorate the visit by Pope John Paul II (see page 198) to the cross at Jarząbcze Szałasiska in June 1983, and passing three other crosses along the way.

The route starts from Schronisko Chochołowska (1148m), together with Red 001. They descend to the path junction at the foot of the clearing, then turn right up the track that gently ascends the Upper Chochołowska Valley, closely following its stream. Entering the side valley Dolina Jarząbcza (Rowan Valley), it climbs more steeply to the final cross at the foot of the clearing Jarząbcze Szałasiska (1265m).

• 802 DZIURA W ZAWIESISTE TO IWANIACKA PRZEŁĘCZ AND SCHRONISKO ORNAK (1037m–1459m)

Grade Moderate	**Distance** 6km	**Average Gradient** 12%
NW–SE Height Gain 422m/**Loss** 351m		**Time** 2h 30m
SE–NW Height Gain 351m/**Loss** 422m		**Time** 2h 25m
Winter/Spring Closed		

A link between the Chochołowska and Kościeliska valleys, via Iwaniacka Przełęcz, a saddle at the foot of the Ornak ridge. It is mostly in forest, but from the saddle you should have good views of the Western Tatras summits. The route is steep nearly all the way, and very steep on either side of the saddle.

The route starts from Green 500A by the shelter at Dziura w Zawiesiste (Hanging Hole, 1037m) in Dolina Chochołowska, together with Black 902, ascending the Starorobociańska valley. In 15 minutes, at Polana Iwanówka (1085m), the black route carries on up the valley, while Yellow 802 turns to the left behind a hut to cross the meadow. It climbs the side valley of a side valley, Iwaniacka Dolina, crossing and recrossing its beck, which is often dry in summer. After a while the route diverts left into a corrie and a small meadow below the minor summit of Kominiarski Wierch (1829m). Eventually you reach the saddle, Iwaniacka Przełęcz (1459m), and the junction with Green 503. *(NW–SE 1h 30, SE–NW 1h 10m.)*

East of the saddle, another usually dry valley is followed most of the way down. Towards the bottom, at the confluence of two streams (or streambeds), the path contours to the right then descends across the Kościeliski stream to **Schronisko Ornak** (1108m, refreshments) and the junctions with Green 505 and Black 905. *(NW–SE 1h 00m, SE–NW 1h 15m.)*

• 803 POLANA PISANA TO SMOCZA JAMA (1018m–1120m)

Grade Mostly easy, but with one strenuous and exposed section
Distance 2km   **Average Gradient** 7%
S–N Height Gain 102m/**Loss** 102m   **Time** 0h 50m
Winter/Spring Closed
This route can only be followed S–N. Torch required.

Not shown on the route map in this book, this is a worthwhile circular side trip from Green 504A at Polana Pisana to the cave Smocza Jama (Dragon's Den) – not to be confused with the more famous cave of the same name in Kraków. There is a one-way system on narrow paths. The route inside the cave goes steeply down, including a fixed chain, and is very muddy in places – each person must bring a torch with spare bulb and batteries.

The approach route passes through the Wąwóz (Ravine) Kraków, which was a huge cave until its roof fell in. You will see hundreds of sticks propped up at the side of the path – a sarcastic gesture by local people to help support the walls from further collapse! One section is steep and exposed, with a fixed chain and a 10m ladder to negotiate.

• 804 DOLINA LEJOWA (922m–1093m)

Grade Easy	**Distance** 4km	**Average Gradient** 5%
N–S Height Gain 171m	**Time** 1h 10m	
S–N Height Loss 171m	**Time** 0h 50m	
Winter/Spring Normally open		

A mostly gently graded route along the peaceful Lejowa valley, beside its beck, with alternate stretches through forest and meadow.

The route starts from Green 501 at Między Ściany (922m), between Siwa Polana and Kiry. Near the top the path leaves the brook and climbs more steeply left-wards to join Black 901A at the meadow Niżnia Polana Kominiarska (1093m).

• 805 DOLINA MAŁEJ ŁĄKI AND KOPA KONDRACKA (938m–2005m)

Grade Moderate	**Distance** 7km	**Average Gradient** 14%
NW–SE Height Gain 965m	**Time** 4h 00m	
SE–NW Height Loss 965m	**Time** 3h 00m	
Winter/Spring Normally open only as far as Rowienki		

A popular and pleasant access route to Giewont and the Czerwone Wierchy, through forest and meadows, and on open rock approaching the top. The start and finish are quite steep, but the central part is gentle. Buses from Zakopane serve the start at Gronik.

From **Gronik** (922m, refreshments) the route follows a forest track for 1.5km up the Małej Łąki valley, beside its stream, together with Blue 202. Where the track ends, the routes diverge onto paths, with Yellow 805 taking the left-hand one, which continues up the valley. At Rówienki (1163m) Black 901B is crossed. (*NW–SE 1h 00m, SE–NW 0h 45m.*)

The path keeps ahead to follow a level course along the left-hand side of the long Wielka Polana (Big Meadow), then starts climbing again in forest. It gets much steeper, tortuously climbing Głazisty Żleb (Rocky Gully), then briefly coming into the open before entering forest again to reach the saddle Przełęcz Kondracka (1725m), where Blue 206 takes traffic for Giewont off to the left. (*NW–SE 2h 00m, SE–NW 1h 30m.*)

Yellow 805 turns right to climb fairly steeply up the crest of a spur to join Red 007 on the border ridge at Kopa Kondracka (2005m). (*NW–SE 1h 00m, SE–NW 0h 45m.*)

806 ZAKOPANE TO DZIANISZ (830m–1129m)

Grade Easy	**Distance** 15km	**Average Gradient** 5%
SE–NW Height Gain 299m/**Loss** 279m		**Time** 2h 55m
NW–SE Height Gain 279m/**Loss** 299m		**Time** 3h 00m
Winter/Spring Normally open		

An easy excursion on paths and lanes into the woods and farmland northwest of Zakopane, finishing at the attractive old village of Dzianisz. The steepest climb can be avoided by taking a mountain lift to the Gubałówka ridge.

The route starts from Kościeliska street in Zakopane, near Stary Cmentarz (Old Cemetery). Approaching from Krupówki, turn right down a lane (Gładkie) that passes underneath the main road flyover. In 400m, turn left across a stream, then immediately turn right, just before the holiday house 'Juhas'.

When the lane ends, keep ahead on a path that steadily ascends the hillside, through woods and meadows, eventually passing under cable-car wires to the road on the Gubałówka ridge, joining Red 014, Blue 203 and Black 906. Turn left along it to Pałkówka, with good views of the Tatras. (*SE–NW 1h 15m, NW–SE 1h 00m.*)

The rest of the route follows lanes, and is a cycle route. The first 1.5km is shared with Red 014 as far as Słodyczki, where the red route goes off on a track to the right, and the yellow continues along the lane through Gruszki to its end at the straggling village of **Dzianisz** (850m). (*SE–NW 1h 40m, NW–SE 2h 00m.*)

Buses go from here to Gubałówka and Zakopane.

• 807 DOLINA BIAŁEGO (SARNIA SKAŁA NATURE TRAIL) (920m–1212m)

Grade Easy   **Distance** 4.5km   **Average Gradient** 7%
NE–SW Height Gain 292m   **Time** 1h 15m
SW–NE Height Loss 292m   **Time** 0h 55m
Winter/Spring Normally open

A popular route that is also a nature trail (Ściezka Przyrodnicza) with interpreta-tion boards – currently only in Polish. Entirely in forest, it ascends the pretty valley called Dolina Białego, following Biały Potok (White Brook), and passing many small waterfalls and cascades. It is aptly named, as the bed is of white limestone. Though the gradient is mostly gentle, there are a couple of steep stretches near the top. The nature trail continues to the summit of Sarnia Skała on Black 901C.

The best way to reach the start from Zakopane is to go up the street called Droga do Białego, past Hotel Belvedere, then follow ascending paths through Las Białego (White Wood), close to Biały Potok. On reaching the lane (Green 501 Droga pod Reglami) turn right for 300m to a sharp right-hand bend, where Yellow 807 turns up to the left.

• 808 UGORY RIDGE AND JAN KASPROWICZ TRAIL (810m–937m)

Grade Easy   **Distance** 4.5km   **Average Gradient** 3%
SW–NE Height Gain 67m/**Loss** 127m   **Time** 1h 10m
NE–SW Height Gain 127m/**Loss** 67m   **Time** 1h 20m
Winter/Spring Open

Part of our 'Zakopane Horseshoe' – see route suggestion number 12. An easy and interesting promenade east of Zakopane along a ridge called Ugory (also called Mrowców Wierch – Ants' Hill), with outstanding views of the Tatras and over the town. It goes through meadows that are filled with flowers in spring and early summer – and presumably ants. The route is called Szlak imienia Jana Kasprowicza (Jan Kasprowicz Trail), after the poet who is commemorated in a museum at Harenda. Waymarking was patchy at the time of writing.

The route starts in Zakopane (870m), near the south end of Jagiellońska street, by the bend at its junction with Bulwary Słowackiego (Slovak Boulevard). Climb the bumpy, narrow path beside a fence and turn right at the top along a lane, passing the Panorama complex. In 100m, before a gate, turn left up a rough track. Keep on up a sheep pasture (a short ski run in winter) heading for a radio mast at the

Typical Góral haystacks on Ugory Ridge, with Havran in the White Tatras, Slovakia (Yellow 808)

top of the hill Antałówka (937m). This is a fine viewpoint, with the rolling hills of Podhale to the north and the Tatras peaks to the south. The slightly isolated peak at the left end is Havran (2152m) in Slovakia's White Tatras.

Ignore the ridge track to your left and continue ahead to join a lane in a settlement, also called Antałówka. Turn left at a road junction (Droga Homolacka) to follow the ridge for the next 2.5km, soon passing a modern chapel with a very pretty interior. When the tarmac ends keep ahead along an earth track, which soon turns to grass, past the machinery of some small ski lifts. Keep ahead at a fork.

You may see a lark ascending, and brimstone and tortoiseshell butterflies fluttering. In late summer, traditional Góral triangular haystacks dot the fields. Away to your left, the distinctive yellow building with a green roof is the Sokolówski Hospital, while to your right is the modern church in Olcza, where visiting choirs sometimes perform. Halfway along, you pass an iron-fenced cross, whose inscription, roughly translated, says 'Lord protect us from plague, hunger, fire and war'.

Towards the end of the ridge, at an icon encased in a concrete pillar, turn sharp left to a track and follow it down to cross the railway line from Kraków. It is unguarded – look both ways. Continue to the main road and keep ahead along a short track between a house and a stream. At a minor road in **Guty** (810m) turn right to a porch, which marks the start of Yellow 809. You can continue along the road for 300m to rejoin the main road, where there are buses back to Zakopane and a McDonald's!

255

• 809 GUTY TO GUBAŁÓWKA (810m–1120m)

Grade Easy to moderate   **Distance** 5.5km   **Average Gradient** 6%
NE–SW Height Gain 310m   **Time** 2h 10m
SW–NE Height Loss 310m   **Time** 1h 40m
Winter/Spring Open

The second part of our Zakopane Horseshoe, providing a longer and quieter route to the popular Gubałówka ridge. It is mostly a gentle ascent, but a very steep section comes soon after the start (black squirrels here). You could make the whole route downhill by taking a mountain lift to Gubałówka, then walk to Guty, but in wet weather the steep slope near the end may be very slippery. Buses from Zakopane call at Guty en route to Poronin and Nowy Targ.

The route starts in **Guty** (810m, refreshments), on a minor road running parallel to the main one, at an unusual porch that leads you across a footbridge over the Zakopianka river. Climb steps to the Jan Kasprowicz Museum, whose entrance is to the left. The route goes round to the right of the building and on to another road, where you turn right (to the left is a pretty wooden church with an onion-shaped spire). Pass a wooden well, then walk through the village for 800m, passing food shops and bars. Where the road bears down to the right (more bars there), take the tarmac lane to your left. Go left of an inhabited shack and climb a long and very steep slope up a wooded combe. Nearing the top, keep ahead at a crossing path to join a track, where you turn left to join Red 014 at the top of a chairlift (refreshments). *(NE–SW 0h 40m, SW–NE 0h 30m.)*

The track follows a ridge called Rafaczańska Grapa, from where you have a fantastic view leftwards, across Zakopane, of the whole Tatras spread – White, High and Western – while to the right are the rolling hills of Podhale. The track soon joins a road through the straggling settlement of Rafaczówki. After 1.5km Green 507 comes in from the left at a road junction, and the three routes run together for 400m to the next junction by the Pope John Paul II memorial (see page 198) at the settlement Eliaszówka (1018m), though a sign says Ząb, which is the village further north. *(NE–SW 0h 45m, SW–NE 0h 35m.)*

The green route goes right, the red and yellow go left, still on a lane, which is the **Droga Papieska** and also a cycle route. It climbs steadily for just over 1km to a junction where Blue 204 crosses. Continue ahead for a further 1km to **Gubałówka** (1020m, refreshments). *(NE–SW 0h 45m, SW–NE 0h 35m.)*

Yellow 809 finishes by the funicular top station, but you can walk down to Zakopane on any of Blue 203, Yellow 806 or Black 906, or take a mountain lift.

810 DOLINA JAWORZYNKA (1025m–1499m)

Grade Easy to moderate   **Distance** 4.5km   **Average Gradient** 12%
NW–SE Height Gain 474m   **Time** 1h 45m
SE–NW Height Loss 474m   **Time** 1h 15m
Winter/Spring Normally open as far as Polana Jaworzynka

Of all the routes from Kuźnice, this one gets out of the forest most quickly, soon reaching the extensive and pretty meadows of Polana Jaworzynka on a gentle path. Higher up it becomes quite steep and rocky.

Approaching from Zakopane, on reaching the steps to the cable-car station at **Kuźnice** (1025m, refreshments), turn left past the restaurant and cross the stream beside the little tarn, together with Blue 207A and Green 509, to the national park entry hut. Turn right, recrossing the stream, and climb gently in forest above the Bystrej valley. You soon bear left into the side valley, Dolina Jaworzynka, to reach the meadows of Polana Jaworzynka, with its collection of summer huts. The stream is usually dry here in summer, as is the little reservoir that you pass at the start of the meadows, though in spring they are filled with meltwater. The valley narrows as you climb, and shortly after a point where the stream beds divide, the path turns right to climb steeply through a forested section. Emerging from the forest, you continue climbing steeply on a zigzag path to Przełęcz między Kopami (Saddle Between the Stacks, 1501m) and the junction with Blue 207.

The Biela river at Kuźnice (Blue 207/Green 509/Yellow 810)

• 811 POLANA OLCZYSKA TO NOSALOWA PRZEŁĘCZ (1038m–1103m)

Grade Easy   **Distance** 1km   **Average Gradient** 2%
SE–NW Height Gain 65m   **Time** 0h 30m
NW–SE Height Loss 65m   **Time** 0h 25m
Winter/Spring Normally open

A short link, mostly in forest, between Green 512 and Green 509, with a large viewing platform at its east and overlooking Olczyski Potok.

• 812A SUCHA PRZEŁĘCZ TO MUROWANIEC (1950m–1500m)

Grade Moderate   **Distance** 3.5km   **Average Gradient** 13%
SW–NE Height Loss 450m   **Time** 1h 10m
NE–SW Height Gain 450m   **Time** 1h 30m
Winter/Spring Closed

A popular route through dwarf pine and on open rock for people taking the easy way to Schronisko Murowaniec, via cable-car to Kasprowy Wierch.

From the cable-car station at **Kasprowy Wierch** (1987m) the route descends fairly gently southwards to Sucha Przełęcz (1950m), then more steeply swings left along a rocky shoulder to the right of the valley Sucha Dolina Stawiańska. The chair-lift opposite serves skiers in winter only. In 30 minutes, now among dwarf pine, you pass the start of Green 511, then the path levels out as you go under the chair-lift wires to the junction with Black 908. The gradient is quite gentle now, as you pass several small tarns to reach **Schronisko Murowaniec** (1500m, refreshments).

• 812B MUROWANIEC TO KRZYŻNE (1500m–2112m)

Grade Easy to Czerwony Staw, strenuous to Krzyżne   **Distance** 6.5km
Average Gradient 5% to Czerwony Staw, 18% to Krzyżne
NW–SE Height Gain 724m/**Loss** 112m   **Time** 2h 55m
SE–NW Height Loss 112m/**Gain** 724m   **Time** 2h 15m
Winter/Spring Closed

A comparatively easy access route to the east end of Orla Perć at the spectacularly situated saddle of Krzyżne, from where there are incredible views in all directions.

The route starts together with Green 513 from **Schronisko Murowaniec** (1500m, refreshments). At first it descends through forest into **Dolina Suchej Wody** (Dry Water Valley) to cross Czarny Potok (Black Brook) at about 1440m, then parts company with the green route. You climb steadily through dwarf pine around Zadni Upłaz, the northern shoulder of the Granaty massif, reaching 1680m. Then a short descent takes you into the broad **Dolina Pańszczyca** and the junction with Black 911 at 1628m. (*NW–SE 1h 00m, SE–NW 0h 50m.*)

A gentle ascent takes you into a corrie to contour around Czerwony Staw (Red Tarn, 1654m). You start climbing more steeply now, on open rock, to **Krzyżne** (Crosswise, 2112m). The last stretch is very steep, but not difficult. (*NW–SE 1h 55m, SE–NW 1h 25m.*)

This is the revered **Orla Perć** – see Red 009B and Yellow 812C.

812C WIELKI STAW POLSKI TO KRZYŻNE (1664m–2112m)

Grade Strenuous	**Distance** 3km	**Average Gradient** 30%
S–N Height Gain 448m	**Time** 1h 30m	
N–S Height Loss 448m	**Time** 1h 15m	
Winter/Spring Closed		

A delightful route linking one of the biggest tarns in the Tatras with one of its finest viewpoints. This is bear country, and you are advised not to tackle this route on your own.

From the junction with Blue 209 on the north shore of **Wielki Staw Polski** (1664m), the route ascends gently at first, following the fringe of the dwarf pine along Dolina Roztoki. After crossing an area of broken rock caused by avalanches, you climb more steeply for a while, then contour around a rock face, which is the southern point of the **Granaty** massif. You descend briefly across a corrie, then cross a stream, with the sound of the Buczynowy Siklawa cascades off to the right. Climbing more steeply now on broken rock up the south side of Buczynowy Turnia, you reach the saddle **Krzyżne** (Crosswise, 2113m) on **Orla Perć** – see Red 009B and Yellow 812B.

813 CZARNY STAW GĄSIENICOWY TO SKRAJNY GRANAT (1637m–2225m)

Grade Strenuous	**Distance** 2km	**Average Gradient** 30%
NW–SE Height Gain 588m	**Time** 2h 10m	
SE–NW Height Loss 588m	**Time** 1h 45m	
Winter/Spring Closed		

A short and comparatively easy route to the Granaty massif and Orla Perć.

From Blue 207B above the east shore of **Czarny Staw Gąsienicowy** (1637m) you start among dwarf pine, but soon reach open rock. The final ascent to the summit is very steep, with a short fixed chain. This is the northernmost peak of the **Granaty** massif, called Skrajny (Outer) Granat (2225m, see Red 009B).

814 ZMARZŁY STAW TO MORSKIE OKO (1406m–2137m)

Plus optional diversion to Szpiglasowy Wierch (2172m)

Grade Strenuous	**Distance** 10km	**Average Gradient** 20%
NW–SE Height Gain 838m/**Loss** 1198m		**Time** 6h 15m
SE–NW Height Gain 1198m/**Loss** 838m		**Time** 6h 35m
Diversion to Szpiglasowy Wierch + 0h 25m		
Winter/Spring Closed		

A long and tortuous route linking the three main tarn areas of the Polish Tatras, almost entirely on open rock. There are two high saddles to cross, each involving very steep climbs with fixed chains.

After leaving Blue 207B at 1766m in company with Green 515, in 20 minutes you pass little Zmarzły Staw (Frozen Tarn). In another 30 minutes the green route goes off to the left, while the yellow climbs to the right up the steep slopes of Kozi Wierch (Goat Peak, 2291m). You cross it at the saddle Kozia Przełęcz (2137m) on **Orla Perć**, with outstanding views. The lower summit immediately to the left is Kozie Czuby (Goat's Tufts, 2266m), while to the right is Zamarła Turnia (2179m, Petrified Crag). There are fixed chains on either side of the saddle, and snow often lies here, hiding the chains and hindering progress – an ice-axe may be helpful. *(NW–SE 1h 40m, SE–NW 1h 20m.)*

You now descend into **Dolina Pięciu Stawów Polskich** (Valley of Five Polish Tarns), one of the most beautiful valleys in the Tatras, briefly joining Blue 209

*Mali Kozi Wierch, beside which Yellow 814 crosses Orla Perć
(Red 009B) (photo: R Turnbull)*

before passing between two of the larger tarns, **Czarny Staw Polski** and **Wielki Staw Polski**, at around 1705m. Climbing again, there is another fixed chain to tackle just before the saddle Szpiglasowa Przełęcz (2110m). (*NW–SE 2h 45m, SE–NW 2h 45m.*)

You now have an opportunity to make a short diversion to the summit of Szpiglasowy Wierch (2172m) on the border ridge, which should take about 25 minutes, plus whatever time you choose to stop there. Slovaks call it Hrubý Štít (Rough Peak), and there are splendid views from here of their summit, Kôprovský Štít (2363m), and down Kôprova Dolina with its tarns.

The descent follows a serpentine route down the slopes of Miedziane (Copper), passing the junction with Red 013. Off to the right is Cubryna (pronounced Tsoobreena), Poland's sixth highest summit at 2376m. The two mountains frame Dolina za Mnichem (Monk Valley), which contains several small tarns. Finally you enter the dwarf pine above the great tarn, **Morskie Oko**, for a gentle descent to the refuge at its north end, Schronisko Morskie Oko (1406m, refreshments). (*NW–SE 1h 50m, SE–NW 2h 30m.*)

• 815 SIKLAWICA (1042m–1100m)

Grade Easy	**Distance** 0.5km	**Average Gradient** 9%
N–S Height Gain 58m	**Time** 0h 15m	
S–N Height Loss 58m	**Time** 0h 15m	
Winter/Spring Normally open		

A very short route, not marked on our map, up a fairly steep path to the impressive cascades of Siklawica.

From the refreshment kiosk at Polana Strążyska, follow Black 901C to the top of the meadow then follow the stream to the cascades.

• 816 KLASZTOR ALBERTYNÓW (1100m–1180m)

Grade Easy	**Distance** 0.7km	**Average Gradient** 10%
SW–NE Height Gain 70m	**Time** 0h 40m	
NE–SW Height Loss 70m	**Time** 0h 30m	
Winter/Spring Open		

The route for visitors to the Albertynów monastery, easily reached from Kuźnice. It is not marked on our map.

The track starts from Blue 206 opposite the gate to **Klasztor Albertynek** at about 1100m and gently climbs Szeroki Żleb (Broad Gully) beside a stream. It rises more steeply towards the end to reach **Klasztor Albertynów** at about 1180m.

BLACK ROUTES

• 900 CHOCHOŁOWSKA POLANA (1120m–1148m)

Grade Easy	**Distance** 0.5km	**Average Gradient** 5%
E–W Height Gain 28m	**Time** 0h 15m	
W–E Height Loss 28m	**Time** 0h 15m	
Winter/Spring Normally open		

A stroll around the sheep pastures of Chochołowska Polana (which become a small ski slope in winter), leading to the little chapel of Święty Jan Chrzciciela (St John the Baptist) at the top of the meadow. The route (not marked on our map) starts at the junction of Red 001, Blue 500A and Yellow 801, and finishes at Schronisko Chochołowska, but can easily be made into a circular walk from the refuge.

• 901 ŚCIEŻKA POD REGLAMI (952m–1377m)

Ścieżka pod Reglami (Path above the Regel) is a long but fascinating route along the lower slopes of the Tatras – regel being local dialect for both the lower slopes and the forest zone (see also Green 501 – Droga pod Regle). The full distance is 18km and could be completed in a long and fairly strenuous day, with a total of 8 hours walking and around 1150m ascent, but note that there is just one place where refreshments can be obtained (Polana Strążyska), so you should take your own. We have divided it into three roughly equal sections (Western, Central and Eastern) that can be incorporated into walks using intersecting routes.

The grade is moderate, though in places quite rough and steep. The route links seven main valleys (Chochołowska, Lejowa, Kościeliska, Małej Łąki, Strążyska, Białego and Bystrej) and crosses six saddles (Kominiarska, Kominiarski, Miętusi, Grzybowcu, Czerwona and Białego). On the eastern section you can make a short diversion to Sarnia Skała, for an outstanding view over Zakopane and Podhale.

• 901A ŚCIEŻKA POD REGLAMI Western Section, Dolina Chochołowska to Dolina Kościeliska (952m–1307m)

Grade Moderate   **Distance** 6.5km   **Average Gradient** 12%
W–E Height Gain 342m/**Loss** 392m   **Time** 2h 20m
E–W Height Gain 392m/**Loss** 342m   **Time** 2h 15m
Winter/Spring Normally open

From Green 500A at Polana pod Jaworki in **Dolina Chochołowska** (1002m), the route crosses a stream then climbs quite steeply through forest to the sheep pasture Polana Jamy (Pits Clearing). It goes round a gully and past the crags of Kobyle Glowy (Mares' Heads), then ascends the small valley, Huciańska Dolina, to the saddle Kominiarska Przełęcz (1307m), which divides two minor, wooded summits. You now descend into the upper part of the Lejowa valley, emerging among the shepherds' huts of Niżnia Kominiarska Polana, on the far side of which is the junction with Yellow 804 (1093m). (*W–E 1h 45m, E–W 1h 30m.*)

    The route climbs very gently to the next saddle, Kominiarski Przysłop (1130m), then descends steadily into **Dolina Kościeliska,** joining Green 504A for the last few hundred metres and across the stream to finish at Polana Cudakowa (952m), the lowest point of Ścieżka pod Reglami. (*W–E 0h 35m, E–W 0h 45m.*)

For Kiry and buses to Zakopane, carry on down the main valley. To continue along Ścieżka pod Reglami, turn right.

• 901B ŚCIEŻKA POD REGLAMI Central Section, Dolina Kościeliska to Strążyska Dolina (952m–1311m)

Grade Moderate	**Distance** 6km	**Average Gradient** 11%
W–E Height Gain 385m/**Loss** 295m		**Time** 2h 30m
E–W Height Gain 295m/**Loss** 385m		**Time** 2h 20m
Winter/Spring Normally open		

Together with Red 004, Ścieżka nad Reglami continues eastwards from Green 504A at Polana Cudakowa in **Dolina Kościeliska** (952m) along the level sheep pasture called Zahradziska in the Miętusia (Mint) side valley. The red route soon diverges to the right, while the black stays in the valley. On entering the forest, the path starts to climb, increasingly steeply, to reach a large meadow called Ogon and the saddle Przysłop Miętusi (Little Mint Saddle, 1189m), a popular picnic spot, from where there are good views. Here is the junction with Red 005 and Blue 202. The route descends almost imperceptibly into **Dolina Małei Łąki**, to cross Yellow 805 at a clearing called Równienki (1163m). (*W–E 1h 15m, E–W 1h 00m.*)

You skirt another clearing (Mała Polanka) then start climbing steeply again on the way to the next saddle, Przełęcz w Grzybowcu (1311m), among forested hills. Here you join Red 008 to tackle a precipitous drop on zigzags, then a stream is followed quite steeply down to Polana Strążyska (1042m, refreshments) in **Dolina Strążyska**. (*W–E 1h 15m, E–W 1h 20m.*)

You have the choice of turning left for Zakopane on Red 008, or right to continue along Ścieżka nad Reglami.

• 901C ŚCIEŻKA POD REGLAMI Eastern Section, Strążyska Dolina to Kuźnice, including Sarnia Skaia (1025m–1377m)

Grade Moderate	**Distance** 5.5km	**Average Gradient** 16%
W–E Height Gain 438m/**Loss** 455m		**Time** 3h 05m
E–W Height Gain 455m/**Loss** 438m		**Time** 3h 05m
Winter/Spring Normally open only as far as Biale		

This section of Ścieżka pod Reglami is a little steeper than the others, as it works its way along the precipitous northern slopes of the Giewont massif. From Red

008 at Polana Strążyska (1042m, refreshments) in **Dolina Strążyska**, it continues up the meadow beside the right-hand stream and into the forest. A rewarding 20-minute diversion can be made along Yellow 815 to the Siklawica cascades. The black route now climbs very steeply, on zigzags at first, to Czerwona Przełęcz (Red Saddle, 1301m). (*W–E 0h 45m, E–W 0h 35m.*)

Though not compulsory, of course, the diversion to **Sarnia Skała** (1377m) is an integral part of the route, though it may be closed in winter, depending on snow conditions. This rocky outcrop has outstanding views over Zakopane and Podhale, and up to Giewont. (*W–E 0h 20m, E–W 0h 20m.*)

Ascending Droga Brata Alberta near Klasztor Albertynek (Blue 206/Black 901C)

From the saddle, the route descends to Białe, briefly following the nature trail that features in Yellow 807, which goes off to the left down the valley. The Ścieżka climbs round the head of **Dolina Białego**, becoming more rocky and a little more exposed than is usual for this route, as it twists and turns around several gullies (this section may also be closed in winter). However, there are great views down the valley, with its many cascades. Eventually you reach the saddle Wyżnia Przełęcz Białego (1325m), then a snaking zigzag path takes you steeply down to Polana Kalatówki, where **Schronisko Kalatówki** (1198m, refreshments) is a short distance to the right. The final stretch of the Ścieżka joins Blue 206 down the cobbled road called Droga Brata Alberta for 1.5km, passing **Klasztor Albertynek**, to **Kuźnice** (1025m, refreshments). (*W–E 2h 00m, E–W 2h 10m.*)

• 902 DOLINA STAROROBIAŃSKA (1037m–1812m)

Grade Moderate	**Distance** 6km	**Average Gradient** 13%
N–S Height Gain 775m	**Time** 2h 45m	
S–N Height Loss 775m	**Time** 2h 10m	
Winter/Spring Closed		

A comparatively easy access route up the forested Starorobiańska valley to the main ridge of the Western Tatras. The ascent is gradual, though it steepens towards the top.

Together with Yellow 802, the route starts from Green 500A by the shelter at Dziura w Zawiesiste (Hanging Hole, 1037m) in **Dolina Chochołowska**. At a clearing called Polana Iwanówka, the yellow route goes off to the left up a side valley. The main stream, Starorobiańska Potok, is always to your right, sometimes quite close, sometimes far below. You cross many side streams and pass many dry gullies. Eventually the forest is left behind and you continue up among dwarf pine and meadows, with the path steepening considerably as you reach Siwa Przełęcz (Grey Saddle, 1812m). Here, Green 503 takes over for the short distance to the main ridge.

• 903 JASKINIA MROŹNA (971m–1100m)

Grade Moderate	**Distance** 1.5km	**Average Gradient** 15%
N–S Height Gain 220m	**Time** 1h 15m	
Winter/Spring Normally open until spring (cave closed)		
This route can only be followed from north to south.		

A short diversion from Green 504A, not shown on our map, this leads to Frosty Cave, one of the longest caves in the area at 530m. It has stalactites and a lake, and there is a small admission charge with a guided tour. The cave is lit, so you do not need a torch.

The route starts from Green 504A by the forge Ośrodek Hutniczy at Stare Kościeliska (971m). Cross the bridge over the stream, then take a level path leading to the small Jaskinia Czynna (Active Cave), from where a steep path leads up to the main cave. You shortly pass Lodowe Źródło (Icy Spring), the source of three streams. Its water, at a constant temperature of about 5°C (41°F), flows at between 245 to 620 litres per second.

The path through Jaskinia Mroźna is level, at about 1100m, and there is one-way traffic. The separate entrance (*wejście*) and exit (*wyście*) are marked on walking maps. A steep, zigzag path leads quickly back down to the valley, some way up from where you started.

• 904 DOLINA KOSCIELISKA – JASKINIA RAPTAWICKA (*c.*1200m)

Grade Strenuous   **Distance** 1.5km round trip   **Time** 1h 00m
Winter/Spring Normally open

A short diversion from Red 003, not shown on our map. The cave is unlit, so you must bring your own torch with spare battery and bulb. A ladder and fixed chains take you down to the bottom of the cave, which is a dead end, so you have to climb up again.

Jaskinia Raptawicka, one of the caves that can be explored in Dolina Koscieliska (Black 904) (photo: R Turnbull)

• 905 SMRECZYŃSKI STAW (1108m–1227m)

Grade Easy   **Distance** 1.5km   **Average Gradient** 8%
NW–SE Height Gain 119m   **Time** 0h 30m
SE–NW Height Loss 119m   **Time** 0h 20m
Winter/Spring Normally open

A dead-end route off Green 504A, which climbs gently through forest from Schronisko Ornak to a small tarn, Smreczyński Staw (1227m). Though muddy and abuzz with flies, there is a good view from the tarn and it may be of interest to naturalists.

• 906 ZAKOPANE TO WITÓW (832m–1165m)

Grade Easy   **Distance** 14km   **Average Gradient** 6%
SE–NW Height Gain 325m/**Loss** 333m   **Time** 3h 20m
NW–SE Height Gain 333m/**Loss** 325m   **Time** 3h 40m
Winter/Spring Open

Apart from the start (which can be avoided by using a mountain lift), this is a gentle route through the low hills and forests on the north side of Zakopane to the straggling village of Witów.

The route is waymarked from Dom Turysty in Zakopane (840m), together with Yellow 806, twisting through back lanes to the main street called Kościeliska. Cross over and go left past the old cemetery (Stary Cmentarz), then turn right down a lane to pass under the main road flyover. The yellow route shortly goes left across a stream, while the black one continues steeply uphill, eventually leaving the road to climb the ski slope. When you reach the bridge over the funicular, you can either continue up to the left of the line, or cross the bridge and follow the right-hand side. Either way brings you to **Gubałówka** (1120m, refreshments). (*SE–NW 1h 00m, NW–SE 0h 50m.*)

Turn left along the ridge and follow the road for 1.75km, together with Red 014 and Blue 203. At **Pałkówka** (1129m, refreshments) keep ahead on a track that gently ascends through forest and meadows over the shoulder of Palenica Kościeliska (1165m). It is now downhill or level all the way to Witów. The track soon levels out, then at a junction you turn right to descend again. At a crossing-track, keep ahead for 500m, then turn left to descend steeply to the chapel at Pilchówka (925m). Turn right along the lane (Zakopane to Witów cycle route) and follow it for 1.5km down until it reaches the Czarny (Black) Dunajec river.

Bear right along a path that contours along the foot of the hillside for 1.5km, then turn left at a junction. In 200m turn left over the river into **Witów** (832m, refreshments). (*SE–NW 2h 20m, NW–SE 2h 50m.*)

• 907 DZIURA (897m–1048m)

Grade Easy	**Distance** 2km (round trip)	**Average Gradient** 11%
N–S Height Gain 50m	**Time** 0h 25m	
S–N Height Loss 50m	**Time** 0h 20m	
Winter/Spring Open		

A suitable route for an evening stroll, or a pre-breakfast appetizer, to Zakopane's nearest public cave, Dziura (Hole), or it can be taken in as a diversion from Green 501.

Head for Bundówki (900m, refreshments), at the south end of Strążyska street from Zakopane. At the car park turn left along Droga pod Reglami (Green 501). In 750m you reach the top of a lane (Droga do Daniela), where you turn right along a path up the valley Dolina ku Dziurze, where the black waymarks start. Near the head of the valley the path turns left to climb the hillside more steeply to the cave, which is accessible and not too deep, though a torch may prove useful.

On the return, for a different route into Zakopane, you could keep ahead at the foot of the valley along Droga do Daniela.

• 908 MUROVANIEC TO ŚWINICKA PRZEŁĘCZ (1500m–2051m)

Grade Strenuous	**Distance** 3.5km	**Average Gradient** 18%
N–S Height Gain 551m	**Time** 2h 00m	
S–N Height Loss 551m	**Time** 1h 35m	
Winter/Spring Closed		

*A steep and rocky path up the western branch of **Dolina Gąsienicowa**. It leads at first through dwarf pine, then above the tree-line to a border saddle with fine views into Slovakia.*

The route starts together with Yellow 812A from **Schronisko Murowaniec** (1500m, refreshments). At a junction take the left fork under the winter chair-lift wires to pass several small tarns, then the larger Litworowy Staw (Angelica Tarn), with a good view of the summits of Kościelec and Świnica ahead. The path levels out as you follow the left-hand shore of Zielony Staw (Green Tarn), then you come to the junction with Blue 208, surrounded by small tarns. The path now steepens considerably and zigzags as it approaches Świnicka Przełęcz (Pig Saddle, 2051m).

Red 009A will take you right, to the cable-car at Kasprowy Wierch, or left, to the top of Świnica and Orla Perć.

• 909 KARB TO KOŚCIELEC (1853m–2155m)

Grade Strenuous	**Distance** 1km	**Average Gradient** 35%
N–S Height Gain 305m	**Time** 0h 45m	
S–N Height Loss 305m	**Time** 0h 45m	
Winter/Spring Closed		

An airy climb to an outlying summit in the Świnica range, providing a challenge for more experienced and confident walkers. There is one fixed chain, a couple of scrambles without the help of a chain, and a few exposed places which require a good head for heights. The summit of Kościelec is a mass of boulders – it is usually very busy, and you may have to settle for an outlying vantage point.

Blue 208 and Green 514 lead to the saddle Karb (1853m), then Black 909 starts in fairly moderate fashion, but soon begins to steepen, on a zigzag route. About halfway up, you come to a fixed chain providing support in a cleft that you climb. The zigzags continue, in some places over bare, convex rock – on the descent this increases the sense of exposure. The final route to the summit of Kościelec (2155m) is comparatively easy. From the summit you have magnificent views of the peaks of Świnica, Kozi Wierch and Granat, while the valley below is sprinkled with tarns of all sizes.

• 910 DOLINA SUCHEJ WODY (996m–1500m)

Grade Easy	**Distance** 7km	**Average Gradient** 7%
NE–SW Height Gain 504m	**Time** 2h 10m	
SW–NE Height Loss 504m	**Time** 1h 50m	
Winter/Spring Normally open		

This is the service road to Schronisko Murowaniec, also a cycle route, with a gravel surface and always in forest. The start is 400m east of the bus stop at Brzeziny. There is no car park.

From Brzeziny (996m, toilets) the route follows the stream Sucha Woda (Dry Water). There is a covered picnic table at Psia Trawka, where Red 010 is crossed.

The route climbs out of the valley (Dry Water Valley), negotiating some hairpin bends, to reach Schronisko Murowaniec (1500m) and the junctions with Blue 207, Green 513 and Yellow 812.

• 911 DOLINA PAŃSZCZYCA (550m–628m)

Grade Easy	**Distance** 1km	**Average Gradient** 8%
N–S Height Gain 78m	**Time** 0h 25m	
S–N Height Loss 78m	**Time** 0h 20m	
Winter/Spring Closed		

*A short link path through dwarf pine in **Dolina Pańszczyca** between Green 513 and Yellow 812B. It is little used, and therefore tends to be overgrown.*

• 912 KOZIA DOLINKA (1936m–225m)

Grade Strenuous	**Distance** 1km	**Average Gradient** 29%
NW–SE Height Gain 289m	**Time** 1h 00m	
SE–NW Height Loss 289m	**Time** 0h 50m	
Winter/Spring Closed		

A short but very steep route on open rock providing a different northern access to (or exit from) Orla Perć.

The fearsome approach to Żleb Kulczyńskiego above Kozia Dolinka (Black 912) (photo: R Turnbull)

The route starts from Green 515 at 1936m and is steep, slippery and exposed at the bottom. Ascending the gully Żleb Kulczyńskiego there are chains, scrambling and more exposure. The route levels out towards the top, and the final approach to the saddle Przełęcz nad Buczynowa Dolina (2225m) is comparatively easy.

If you are continuing on **Orla Perć** (Red 009B) towards Krzyżne, the route leads off to the left shortly before the saddle. If heading for Świnica and Kasprowy Wierch, continue to the saddle and go right.

• 913 SZEROKI ŻLEB (1710m–2291m)

Grade Strenuous	**Distance** 1.5km	**Average Gradient** 38%
SE–NW Height Gain 581m	**Time** 1h 45m	
NW–SE Height Loss 581m	**Time** 1h 15m	**Winter/Spring** Closed

*A very steep but comparatively easy access route on open rock to **Orla Perć** (Red 009B), this time from the south, leading off Blue 209 a little way above **Wielki Staw Polski** (1710m). It is not difficult, with a zigzag climb up the side of Szeroki Żleb (Broad Gully) to the summit of Kozi Wierch (2291m).*

• 914 NIŻNIA KOPA (1435m–1672m)

Grade Moderate	**Distance** 1.5km	**Average Gradient** 18%
N–S Height Gain 237m	**Time** 0h 40m	
S–N Height Loss 237m	**Time** 0h 30m	**Winter/Spring** Closed

*A steep but not difficult short cut from Green 516 in Dolina Roztoki to **Schronisko Pięciu Stawów** and Przedni Staw Polski on Blue 209.*

The path starts with a long series of short zigzags on the lower slope of Niżnia Kopa (Lower Stack). Towards the top, it levels out a little to traverse below the cliff face.

• 915 RUSINOWA POLANA TO POLANA POD WOŁOSZYNEM (1190m–1250m)

Grade Easy	**Distance** 2km	**Average Gradient** 3%
N–S Height Loss 10m/**Gain** 60m		**Time** 0h 30m
S–N Height Loss 60m/**Gain** 10m		**Time** 0h 30m
Winter/Spring Normally open		

A short and easy link between Blue 210 and Red 010.

A large black spot and arrow painted on top of a flat boulder marks the start of this route from Blue 210 at the south end of **Rusinowa Polana** (1200m). It goes first along a broad track, then into the forest, contouring at the same level before descending into **Dolina Waksmundzka**. After crossing its brook, the path gradually climbs around a shoulder (which eventually becomes Wołoszyn) to reach Polana pod Wołoszynem and Red 010 (1250m).

Two short black routes have recently been added to the network: 916 from Green 500A at Schronisko Chochołowska to the Chapel of St.Jan Chrcziciel and 917 from Yellow 800 to Bobrowiecka Przełęcz.

SELECTED TIMINGS

This section provides a quick-reference, rough guide to selected approximate walking times. Always allow extra time for your journey, in case of unforeseen difficulties. **By adding together the various sections, these tables can be used to compute the total times for your own routes**.

Of course, people walk at differing speeds. On your first day of walking, you can compare your times with those shown to get an idea of whether you are faster or slower. This is only for information – there is no point in racing the signposts!

Approaching Giewont at Wyznia Kondracka Przełęcz (Blue 206)

Remember that routes beginning with 0 = Red, 2 = Blue, 5 = Green, 8 = Yellow, 9 = Black.

From/to	Time	Via routes
BUŃDÓWKI to		
Giewont	3h 30m	008, 206
Polana Strążyska	0h 40m	008
Przełęcz w Grzybowcu	1h 30m	008
Sarnia Skała	1h 35m	008, 901C
CZARNY STAW GĄSIENICOWY to		
Granaty	2h 10m	207B, 813
Karb	0h 35m	514
Kościelec	1h 20m	514, 909
Zawrat	2h 00m	207B
GRONIK to		
Przysłop Miętusi	1h 00m	202
Małołaczniak	4h 00m	202
HOTEL GORSKI KALATÓWKI to		
Giewont	2h 25m	206
Kopa Kondracka	2h 40m	206, 508, 007
Kuźnice	0h 30m	206
Schronisko Kondratowa	0h 50m	206
KASPROWY WIERCH to		
Ciemniak	3h 00m	007
Kuźnice	2h 55m	510
Schronisko Murowaniec	1h 10m	812A
Świnica	1h 55m	009A
KIRY to		
Ciemniak	4h 20m	504A, 004
Gubałówka	2h 05m	504B
Polana Pisana	1h 00m	504A
Schronisko Ornak	1h 30m	504A
Stare Kościeliska	0h 30m	504A
Tomanowa Przełęcz	3h 35m	504A, 505, 006

KUŹNICE to

Giewont	3h 05m	206
Hotel Gorski Kalatówki	0h 40m	206
Kasprowy Wierch	3h 45m	510
Polana Strążyska	2h 50m	901C
Schronisko Kondratowa	1h 20m	206
Schronisko Murowaniec	2h 10m	207A or 810, 207A
Nosal	0h 40m	509
Sarnia Skała	2h 25m	206, 901C

NĘDZÓWKA to

Małołaczniak	4h 00m	005, 202
Przysłop Miętusi	1h 30m	005

POLANA HUCISKA to

Schronisko Chochołowska	1h 10m	500A
Siwa Polana	0h 50m	500A
Trzydniowiański Wierch	3h 00m	500A, 001
Wołowiec	4h 05m	500A, 500B, 200

POLANA PALENICA to

Rusinowa Polana	0h 50m	210
Rysy	6h 40m	011, 012
Schronisko Morskie Oko	2h 35m	011
Schronisko Pięciu Stawów	3h 00m	011, 516, 914
Wodogrzmoty Mickiewicza	0h 50m	011
Zazadnia Polana	1h 45m	210

RONDO KUŹNICKIE to

Hotel Gorski Kalatówki	1h 05m	205, 206
Kuźnice	0h 25m	205
Kuźnice	1h 10m	509
Nosal	0h 50m	205, 509
Nosalowa Przełęcz	1h 00m	205, 509
Polana Olczyska	1h 25m	205, 509, 811
Schronisko Murowaniec	2h 35m	205, 207A

RUSINOWA POLANA to

Polana Palenica	0h 40m	210
Wodogrzmoty Mickiewicza	1h 05m	915, 010, 011
Zazadnia Polana	0h 55m	210

SCHRONISKO CHOCHOŁOWSKA to

Kończysty Wierch	3h 30m	001, 502
Schronisko Ornak	3h 00m	500A, 802
Siwa Polana	1h 40m	500A
Trzydniowiański Wierch	2h 30m	001
Wołowiec direct	2h 55m	500B, 200
Wołowiec via Grześ	3h 30m	801, 200

SCHRONISKO KONDRATOWA to

Giewont	1h 45m	206
Kopa Kondracka	1h 50m	206, 805
Kuźnice	1h 00m	206
Przełęcz pod Kondracką Kopą	1h 30m	508

SCHRONISKO MORSKIE OKO to

Schronisko Pięciu Stawów	2h 00m	209
Mięguszowiecka Przełęcz	3h 40m	012, 518
Rysy	4h 05m	012
Szpiglasowa Przełęcz	2h 30m	814

SCHRONISKO MUROWANIEC to

Brzeziny	1h 50m	910
Granaty	2h 45m	207B, 813
Kasprowy Wierch	1h 30m	812A
Kościelec	1h 55m	207B, 514, 909
Kozia Przełęcz	2h 00m	207B, 814
Krzyżne	2h 55m	812B
Kuźnice	1h 40m	207 or 207, 810
Liliowe	1h 40m	812A, 511
Polana Palenica	3h 45m	513, 210
Świnica	3h 00m	812A, 908, 009A
Zawrat	2h 35m	207B

SCHRONISKO PIĘCIU STAWÓW to

Kozi Wierch	2h 05m	209, 913
Kozia Przełęcz	1h 55m	209, 814
Krzyżne	2h 10m	209, 812C
Schronisko Morskie Oko	1h 40m	209
Szpiglasowa Przełęcz	2h 20m	209, 814
Zawrat	1h 50m	209

SIWA POLANA to

Kiry	1h 05m	501
Schronisko Chochołowska	2h 05m	500A

TOPOROWA CYRHLA to

Kuźnice	2h 10m	512, 811, 509
Schronisko Murowaniec	2h 45m	010, 910
Wodogrzmoty Mickiewicza	3h 40m	010, 011

WIERCH PORONIEC to

Gęsia Szyja	1h 30m	513
Rusinowa Polana	1h 00m	513
Schronisko Murowaniec	4h 15m	513
Wodogrzmoty Mickiewicza	2h 05m	513, 210, 915, 010, 011

WODOGRZMOTY MICKIEWICZA to

Schronisko Morskie Oko	1h 45m	011
Schronisko Pięciu Stawów	2h 10m	516, 914
Schronisko Stara Roztoka	0h 10m	517

ZAZADNIA POLANA to

Polana Palenica	1h 55m	210
Rusinowa Polana	1h 15m	210
Wodogrzmoty Mickiewicza	2h 20m	210, 915, 010, 011

HIGHEST SUMMITS (2000m AND ABOVE)

See also Altitudes, page 21. Some translations are approximate.

★ = shared with Slovakia   + = accessible to walkers

Summit	Translation	Height
Rysy ★+	Scars	2499m
Mięguszowiecki Szczyt ★	Mengusovce Peak	2438m
Niżnie Rysy ★	Lower Scars	2430m
Czarny Mięguszowiecki Szczyt ★	Black Mengusovce Peak	2410m
(also called Chlopek – Little Peasant)		
Pośredni Mięguszowiecki Szczyt ★	Middle Mengusovce Peak	2393m
Cubryna ★	(No translation)	2376m
Wołowa Turnia ★	Ox Crag	2373m
Hinczowa Turnia ★	Hincova Crag	2378m
Żabia Turnia ★	Frog Crag	2336m
Świnica ★+	The Pig	2301m
Żabi Koń ★	Frog Horse	2291m
Kozi Wierch +	Goat Peak	2291m
Gąsienicowa Turnia	Caterpillar Crag	2280m
Kozie Czuby +	Goats' Tufts	2266m
Niebieska Turnia	Heavenly Crag	2262m
Wyżni Żabi Szczyt ★	Higher Frog Peak	2259m
Kopa Spadowa ★	Drop Stack	2250m
Zawratowa Turnia	Zawrat Crag	2247m
Zadni Granat +	Back Grenade	2240m
Pośredni Granat +	Middle Grenade	2234m
Skrajny Granat +	Front Grenade	2225m
Miedziane	Copper	2233m
Mali Kozi Wierch +	Little Goat Hill	2228m
Wielka Koszysta	Great Koszysta	2193m
Waksmundzki Wierch	Waksmund Peak	2189m
Małe Miedziane	Little Copper	2186m
Wielka Buczynowa Turnia	Great Beech Crag	2184m
Zamarła Turnia +	Petrified Crag	2179m
Starorobociański Wierch ★	Old Works Peak	2176m
Orla Baszta +	Eagle Tower	2175m

Szpiglasowy Wierch ★+	Spiglas Peak	2172m
Zadni Mnich ★	Back Monk	2172m
Mała Buczynowa Turnia +	Little Beech Crag	2172m
Zadni Kościelec	Back Church or Bones	2162m
Błyszcz ★	Sparkle	2159m
Kazalnica	Pulpit	2159m
Walentkowy Wierch ★	Valentine Peak	2156m
Kościelec +	Church or Bones	2155m
Wielki Wołoszyn	Great Woloszyn	2155m
Żabi Mnich ★	Frog Monk	2146m
Mali Woloszyn	Little Woloszyn	2144m
Ciemnosmreczynska Turnia ★	Dark Spruce Crag	2142m
Jarząbczy Wierch	Rowan Peak	2137m
Wierch pod Fajki	Peak below Pipes	2134m
Pośrednia Turnia ★	Middle Crag	2128m
Krzesanica ★+	Craggy	2122m
Kamienista	Stony	2121m
Pośredni Woloszyn	Middle Woloszyn	2117m
Opalony Wierch	Burnt Peak	2115m
Kołowa Czuba	Round Tuft	2105m
Niżni Żabi Szczyt	Lower Frog Peak	2098m
Skrajna Turnia ★+	Furthest Crag	2096m
Ciemniak ★+	Potato	2096m
Małołacniak ★+	Little Meadow	2096m
Skrajny Wołoszyn	Furthest Woloszyn	2092m
Kopa Mnichowa	Monk Stack	2090m
Żolta Turnia	Yellow Crag	2087m
Wyżni Liptowski Kostur ★	Higher Liptov Stave	2083m
Żabia Czuba ★	Frog Tuft	2079m
Mnich	Monk	2067m
Smreczyński Wierch	Spruce Peak	2066m
Gładki Wierch ★	Smooth Peak	2065m
Wołowiec ★ +	The Ox	2064m
Niżni Liptowski Kostur ★	Lower Liptov Stave	2055m
Wierch nad Zagonnym Żlebem	Peak above Clump Gully	2039m
Mała Koszysta	Little Koszysta	2014m
Beskid ★+	-	2012m
Kopa Kondracka ★+	Kondracka Stack	2005m
Kończysty Wierch ★	End Peak	2002m

TRAVEL

Public Transport To and From the Polish Tatras

The nearest airport to Zakopane in Poland is at Kraków, about 100km northeast, from where there are trains and buses to Zakopane. Kraków is served by several airlines (see Appendix C) and has a rail link to the city centre. Many international airlines fly to Warsaw, from where there are connecting flights to Kraków, or trains and express buses to Zakopane.

If you wish to approach from Slovakia, Czech Airlines (020 7365 9189, www.czechairlines.co.uk) have started a service from Prague to Poprad. They do not currently serve UK airports so travellers from the UK would have to book connecting flights to Prague. Alternatively you could fly to Bratislava or Vienna, continue by train to Poprad then bus to Zakopane (see page 158).

There are trains from Kraków to Zakopane, though they are rather slow, taking 3–4 hours for the 100km journey. There is also a sleeper from Warsaw to Zakopane. Details of services can be obtained from the website of PKP (Polskie Koleje Państwowe – Polish State Railways) on www.pkp.pl or http://rozklad.pkp.pl, and there is a helpful unofficial site, www.polrail.com.

Long-distance buses operated by Polskie Express serve Zakopane from Warsaw and Kraków. Their website is www.polskiexpress.pl.

The Sleeping Giant (Giewont) keeps watch over Zakopane

A dorożka *(horse-drawn cab) waits for customers in Krupówki street, Zakopane*

Public Transport Within the Polish Tatras

Frequent buses link Zakopane with its outskirts, outlying villages and walk starting points. Most services start from the main bus station (*dworzec autobusowy*) in Tadeusza Kościuszki street near the railway station. There is a smaller bus station at Targowica, by the subway near the foot of Krupówki street. This is better for services to the west as they avoid the town centre. No timetables are published as such, but times of departures to each destination are shown. Some services do not operate daily, as indicated on the departure lists (in Polish). There is an enquiry office at the bus station. Fares are paid to the driver.

As well as motor taxis, Zakopane has a large fleet of horse-drawn ones (*dorożki*). They operate from several stands, including one near the post office in Krupówki street, one at the railway station, and another at the foot of the road leading to Kuźnice. It is advisable to agree the fare in advance.

The three main valleys have horse-drawn transport (bus or taxi), which operate as follows.

- Dolina Chochołowska (bus and taxi – Siwa Polana to Schronisko Chochołowska).
- Dolina Kościeliska (taxi – Kiry to Polana Pisana).
- Dolina Białki (bus – Polana Palenica to Włosienica).

In Dolina Chochołowska there is also a 'road train' from Siwa Polana to Polana Huciska, and cycles can be hired at three points – on a one-way basis if required.

Mountain Transport

A cable-car (rebuilt in 2007) climbs from Kuźnice to the summit of Kasprowy Wierch, from dawn to dusk. The journey takes 15 minutes and you must change cars halfway up. It is always very busy, and unless you have an advance reservation (groups only, bookable through hotels and travel agencies) you may have to queue for at least an hour. For individuals, it is more practical to plan for an ascent in the afternoon, when the queue should have subsided, still leaving plenty of time if you wish to walk down.

Several lifts operate to the Gubałówka ridge to the north of Zakopane:
- A funicular railway runs from the street called Na Gubałówka, which in effect is a continuation of the main Krupówki street crossing the river.
- A cable-car and two chair-lifts (one only in winter) run from Powstańców Ślańskich street, the main road from Zakopane to Kościelisko, near Hotel Mercure Kasprowy.

By Car

At the time of writing, the A4 motorway (also Euroroute E40) had been completed most of the way from Berlin to Kraków. From there follow Highway 7 (also Euroroute E77) south to Chabówka, then Highway 47 through Nowy Targ to Zakopane – some of this is dual carriageway (but expect long traffic jams).

Coming from the south, through Slovakia, head for Ružomberok, take Highway 59 (also Euroroute E77) to the frontier station at Chyżne, then Poland's Highway 7 to Chabówka, then Highway 47 through Nowy Targ to Zakopane. Alternatively, head for Poprad then take Highway 67 to the frontier station – Lysá Poľana in Slovak, Łysa Polana in Polish. From there follow signs to Poronin then Zakopane. These are all single-carriageway roads, much used by heavy vehicles.

Within the Polish Tatras, private vehicles are banned from roads within the national park, including the one from Zakopane to Kuźnice – see above regarding public transport within the Polish Tatras. There are large car parks at the foot of most of the walk starting points, where a charge is made. Some of the minor starting points do not have car parks, just space for a few cars.

Self-drive cars can be rented in Kraków and Zakopane.

Passports and Visas

Poland is now, like Slovakia, a member of the Schengen Convention, in which all member countries share the same passport and visa arrangements. See page 162.

DIVERSIONS

If you need a break from walking, or if the weather is bad, or you have enough energy left to do something in the evening, Zakopane offers the following.

Sightseeing Excursions
The following can be booked through travel agencies in Zakopane.

* Kraków – historic city centre; Wawel – royal castle where most Polish kings were crowned and are buried; Wieliczka – 13th-century salt mine.
* Auschwitz (Oswieńcim) – former military barracks, converted during the Second World War into a notorious concentration camp. Now a museum and memorial to those who perished there.
* Wadowice – birthplace of Pope John Paul II; can be included en route to Auschwitz.
* Gentle rafting on Dunajec river, including a tour of the Pieniny mountains (a limestone range considerably different from the Tatras).
* Debno – town with a unique wooden church and a castle (can be included en route to rafting).
* Tour into Slovakia to visit eg Demänovská and other caves, Low Tatras, Levoce, Spišsky Hrad castle.

The following facilities are in or near Zakopane, and can be visited on foot or by bus or taxi.

Museums and Art Galleries
There are nine museums in Zakopane, including the following.

* Muzeum Tatrzańskie, Krupówki 10 – a reconstructed wooden cottage containing folk costumes, features on shepherding, geology, fauna and flora.
* Muzeum TPN (National Park Museum), Rondo Kuźnickie (look for the carved wooden columns) – fauna and flora of the Tatras.
* Willa Koliba, Kościeliska street (near cemetery) – exhibition of Zakopane style architecture.
* Muzeum Karola Szymanowskiego, Willa Atma, Kościeliska street – dedicated to the composer Karol Szymanowski.

There are about 30 art galleries of various sizes in Zakopane. They include Galeria Władisława Hasiora in Jagiellońska street, dedicated to the artist whose monumental sculpture can be seen on the road to Kuźnice.

Sw Krzyża (St Cross) Church in Zamoyskiego street, Zakopane

Sports
Swimming Pools (*Pływalnie*) Olympic-size pool at the COS Stadium near Rondo Kuźnickie; Aquapark (several indoor pools, east side of Zakopane, fed by a thermal sulphuric spring); some hotels have small indoor pools.

Tennis Courts (*Korty Tenisowe*) Sports Centre (COS Centralny Ośrodek Sportu) near Rondo Kuźnickie; Hotel Mercure Kasprowy (open to the public).

Horse Riding (*Jazda Konna*) Polana pod Nosalem, Bystre (at the foot of the ski jump).

Dining with Entertainment
Several restaurants provide live Góral or old Zakopane-style folk music, including Czarci Jar, Obrochtówka and Redykolka.

Theatres (teatri) and Cinemas (kini)
Teatr Witkacy, Chramkówki street, dedicated to local artist Ignacy Witkiewicz, with its own highly respected repertory company.
Sokól Kino (cinema), Orkana 2.
Giewont Kino (cinema), Kościuszki 4.

SHOPPING AND LOCAL SERVICES

Zakopane has a wide range of shops and other facilities. Shops generally open from 10am to 6pm, but food shops usually open at 7am. There are a few 'convenience' shops that are open for 24 hours.

A growing number of local people, especially the younger ones, speak English. German is not widely spoken. A Polish phrasebook or dictionary may be useful.

A word about streets in Zakopane and their names. The Polish word for street is *ulica* (pronounced 'oolitsa'), but this rarely appears on maps or street-name signs. Many streets are named after local dignitaries or historical figures, but these can be long, and usually only the surname is used. On street-name signs the initial of the given name is also shown. For example, Ulica Józefa Piłsudskiego appears on maps as Józefa Piłsudskiego, on street-name signs as J Piłsudskiego, and in most guidebooks, directories and conversation as plain Piłsudskiego. In this book we follow the latter practice. Some streets are called *droga* (road), and we show their names in full.

The following is a selection of services available. For more details enquire at the tourist information centre.

Tourist Information

There are two tourist information (*informacji turystycznej*) offices.

Kościuszki 17, 34500 Zakopane (phone 018 201 2211, e-mail info@um.zakopane.pl), near the rail and bus stations. Run by the town council and provides information on accommodation and tourist facilities.

Chałubinskiego (next to Rondo Kuźnickie, phone 018 206 3799). Run by the Tatras National Park (TPN) and provides information on walking in the mountains.

Zakopane currently has no official tourist information website, but several unofficial ones offer English pages eg www.zakopane.pl, www.discoverzakopane.com, www.ezakopane.pl.

Books, Maps and Dictionaries

Maps can be bought at many places in Zakopane (including hotels, information centres and street kiosks). There are two good bookshops (*księgarnia*) in the lower part of Krupówki street – they sell a wide variety of books on local flora and fauna, maps and dictionaries.

Car Rental

Value24 Rent a Car, Kościuszki 10, 34500 Zakopane (phone 018 201 2181, e-mail biuro@value24rentacar.eu, www.value24rentacar.pl). Otherwise the nearest facilities are in Kraków.

Car Service Stations

There are several car service stations (*stacje obslugi samochódow*) in or near Zakopane – for details enquire at the tourist information centre.

Currency Exchange

Many hotels and all banks and travel agencies offer currency exchange (*kantor*) facilities (see also Other Useful Information, page 289). Most banks have cash machines.

Department Store

The department store (*dom towarowy*) in Zakopane is called Granit (see Supermarkets).

Filling Stations

There are several filling stations (*stacje benzynowe*) in Zakopane town centre and on the main road into Zakopane from the northeast.

General store
A shop called Zakfol sells all kinds of useful items such as stationery and hardware. It is at Kościeliska 2, near the foot of Krupówki.

Internet Cafés
The Granit internet café (*kawiarnie internetowe*) is situated next to the post office in Krupówki street. Some hotels offer internet facilities.

Markets and Malls
There is a large outdoor market in the area between the foot of Krupówki street and the Gubałówka funicular. An open-air shopping mall called Pasaż Handlowy leads off to the right, halfway down Krupówki street.

Mountain Guides
Mountain guides (*przewodnik gorski*) can be found via PTTK/BORT, Krupówki 12, 34500 Zakopane (phone 018 201 2429).

Outdoor Equipment
There are many outdoor equipment shops (*wyposażenie górskie*) in Zakopane.

Orla Perć – on Kozi Wierch
(Red 009B) (photo: R Turnbull)

Pharmacies
There are many pharmacies (*apteka*) in Zakopane.

Post Offices
The central post office is at the junction of Krupówki and Kościuszki streets, opposite Orbis Hotel Giewont. There are several sub-post offices (*poczta*) in outlying districts.

Souvenirs
Many shops and kiosks in the town centre sell a variety of souvenirs (*pamiatka*).

Supermarkets/Foodshops
There are many small supermarkets and food shops (*sklep zywnościowe*) throughout Zakopane and in the outlying villages. There is a Tesco Express in Chramcówki street (near the railway station) and a Carrefour Express in Orkana street (opposite the football stadium).

Taxis
There are taxi-ranks (*postóje taksówek*) at several locations. There are also ranks (*postóje dorożek*) for horse-drawn taxis (*dorożki*) at several locations, but these are much more expensive.

Travel Agencies
There are several travel agencies (*biuro podrózy*), but the main ones are:
Orbis Travel, Krupówki 22
(phone 018 201 5051, e-mail travel@orbis.zakopane.pl,
www.orbis.zakopane.pl).
Pomian Travel, Kościuszki 1 (at Orbis Hotel Giewont)
(phone 018 201 5204, e-mail info@pomiantravel.com, www.pomiantravel.pl)
Tatra Travel, Krupówki 16
(phone 018 206 4201, e-mail biuro@tatratravel.com.pl,
www.tatratravel.com.pl)

OTHER USEFUL INFORMATION

Cost of Living
Public transport, accommodation and food are moderately priced in comparison with most English-speaking countries. Woollen sweaters are good value, but other clothing and luxury goods are expensive.

Currency

The Polish currency unit is the *złoty*, pronounced 'zwotty' and meaning 'golden'. The official international abbreviation is PLN, but inside Poland you will usually see it written as Zł. It is freely exchangeable at banks and currency exchange offices within and outside the country. If you are also visiting Slovakia, there is a currency exchange office at the Łysa Polana frontier station.

Electricity

220 volts. Two-pin plugs are used – you may need an adaptor.

Meals

There is a wide choice of restaurants (*restauracje*) and cafés (*kawiarnie*) in Zakopane, as well as street kiosks. For better or worse (depending on your lifestyle) some of the major international chains have reached Zakopane, such as Costa Coffee, Kentucky Fried Chicken, McDonald's and Pizza Hut. Food and drink in cafés, mountain refuges and restaurants is reasonably priced. Meat tends to be quite spicy. Vegetarians may struggle to find much other than pizzas, cheese and egg dishes.

Specialities include trout (*pstrag*), lamb (*czaczlyk*), goats' cheese (*oścypek*). Hot spiced wine is sold at many bars and restaurants and there is also a powerful brew called *herbata z pradem* (electric tea) – a hot, sweet tea with very alcoholic spirit added.

News

Few English-language newspapers are available in the Polish Tatras, though international editions of American ones may be available. You can keep in touch online at an internet café (see above) through http://news.bbc.co.uk or other international news agencies. You can also listen online to the news bulletins of most major radio stations. The BBC World Service may be obtainable on various radio frequencies (details on www.bbc.co.uk/worldservice).

Phoning Home from Poland

Calls are easily made from most hotels, or at the central telephone and telegraph office, at the rear of the main post office in Krupówki street. On hearing the dialling tone, you first dial a 0 (zero) and wait for a second tone, then another 0 followed by the appropriate national prefix (UK 44, Irish Republic 353, Australia 61, New Zealand 64, South Africa 27, USA/Canada 1), followed by the area code (for the UK omit the initial 0), then the personal number. If you wish to use your mobile phone abroad, you should contact your service provider beforehand as special 'roaming' arrangements may need to be made to ensure that it will work.

Public Holidays in Poland

January 1	New Year's Day
Variable	Easter Sunday and Monday (March or April)
May 1	May Day
May 3	Constitution Day
Variable	Whit Sunday (May or June)
Variable	Corpus Christi Day (a Thursday in May or June)
August 15	Assumption Day
November 1	All Saints' Day
November 11	Independence Day
December 25	Christmas Day
December 26	Second Day of Christmas

Tipping
Generally 10%.

Toilets
Men – *męska*   Women – *damska*
Some toilets (*toaleta*) have a triangle symbol for men and a circle for women. There is sometimes a guardian who collects a nominal charge.

GAZETTEER

Beskid (2012m) The first of the Polish High Tatras peaks, as viewed from Zakopane. Because of its proximity to the cable-car at Kasprowy Wierch, it is usually crowded.

Brzegi (800m–1000m) A straggling village, one of the highest in Podhale, occupying a ridge in the hills to the northwest of Zakopane and north of Łysa Polana. It is served by bus from Zakopane and has a pretty wooden church.

Bukowina Tatrzańska (800m–1000m) Close to Brzegi, this village climbs the northern slope of Wysoki Wierch, and is the second highest in Poland. It is served by bus from Zakopane. Its Aquapark swimming complex is worth a visit.

Buńdówki (898m) A location on the southwestern outskirts of Zakopane and at the foot of Strążyska Dolina. It is a popular starting or finishing point for walks, with a bus service from the town centre, car park, buffets and toilets.

On Skupniów Upłaz en route to Schronisko Murowaniec (Blue 207A)

Bystre (Swift, 920m) The southern part of Zakopane, with a hotel, a trade union holiday centre, a few shops and bars. The Galeria Sztuki im. W J Kulczyckich (Kulczyckich Art Gallery) displays tapestries by local artists. Near the Kuźnickie Rondo (roundabout) are the stadia of the COS (Centralny Osrodek Sportu – Central Sport Centre) and the museum of the TPN (Tatrzanski Park Narodowy – Tatras National Park), while a little way towards the centre of Zakopane lies the memorial to Tytus Chalubiński, the founder of Zakopane. The large building on the eastern outskirts is an orthopaedic rehabilitation centre for children, and is the largest building constructed in traditional Zakopane style.

Chochołowska Dolina See Dolina Chochołowska.

Czarny Staw (Black Tarn) The name for three large tarns in the Polish High Tatras, all so called because they spend much of the time in the shadow of high mountains. They are referred to as follows (in order from northwest to southeast):

- Czarny Staw Gąsienicowy (1624m) In the shadow of Orla Perć. Covers nearly 18 hectares and is 51m deep.
- Czarny Staw Polski (1722m) Lies below the group of summits called Kotelnica in the Liptowskie Mury range. Covers a little over 12.5 hectares and is 50m deep. Also known as Czarny Staw pod Kotelnica.
- Czarny Staw pod Rysami (1583m) Largest and deepest of the three, at 20.64 hectares and 76m respectively. It obviously lies in the shadow of Rysy, Poland's highest summit.

Czerwone Wierchy (Red Peaks) The name of a range of rounded, grass-topped mountains in the Western Tatras, southwest of Zakopane, so called because the grass turns a reddish-brown in the autumn. The range has four peaks (from east to west): Ciemniak (2096m), Krzesanica (2122m), Małołaczniak (2096m) and Kondracka Kopa (2005m).

Dolina Polish for 'valley'. On some maps and signs you may variously see names written as 'Dolina X' or 'X Dolina', but the former is standard Polish, and that is what we normally use in this book.

Dolina Białego The pretty, cascade-filled valley that runs due south from Zakopane town centre. It contains a nature trail (Yellow 807).

Dolina Białki The valley of the Białka river, which forms part of the border with Slovakia, and runs through Łysa Polana. Towards its head it divides into three branches – Dolina Roztoki, Dolina Rybiego Potoku (both in Poland) and Dolina

Białej Wody (or Bielovodská Dolina) in Slovakia. The Białka is one of the main tributaries of the Dunajec, itself one of the major rivers of southern Poland, flowing into the Wisła (Vistula) and thus to the Baltic. It is fed by streams that rise in the High and White Tatras.

Dolina Bystrej Also known as Dolina Bystrej Wody (Swift Water Valley), this valley includes Schronisko Kondratowa, Kuźnice and central Zakopane. Its Bystra stream rises in the slopes around Kasprowy Wierch, and joins Cicha Woda (Quiet Water) in Zakopane to form the Zakopianka river.

Dolina Chochołowska The most remote valley (from Zakopane) in the Polish part of the Western Tatras, taking its name from the village of Chochołów. Together with Kościeliska Dolina, its streams rise in the Western Tatras and flow into the Czarny (Black) Dunajec river, while those of the valleys further east flow into the Biały (White) Dunajec (see also Dolina Białki).

Dolina Gąsienicowa (Caterpillar Valley) One of the most visited valleys in the Polish Tatras, actually the upper part of Dolina Suchej Wody, southeast of Zakopane, and south of Schronisko Murowaniec. It is divided into two by the Kościelec ridge – the western part, Sucha Dolina (Dry Valley), has Kasprowy Wierch at its head, the eastern part, Kozia Dolina (Goat Valley), has the Granaty peaks at its head.

Dolina Goryczkowa Though traversed by ski routes in winter, this valley is not accessible to walkers, being off the waymarked routes, but its lower regions can be seen from the cable-car to Kasprowy Wierch. The upper part is called Świńska Dolina (Pig Valley).

Dolina Kościeliska A popular, pretty valley running south from Kiry. The refuge called Schronisko Ornak lies at the point where it divides into several branches. It takes its name from the Kościeliska ridge, the watershed between the Czarny (Black) Dunajec and Biały (White) Dunajec river basins.

Dolina ku Dziurze A short valley close to Zakopane on its southwestern side. It has the cave called Dziura (Hole) at its head.

Dolina Małej Łąki (Little Meadows Valley) The shortest of the main valleys leading directly off the Zakopane basin. Its upper regions are peppered with small caves, while its stream, Małołącki Potok, is fed by springs that rise on the western shoulder of Giewont.

Dolina Olczyska A short and well-populated valley immediately to the east of Zakopane, taking its name from a farming community called Olcza.

Dolina Pańszczyca A side valley of Dolina Suchej Wody, to the east of Schronisko Murowaniec. It is very quiet, with a rather dejected atmosphere – it is said that no birds will sing here.

Dolina Pięciu Stawów Polskich (Valley of Five Polish Tarns) One of the prettiest valleys in the Polish Tatras – actually the upper part of Dolina Roztoki – with Orla Perć at its head. The 'five tarns' are Przedni (Front), Mały (Little), Wielki (Big), Czarny (Black) and Zadni (Back). Mały is tiny, compared to the others, and not much bigger than several others near the head of the valley.

Dolina Roztoki The valley that connects Dolina Białki with Dolina Pięciu Stawów Polskich. Its stream, fed from the Five Polish Tarns, plunges down the cascades of Wodogrzmoty Mickiewicza, and the refuge called Schronisko Roztoka is situated near its foot, by the border with Slovakia.

Dolina Rybiego Potoku (Fish Brook Valley) One of the most popular valleys in the Polish Tatras, despite its remoteness from Zakopane, as it contains the beautiful tarn called Morskie Oko, and has at its head the country's highest mountain, Rysy. It is the central branch at the head of Dolina Białki.

Dolina Strążyska A short valley leading southwestwards directly out of the centre of Zakopane. It is much frequented by tourists, as the beautiful cascade called Wodospad Siklawica lies at its head, and refreshments can be obtained en route at Buńdówki (served by bus from Zakopane) and the farm at Polana Strążyska.

Dolina Suchej Wody (Dry Water Valley) So called because its stream disappears into the limestone bedrock for about 1km of its length. It is one of the main valleys of the Polish High Tatras, southeast of Zakopane. It contains the busy refuge called Schronisko Murowaniec, above which the valley is known as Dolina Gąsienicowa.

Dolina Tomanowa A side valley of Dolina Kościeliska, leading eastwards from Schronisko Ornak. It is very quiet, and much frequented by bears.

Dolina Waksmundzka The upper part of this quiet side valley of Dolina Białki, southeast of Zakopane, is a strict nature reserve with no marked paths – it is a haunt of bears – though two routes cross the lower part.

Droga Oswalda Balzera The road leading up Dolina Białki from Bukowina Tatrzańska towards Morskie Oko, the upper part of which (closed to motorised traffic) forms our route Red 011. It is named after Oswald Balzer (1858–1933), a renowned Polish historian and professor at the University of Lwów.

Droga Papieska (the Pope's Road) Mostly on country lanes, this commemorative route was named in honour of Pope John Paul II, who travelled this way on a visit to Zakopane in 1997. It leads for about 25km from Nowy Targ to Gubałówka, on the ridge northwest of Zakopane. A monument to his visit stands beside the road just outside Ząb, on routes Red 014, Green 507 and Yellow 809.

Dzianisz (850m–1000m) A farming village in the hills to the northwest of Zakopane, beyond the Gubałówka ridge. It has many old houses and a pretty wooden church.

Five Polish Tarns (Valley of) See Dolina Pięciu Stawów Polskich.

Gaborowa Przełęcz Wyżnia See Raczkowa Przełęcz.

Gąsienicowa Dolina See Dolina Gąsienicowa.

Gęsia Szyja (Goose Neck, 1490m) A high knoll in the foothills of the High Tatras, southeast of Zakopane. It makes a marvellous picnic spot and viewpoint, from where you can see the High, White and Western Tatras. From the grassy northeast end, looking east you can see Rusinowa Polana, the slate-roofed border post of Łysa Polana, the Białka valley, the town of Nowy Targ, and the White Tatras in Slovakia. Looking west, you can see Zakopane, Giewont and the rounded summits of the Western Tatras, with the cable-car station on Kasprowy Wierch visible. The craggy southwest end of Gęsia Szyja looks up to the High Tatras peaks.

Giewont (1894m) The twin-humped peaks of this mountain, the nearest to and most visible from Zakopane, gave rise to the legend that it is in fact a sleeping giant, who will rise when Poland needs his help. Unfortunately he was in such deep sleep during the Second World War that he could not be woken. Only the higher, eastern summit is accessible to walkers, and this is surmounted by a huge, iron-frame cross – the altitude is sometimes shown as 1909m, which is in fact that of the top of the cross. The lower western summit (Mały Giewont) is 1728m.

Głodówka (1130m) A popular viewpoint on the road from Łysa Polana to Nowy Targ, east of Zakopane. There is a small car park and a café (Schronisko Głodówka), with a fine view of the High Tatras.

Goryczkowa Dolina See Dolina Goryczkowa.

Granaty A trio of peaks on Orla Perć. Zadni (Inner) Granat is the highest at 2240m, then Pośredni (Middle) Granat at 2234m and Skrajny (Outer) Granat (2225m). The meaning of the name is a matter of some dispute – it could be either 'grenades', 'pomegranates' or even 'navy blue'! All three summits are comparatively easily accessible, though with some use of fixed chains.

Gronik (940m) A hamlet in Kościelisko municipality, southwest of Zakopane, at the foot of Dolina Małej Łąki. It is the location of the Zakopane Military Training Centre (Wojskowy Ośrodek Szkoleniowo-Kondycyjny).

Gubałówka (1120m) A popular ridge in the hills northwest of Zakopane, with a pleasant and relaxed atmosphere – if you don't mind the smoke from numerous charcoal grills. It is easily reached from Zakopane by bus or several mountain lifts, or on foot via six fairly steep waymarked routes. There are restaurants, pizzerias, bars, kiosks and pay-telescopes (Tatras, for the viewing of). A stroll along the ridge is rewarding, so if you would rather walk in the mountains during the day, an evening up here would make an attractive change.

Harenda (760m) A straggling village just off the main road 3km northeast of Zakopane. It has several bars, shops, and an attractive onion-spired church. At the southwest end of the village (on Yellow 809) is a museum commemorating the poet Jan Kasprowicz (1860–1926), located in the house where he spent the last years of his life. Next to this is a mausoleum containing his ashes and those of his wife.

Hotel Górski Kalatówki See Kalatówki.

Jaszczurówka (900m) A village at the foot of Nosal and Dolina Olczyska to the southeast of Zakopane, its name means 'spotted salamander'. A little to the east along the main road is Kaplica Witkiewicza, a beautiful wooden chapel set on a rise above the road, and well worth a visit. Don't miss the gallery of religious art and icons, some of it for sale, in the crypt. Also of interest to walkers are the refreshments obtainable at Bar Gawra and Hotel pod Piorem.

Kalatówki (1198m) A sloping mountain pasture above Dolina Bystrej, southwest of Kuźnice, where sheep and cattle graze. It makes a small but popular ski slope in winter. The dry valley above it (Kalackie Koryto) leads up to Kalacka Kopa (1592m), the easternmost crag of the Giewont range.

Here is located Hotel Górski Kalatówki, run by PTTK (see Schronisko) and open all year. It is shown on some maps as Hotel Górski na Kalatówkach, and sometimes called Schronisko na Kalatówkach. It has a café, restaurant and toilets, also accommodation of a higher standard than the refuges, with bedrooms rather than dormitories. Its phone number is 018 201 2827, e-mail hotel@kalatowki.pl, website www.kalatowki.pl.

Kasprowy Wierch (1987m) The easternmost of the Western Tatras peaks, with an observatory at the summit. The top station of the cable-car from Kuźnice is a little way down at about 1940m, and has a café, souvenir shop and toilets. The cable-car, built in 1936, is 4181m long, rises 908m and reaches nearly 200m above ground level at one point. In winter this area is buzzing with skiers, being the start of several runs into adjoining valleys.

Kiry (927m) A hamlet 7km west of Zakopane at the foot of Kościeliska Dolina. It is a popular starting point for walks, with a bar and a refreshment kiosk. It is served by bus from Zakopane, and there is a large car park and toilets. From here horse-drawn taxis ply along Kościeliska Dolina as far as Polana Pisana. On the other side of the road is Hotel Halit, whose name comes from halite, a type of rock salt, reflecting its previous ownership by a salt mining company.

Klasztor Albertynek (Albertine Convent, 1100m) A small convent in the forest above Kuźnice, established in 1898 on the site of the hut in which lived Brother Albert. This was the monastic name taken by Adam Chmielówski (1845–1916), a freedom fighter who in later life took on the task of caring for the poor and homeless people of Kraków. He was canonised in 1989. The convent is open to visitors.

Klasztor Albertynow (Albertine Monastery, 1180m) The counterpart of the above, for monks rather than nuns, established in 1902. It is situated up a side track opposite the entrance to the convent, and also open to visitors.

Kościelec (2155m) One of the more accessible peaks of the Polish Tatras, standing on a spur of Świnica, though reaching its summit is quite hard work, with some exposure and a length of fixed chain. Looking north from the top you have an excellent view across Czarny Staw Gąsienicowy and down Dolina Suchej

Wody, while Giewont and Zakopane can be seen to the northwest. To the west are Kasprowy Wierch and the frontier ridge with Slovakia, and to the east the Orla Perć ridge.

Kościeliska Dolina See Dolina Kościeliska.

Kościelisko A sprawling community occupying the low hills around 900m–1000m to the west of Zakopane, with which it is connected by several bus routes. Formerly part of Zakopane, it is now a separate municipality, consisting of a large number of adjoining hamlets. The chief one is Wojdyłówka, which has shops, several bars and restaurants. Neighbouring Szeligówka has a bar, while Myśliwsky has a pretty wooden church. The community centre offers folklore evenings for visitors. Kościelisko has connections with Marie Curie and her family, who established a large sanatorium here in 1902. (Not to be confused with Kościeliska street in Zakopane.)

Koszysta A massif north of the saddle Krzyżne, which includes the summits Wielka Koszysta (2193m) and Mała Koszysta (2014m). There used to be a way-marked path along its ridge, but this has been closed to walkers to protect the strict nature reserve in the adjoining Dolina Waksmundzka.

Kozi Wierch (Goat Peak, 2291m) One of the Orla Perć summits, this is the highest mountain that is totally within Poland – the higher ones being shared with Slovakia.

Krzyżne (2112m) A high saddle at the east end of the waymarked Orla Perć route. It has comparatively easy access and some of the finest views in the Polish Tatras.

Kuźnice (Smithy, 1025m) The main starting point for walks in the Polish Tatras. As the name suggests, it was once the centre of the local iron-smelting industry – a huge waterwheel remains as evidence. Here is located the bottom station of the cable-car to Kasprowy Wierch, and there are usually huge crowds of people waiting to get on it. There are refreshment kiosks, a restaurant, a small supermarket, and usually several itinerant vendors of nicknacks. Normally Kuźnice can only be reached on foot, or by bus, taxi or horse-drawn taxi, consequently it has a large bus terminus. At the end of the day a large fleet of minibuses awaits hordes of walkers – you just pile into the first in line and pay the driver when you alight. In the lower part, near the fountain, is the headquarters of TNP, the Polish Tatras National Park.

Liliowe (Lily, 1952m) See Ľaliové Sedlo in the Slovak gazetteer.

Łysa Polana (971m) The main border crossing in the Tatras between Poland and Slovakia. Note that in Polish the first word is pronounced 'weessa', while in Slovak (as Lysá Poľana) it is 'leessa'.

Miedziane (Copper) A double summit in the High Tatras, on the spur leading northeastwards from Szpiglasowy Wierch on the Slovak border. Neither summit (2186m and 2233m) is accessible to walkers. The name comes from the 18th-century discovery of veins of copper, though these turned out to be unviable.

Morskie Oko (Eye of the Sea, 1395m) Considered to be Poland's most beautiful tarn, whose still waters reflect the summit of Rysy. It used to be the largest in the Tatras, but infilling by scree led to its being overtaken during the 1990s by Wielki Staw Polski, one of the Five Polish Tarns. It currently occupies 33 hectares and is 51m deep. At the north end of the tarn is Schronisko Morskie Oko (qv).

The original name was Rybi Staw (Fish Tarn), and the stream that issues from its north end is still called Rybi Potok. In German folklore large tarns were described as Meeraugen (Eyes of the Sea). At the time when this area was part of the Austro–Hungarian province of Galizien, this was adopted as the tarn's official name, and has been carried on through its Polish equivalent, Morskie Oko. This gave rise to the improbable legend of an underground connection to the Adriatic Sea.

This area was the subject of a long-standing internal border dispute, which lasted for 150 years. For centuries shepherds from the northern side of the Tatras brought their livestock here for summer grazing. However, the border between the two Austro–Hungarian provinces of Galizien (to the north) and Zips (to the south) ran along Rybi Potok and across the tarn, causing considerable inconvenience. Eventually in 1902 the matter was referred to arbitration and, sensibly, the border was shifted to run along the mountain tops, leaving the whole valley in the hands of Galizien, which eventually became part of modern Poland.

Murowanica (Bricks, 935m) A locality on the road to Kuźnice, not to be confused with Murowaniec.

Murowaniec See Schronisko Murowaniec.

Murzasichle (800m–900m) A village draped along a ridge to the east of Zakopane, with a pretty wooden church, several bars and pensions.

Myślenickie Turnie (1360m) A minor summit to the south of Kuźnice, which serves as the station where you change cable-cars on the way to or from Kasprowy Wierch. It is not much use to walkers, with no facilities, but in winter this is the starting point of one of the ski-pistes.

Nędzówka (952m) A hamlet 6km southwest of Zakopane, the starting point of Red 005, served by bus. It is part of Kościelisko municipality, and has a grocery.

Orla Perć (Eagle Edge) The High Tatras ridge route *par excellence*, to which adventurous walkers aspire – see Red 009B. It leads from the peak Świnica (2301m) to the saddle Krzyżne (2112m), climbing or passing seven other major peaks, all around 2200m. The route used to continue eastwards from Krzyżne along the Wołoszyn massif, but has been closed to walkers to protect the strict nature reserve in the adjoining Waksmundzka Dolina.

Palenica Białczańska See Polana Palenica.

Pałkówka (1129m) A small settlement at the west end of the Gubałówka ridge, to which two chair-lifts come up from Zakopane during the ski season. It has a buffet, toilets, car park and a bus service from Zakopane.

Podhale The geographical region north of Zakopane. It has its own dialect and architectural style, culture and folklore.

Polana Polish for 'clearing'. On some maps and signs you may variously see names written as 'Polana X' or 'X Polana', but the former is standard Polish, and that is what we normally use in this book. The word *hala* (mountain pasture, equivalent to the German *alm*) is sometimes used instead, though the surroundings are similar.

Polana Chochołowska See Schronisko Chochołowska.

Polana Huciska (982m) A clearing in Dolina Chochołowska. Until the 1990s motorised vehicles were allowed up to here, then they were banished to Siwa Polana lower down. The empty car park is used as a terminus by the road train that chugs up to here from Siwa Polana, and there are still toilets.

Polana Kalatówki See Kalatówki.

Polana Kondratowa See Schronisko Kondratowa.

Polana Palenica (984m) Also known as Palenica Białczańska. Served by bus from Zakopane. Subsidence has resulted in the closure of the road higher up, and only service vehicles and horse-drawn buses are now allowed to use it. The horse-drawn buses are inexpensive, but wrap up well – they are open to the elements, the journey lasts 45–60 minutes, and you may get cold. There is a large car park, a buffet and several refreshment kiosks.

Polana Pisana (1018m) A clearing in Dolina Kościeliska, where horse-drawn taxis turn round. Here can be found the remains of a furnace used for smelting iron ore during the 18th and 19th centuries. There are toilets here.

Przedni Staw Polski (Front Polish Tarn, 1669m) The first and lowest of the 'Five Polish Tarns' in Dolina Pięciu Stawów Polskich. The lake occupies 8 hectares and is 35m deep. At its north end, slightly above the tarn at 1672m, lies the Five Lakes Refuge – see Schronisko Pięciu Stawów.

PTTK See Schronisko.

Raczkowa Przełęcz (1959m) A saddle in the Western Tatras between Starorobociański Wierch and Błyszcz. Some maps (including Sygnatura) call it Gaborowa Przełęcz Wyżnia, with a note that Raczkowa Przełęcz is incorrect. However, we are reliably informed that the latter is how it is known to local people – and anyway, it is easier to say and write!

Rusinowa Polana (1210m) A steep summer pasture with a scattering of shepherds' huts. At one of the huts, by the junction of the blue and green routes you can buy sheep's and goats' cheese (sadly, no refreshments).

Sarnia Skała (1377m) A rocky outcrop lying a little way off Ścieżka nad Reglami (Black 901C) due south of Zakopane. From here you can get a grandstand view of the town, and looking back you have a close-up view of the north wall of Giewont.

Schronisko This means 'refuge' in Polish, and is applied to the mountain refuges where refreshment and accommodation are provided for walkers. There are eight in the Polish Tatras, if you include Hotel Górski Kalatówki. Their names as shown on maps are rather long winded, and usually shortened in conversation to those shown below. Some had alternative names thrust on them during the communist era, usually commemorating a local dignitary – they were unpopular and are no longer used.

All the refuges have at least a dining room and toilets, though they may be fairly basic, and accommodation is provided in bunks in bedrooms of various sizes, or on mattresses in dormitories. In the larger refuges you order and pay for your meal at the bar, then collect it at the kitchen counter.

Most of the refuges (also Hotel Górski Kalatówki) are operated by PTTK (Polskie Towarzystwo Turystyczno Krajoznawcze), which translates roughly as Friends of the Polish Tourist Countryside, or by some English speakers as Polish Alpine Club. This was formed by the merger of the Polish Tatras Society (established 1873) and the Polish Country Lovers Society (established 1906). They have an English language website, http://english.pttk.pl.

Schronisko Chochołowskie (Schronisko na Chochołowskiej Polanie, 1148m) A large refuge in a large clearing in Dolina Chochołowska, where livestock graze. The horse-drawn taxi service from Siwa Polana stops 250m short of the refuge, where the road steepens considerably. Schronisko Chochołowskie was built for the Warsaw Ski Club in 1933, and was visited in 1983 by Pope John Paul II during his trek into Dolina Jarząbcza. Dormitory accommodation for 121 people. Phone 018 207 0510, website www.Chochołowska.zakopane.pl.

Schronisko Kalatówki See Kalatówki.

Schronisko Kondratowa (Schronisko na Kondratowej Hali, 1333m) A small and congenial refuge in the large meadow that is variously described as Hala or Polana Kondratowa, though livestock no longer graze here. The first refuge on this site was built in 1910, but it has been rebuilt several times. Owned by the TPN (Tatras National Park) but operated by PTTK, Schronisko Kondratowa is very busy, on the routes from Kuźnice to Giewont and Kondracka Kopa, and the lush grass provides a popular picnic spot. Accommodation for 20 people in 6 or 8 bunk rooms. Phone 018 201 5214 or 9114, website www.kondratowa.com.

Schronisko Morskie Oko (Schronisko przy Morskim Oku, 1406m) A large refuge on the slope above the north end of Morskie Oko (qv), which is very busy because of its magnificent location on a beautiful tarn, and as the starting point for ascents of Rysy and other High Tatras summits. It was built in 1908 and received a complete refurbishment in 1992. At various times it has been known as Schronisko w Dolinie Rybiego Potoku (Refuge in the Valley of Trout Brook), or Schronisko imienia Stanisława Staszica, after the great Polish scientist, reformer and philanthropist, Stanisław Staszic (1755–1826). Dormitory accommodation for 104. Phone 018 207 7609.

Schronisko Murowaniec (Schronisko Murowaniec na Hali Gąsienowicej, 1500m) A substantial and picturesque refuge of brick and stone in the traditional local style – its full name means 'Brick Refuge in Caterpillar Pasture'. Walkers beat a path to this spot from six directions, and being easily accessible from Kuźnice and the cable-car at Kasprowy Wierch it is always busy. Built in 1923 for the Warsaw Section of the Polish Tatras Society, the refuge was enlarged in 1952, but a fire in 1962 severely damaged the building, and it had to be rebuilt. There is a very large dining room, and outside is a large terrace with picnic tables. Dormitory accommodation for 116. Phone 018 201 2633, e-mail murowaniec@poczta.fm.

Schronisko Ornak (Schronisko na Hali Ornak, 1108m) A medium-sized refuge situated in an idyllic meadow at the head of Kościeliska Dolina, and the meeting point of several routes. Built in 1949 on the site of an earlier refuge, at various times it has been known as Schronisko przy Małej Polance Ornaczanskiej (Refuge near Little Ornak Clearing) or Schronisko imienia Walerego Goetela, after a former PTTK president and nature conservationist. Accommodation for 80 people in 2 to 14 bunk rooms. Phone 018 207 0520, e-mail ornak@tatrynet.pl, website www.ornak.tatry.net.pl.

Schronisko Pięciu Stawów (Schronisko w Dolinie Pięciu Stawów Polskich, 1672m) The medium-sized Five Tarns Refuge is the highest in the Polish Tatras, situated in a spectacular location beside Przedni Staw Polski (Front Polish Tarn). The present building was completed in 1953 on or near the sites of earlier refuges. For a time it was known as Schronisko imienia Leopolda i Mięczysława Swierzow, after father and son Leopold (1835–1911) and Mięczysław (1891–1929) Swierz, leading mountaineers and explorers of the Tatras. Dormitory accommodation for 70. Phone 018 207 7609.

Schronisko Roztoka (Schronisko w Dolinie Roztoki, 1031m) The lowest of the Polish Tatras refuges, it is also slightly off the beaten track and consequently less busy than most. It is located in a clearing known as Stara (Old) Roztoka, not far from the Białka river. The track that approaches from the north via Niżnia Polana pod Wołoszynem is not currently accessible to walkers. The building dates from 1913 but was modernised in 1938. For a while during the communist era it was closed to tourists. In the past it has been known as Schronisko Starej Roztoce or Schronisko imienia Wincentego Pola, after the poet Wincenty Pol (1807–77). Accommodation for 77 people in 2 to 8 bunk rooms. Phone 018 207 7442.

Siklawa (1600m) Sometimes called Wielka (Big) Siklawa, this is a huge waterfall in Dolina Roztoki, a little below Wielki Staw Polski. With a fall of 70m it is the biggest in all the Tatras.

Siwa Polana (Grey Clearing, 907m) The highest point in Chochołowska Dolina that can be reached by motorised traffic. It is served by buses from Zakopane and has a large car park, refreshment facilities and toilets. A horse-drawn taxi service runs further up the valley to Schronisko Chochołowska, and a road train goes as far as Polana Huciska.

Skibówki (860m) A district on the west side of Zakopane on the road to Kiry. It is noted for its handsome, modern church – Sanktuarium Matki Bozej Fatimskiej (Sanctuary of Divine Mother Fatima, usually abbreviated to Sanktuarium Fatimskie or Fatima Sanctuary) – which was opened in 1981 and visited in 1983 by Pope John Paul II.

Strążyska Dolina See Dolina Strążyska.

Sucha Przełęcz (Dry Saddle, 1950m) Considered in Poland to be the dividing point between the High and Western Tatras, though in Slovakia L'aliové Sedlo (Liliowe in Polish) to the southeast is the official break. This means that the intervening peak, Beskid/Beskyd, may be in the High or Western Tatras, depending on whose authority you accept.

Szałasiska (1360m) A campsite on the road to Morskie Oko, which is reserved for members of mountaineering clubs. It serves as a base camp for climbing expeditions into the High Tatras.

Tomanowa Dolina See Dolina Tomanowa.

Toporowa Cyrhla (Axe Clearing, 950m–1040m) A village on the road to Łysa Polana, east of Zakopane, from where it is served by bus. There is a beautiful church in the lower part of the village, while the popular restaurant Siedem Kotów (Seven Tomcats) lies on the main road at the top end. Accommodation can be obtained in a number of pensions and private houses.

Waksmundzka Dolina See Dolina Waksmundzka.

Wielki Staw Polski (Big Polish Tarn, 1664m) Now the largest tarn in the Polish Tatras, at 35 hectares, having overtaken Morskie Oko, which is slowly filling with scree. It is one of the Five Polish Tarns (Pięciu Polskich Stawów). At the north end of the tarn, a high rocky islet, like a miniature sugarloaf, provides a popular photo-opportunity for the agile.

Wiktorówki (1140m) A charming, lonely chapel and monastery in the forest southeast of Zakopane. It is situated in Złota Dolina (Golden Valley) and can be reached on Blue 210 from Zazadnia. Visitors are welcomed, and cups of tea can be obtained. On maps it is variously shown as Kaplica Matki Boskiej Jaworzyńskie, or Witamy na Wiktorówkach Matka Boza Jaworzyńska, loosely translated as the Chapel of Our Lady the Queen of the Tatras, whose statue is located inside. On his visit in 1983, Pope John Paul II described this as one of his favourite places in the Tatras. The monastery is also a mountain rescue point.

Witów (832m) A straggling village to the northwest of Zakopane on the way to Chochołów. It consists almost entirely of wooden buildings in traditional Podhale style. There is a bar (Hanka) in the village centre, and at its north end a grocery kiosk.

Włosienica (1315m) A huge, former car park on the road to Morskie Oko, now grassed over and usually deserted, except for the horse-drawn buses from Polana Palenica, which turn round here. There are toilets, and nearby is the big, barn-like Pawilion Turystyczny na Włosienicy (Włosienica Tourist Pavilion), where refreshments can be obtained.

Wodogrzmoty Mickiewicza (1100m) A picturesque waterfall that performs a couple of right-angled bends during its descent, before cascading beneath the road from Polana Palenica to Morskie Oko. Wodogrzmoty means 'water thunderclap'; Adam Mickiewicz (1798–1855) was a 19th-century romantic poet who inspired Polish nationalism. The large former car park, now deserted, is a popular picnic site.

Zakopane (855m) The largest holiday resort in all the Tatras, with a resident population of 30,000. Its economy is largely dependent on tourism, although it is also a market town serving much of Podhale. It offers a good choice of accommodation in hotels, pensions and private houses, and there are good shopping and currency exchange facilities.

The main street, Krupówki, is now pedestrianised. What would the great Polish patriot and nature lover Władysław Zamoyski (1853–1924) have made of it? His statue gazes in bemusement down Krupówki, surrounded by amusements, a carnival atmosphere and jolly, strolling tourists who are probably completely unaware that they are here because of him. When the Tatras forests were auctioned in 1889, Zamoyski bought them to prevent destruction through logging and mining, otherwise things could have been very different now. In 1924 he established the Tatra Mountains National Foundation, which eventually became the Tatras National Park. He was inspired by the local physician and botanist Tytus Chałubiński (1820–89), who enthusiastically promoted Zakopane as a health resort, and whose name is perpetuated in the main street that leads towards Kuźnice.

Throughout the town you come across attractive wooden buildings in two traditional styles, Podhale and Góral, though it is difficult for visitors to discern the difference. Some modern buildings are being refurbished or extended in the old style. Church architecture is an intriguing mixture of traditional and modern – the latter often being highly original in design. Public transport within the town and to outlying villages is provided by frequent buses and minibuses. For something more unusual, try the horse-drawn taxis (*dorożki*) – they are to be found principally at the north end of Krupówki street (near the post office), by Kuźnickie Rondo (the roundabout on the road to Kuźnice) and at the railway station.

Polana Kondratowa and Sucha Czuba (Blde 206) (photo: C Saunders)

APPENDIX A
GLOSSARY

See Languages, page 30, for a general introduction to Polish and Slovak – what follows here is a guide to pronunciation.

Letters are pronounced as in English except as shown below. Some sounds in both languages have no exact equivalent in English. There are distinctions between similar sounds that an 'English-speaking ear' would be incapable of detecting, and which are impossible to explain in a book such as this, so the explanations that appear below can be no more than a rough guide.

Slovak

Diacritics There are four kinds of diacritic (accent) in Slovak, affecting the way a letter is pronounced. One, similar to the German umlaut, sharpens the vowels ä and ö. Another, similar to the French circumflex, flattens the vowel ô. A third, called *dĺžeň* (pronounced 'dlzhain'), lengthens the vowels on á, é, í, ó, ú and ý. The fourth, called *mäkčeň* (pronounced 'maikchen') softens the consonants č, ň, š and ž. The mäkčeň is also used in different ways on ď, ľ and ť in lower case or Ď, Ľ and Ť in upper case.

Vowels A as in 'map'; Á as in 'father'; Ä like 'ai' in 'hair'; AJ like 'ie' in 'tie'; E as in 'bed'; É like 'a' in 'cat'; EJ like 'ai' in 'rain'; I and Y like 'i' in 'pit'; Í and Ý like 'i' in 'police'; O as in 'dog'; Ô like 'aw' in 'paw'; OU like 'oa' in 'boat'; U as in 'bull'; Ú as in 'rule'.

Consonants C like 'ts' in 'tsar'; Č like 'ch' in 'char'; Ď like 'd' in 'due'; CH like 'ch' in Scottish 'loch'; J like 'y' in 'yes'; Ľ like 'li' in 'lieu'; Ň like 'ni' in 'onion'; Š like 'sh' in 'cash'; Ť like 't' in 'picture'; Ž like 's' in 'leisure'. H is always aspirated, even before another consonant.

'R' and 'L' are used both as consonants and vowels. As consonants, 'L' is as in English, 'R' is rolled as in Scotland. As vowels, a short 'e' as in 'meringue' or 'model' is implied.

Note that in the Slovak alphabet 'č' comes after 'c', 'ch' after 'h', 'š' after 's' and 'ž' after 'z'.

Here are some examples using places you will find on the maps:

Štrbské Pleso – 'shturrbska plesso'
Starý Smokovec – 'starree smockovets'
Tatranská Lomnica – 'tatranskah lomnitsa'
Ľaliové Sedlo – 'lialiova sedlo'
Jahňací Štít – 'jahh-niatsi shteet'
Ždiar – 'zhdee-arr'.

Here is a translation of some of the words you are likely to come across in the Tatras. Note that most of these have varying endings, depending on gender and case. Where some help with pronunciation is needed, this is shown in brackets (xh:'ch' as in Scottish 'loch'; do not forget to roll your Rs). In both Polish and Slovak, the stress tends to go on the first syllable.

biely ('byellee')	white
červený ('chervenee')	red
chata ('xhata')	mountain chalet
čierny ('chernee')	black
dobrý deň	good morning, hello (see note below)
dolina	valley
dolinka	little valley
hnedý	brown
hora, horský	mountain
hrebeň	ridge
jaskyňa ('yaskinya')	cave
juh ('yooh')	south
južný ('yoozhnee')	southern
kabínková lanovka	gondola (mountain lift)
kopa	stack (bulky summit)
koruna	crown (Slovak currency)
kotlina	basin (geographical)
malý ('mahlee')	little, small
modrý	blue
na	by, at
nad	above
nebezpečenstvo	danger
nízky	low
nižný ('nizhnee')	lower
nový	new
obchod ('obxhod')	shop

pleso	tarn
pod	below
poľana	clearing
poľský	Polish
pošta	post, post office
potok	brook, stream
potraviny	grocery
prameň	spring, source
predný	front, foremost, outer
prostredný	middle
sedačková lanovka	chair-lift
sedielko	little saddle, pass
sedlo	saddle, pass
šedý ('shedee')	grey
sever	north
severný	northern
skała	cliff
slovenská	Slovak
starý	old
štít ('shteet')	peak, summit
suchý ('sooxhee')	dry
úplaz	slope (steep, narrow)
vchod ('vxhod')	entrance
veľký	big, large, great
veža ('vayzha')	tower
voda	water
vodopád	waterfall
vrch ('verxh')	hill
východ ('veexhod')	exit, east
východný	eastern
vyhliadka	viewpoint
vysoký	high
vyšný ('veeshnee')	upper
zadný	back, hindmost, inner
západ	west
západný	western
zastávka	bus stop
zelený	green
žľab ('zhlyab')	flood stream (usually dry in summer)
žltý ('zhultee')	yellow

Polish

Diacritics There are three kinds of diacritic (accent) in Polish – the *kreska* (stroke), which lengthens (ó) or softens (ć, ł, ń, ś and ź), the *kropka* (dot), which also softens (ż) in a slightly different way, and the *ogonek* (tail), which has a nasal effect on ą and ę.

Vowels A as in 'rather'; Ą like 'on' in French 'bon'; E as in 'bed'; Ę like 'ien' in French 'chien'; I as in 'police'; IE like 'ye' in 'yes'; O as in 'dog'; Ó as in 'shoe'; U as in 'rule'; Y as in 'cryptic'.

Consonants C like 'ts' in 'tsar'; Ć like 'j' in 'jug'; CH like 'ch' in Scottish 'loch'; CI like 'ci' in cigar; CZ like 'ch' in 'chat'; J like 'y' in 'yes'; Ł like 'w' in 'water'; Ń like 'ni' in 'onion'; Ś, SI and SZ like 'sh' in 'ship'; W like 'v' in 'vat'; Ź, Ż and RZ are all like 's' in 'leisure'.

A soft consonant at the end of the word becomes hard, so B = P, G = K, D = T, W = F.

Note that in the Polish alphabet ą comes after a, ć after c, ę after e, ł after l, ń after n, ó after o, ś after s, ż after ź after z.

Here are some examples using places you will find on the maps:

Kuźnice – 'koozhnits-e'
Świstowa Czuba – 'shvistova chooba'
Łysa Polana – 'weesa polana' (but note that in Slovak the 'L' in Lysá is pronounced as in English).

biały ('byawee')	white
brązowy ('brongzovee')	brown
czarny ('charnee')	black
czerwony ('chervonee')	red
czuba ('chooba')	tuft
dolina	valley
dolinka	little valley
dzień dobry ('jean dobree')	good day, hello (see note below)
góra (noun), *górsky* (adjective)	mountain
grzbiet ('gurzbyet')	ridge
hala	mountain pasture (alm)
hruby ('hroobee')	thick
jaskinia ('yaskinya')	cave
kolejka linowa ('kolika linova')	cable-car
kopa	stack (bulky summit)

kopka	little stack
łąka ('wongka')	meadow
mali ('mawee')	little, small
na	on, by, at
nad	above
niebezpieczeństwo	danger
niebieski ('nyebyeskee')	blue
niski	low
niżnia ('nizhnya')	lower
nowy ('novee')	new
poczta ('potchta')	post, post office
pod	below
polana	clearing
polanka	little clearing
północ ('pouwnots')	north, midnight
polski	Polish
południe ('pouwoodniye')	south, midday
pośredni ('poshredni')	middle
potok	brook, stream
przedni ('pshednyi')	front, foremost
przełącka ('pshewongchka')	little pass
przełęcz ('pshewangch')	pass, saddle
przysłop ('psheeswop')	a kind of saddle
przystanek ('psheestanek')	bus stop
schronisko ('sxhronisko')	mountain refuge
siwy ('sivvee')	grey
skała ('skahwa')	cliff
sklep	shop
słowak ('swovak')	Slovak
spożywczy ('spozheevchee')	grocery
stary ('starree')	old
staw ('staf')	tarn
suchy ('sooxhee')	dry
szczyt ('shcheet')	peak, summit
turnia ('toornya')	crag
upłaz ('oopwaz')	slope
wejście ('vieshtche')	entrance (to cave)
widzenie ('vidzenye')	viewpoint
wielki ('vyelky')	large, big, great
wierch ('veerxh')	hill

wjazd ('vyazd')	entrance (to building)
woda ('voda')	water
wodospad ('vodospad')	waterfall
wschod ('vsxhod')	east
wyjście ('veeshtche')	exit
wysoki ('veesoki')	high
wyżnia ('veezhnya')	upper
zachod ('zaxhod')	west
zadni	back, hindmost, inner
zielony ('zhelonee')	green
złoty ('zwotee')	gold, Polish currencey
źródło ('zhrodwo')	spring, source
żleb ('zhleb')	gully
żółty ('zhouwtee')	yellow

Useful Words and Phrases

English	Polish	Slovak
food	*żywność*	potraviny
meal	*posiłek*	jedlo
breakfast	*sniadanie*	raňajky
lunch	*lunch*	obed
dinner	*obiad*	večera
beer	*piwo*	pivo
coffee	*kawa*	káva
juice	*sok*	džús
milk	*mleko*	mlieko
tea	*herbata*	čaj
water	*woda*	voda
wine	*wino*	víno
bread	*chleb*	chlieb
butter	*masło*	maslo
jam	*dżem*	džem
honey	*miód*	med
soup	*zupa*	polievka
omelette	*omlet*	omeleta
bacon	*boczek*	slanina
beef	*wołowina*	hovädziemäso
beefsteak	*befsztyk*	biftek
chicken	*kurczę*	kurča
egg	*jajko*	vajce

312

ham	*szynka*	*šunka*
kidney	*nerka*	*oblička*
lamb	*jagnię*	*jahňacie mäso*
liver	*wątroba*	*pečeň*
pork	*wieprzowina*	*bravčové mäso*
sausage	*kiełbasa*	*klobása*
veal	*cielęcina*	*teľacie mäso*
bean	*fasola*	*fazuľa*
cabbage	*kapusta*	*kapusta*
carrot	*marchewka*	*mrkva*
cauliflower	*kalafior*	*karfiol*
pea	*groch*	*hrach*
potato	*ziemniak*	*zemiak*
salt	*sól*	*soľ*
pepper	*pieprz*	*čierne korenie*
vinegar	*ocet*	*ocot*
apple	*jabłko*	*jablko*
cake	*placek*	*koláč*
fruit	*owoc*	*ovocie*
orange	*pomarańcza*	*pomaranč*
pudding	*budyń*	*puding*
cream	*śmietana*	*smotana*
ice cream	*lody*	*zmrzlina*
bill please	*proszę płacić*	*platím prosím*

Days of the Week, Times of Day

Monday	*poniedzialek*	*pondelok*
Tuesday	*wtorek*	*utorok*
Wednesday	*środa*	*streda*
Thursday	*czwartek*	*štvrtok*
Friday	*piatek*	*piatok*
Saturday	*sobota*	*sobota*
Sunday	*niedziela*	*nedeľa*
morning	*rano*	*ráno*
midday	*południe*	*poludnie*
afternoon	*popołudnie*	*popoludnie*
evening	*wieczór*	*večer*
midnight	*północ*	*polnoc*
night	*noc*	*noc*
o'clock	*godzina*	*hodina*

Numbers

one	*jeden*	*jeden*
two	*dwa*	*dva*
three	*trzy*	*tri*
four	*cztery*	*štyri*
five	*pięć*	*päť*
six	*sześć*	*šest*
seven	*siedem*	*sedem*
eight	*osiem*	*osem*
nine	*dzewięć*	*deväť*
ten	*dzesięć*	*desať*

Greetings

hi	*cześć*	*ahoj, servus*
hello	*dzień dobry* ★	*dobrý deň* ★
good morning	*dzień dobry* ★	*dobrý deň* ★
good afternoon	*dzień dobry* ★	*dobrý deň* ★
good evening	*dobry wieczór*	*dobrý večer*
goodnight	*dobranoc*	*dobrú noc*
goodbye	*do widzenia*	*dovidenia*
cheers!	*sto lat!*	*na zdravie!*
good appetite!	*smacznego!*	*dobrú chuť!*
please	*prosze*	*prosím*
thank you	*dziękuję*	*ďakujem*

★**Note** In the Tatras a common greeting as you meet others on a path is plain *dobry* (pronounced 'dobbree'), which just means 'good'. This gets over the possibility that the other person may be Polish (*dzień dobry*) or Slovak (*dobrý deň*).

Others

ladies	*kobieti*	*ženy/dámy*
gents	*człowieki*	*muži/pany*

APPENDIX B
ACCOMMODATION

See also Accommodation, page 35.

Hotels and Guest Houses in the Villages
This section lists accommodation available for visitors who wish to book direct rather than on a package tour. **Inclusion in these lists does not imply a recommendation**, and before booking you are advised to obtain further information about places that interest you.

Alternatively you could contact one of the travel agents in the Tatras shown under Shopping and Local Services for the country you are visiting, as they may hold allocations at hotels, and can offer alternatives if your first choice is full. Having helped with the preparation of the Polish section of this book, Trip Travel in Zakopane will be very pleased to help readers with accommodation and sightseeing requirements there (phone 018 202 0200, e-mail biuro@trip.pl, website www.trip.pl). Say that you are using this book.

Another option is to use one of the online accommodation booking services that specialise in the Tatras, and sometimes have special offers. In Slovakia these include, www.bookings.sk, www.enjoyslovakia.com and www.tatry.net. In Poland, www.accommodation.pl, www.hotele.pl and www.hotelspol.com.

Postcodes (zip codes), shown below, go before the place name on your envelopes, on the same line, eg 06201 Starý Smokovec.

The telephone dialling code (phone code) is given for each place. If dialling from outside Slovakia or Poland, you will usually need to omit the initial zero after dialling the country code.

The categories are indicated as follows:
★★★★★ deluxe hotel, ★★★★ first-class hotel, ★★★ superior hotel, ★★ medium-grade hotel, P pension, YH youth hostel.

(+) after the stars indicates that the hotel is reckoned to be better than its grade implies, but not quite measuring up to the higher grade.

Camping
Campsites are sometimes shown on maps and signs as *Kemping* in both Polish and Slovak.

There are two large campsites on the Slovak side:

Tatracamp, run by Hotel Tatranec, is situated a little to the south of Tatranská Lomnica (phone 052 446 7092) www.hoteltatranec.com.

RIJO Camping at Stará Lesná (phone 052 446 7493) is smaller but has good facilities. Further details are shown on website www.rijocamping.eu.

There are three campsites in or near Zakopane. At each of these you must provide your own tent (there are no 'tent-camps', where tents are provided, in the Polish Tatras). They are: Tatry Pod Krokwia – the largest – in Zeromskiego Stefana near the Bystre Rondo (1.5km southeast), Tatry, at Harenda (3km northeast), and Za Strugiem (1km southwest).

Self-catering

There is a rapidly expanding market in self-catering facilities in the Tatras, though much of it is on long-term lets and it may be difficult to find vacancies. Contact the local tourist information office for more information.

Accommodation List

Due to space limitations we can only provide basic details of the hotels and larger guest houses. Places are listed under their location, progressing from west to east. The name is followed by the star rating, number of bedrooms, phone number and e-mail address, and website if available. All details are subject to change.

Slovakia

Podbanské (postcode 03242 Pribylina):

Grand Hotel Permon ★★★★ (150), 052 471 0111, hotelpermon@hotelpermon.sk, www.hotelpermon.sk

Hotel Kriváň ★★ (75) – contact via Grand Hotel Permon

Štrbské Pleso (postcode 05985):

Grand Hotel Kempinski High Tatras ★★★★★ (117), 052 3262 222, reservations.hightatras@kempinski.com, www.kempinski.com/hightatras.

Hotel Patria ★★★★ (152), 052 449 2591, recepcia@hotelpatria.sk, www.hotelpatria.sk

FIS Hotel ★★★ (60), 052 449 2221, hotelfis@hotelfis.sk, www.hotelfis.sk

Hotel Panoráma ★★★ (96), 052 449 2111

Hotel Toliar ★★★ (60), 052 449 2690, kanc@tatry-toliar.sk, www.hoteltoliar.sk

Hotel Sorea Baník ★★ (101), 052 449 2541, banik@sorea.sk, www.sorea.sk

Tatranská Štrba (postcode 05941):
    Hotel Nezábudka ★★★ (26), 052 448 4838, rezervacie@hotelnezabudka.sk,
    www.hotelnezbudka.sk
    Hotel Rysy ★★★ (80), 052 448 4845, info@hotel-rysy.sk, www.hotel-rysy.sk
    Hotel Meander ★★★ (70), 052 478 1051, www.hotelmeander.sk

Batizovce (postcode 05935):
    Hotel Guľa ★★ (15), 052 775 6942, slovakiainn@hotelgula.sk,
    www.hotelgula.sk

Gerlachov (postcode 05942):
    Hotel Hubert ★★★★ (49), 052 478 0811, hubert@hotel-hubert.sk,
    www.hotel-hubert.sk

Tatranské Zruby (postcode 06201):
    Hotel Tatranské Zruby ★★ (86), 052 442 2751, recepcia@tatranskezruby.sk,
    www.tatranskezruby.sk

Nový Smokovec (postcode 06201):
    Atrium Hotel ★★★ (92), 052 442 2342, recepcia@atriumhotel.sk,
    www.atriumhotel.sk
    Hotel Palace Grand ★★★★ (77), 052 442 2342, kupelens@sinet.sk,
    www.kupelens.sk
    Hotel Branisko ★★★ (21) – contact Hotel Palace
    Aparthotel Família Smokovec ★★★ (30), 052 442 2791, recepcia@
    familiasmokovec.sk, www.familiasmokovec.sk
    Villa Dr. Szontag (P) (16), 052 442 2061, szontagh@isternet.sk
    Villa Siesta (P) (23), 478-0931, recepcia@villasiesta.com,
    www.villasiesta.com

Starý Smokovec (postcode 06201):
    Grand Hotel ★★★+ (79), 052 478 0000, reserve@grandhotel.sk,
    www.grandhotel.sk
    Hotel Smokovec ★★★ (31), 052 442 5191, recepcia@hotelsmokovec.sk,
    www.hotelsmokovec.sk
    Horný Smokovec (postcode 06201):
    Grand Hotel Bellevue ★★★★ (70), 052 442 2941, hotelbellevue@
    hotelbellevue.sk, www.hotelbellevue.sk
    Hotel Garni Sorea Skalnička ★★★ (15), 052 442 3114, skalnicka@sorea.sk,
    www.sorea.sk

Penzión Poľana (P) (25), 052 442 2516, polana@slovakiatatry.sk, www.slovakiatatry.sk
Hotel Tatrapeak ★★ (14), 052 442 5026, tatrapeak@tatry.sk
Penzión Partizán (P) (22), 052 442 2161, partizan@sinet.sk , www.penzionpartizan.sk
Vila Marta (P), (20), 0910 777666, rezervacia@vilamarta.sk, www.vilamarta.sk
Penzión Vila Klara (P), 0917 287182, e-mail vilaklara@stonline.sk

Dolný Smokovec (postcode 05981):
Hotel Autis ★★ (18), 052 442 5331, info@hotelautis.sk, www.hotelautis.szm.sk

Hrebienok (postcode 06201 Starý Smokovec):
Horský Hotel Sorea Hrebienok ★★★ (50), 052 442 5060, hrebienok@sorea.sk, www.sorea.sk

Tatranská Lesná (postcode 05960):
Penzión Erika (P) (23), 052 442 2397, erikapenzion@erikapenzion.sk, www.erikapenzion.sk
Penzión Karpátia (P) (28), 052 442 2516

Nová Lesná (postcode 05986);
Hotel Amalia ★★★ (14), 052 478 0110, hotelamalia@hotelamalia.sk, www.hotelamalia.sk

Stará Lesná (postcode 05960):
Hotel Horizont ★★★ (43), 052 446 7881, recepcia@hotel-horizont.sk, www.hotel-horizont.sk
Hotel Kontakt ★★★ (37), 052 446 8185, recepcia@hotelkontakt.sk, www.hotelkontakt.sk
Hotel Lesná ★★★ (44), 052 446 7556, lesna@stonline.sk, www.hotellesna.sk
Hotel Tatrania ★★ (12), 052 446 7969, tatrania@tatrania.sk, www.tatrania.sk

Poprad (postcode 05801):
Aquacity Hotel ★★★ (41), 052 785 1222, recepcia@aquacity.sk, www.aquacity.sk
Hotel Poprad ★★★ (58), hotel-poprad@pp.psg.sk, www.hotel-poprad.sk

Hotel Satel ★★★ (127) 052 716 1111, satelpp@hotelsatel.com,
www.hotelsatel.com
Hotel Europa ★★★ (45), 052 772 1897, kancelaria@hotel-europa.sk,
www.hotel-europa.sk
Hotel Gerlach ★★★ (98), 052 772 1945, hotelgerlach@hotelgerlach.sk,
www.hotelgerlach.sk
Tatra Hotel ★★ (87), 052 787 1700, recepcia@tatrahotel.com,
www.tatrahotel.com

Spišská Sobota (postcode 05801):
Penzión Atrium a Dagmar (P) (30), 952 776 9522, atrium@sinet.sk,
www.penzion-atrium.sk
Penzión Juraj (P) (20), 052 776 9517, info@svjuraj.sk, www.svjuraj.sk

Tatranská Lomnica (postcode 05960):
Best Western Hotel Tulipan ★★★★ (14), 052 478 0611,
www.tatry.net/tulipan
Grandhotel Praha ★★★★ (97), 052 446 7941, grandpraha@tatry.sk,
www.grandhotelpraha.sk
Hotel Slovakia ★★★ (35), 052 446 7961, recepcia@hotel-slovakia.sk,
www.hotel-slovakia.sk
Hotel Slovan ★★★ (85), 052 446 7851, hotel-slovan@hotel-slovan.sk,
www.hotel-slovan.sk
Hotel Sorea Titris Odborár ★★★ (85), 052 446 7351, odborar@sorea.sk,
www.sorea.sk
Hotel Sorea Urán ★★★ (107), 052 446 7841, uran@sorea.sk,
www.sorea.sk
Hotel Morava ★★ (80), 052 446 7641, recepcia@hotel-morava.sk,
www.hotel-morava.sk
Penzión Horec (P) (40), 052 446 7261

Tatranské Matliare (postcode 05953):
Hotel Sorea Hutník I ★★★ (127), 052 446 7441, hutnik@sorea.sk,
www.sorea.sk
Hotel Sorea Hutník II ★★ (85) – contact Hotel Sorea Hutník I

Tatranská Kotlina (postcode 05954):
Penzión Koliba (P) (37), 052 446 8274, info@penzion-koliba.sk,
www.penzion-koliba.sk
Penzión Limba (P) (9), 0918 723404, penzionlimba@post.sk

Ždiar (postcode 05955):
  Hotel Bachledka-Strachan ★★★ (20), 052 4498 206, info@bachledka.sk,
  www.bachledka.sk
  Hotel Magura ★ (80), 052 478 0511, recepcia@magurahotel.sk,
  www.magurahotel.sk
There is also a large number of pensions (*penzión*) in Ždiar.

Javorina (postcode 05956):
  Hotel Kolowrat ★★★★ (58), 052 476 3111, kolowrat@hotelkolowrat.sk,
  www.hotelkolowrat.sk

Poland
Zakopane (postcode 34500):
There is a large number of hotels in Zakopane – the following is a selection.
  Hotel Litwor ★★★★★ (53), 018 202 4200, rezerwacja@litwor.pl, www.litwor.pl
  Hotel Villa Marilor ★★★★★ (20), 018 200 0670, rezerwacja@hotelmarilor.com,
  www.hotelmarilor.com
  Hotel Belvedere ★★★★ (175), 018 202 0211, belvederehotel@trip.pl,
  www.belvederehotel.pl
  Grand Hotel Stamary ★★★★ (53), 018 202 4510, hotel@stamary.pl,
  www.stamary.pl
  Hotel Czarny Potok ★★★ (44), 018 202 0204, rezerwacja@czarnypotok.pl,
  www.czarnypotok.pl
  Hotel Gromada ★★★ (55), 018 201 5011, www.gromadazakopane.com
  Hotel Mercure Kasprowy ★★★ (288), 018 202 4000, H3399@accor.com,
  www.mercure.com
  Hotel Nosalowy Dwór ★★★ (30), 018 201 1400, hotelgrand@nosalowy-dwor.eu,
  www.nosalowydwor.eu
  Hotel Orbis Giewont ★★★ (44), 018 201 2011, giewont@orbis.pl,
  www.giewont.net.pl
  Hotel Sabała ★★★ (20), 018 201 5092, recepcja@sabala.zakopane.pl,
  www.sabala.zakopane.pl
  Hotel Skalny ★★★ (32), 018 201 9100, skalny@skalny.com.pl,
  www.skalny.com.pl
  Hotel Wersal ★★★ (45), 018 202 3123, reservation@hotelwersal.pl,
  www.hotelwersal.pl
  Hotel Helios ★★ (40), 018 201 3808, reserwacja@hotel-helios.pl,
  www.hotel-helios.pl

Hotel Kasprowy Wierch ★ ★ (20), 018 201 2738, kasprowy@mati.zakopane.pl, www.kasprowy.zakopane.pl
There is also a large number of pensions (*pensjonat*) in Zakopane.

Murowanica-Kuźnice
    Apartment Hotel Murowanica ★ ★ ★ (40), 601 766 677, kontakt@ zakopanemurowanica.pl, www.zakopanemurowanica.pl

Kiry (postcode 34511 Kościelisko):
    Hotel Halit ★ ★ ★ (30), 018 207 9282, biuro@halit.pl, www.halit.pl

Jaszczurówka (postcode 34500 Zakopane):
    Hotel Pod Piorem ★ ★ (11), 018 201 1001, pp@gabrysia.com.pl, www.polhotels.com/zakopane/podpiorem

Murzasichle (postcode 34531):
    Hotel Misiówka (12), 018 201 9756, murzasichle@poczta.onet.pl

Zgorzelisko (postcode 34531 Male Ciche):
    Hotel Tatry ★ ★ ★ (50), 018 207 7011, polanazgorzelisko@polskietatry.pl, www.polskietatry.pl

Bukowina Tatrzańska (postcode 34530)
    Hotel Bukovina ★ ★ ★ ★ (146), www.hotelbukovina.pl

APPENDIX C
USEFUL CONTACTS

Airlines

The following list shows services available at the time of writing, which are subject to alteration and may be discontinued. New services are frequently introduced – you should check what is currently available with a travel agent or on the internet.

Phone numbers are only shown for airlines that accept reservations by this method and may be charged at higher rates than normal landlines. Where no phone number is shown airlines will only accept reservations online via the website address shown, or through a travel agent.

At the time of writing, no airlines were serving Poprad but services may be restarted – try searching online.

Aer Lingus (Dublin to Vienna), Irish Republic 0818 365000, www.aerlingus.com

Austrian Airlines (London Heathrow, New York, Washington and Toronto), www.austrian.com

British Airways (London Heathrow to Vienna). UK 0844 493 0787, Australia 1300 767 177, Canada/USA 1-800-AIRWAYS or 1-800-247-9297, India 1800 102 35922, New Zealand 09 966 9777, South Africa 011 441 8600, www.britishairways.com

EasyJet (London Gatwick to Vienna; London Gatwick, Belfast International, Bristol, Edinburgh and Liverpool to Kraków), www.easyjet.com

LOT Polish Airlines (London Heathrow to Warsaw; Chicago and New York to Kraków). UK 0845 601 0949, Canada/USA 1-212-789-0970, www.lot.com

RyanAir (London Stansted, Dublin, Birmingham, Edinburgh and Liverpool to Bratislava and Kraków; London Luton to Bratislava and Rzeszów; Bristol to Bratislava, Rzeszów and Wrocław; East Midlands, Leeds/Bradford and Malta to Kraków; Glasgow Prestwick and Shannon to Wrocław). UK 0871 246 0000; Irish Republic 0818 303030

Wizz Air (London Luton to Brno, Katowice and Wrocław; Cork and Doncaster/ Sheffield to Katowice and Wrocław; Glasgow Prestwick to Warsaw; Liverpool to Katowice). UK 0906 959 0002, Irish Republic 1550 475970, www.wizzair.com

Embassies Abroad
Slovak Republic
UK: 25 Kensington Palace Gardens, London, W8 4QY, phone 020 7313 6470, e-mail emb.london@mzv.sk

Irish Republic: 20 Clyde Road, Ballsbridge, Dublin 4, phone 01 660 0012, e-mail slovak@iol.ie

Australia: 47 Culgoa Circuit, O'Malley, Canberra ACT, 2606, phone 02 6290 1516, e-mail emb.canberra@mzv.sk

Canada: 50 Rideau Terrace, Ottawa, K1M 2A1, phone 613-749-4442, e-mail ottawa@slovakembassy.ca

New Zealand: no representation at time of writing – contact office in Australia

South Africa: 930 Arcadia Street, 0083 Tshwane (Pretoria), phone 012 342 2051, e-mail emb.pretoria@mzv.sk

USA: 3523 International Court NW, Washington DC, 20008, phone 202 237 1054, e-mail emb.washington@mzv.sk

Poland
UK: 47 Portland Place, London, W1B 1JH, phone 020 7580 4324, e-mail londyn. konsulat@msz.gov.pl

Irish Republic: 5 Ailesbury Road, Ballsbridge, Dublin 4, phone 01 283 0855, e-mail info@dublin.polemb.net

Australia: Consulate General, 10 Trelawney Street, Woollahra, NSW 2025, phone 0419 488 677, e-mail sydney.kg.sekretariat@msz.gov.pl

Canada: 443 Daly Avenue, Ottawa, K1N 6H3, phone 613 789 0468, e-mail ottawa@ottawa.polemb.net

New Zealand: 142 Featherston Street, Wellington 6143, phone 04 475 9453, e-mail polishembassy@xtra.co.nz

South Africa: 14 Arnos Street, Colbyn, Tshwane (Pretoria) 0083, phone 012 430 2631, e-mail konsulat@mweb.co.za

USA: 2224 Wyoming Avenue NW, Washington DC 20008-3992, phone 202 234 3800, e-mail washington.consular@msz.gov.pl

Tourist Information
The Polish National Tourist Office has offices in:

UK: Westgate House, West Gate, London, W5 1YY, phone 0870 067 5010, e-mail info@visitpoland.org, website www.poland.travel/en-gb

USA: 5 Marine View Plaza, Hoboken, NJ 07030, phone 201 420 9910, e-mail pntony@polandtour.org, website www.poland.travel/en-us

The Slovak Tourist Board has an information office in the UK at 25 Kensington Palace Gardens, London, W8 4QY, phone 020 7313 6470, www.slovakia.travel.

In the UK, the following travel agencies organise holidays in the Tatras:
- Exodus Travels (walking in the Polish and Slovak Tatras), Grange Mills, Weir Road, London SW12 0NE, phone 0845 869 9174, e-mail sales@exodus.co.uk, www.exodus.co.uk
- Explore Worldwide (walking in the Polish and Slovak Tatras), 55 Victoria Road, Farnborough, Hampshire, GU14 7PA, phone 0845 013 1537, e-mail res@explore.co.uk, www.exploreworldwide.com
- Inntravel (walking holidays in Slovak Tatras), Whitwell Grange, Castle Howard, Yorkshire, YO60 7JU, phone 01653 617001, e-mail inntravel@inntravel.co.uk, www.inntravel.co.uk
- Mountain Paradise (walking in the Slovak Tatras), Station House, Stamford New Road, Altrincham, WA14 1EP, phone 0161 408 8988, e-mail info@mountainparadise.co.uk, www.mountainparadise.co.uk
- Polorbis Holidays (general holidays in Poland), 25 Maude Crescent, Watford, WD24 6DE, phone 01923 803006, e-mail sales@polorbis.co.uk, www.polorbis.co.uk
- Slovakia Holidays (general holidays in Slovakia), 10 Birch Road, Stowmarket, IP14 3EZ, phone 01844 339754, e-mail slovakiaholidays@aol.com, www.slovakiaholidays.org

APPENDIX D
SUGGESTED KIT LIST

See also Clothing and Equipment, page 38.

Essential Items for Walking in the Mountains
- [ ] Compass (also useful for identifying places from viewpoints)
- [ ] Emergency food rations
- [ ] First aid kit (including a blister kit and tick remover)
- [ ] Handkerchiefs
- [ ] Maps
- [ ] Pullovers
- [ ] Rucksack
- [ ] Shirts with long sleeves
- [ ] Socks
- [ ] Torch, spare batteries and bulb (especially if you intend to explore the caves in the Polish Tatras)
- [ ] Underwear
- [ ] Walking boots
- [ ] Walking trousers or breeches
- [ ] Water-bottle
- [ ] Waterproof clothing (jacket, overtrousers, gaiters)
- [ ] Whistle
- [ ] Windproof jacket

Optional Items for Walking
- [ ] Mobile phone (check availability in Poland/Slovakia with your service provider)
- [ ] GPS
- [ ] Shorts or skirt

Suggested Items for Evenings
- [ ] Footwear
- [ ] Jacket or pullover
- [ ] Nightwear
- [ ] Shirts or blouses
- [ ] Socks
- [ ] Toilet gear
- [ ] Trousers or skirts, etc.

Miscellaneous

- [ ] Camera
- [ ] Dictionary or phrase book (Polish or Slovak as appropriate)
- [ ] Food container
- [ ] Insect repellent
- [ ] Knife (for cutting food)
- [ ] Sleeping bag (if staying overnight at mountain chalets or refuges)
- [ ] Sunglasses
- [ ] Thermos flask
- [ ] Washing powder

Note Any sharp objects such as a penknife or scissors should be packed in your checked-in baggage. If taken through airport security in hand baggage, they will probably be confiscated.

APPENDIX E
THE TATRAS MOUNTAIN CODE AND
VISITORS' CHARTER

The following requests and advice combine common sense with the visitors' charter devised by TANAP (the Tatras National Park in Slovakia).

Before You Set Out
* Check the weather forecast and state of the paths.
* Tell your hotel reception or accommodation manager where you will be going, or write it in the 'walks book'.
* Never go into the mountains alone.
* Don't plan a difficult walk above 2000m until you have had time to adjust to the altitude (2–3 days).

In the Mountains
* Make an early start.
* Always keep a steady pace – don't push yourself too far or go too fast.
* Keep in close touch with your map – always know where you are.
* Go down if the weather turns bad.
* Keep to the waymarked paths.
* Don't use any paths that are closed during the winter and spring (1 November to 15 June).
* Don't take short cuts.
* Don't cause rocks to roll down the mountain.
* Avoid steep snowfields.
* Avoid difficult terrain with inexperienced walkers or children.
* Always help those in distress.
* Don't pick or disturb plants or wildlife.
* Don't drop litter – put it in a bin or take it back to where you are staying.
* Don't damage information boards or other signs.
* Don't play loud music, or make any other loud noise, or shine bright lights at night (unless for safety reasons), as this disturbs wildlife.
* Don't camp or undertake any other activity that may cause disturbance to wildlife, except in permitted areas.
* In Slovakia, don't take your dog into the Tatras National Park unless it is muzzled and on a lead. Dogs must not be taken into designated nature reserves at all. In Poland, dogs are not allowed into the Tatras National Park at all.

APPENDIX F
HELP!

The following addresses and telephone numbers may be useful in an emergency.

Hospitals and Clinics

Nový Smokovec
Policlinic, on Cesta Slobody highway, opposite Slovakia holiday centre
(phone 052 442 2444, open daily 24 hours)

Tatranská Lomnica
Zdravotné Stredisko (Health Centre), opposite TANAP museum (phone 052
446 7349, open Mon–Fri mornings)

Poprad
Poprad's hospital and polyclinic (Nemocnica s Poliklinik) is located at
Banicka 28 on the south side of the town, phone 052 712 5111.

Zakopane
Szpital Miejski (Municipal Hospital), Kamieniec 10 (in Stary Kamieniec on
the north side of the town centre)

Encountering a Bear

There are thought to be around 80 to 100 European brown bears on either side of
the Tatras border. Most are shy and keep well away from human activity, keeping
to the remoter parts, but some are losing their fear of humans and have occasionally been seen rummaging in dustbins around the mountain huts and even in the
villages in broad daylight. It is as well to be aware that they are around, and what
to do if one is encountered.

We quote from the *Small Illustrated Guide to the High Tatras* by Juraj Ksiažek,
in which it is suggested: not to leave the marked hiking paths; to warn of your
presence in a normal voice, especially early in the morning or in the evening
when the bears are still active; not to approach a bear even if it appears peaceful; if an attack occurs, do not actively defend yourself but stay motionless on the
ground until the bear moves away.

Mountain Rescue

Mountain rescue centres can be found in many places throughout the High Tatras, including all the chalets or refuges. If someone in your party is unlucky enough to suffer an accident, or if you are in a position to help someone else, go to the nearest mountain rescue station, or any place from where help may be summoned.

If you can telephone (though you may not get an English speaker) call 18300 if in Slovakia, or 0603 100 100 if in Poland. You could also call the international emergency number 112, but this may be slower than calling mountain rescue direct.

In **Slovakia** there are mountain rescue posts at all the chalets (*chaty*), plus:
TANAP offices at Podbanské, Javorina, Lysá Poľana;
at or near the chair-lift/cable-car/funicular stations (including Štart middle station);
Dom Horskej Sluzby (Mountain Rescue Office) in Starý Smokovec;
Tichá forest house, near Podbanské;
Pod Muráňom forest house, near Javorina.
On Slovak maps they are indicated by a red cross.

In **Poland** there are mountain rescue posts at all the refuges (*schroniskî*), at Hotel Kalatówki, plus Wiktorówki monastery and cable-car stations.
On Polish maps they are indicated by a blue cross.

Consulates and Embassies

If you need advice in an emergency while in Slovakia or Poland, contact the nearest consulate or embassy for the country.

UK

Poland: British Embassy, Consular Section, Ulica Kawalerii 12, 00468 Warszawa/Warsaw, phone 022 311 0000, fax 022 311 0250, e-mail consular@britishembassy.pl

Slovakia: British Embassy, Consular Section, Panská 16, 81101 Bratislava, phone 02 5998 2000, fax 02 5998 2237, e-mail consular@britishembassy.sk

Irish Republic

Poland: Irish Embassy, Ulica Mysia 5, 00496 Warszawa/Warsaw, phone 022 849 6633, fax 022 849 8431, e-mail ambasada@irlandia.pl

Slovakia: Carlton Savot Building, Mostova 2, 81102 Bratislava, phone 02 5930 9611, fax 02 5443 0690, e-mail bratislavaembassy@dfa.ie

USA
Poland: American Consulate General, Ulica Stolarska 9, 31043 Kraków, phone 012 424 5100, fax 012 424 5103, e-mail publicwrw@state.gov

Slovakia: American Embassy, PO Box 309, 81499 Bratislava, phone 02 5443 3338, fax 02 5441 8861, e-mail cons@usembassy.sk

Canada
Poland: Canadian Embassy, Ulica Jana Matejki 1, 00481 Warsaw, phone 022 584 3100, fax 022 584 3192, e-mail wsaw@international.gc.ca

Slovakia: No representation in Slovakia at time of writing; contact Canadian Embassy, Muchova 6, 16000 Prague, Czech Republic, phone 020 27210 1800, e-mail canada@canada.cz.

Australia
Poland: Australian Embassy, Ulica Nowogrodzka 11, 00513 Warszawa/Warsaw, phone 022 521 3444, e-mail ambasada@australia.pl

Slovakia: no representation in Slovakia at time of writing; contact Australian Embassy, Mattiellistrasse 2, 1040 Wien/Vienna, Austria, phone 01 506 740, fax 01 504 1178, e-mail austemb@aon.at

New Zealand
Poland: New Zealand Embassy, Ulica Ujazdowskie 51, 00536 Warszawa/Warsaw, phone 022 521 0500, fax 022 521 0510, e-mail nzwsw@nzembassy. pl

Slovakia: no diplomatic representation at the time of writing; contact New Zealand Embassy, Atrium, Friedrichstrasse 60, 10117 Berlin, Germany, phone +49 30 206 210, fax +49 30 206 21114, e-mail nzembassy. berlin@t-online.de

South Africa
Poland: South African Embassy, IPC Business Centre, 6th Floor, Ulica Koszykowa 54, 00675 Warszawa/Warsaw, phone 022 625 6228, fax 022 625 6270, e-mail admin@southafrica.pl

Slovakia: South African Honorary Consulate, Frana Krala 1, 81101 Bratislava, phone 02 2077 1025, e-mail rsa.consulate.sk@mail.t-com.sk

NOTES

LISTING OF CICERONE GUIDES

Roads and Tracks of the Lake
  District
Rocky Rambler's Wild Walks
Scrambles in the Lake District
  North & South
Short Walks in Lakeland
  1 South Lakeland
  2 North Lakeland
  3 West Lakeland
The Cumbria Coastal Way
The Cumbria Way and the
  Allerdale Ramble
Tour of the Lake District

DERBYSHIRE, PEAK DISTRICT AND MIDLANDS

High Peak Walks
The Star Family Walks
Walking in Derbyshire
White Peak Walks
  The Northern Dales
  The Southern Dales

SOUTHERN ENGLAND

A Walker's Guide to the Isle
  of Wight
London – The definitive
  walking guide
The Cotswold Way
The North Downs Way
The South Downs Way
The South West Coast Path
The Thames Path
Walking in Berkshire
Walking in Kent
Walking in Sussex
Walking in the Isles of Scilly
Walking in the Thames Valley
Walking on Dartmoor
Walking on Guernsey
Walking on Jersey
Walks in the South Downs
  National Park

WALES AND WELSH BORDERS

Backpacker's Britain – Wales
Glyndwr's Way
Great Mountain Days in
  Snowdonia
Hillwalking in Snowdonia
Hillwalking in Wales
  Vols 1 & 2

Offa's Dyke Path
Ridges of Snowdonia
Scrambles in Snowdonia
The Ascent of Snowdon
The Lleyn Peninsula Coastal
  Path
The Pembrokeshire Coastal
  Path
The Shropshire Hills
The Wye Valley Walk
Walking in Pembrokeshire
Walking on the Brecon
  Beacons
Welsh Winter Climbs

INTERNATIONAL CHALLENGES, COLLECTIONS AND ACTIVITIES

Canyoning
Europe's High Points
The Via Francigena
  (Canterbury to Rome):
  Part 1

EUROPEAN CYCLING

Cycle Touring in France
Cycle Touring in Ireland
Cycle Touring in Spain
Cycle Touring in Switzerland
Cycling in the French Alps
Cycling the Canal du Midi
Cycling the River Loire
The Danube Cycleway
The Grand Traverse of the
  Massif Central
The Way of St James

AFRICA

Climbing in the Moroccan
  Anti-Atlas
Kilimanjaro: A Complete
  Trekker's Guide
Mountaineering in the
  Moroccan High Atlas
Trekking in the Atlas
  Mountains
Walking in the Drakensberg

ALPS – CROSS-BORDER ROUTES

100 Hut Walks in the Alps
Across the Eastern Alps: E5
Alpine Points of View

Alpine Ski Mountaineering
  1 Western Alps
  2 Central and Eastern Alps
Chamonix to Zermatt
Snowshoeing
Tour of Mont Blanc
Tour of Monte Rosa
Tour of the Matterhorn
Trekking in the Alps
Walking in the Alps
Walks and Treks in the
  Maritime Alps

PYRENEES AND FRANCE/SPAIN CROSS-BORDER ROUTES

Rock Climbs in The Pyrenees
The GR10 Trail
The Mountains of Andorra
The Pyrenean Haute Route
The Pyrenees
The Way of St James
  France & Spain
Through the Spanish Pyrenees:
  GR11
Walks and Climbs in the
  Pyrenees

AUSTRIA

Trekking in Austria's Hohe
  Tauern
Trekking in the Stubai Alps
Trekking in the Zillertal Alps
Walking in Austria

EASTERN EUROPE

The High Tatras
The Mountains of Romania
Walking in Bulgaria's National
  Parks
Walking in Hungary

FRANCE

Ecrins National Park
GR20: Corsica
Mont Blanc Walks
Mountain Adventures in the
  Maurienne
The Cathar Way
The GR5 Trail
The Robert Louis Stevenson
  Trail
Tour of the Oisans: The GR54

Tour of the Queyras
Tour of the Vanoise
Trekking in the Vosges and Jura
Vanoise Ski Touring
Walking in Provence
Walking in the Cathar Region
Walking in the Cevennes
Walking in the Dordogne
Walking in the Haute Savoie North & South
Walking in the Languedoc
Walking in the Tarentaise and Beaufortain Alps
Walking on Corsica

GERMANY
Germany's Romantic Road
Walking in the Bavarian Alps
Walking in the Harz Mountains
Walking the River Rhine Trail

HIMALAYA
Annapurna: A Trekker's Guide
Bhutan
Everest: A Trekker's Guide
Garhwal and Kumaon: A Trekker's and Visitor's Guide
Kangchenjunga: A Trekker's Guide
Langtang with Gosainkund and Helambu: A Trekker's Guide
Manaslu: A Trekker's Guide
The Mount Kailash Trek

IRELAND
Irish Coastal Walks
The Irish Coast to Coast Walk
The Mountains of Ireland

ITALY
Gran Paradiso
Italy's Sibillini National Park
Shorter Walks in the Dolomites
Through the Italian Alps
Trekking in the Apennines
Trekking in the Dolomites
Via Ferratas of the Italian Dolomites: Vols 1 & 2
Walking in Abruzzo
Walking in Sardinia
Walking in Sicily
Walking in the Central Italian Alps

Walking in the Dolomites
Walking in Tuscany
Walking on the Amalfi Coast

MEDITERRANEAN
Jordan – Walks, Treks, Caves, Climbs and Canyons
The Ala Dag
The High Mountains of Crete
The Mountains of Greece
Treks and Climbs in Wadi Rum, Jordan
Walking in Malta
Western Crete

NORTH AMERICA
British Columbia
The Grand Canyon
The John Muir Trail
The Pacific Crest Trail

SOUTH AMERICA
Aconcagua and the Southern Andes
Hiking and Biking Peru's Inca Trails
Torres del Paine

SCANDINAVIA
Trekking in Greenland
Walking in Norway

SLOVENIA, CROATIA AND MONTENEGRO
The Julian Alps of Slovenia
The Mountains of Montenegro
Trekking in Slovenia
Walking in Croatia

SPAIN AND PORTUGAL
Costa Blanca Walks 1 West & 2 East
Mountain Walking in Southern Catalunya
The Mountains of Central Spain
Trekking through Mallorca
Walking in Madeira
Walking in Mallorca
Walking in the Algarve
Walking in the Canary Islands 2 East
Walking in the Cordillera Cantabrica
Walking in the Sierra Nevada

Walking on La Gomera and El Hierro
Walking on La Palma
Walking on Tenerife
Walking the GR7 in Andalucia
Walks and Climbs in the Picos de Europa

SWITZERLAND
Alpine Pass Route
Central Switzerland
The Bernese Alps
Tour of the Jungfrau Region
Walking in the Valais
Walking in Ticino
Walks in the Engadine

TECHNIQUES
Geocaching in the UK
Indoor Climbing
Lightweight Camping
Map and Compass
Mountain Weather
Moveable Feasts
Outdoor Photography
Rock Climbing
Sport Climbing
The Book of the Bivvy
The Hillwalker's Guide to Mountaineering
The Hillwalker's Manual

MINI GUIDES
Avalanche!
Navigating with a GPS
Navigation
Pocket First Aid and Wilderness Medicine
Snow

For full information on all our guides, and to order books and eBooks, visit our website:
www.cicerone.co.uk.

Walking – Trekking – Mountaineering – Climbing – Cycling

Over 40 years, Cicerone have built up an outstanding collection of 300 guides, inspiring all sorts of amazing adventures.

Every guide comes from extensive exploration and research by our expert authors, all with a passion for their subjects. They are frequently praised, endorsed and used by clubs, instructors and outdoor organisations.

All our titles can now be bought as **e-books** and many as iPad and Kindle files and we will continue to make all our guides available for these and many other devices.

Our website shows any **new information** we've received since a book was published. Please do let us know if you find anything has changed, so that we can pass on the latest details. On our **website** you'll also find some great ideas and lots of information, including sample chapters, contents lists, reviews, articles and a photo gallery.

It's easy to keep in touch with what's going on at Cicerone, by getting our monthly **free e-newsletter**, which is full of offers, competitions, up-to-date information and topical articles. You can subscribe on our home page and also follow us on **Facebook** and **Twitter**, as well as our **blog**.

Cicerone – the very best guides for exploring the world.

CICERONE

2 Police Square Milnthorpe Cumbria LA7 7PY
Tel: 015395 62069 info@cicerone.co.uk
www.cicerone.co.uk